Crafts with Kids

OVER 40 FUN AND FABULOUS PROJECTS

SUSIE JOHNS

Published in 2010 by New Holland Publishers (UK) Ltd
London • Cape Town • Sydney • Auckland
www.newhollandpublishers.com

Garfield House, 86–88 Edgware Road,
London W2 2EA, United Kingdom

80 McKenzie Street, Cape Town 8001, South Africa
Unit 1, 66 Gibbes Street, Chatswood, NSW 2067, Australia
218 Lake Road, Northcote, Auckland, New Zealand

10 9 8 7 6 5 4 3 2 1

A catalogue record for this book is available from the British Library

ISBN 978 1 84773 597 3

Publisher: Clare Sayer
Design: Simon Daley
Photography: Roddy Paine
Production: Laurence Poos
Editorial Direction: Rosemary Wilkinson

Reproduction by Pica Digital PTE Ltd, Singapore
Printed and bound in Malaysia by Times Offset (M) Sdn Bhd

The paper used to produce this book is sourced from sustainable forests.

Crafts with Kids

contents

introduction

Though toddlers and young children need to be given the freedom to explore their environment and to develop basic skills at their own pace and through trial and error, organized activity sessions can also be very enjoyable and educational.

It is widely believed that children learn more during their pre-school years than at any other time in their lives, so it is important that parents and carers provide plenty of creative materials for them to experiment with and explore.

If you give crayons to very young children, the chances are that they will put them in their mouths. But from about 15 to18 months onwards, most children start to understand that they can use a crayon to make marks on a piece of paper – random scribble. By the age of about two and a half, they may start to make more deliberate marks. At this age, they will also enjoy using paint: poster paints are the best kind to start with, while older children may enjoy using acrylics, which can be used not only on paper but on other surfaces such as wood and stone, and to paint clay flowerpots and papier maché models.

play together, learn together

All the projects in this book have been designed as activities for adults and children to enjoy together and they can easily be adapted for children of all ages and abilities. During supervised art and craft activities, children will enjoy receiving their parent's full attention, even if it is only for a short period, and parents will learn a lot from observing their children's creative output.

No guidelines have been given regarding age groups, though most of the projects can be attempted from about the age of three or four years upwards, with varying degrees of adult participation. Obviously, the younger the child, the more the supervising adult will have to do, but as children become older and more able, it is important to strike a balance between helping or instructing and interfering. And don't forget that it is important to offer praise for even the smallest achievement, whether it is cutting out a shape or sewing a neat line of stitches, as this will help to boost children's confidence and make them more willing and eager to learn new skills.

Creative play helps to develop other skills. When painting and drawing, for instance, very young children might arrange the crayons or paint pots in a particular colour order, or learn to name the colours. Many of the projects in this book involve measuring, which helps children to learn numbers and to add and subtract. Some activities involve cutting and sticking, which helps to improve hand-eye coordination and manual dexterity. A number of the projects also involve designing, colour matching and copying shapes, which develops creativity, while others – such as the magic wand (page 42), the hula-hula garlands (page 100), the wooden spoon puppet (page 58), the sock puppet (page 77) and the finger puppets (page 74) – encourage dressing up and imaginative play, which in turn helps to develop speech. And most of the projects involve problem solving as you and your child interpret the words and pictures on each page and translate them into your own handcrafted objects.

skills and techniques

Skills of holding and using a paintbrush or scissors are developed over time. If your child finds it too difficult to cut paper with scissors, for a project such as the mosaic frame on page 20, you could suggest that they tear up the pieces instead.

Younger children may lack the dexterity to manoeuvre a needle and thread through fabric or to manipulate a pair of knitting needles but they may still want to try.

Adults can play an invaluable role in helping their young children to learn new skills. Things you take for granted as an adult, such as being able to measure accurately and cut a piece of paper or fabric, or sticking two surfaces together and holding them in place until the glue dries, are useful things that children need to learn. You should, however, try to choose an activity that you will enjoy or your child may well sense the fact that you are not fully engaged or happy.

be prepared

Don't wait for a rainy day; these activities can be enjoyed at any time and though some are best done indoors, others can be done outside and some (such as painted pebbles, page 116, painted flowerpots, page 108 and leaf prints, page 106) would be ideal for group play, at a party or playgroup, or on holiday.

SECRET SERVICE

The book is divided into five sections – Papercraft, Recycling, Painting and Printing, Needlecraft and Naturecraft – to make it easier to find and choose projects.

Do bear in mind that activities involving paint and glue create mess, so cover work surfaces with plenty of newspapers, or a sheet of plastic taped in place using masking tape. You may want to cover the surrounding floor area as well. Keep a damp cloth or a packet of wet wipes handy for mopping up spills and wear old clothes or a protective apron. Some felt-tip pens and paints are washable but most will stain clothing, so it is best to be on the safe side and dress your children and yourself in old clothes. If you are worried about making a mess, it will take the fun out of the activity.

be creative

Don't expect your creations to look exactly like the ones in this book: the instructions and the pictures of the finished projects are intended as a guideline or a starting point for your own creative activities.

For example, with the string prints on page 60, if you haven't got a suitable block of wood, you could glue string on to a cotton reel or a scrap of thick cardboard. For the paper plate tambourine, on page 50, if you haven't got paper plates, you could use two aluminium foil dishes, or perhaps make a rattle from a plastic cup or yogurt pot instead.

For the potato prints on page 112, instead of printing on a pillowcase, you could decorate a T-shirt, or perhaps print on to plain scraps of fabric then turn these into bean bags (see page 88) or a patchwork cushion (see page 95).

See if you can think of other ideas for using some of the projects in this book. If you enjoy making the fish cutouts for the fishing game, for example, you could stick one on a folded card to make a birthday card or invitation, or suspend a few from strings to make a mobile. And you could think of other ways of decorating the fish, such as sticking on circles of shiny paper for scales.

All the ideas have been tried out and tested on my own children over time and I am pleased to say that my daughters had a hand in producing the projects featured on the following pages. The children who helped to put the book together and whose hands and faces appear in the photographs had great fun in the studio and couldn't wait to get home to try out the ideas for themselves – so we all hope that you will be inspired to have lots of fun too.

papercraft

materials

Matt or shiny, metallic, corrugated, textured and recycled, printed or plain – paper is marvellous stuff. In this chapter there are some great ideas for party decorations, gifts, games and things to decorate your home.

When it comes to papercraft, it pays to be resourceful. Craft shops and stationers offer a dazzling array of papers for cutting, drawing, wrapping, folding and scrapbooking; but you can also save scraps from other projects, used giftwrap and cards from birthdays and other occasions, sweet wrappers, packaging, old letters and envelopes, discarded photocopies from the office and pages from newspapers, magazines and catalogues.

Keep all your paper pieces in a box and you will have a wide variety from which to choose whenever you want to make something.

For the projects in this chapter you will also need string, glue, sticky tape, ribbons and beads, among other things.

checklist

- old magazines or catalogues
- tissue paper
- string
- beads
- coloured paper scraps
- glue stick
- cardboard
- ribbon
- wooden sticks
- plastic drinking straws
- self-adhesive clear plastic film
- paper punch
- stapler
- paper clips
- sticky tape
- ruler
- pens and pencils

rolled paper beads

Recycle wrapping paper or the pages from magazines to make colourful jewellery.

you will need

MATERIALS

- sheets of A4 (11¾ x 8¼ in) coloured paper
- glue stick or double-sided sticky tape
- plastic beads (optional)
- string
- cord elastic

TOOLS

- ruler
- pencil
- scissors
- knitting needle or bamboo skewer

LEARNING THROUGH PLAY

- Measuring
- Cutting and sticking
- Threading

ADULT SUPERVISION

Rolling the beads can be fiddly, so be prepared to help.

handy hint

Stick a length of double-sided sticky tape along one of the shorter edges of a sheet of paper. Once the strips have been cut, roll the bead from the untaped end.

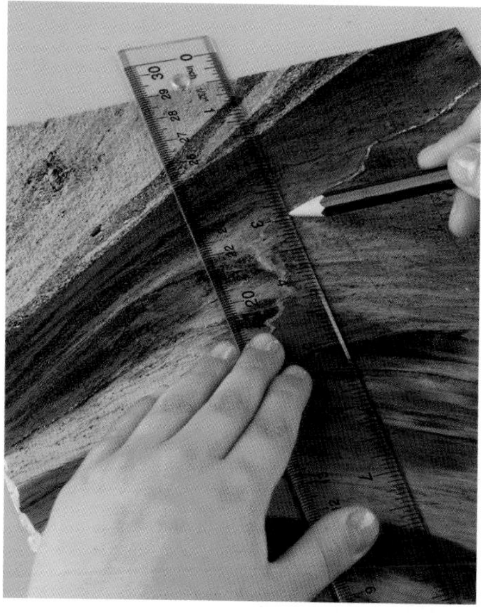

1 Draw lines along the length of a sheet of paper or magazine page, using a pencil and ruler. The lines can be parallel or at angles to one another.

2 Cut along the lines you have drawn, to form strips; some will be straight and others tapered (with one end wider than the other).

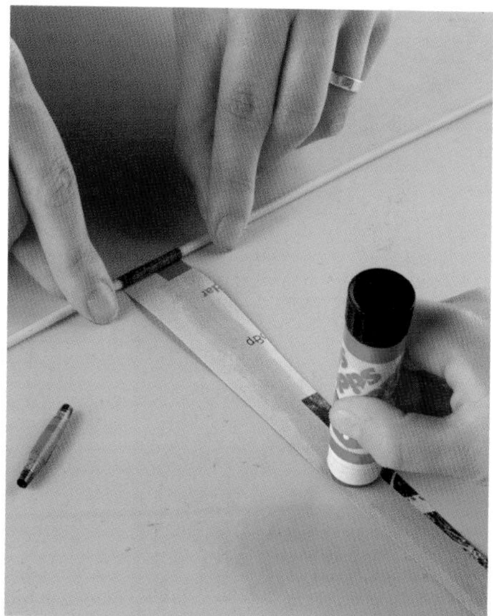

3 Roll one of the strips tightly around a knitting needle or skewer and stick the end of the paper down with a glue stick or double-sided tape.

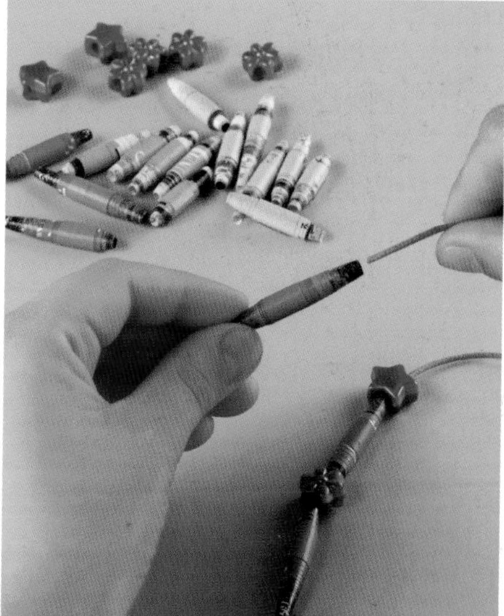

4 Make lots of beads, then thread them on to a length of string to make a necklace, or on to cord elastic to make a stretchy bracelet.

mexican fiesta flags

Make a line of colourful flags from rectangles of coloured tissue paper and use them as a party decoration.

you will need

MATERIALS

- tissue paper
- string
- glue stick or double-sided sticky tape

TOOLS

- scissors
- ruler
- hole punch (optional)

LEARNING THROUGH PLAY

- Measuring
- Cutting and sticking
- Folding

ADULT SUPERVISION

Show children how to make small cuts without cutting right across the paper. Help with attaching the flags to the string.

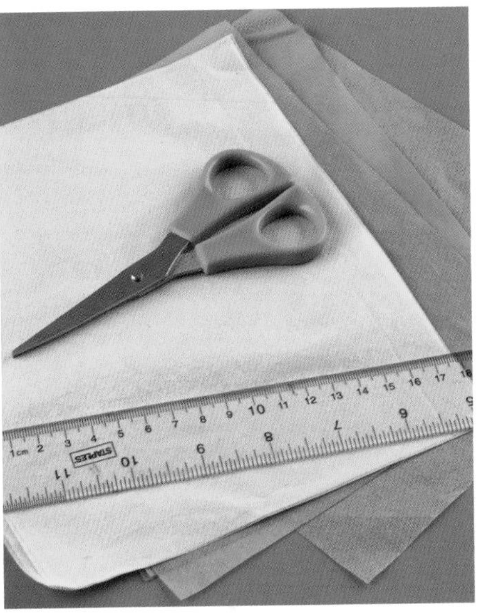

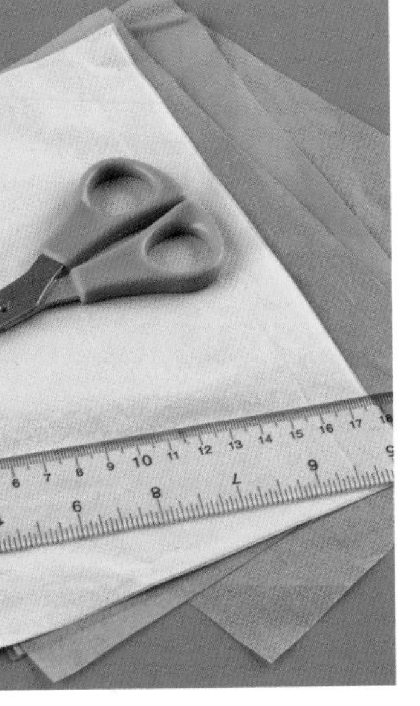

1 Cut rectangles of tissue paper measuring approximately 21 x 19 cm (8¼ x 7½ in). Alternatively you can make the flags any size you prefer.

2 Fold a piece of tissue in half and then in half again. Make little cuts into the folds in the paper – small cuts work best.

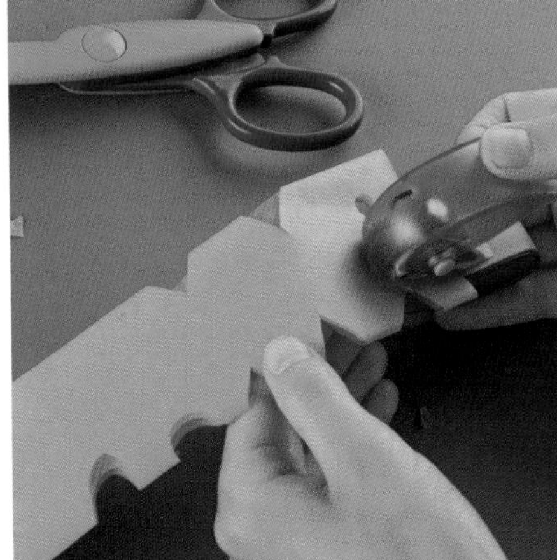

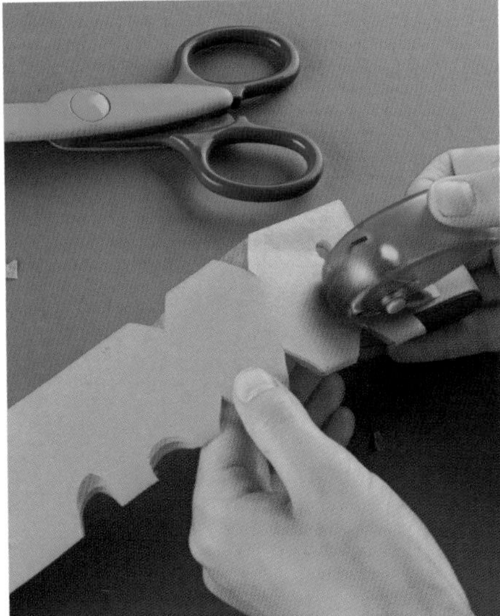

3 You can use a paper punch to create small circles or other shapes and scissors with decorative blades to make fancy edges.

4 When you have made lots of flags, fold over about 1 cm (½ in) at the top of each one, place the fold over a length of string and glue in place.

handy hint

The flags can be hung outside on a dry day but do not leave them out in the rain or they will fall apart.

mosaic picture frame

Use small scraps of coloured paper to decorate a card mount, ideal for displaying a drawing or a family photograph.

you will need

MATERIALS

- thick card or pre-cut cardboard mount
- scraps of coloured paper
- PVA glue or glue stick

TOOLS

- scissors
- ruler
- pencil

LEARNING THROUGH PLAY

- Measuring
- Cutting and sticking

ADULT SUPERVISION

For smaller children, you may want to cut out the paper 'mosaics' in advance. Instead of a frame, children could make a mosaic picture.

handy hint

You don't have to spend lots of money on coloured papers; magazines and catalogues are a good source, or save scraps of gift wrapping paper. Collect suitable papers as you find them and store in a box ready to use.

1 If you are starting with a sheet of cardboard, cut it into a rectangle and cut out a rectangular window in the centre. The mount shown measures 30 x 23 cm (12 x 9 in) with a 20 x 13 cm (8 x 5 in) aperture. Snip coloured paper into small pieces: squares or strips.

2 Try out patterns before you stick them on the frame to see what works best.

3 Either apply glue to the back of each paper piece or apply to a small area of the frame then press paper pieces in position.

4 Finally, position your picture behind the frame and stick in place.

paper heart

Make one of these for Valentine's Day, or as a present for someone you love. Or make lots as party decorations.

you will need

MATERIALS

- coloured cardboard
- tissue paper
- short length of ribbon or cord
- sticky tape
- glue
- coloured foil sweet wrappers
- paper cutouts
- gem stones

TOOLS

- scissors

LEARNING THROUGH PLAY

- ▶ Measuring
- ▶ Cutting and sticking

ADULT SUPERVISION

Look for self-adhesive gem stones in craft shops, or use a suitable adhesive.

handy hint

You could use shapes other than a heart – a circle, square or diamond, for example – and have fun combining colours and using of decorations such as stickers, buttons, sequins and beads.

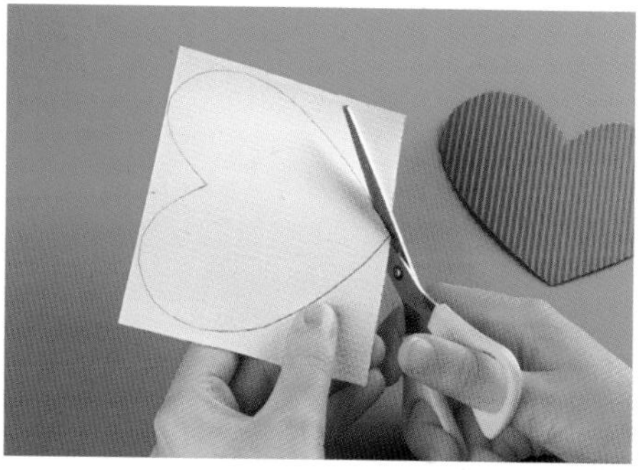

1 Cut two identical heart shapes from card; cut larger heart shapes from tissue paper. You will find templates on page 120.

2 Form a piece of ribbon into a loop and tape the ends to the back of one of the heart shapes, at the top.

3 Apply glue to this heart shape, place two or more tissue paper hearts on top, then glue the other heart shape on top. Press down until they are all firmly stuck together. If you like, you can cut out and stick one or two more card hearts on top, to make your decoration really thick.

4 Now decorate the hearts – both sides or just the front – using pieces of coloured foil, paper cutouts and gems.

5 Snip the tissue paper to form a fringe all round. Your decoration is now ready to hang up.

paper flowers

Made from crêpe paper, these colourful flowers make a lovely gift and will last longer than real ones.

you will need

MATERIALS

- yellow tissue paper
- plastic drinking straws
- sticky tape
- crêpe paper, pink, blue and green

TOOLS

- scissors

LEARNING THROUGH PLAY

- ▶ Cutting and sticking
- ▶ Using templates
- ▶ Binding

ADULT SUPERVISION

Wrapping the petals around the stem can be fiddly so be prepared to help.

1 Cut a strip of yellow tissue paper about 6 cm (2½ in) wide and snip the strip with scissors to form a fringe.

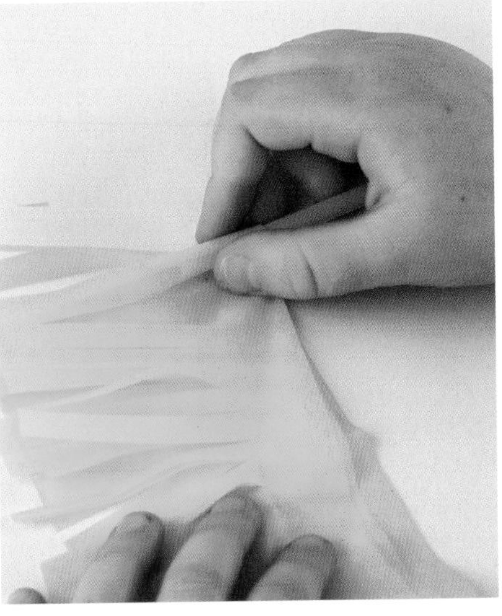

2 Wind the tissue paper fringe around the top of a drinking straw and wrap the bottom edge with a piece of sticky tape, to hold it in place.

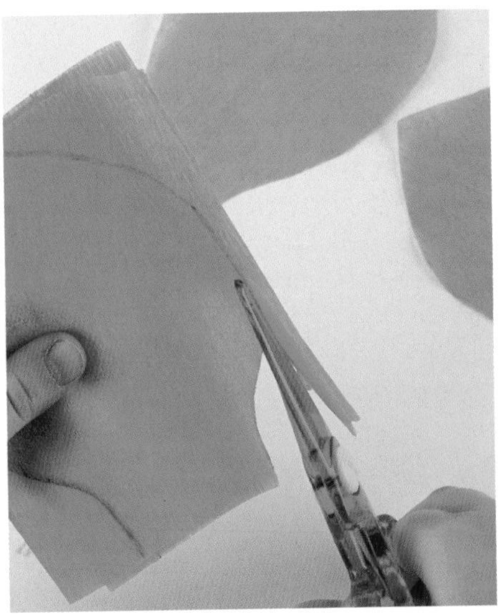

3 Cut petal shapes from crêpe paper. Use ordinary scissors or scissors with zigzag blades to cut out the petals.

4 Wrap the base of each petal, one by one, around the drinking straw 'stem', holding them in place with short lengths of sticky tape.

handy hint

Instead of ordinary sticky tape, you could use double-sided tape for a neat finish.

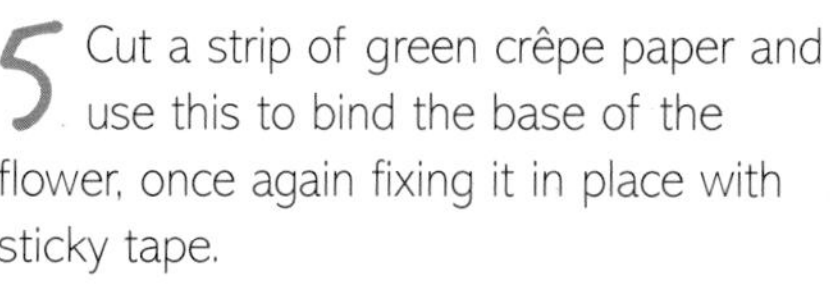

5 Cut a strip of green crêpe paper and use this to bind the base of the flower, once again fixing it in place with sticky tape.

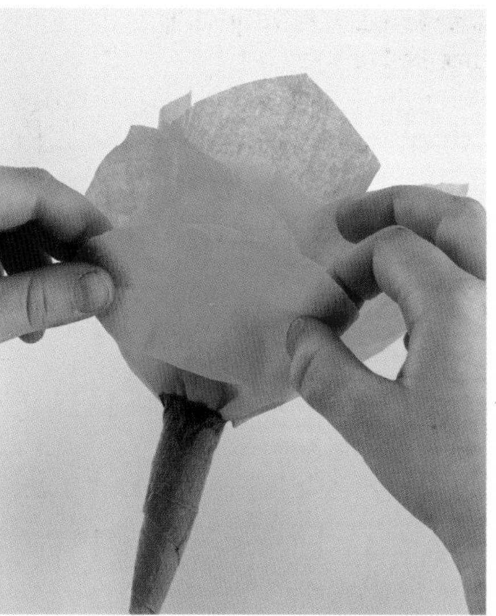

6 Finally, gently pull each petal into shape: because crêpe paper can be stretched, you can make the petals curve.

badge

Make a single badge to pin to a birthday card, or make lots for party guests or members of a team.

you will need

MATERIALS

- plain paper
- felt tip pens
- scraps of cardboard
- glue stick
- fine cord or thick thread
- beads
- short length of ribbon
- safety pin
- sticky tape

TOOLS

- scissors
- hole punch
- large needle

LEARNING THROUGH PLAY

- Measuring and cutting
- Decorating
- Sticking
- Threading beads

ADULT SUPERVISION

Younger children may need help with the more fiddly aspects such as sticking down the pieces of ribbon and threading cord through the holes.

1 Decorate a piece of paper with your design, such as a number for a birthday.

2 Cut two rectangles of cardboard the same shape and size as the design for your badge. Cut out the design and glue to one of the cardboard pieces.

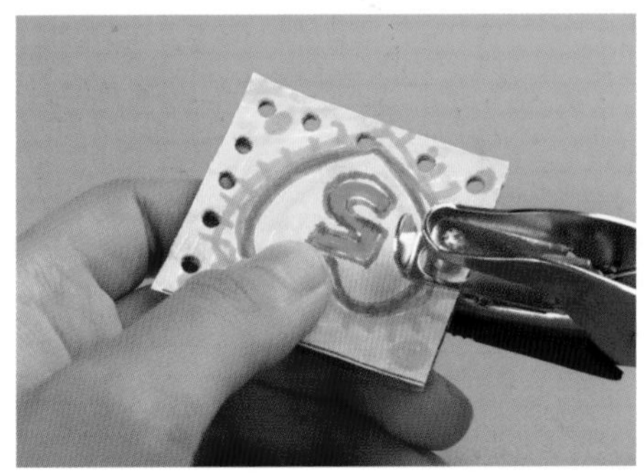

3 Punch holes all around the sides and base of the badge. top so that the ribbon is sandwiched between the two.

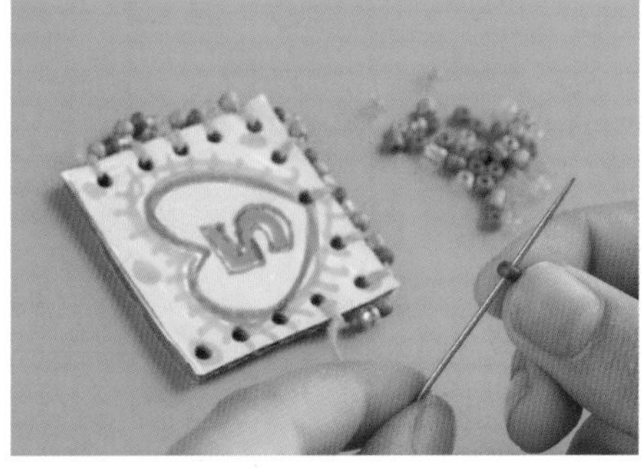

4 Tie the end of a length of cord to the first hole at the top corner of the badge. Thread a needle on to the cord and then thread on a few beads. Push the cord through the next hole and pull up tightly. Repeat until you have decorated the edge of the badge with beads.

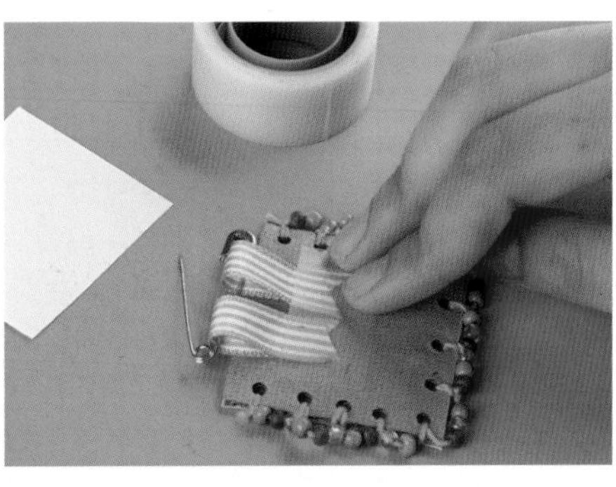

5 Loop two short lengths of ribbon over the bar of the safety pin (on the side of the pin that doesn't open) and tape the ribbon ends to the back of the card you have just decorated; glue the other piece of card on top so that the ribbon is sandwiched between the two.

5

table mat

Make tea-time fun with a personalized place mat. By laminating it, you can wipe it clean and use again and again.

you will need

MATERIALS

- pencil
- white paper
- large piece of coloured card
- scraps of coloured paper
- glue stick
- felt tip pens
- clear self-adhesive film

TOOLS

- scissors

LEARNING THROUGH PLAY

- ▶ Measuring
- ▶ Cutting shapes
- ▶ Sticking

ADULT SUPERVISION

You will probably need to apply the self-adhesive film, as it can be tricky to do without creating creases and air bubbles. Or you may prefer to take it to your local copy shop or office suppliers and have it professionally laminated.

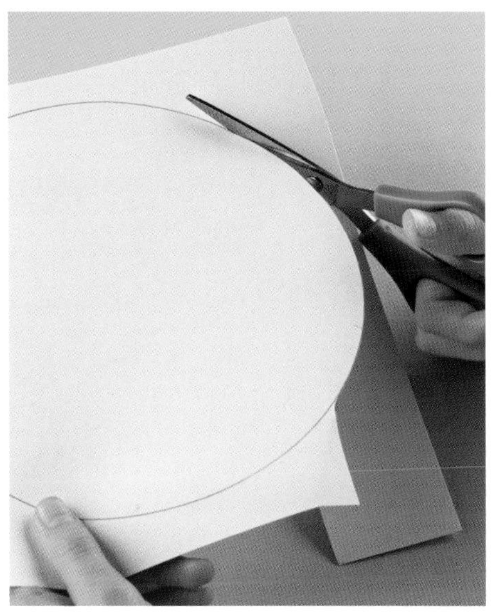

1 Draw a round shape on a piece of paper. To create a neat circle, draw around a plate. Cut out the circle. Draw a slightly smaller circle inside it to make it look like the rim of a plate.

2 Stick the circle in the centre of your large sheet of card. Make sure the sheet of card is the size and shape you want your finished table mat to be. Cut out shapes to represent your favourite foods.

3 Now cut out knife, fork and spoon shapes and stick all the shapes in place on the plate.

4 You can add any extra details using felt tip pens. Then apply self-adhesive film to the back and front and trim edges.

fishing game

Make a pond full of fish then try to catch them with your magnetic rod.

you will need

MATERIALS

- thick paper or thin card
- wax crayons
- brush pens or watercolour paints
- paper clips
- string
- wooden stick
- coloured sticky tape
- a magnet

TOOLS

- scissors

LEARNING THROUGH PLAY

- ▶ Drawing
- ▶ Cutting
- ▶ Counting

ADULT SUPERVISION

You may wish to draw basic fish shapes for younger children to colour in; you will find a template on page 121. To make the game more challenging, older children can draw a number on each fish, then count up each player's score.

1 Draw fish outlines on paper or card. You can invent your own shapes or copy the shape from page 121 and make a template.

2 To decorate the fish, draw patterns with wax crayon. If you like, write a number on each fish.

3 Paint the fish using brush pens or watercolour paints; the wax lines will resist the paint and show through.

(continued overleaf)

photo album

continued

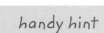

handy hint

Albums can be made in different shapes and sizes. Use A5 (8¼ x 6 in) paper and card for a smaller album, or custom-cut paper to the size you prefer.

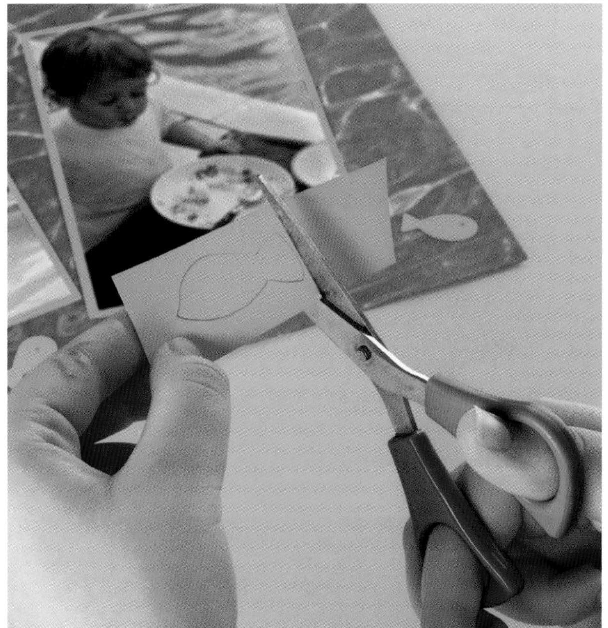

4 Make up more pages – as many as you like – being creative with background colours, paper scraps and stickers.

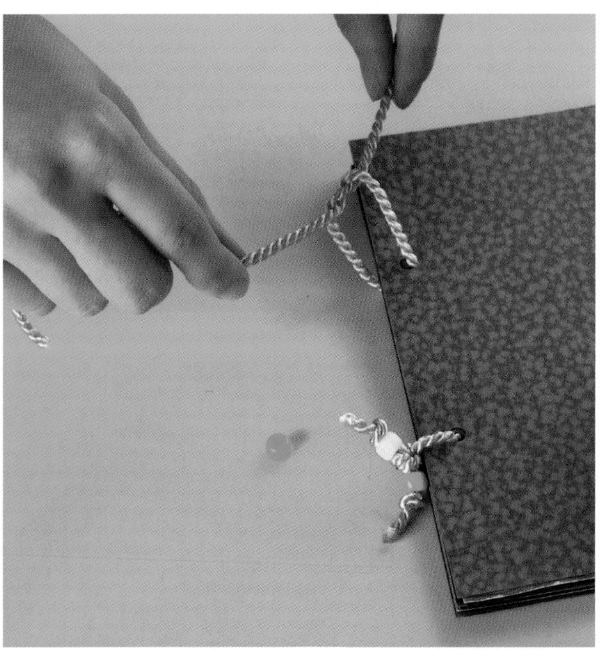

5 Assemble the book. Use colourful card for covers – in a slightly heavier weight than the pages – and include the pages you have made as well as some plain pages to fill in later. Thread ribbon or cord through the holes and add a couple of beads. Knot to hold the pages together. Choose a favourite picture to put on the cover and add a border and stickers to make it eye-catching.

recycling

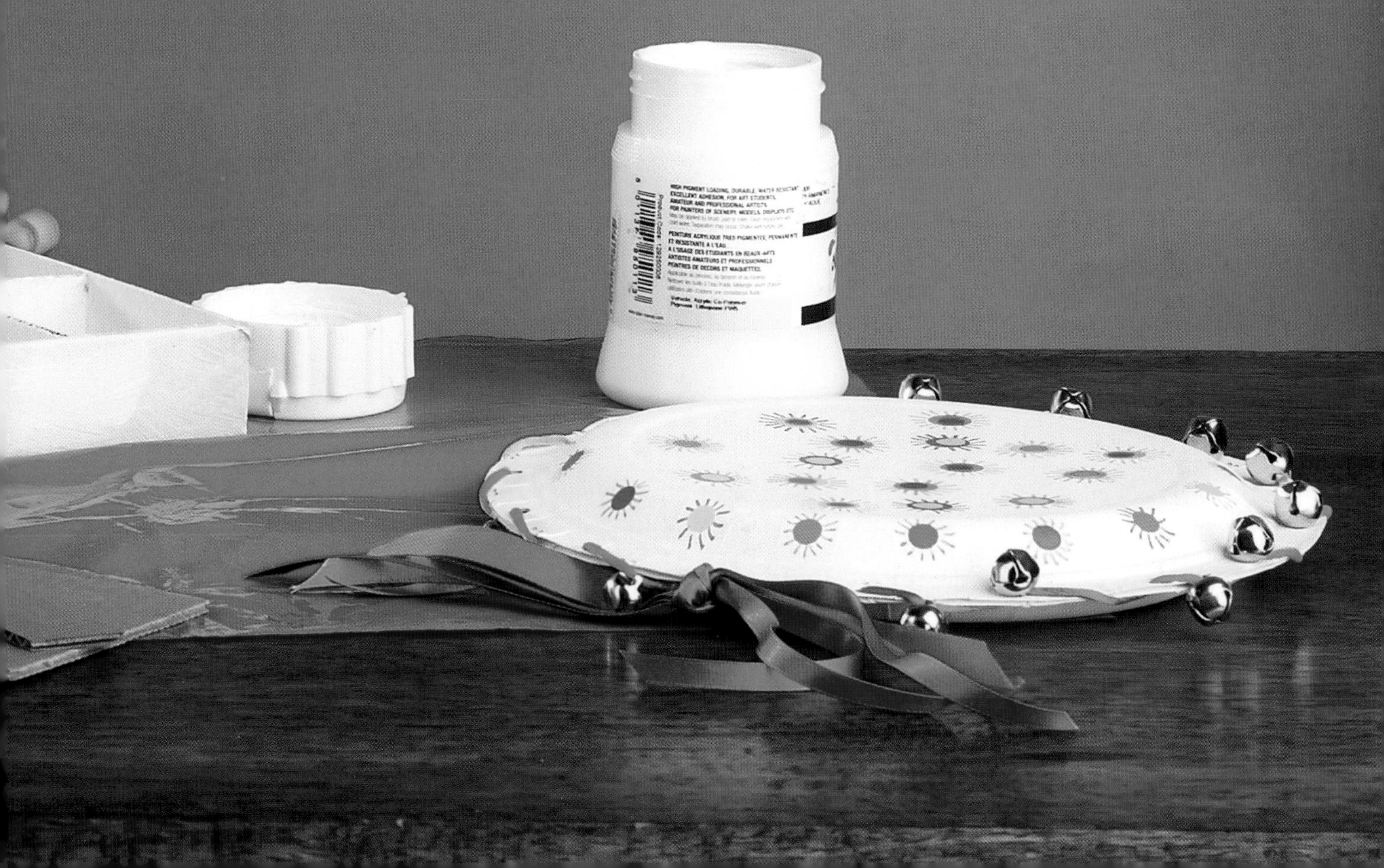
HIGH PIGMENT LOADING, DURABLE, WATER RESISTANT
EXCELLENT ADHESION, FOR ART STUDENTS,
AMATEUR AND PROFESSIONAL ARTISTS
FOR PAINTERS OF SCENERY, MODELS, DISPLAYS ETC
PEINTURE ACRYLIQUE TRES PIGMENTEE, PERMANENTE
ET RESISTANTE A L'EAU
A L'USAGE DES ETUDIANTS EN BEAUX-ARTS
ARTISTES AMATEURS ET PROFESSIONNELS
PEINTRES DE DECORS ET MAQUETTES.

materials

There is a great tradition of make do and mend which applies to all kinds of creative pursuits. Hunt around the house and you will undoubtedly find all manner of things that can be incorporated into your craft projects: plastic bags, newspapers and magazines, food packaging, scraps of paper, cardboard and fabric, even old clothes need not be thrown away but can be utilized in all sorts of ways.

So next time the refuse collectors are due to call, don't consign all your old clutter to the recycling bin but sort through it for items that can be re-used.

In this chapter you will find uses for plastic bottles, old box lids, paper scraps, aluminium foil, cardboard tubes, paper plates and wooden spoons, among other things, all of which would otherwise be discarded. There are also projects in other chapters that make use of old clothes such as odd socks and gloves, leftover lengths of yarn and remnants of fabric, magazines and plastic carrier bags.

So at the same time as teaching your children new craft skills and encouraging them to be creative, you can also engender a need to avoid waste and make good use of what might otherwise end up as landfill.

checklist

- plastic bottles
- scrap paper
- glue stick
- PVA glue
- glitter
- cardboard boxes
- plastic packaging
- cardboard tubes
- paper plates
- sweet wrappers
- paints
- paintbrushes
- ribbons
- bells
- sticky tape
- scissors

skittles

This game is fun to play indoors, in the garden or even on the beach. Line them up and try to knock them over.

you will need

MATERIALS

- plastic bottles
- paper
- crayons or felt tip pens
- glue or double-sided tape

TOOLS

- tape measure
- ruler
- scissors

LEARNING THROUGH PLAY

- Measuring
- Cutting and colouring
- Counting

ADULT SUPERVISION

For younger children, cut out the strips of paper beforehand for them to decorate, then help them to wrap the paper around the bottles. Older children can measure and cut the paper themselves.

handy hint

To add weight to the skittles, place a small lump of modelling clay inside each one. If the bottles have lids, then pour in water or sand and screw lids on tightly.

1 Measure around each bottle and draw rectangles this length on paper, adding 2 cm (¾ in) for overlap. Calculate how wide the rectangles should be and then cut them out.

2 Decorate each rectangle using crayons or felt-tip pens.

3 If you wish, you can number the skittles.

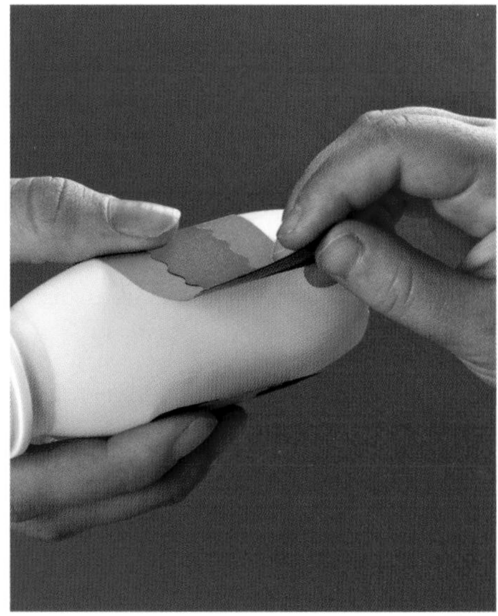

4 Wrap a strip of paper around each bottle, sticking the ends together with glue or double-sided tape.

8
4

magic wand

Every fairy, witch or wizard needs a wand in order to cast magical spells.

you will need

MATERIALS

- fancy sticky tape
- wooden stick
- thick cardboard
- masking tape
- gem stones
- PVA glue
- glitter
- ribbons

TOOLS

- scissors

LEARNING THROUGH PLAY

- ▶ Cutting and sticking
- ▶ Decorating using a variety of materials

ADULT SUPERVISION

Children will need a bit of patience while the glue is drying. Take care when using glitter with younger children.

1 Decorate the stick by wrapping it with fancy sticky tape.

2 Cut out two identical star shapes from cardboard. You will find a template for the star on page 121.

3 Tape one end of the stick to one of the stars, then tape the two stars together by wrapping masking tape around each point of the star.

4 Apply PVA glue all over one side of the star and position the gem stones, then sprinkle glitter all over. Allow the glue to dry before shaking off any excess glitter. Decorate the other side in the same way.

5 Finally, tie ribbons around the top of the stick, at the base of the star.

handy hint

When applying glitter, be generous. Any excess can be shaken off when the glue has dried and returned to its container, to reduce wastage.

108

box lid frames

Save the lids from cardboard boxes, such as shoe boxes, to create a display of treasured collections.

you will need

MATERIALS

- box lid
- cardboard
- PVA glue
- acrylic paints or poster paints
- coloured paper scraps

TOOLS

- ruler
- pencil
- scissors

LEARNING THROUGH PLAY

- Measuring
- Cutting
- Painting

ADULT SUPERVISION

Accurate measuring is essential for good results so supervise the measuring, cutting and assembling of the cardboard strips.

1 Measure the box lid then measure and mark out four strips the same width as the depth of the lid. One of these strips should be the same length as the inner dimension of the box and the other three the same length as the width of the box.

2 Cut out the strips and cut a notch in the centre of each one so that they will slot together. Apply PVA glue to the edges and slot the pieces in place. Leave to dry completely.

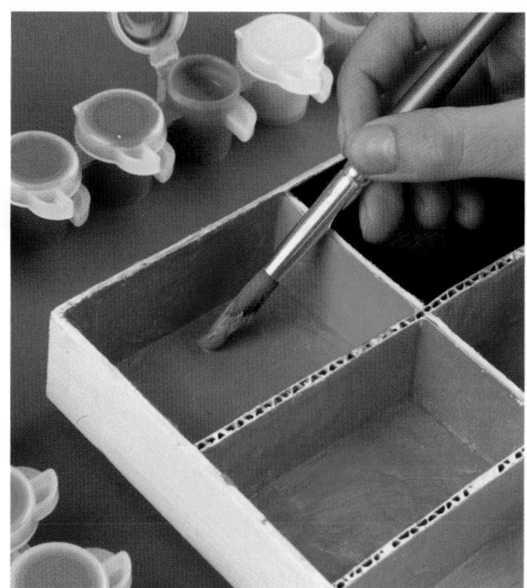

3 Paint the box and its divisions white all over. Leave to dry. Paint the frame in your choice of colours; you could paint each section a different colour, like the one in the picture.

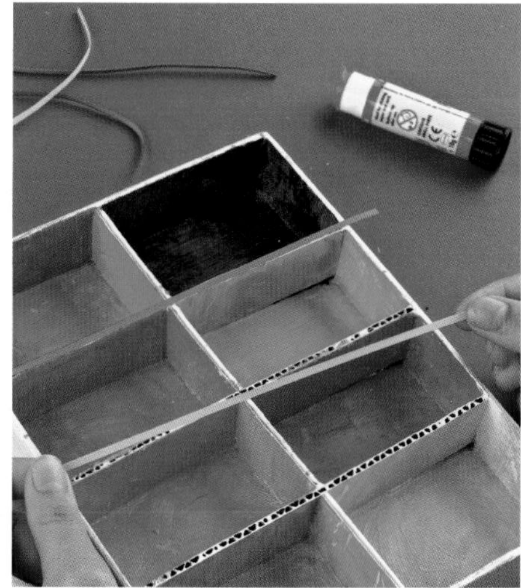

4 When the paint is dry, stick strips of paper along the edges of the dividers, if you like, to create a neat finish.

handy hint

Make a simpler box frame, without dividers, by simply painting a sturdy shallow box or lid.

robot collage

This is collage with a difference: the shiny robot has moving parts, easily achieved with the help of paper fasteners.

you will need

MATERIALS

- small cardboard box lid
- aluminium foil
- pipe cleaner
- A4 (11¾ x 8¼ in) card or thick paper
- foam sticker pads
- assorted metallic or textured card scraps
- paper fasteners
- glitter glue or dimensional paint
- sequins or gem stones

TOOLS

- hole punch
- scissors

LEARNING THROUGH PLAY

► Measuring; cutting; sticking; designing.

ADULT SUPERVISION

Smaller children may find punching holes and inserting paper fasteners a bit fiddly.

handy hint

Collect the materials needed before you start. The more variety, the better.

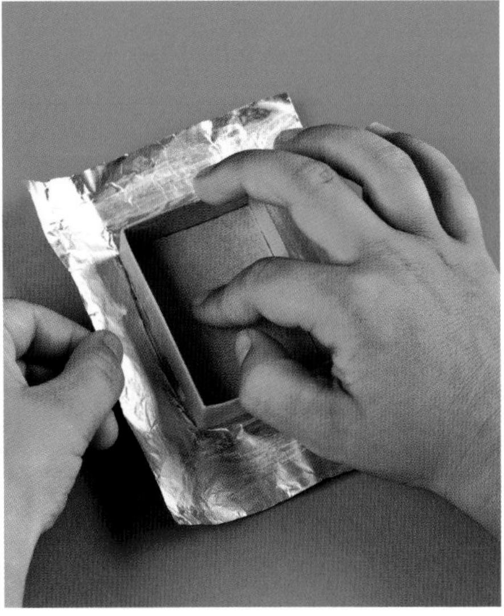

1 Cover the small box lid with aluminium foil to make a head, then punch two holes in one long edge and insert a short length of pipe cleaner.

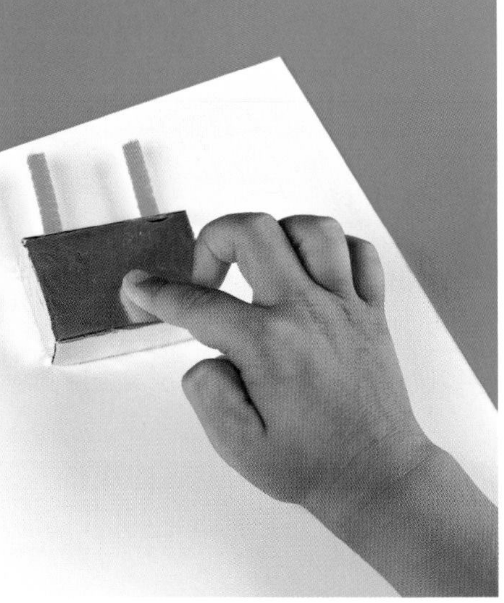

2 Stick the head in place on the card using foam sticker pads. Cut out a rectangle of textured card for the body and stick in place.

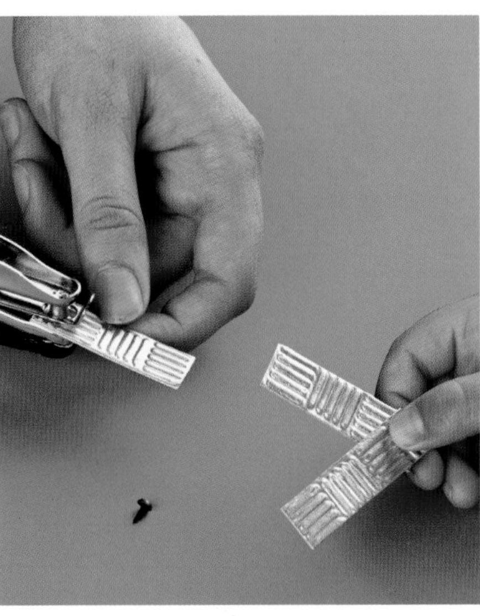

3 Cut strips of textured card for body parts. Punch holes in the ends of arm and leg components then join two arm or leg pieces using a paper fastener.

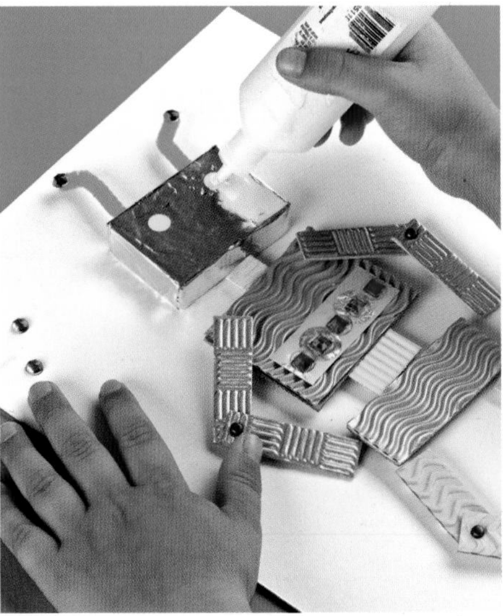

4 Attach the arms and legs to the body using foam sticker pads then, using glitter glue or dimensional paint, stick on sequins and gem stones to look like lights and controls.

maze puzzle

Have a double dose of fun by creating your own little puzzle then playing with it or challenging your friends.

you will need

MATERIALS

- printed picture or wrapping paper
- 1 round cardboard cheese box
- scrap cardboard
- PVA glue
- edible silver cake decorations
- clear acetate
- double-sided sticky tape
- scrap paper

TOOLS

- scissors
- hole punch

LEARNING THROUGH PLAY

- ▸ Measuring and cutting
- ▸ Sticking
- ▸ Decorating

ADULT SUPERVISION

Help is needed at all stages. It is important that the acetate lid fits, without gaps.

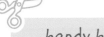

handy hint

Some cheese boxes may have a clear lid, which can be replaced on the box in step 5 and simply taped in place.

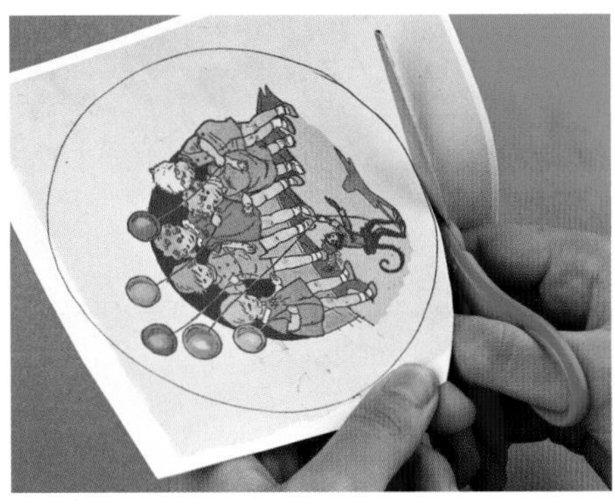

1 Choose a picture, place the cheese box on top and draw around it. Stick the picture to some card; cut it out and trim so that it fits snugly inside the box.

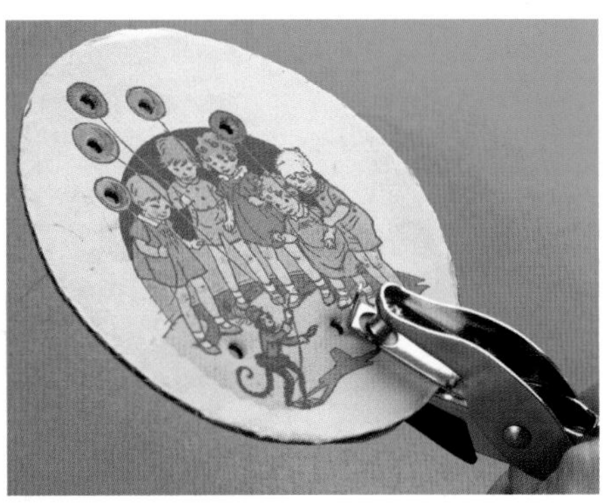

2 Punch holes in the picture – as many as you like.

3 Apply glue to the box base and place the circle in the box; put a weight on top to hold it firmly in place until the glue dries completely.

4 Add silver cake decorations – one for each punched hole – then glue a circle of acetate on to the edge of the box and leave it to dry.

5 Measure the circumference of the box and cut a length of double-sided tape to the same measurement plus about 1 cm (½ in) to allow for overlap. Apply the tape to a piece of scrap paper and cut out around the edges of the tape. Peel off backing and stick the paper strip in place, then snip into the edge of the paper and fold down the strips; this helps to hold the acetate in place and produces a neat finish to the top of the puzzle.

paper plate tambourine

Fun to create and to play with, this simple music maker takes no time at all to make.

you will need

MATERIALS

- 2 plastic drinking straws
- 2 paper plates
- stickers
- felt tip pens
- 1 m (39 in) of cord
- about 16 bells
- short lengths of ribbon

TOOLS

- scissors
- stapler
- hole punch

LEARNING THROUGH PLAY

- Measuring
- Cutting and decorating
- Making music

ADULT SUPERVISION

Stapling is a quick way to join the plates, but for young children you may prefer to use sticky tape or glue, since staples can be sharp.

handy hint

Instead of drinking straws, try using other things to create different sounds: dried peas, beans, lentils or rice, for example.

1 Snip the drinking straws into short lengths and place on one of the plates. Place the other plate on top.

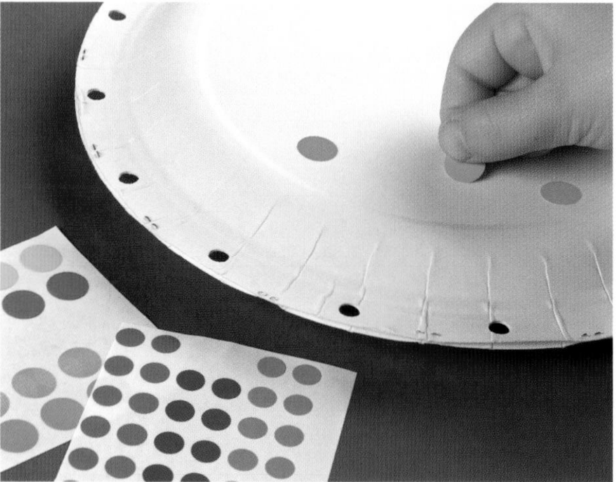

2 Staple the edges of the plates together; then punch holes, evenly spaced, all round. Decorate the base of each plate with stickers. Add a few more decorations using felt tip pens.

3 Thread the cord through the holes in the edge of your tambourine, adding bells as you go, then tie on a few coloured ribbons.

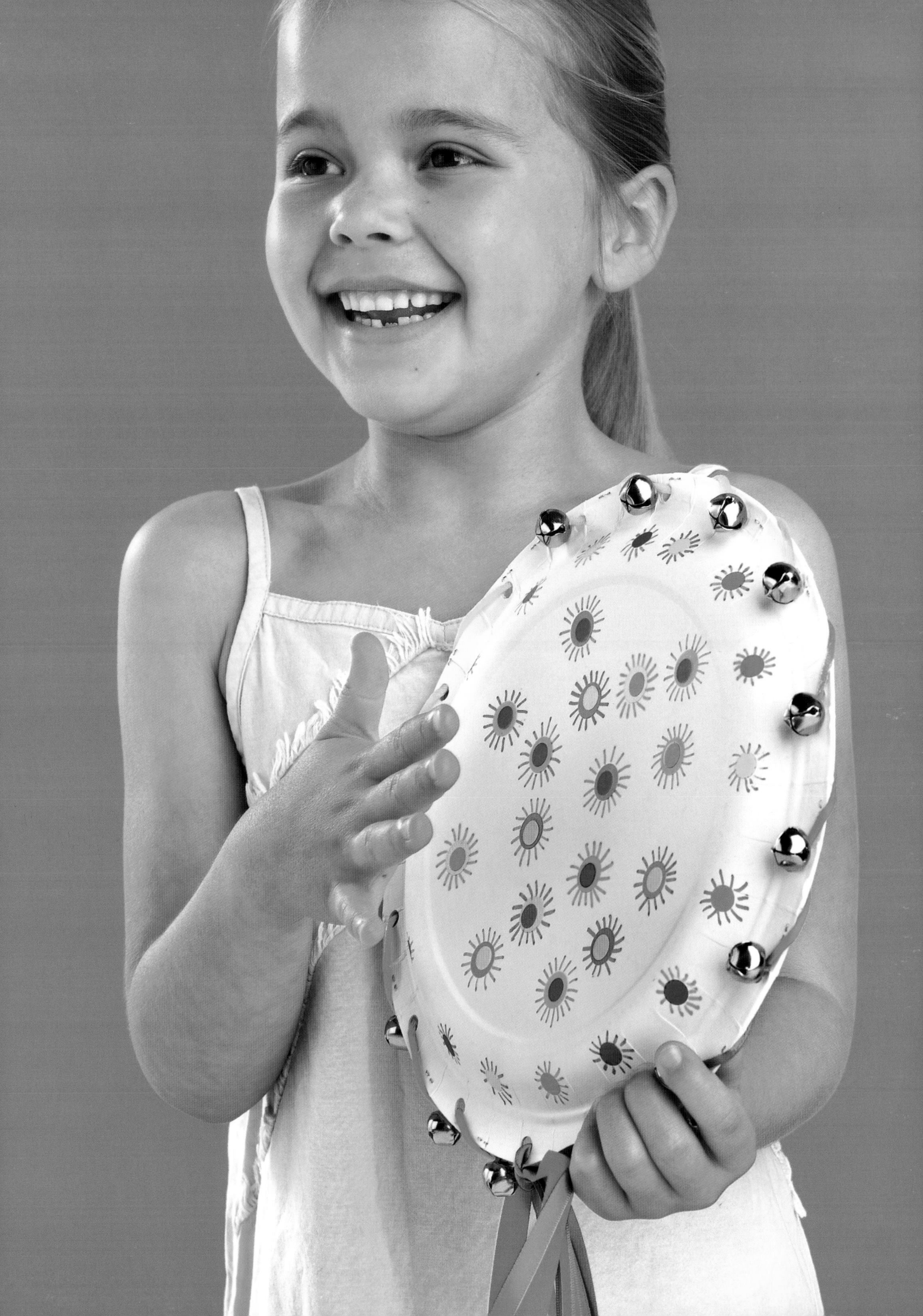

rocket

Turn a plastic bottle into a space rocket ready to zoom off and explore distant planets.

you will need

MATERIALS

- plastic bottle
- aluminium foil
- foil sweet wrappers
- glue stick
- 3 small cardboard tubes
- stickers
- thick paper or thin cardboard
- sticky tape

TOOLS

- scissors

LEARNING THROUGH PLAY

- ▸ Measuring
- ▸ Cutting
- ▸ Decorating

ADULT SUPERVISION

Cutting off the base of the bottle can be done with scissors but is best done by an adult.

1 Cut off the base of the plastic bottle. Glue pieces of aluminium foil and foil sweet wrappers all over the bottle.

2 Cover each of the cardboard tubes with foil.

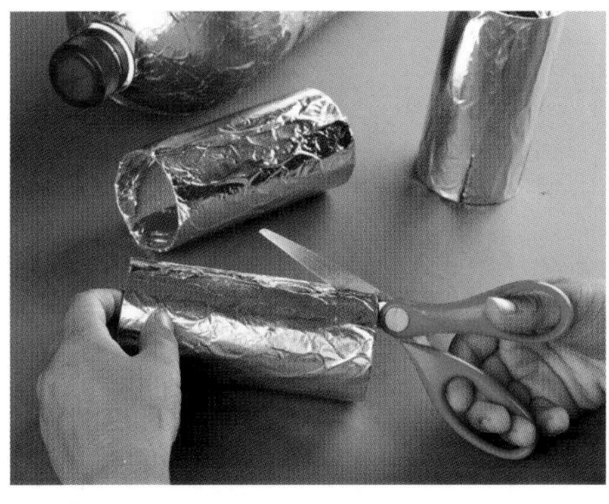

3 Snip notches in opposite sides of each tube, about 3 cm (1¼ in) in length.

4 Slot the three tubes on to the base of the rocket, spacing them evenly. Decorate the rocket with stickers – star shapes are good.

5 To make a nose cone, cut a semi-circle of paper or card, apply glue to one straight edge, curl to make a cone and stick edges together. Attach to the rocket with sticky tape or glue.

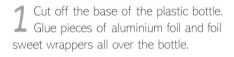

painting and printing

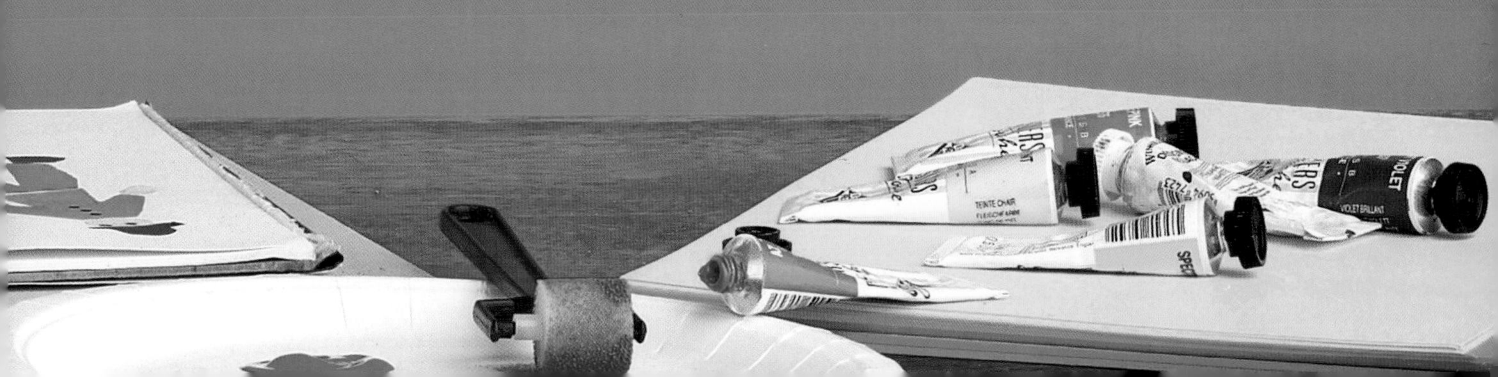

materials

Painting is one of the most enjoyable and creative activities for children – and one that requires very little in the way of equipment and materials. With just a few tubes or pots of paint, a brush and a supply of paper, you are all set. But this chapter includes a few other suggestions to stretch the imagination.

First of all, when buying paints, there is no need to buy dozens of colours: most colours can be mixed from just red, blue, yellow, white and black. So instead of buying the biggest set of paints in the shop, consider buying different types of paint, to extend your child's creative possibilities.

Poster paints and watercolours are great for basic painting and printing on paper.

Acrylics can be used not only on paper and card but on canvas, wood and stone, and also to decorate papier maché models.

To decorate clothing, you will need fabric paints and to decorate china and glass, you will need ceramic and glass paints – just make sure you select the water-based types, which are safer for children to use and make cleaning up easier too.

On the subject of cleaning up, it makes sense to protect work surfaces

and clothing when indulging in messy pursuits such as painting and printing, especially when using acrylic paints which can be impossible to remove from clothing.

Then there is the subject of brushes. Once again, acrylics can ruin brushes if you don't wash them before the paint has had time to dry. It's a good idea to buy cheap brushes for acrylics and save your best brushes for watercolours. Sponge-tipped paint applicators and rollers are great for applying paint to all kinds of surfaces and cotton buds are not only useful but also disposable.

checklist

- acrylic and poster paints
- fabric paints and dyes
- china and glass paints
- paint brushes
- small roller
- cotton buds
- paper towels
- plastic sheet
- old clothes
- paper and cardboard
- string

wooden spoon puppet

A simple wooden spoon is the ideal shape for a puppet head. Clothes are optional.

you will need

MATERIALS

- wooden spoon
- acrylic paints
- coloured fabric
- sewing thread
- ribbon
- glue
- scrap of yarn

TOOLS

- paintbrushes
- scissors
- needle

LEARNING THROUGH PLAY

- Painting
- Stitching
- Sticking

ADULT SUPERVISION

You may wish to hold the spoon steady while your child paints it. Make sure the work surface is protected and wear old clothes.

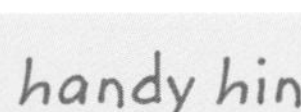

handy hint

Acrylic paint dries quite quickly but if you are impatient, skip step 1 and start at step 2.

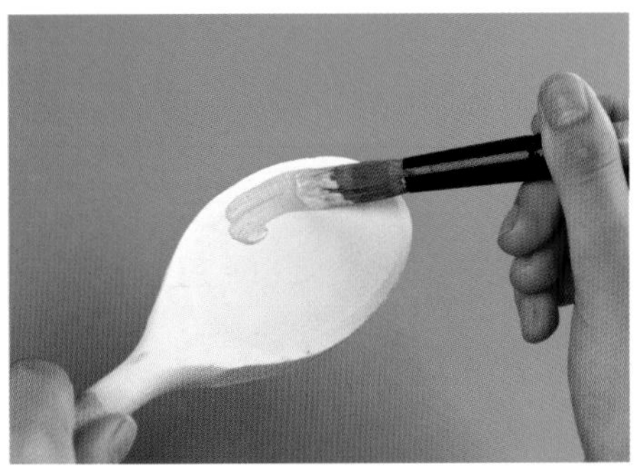

1 Protect your surface with newspapers. Using a medium-sized paintbrush, paint the head of the spoon white, let it dry, then paint in your chosen colour.

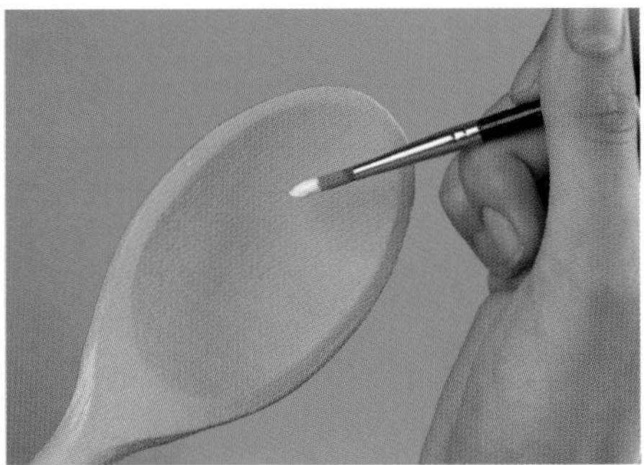

2 Once your chosen colour is dry, use a smaller brush to paint eyes and other features. If you like, paint both sides, each with a different expression.

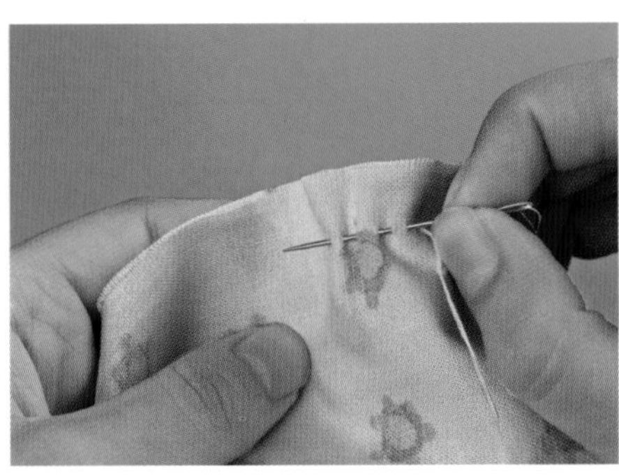

3 To dress your puppet, cut a rectangle shape from brightly coloured fabric. Stitch the short sides together to make a 'tube' of fabric. Make a running stitch all round the top.

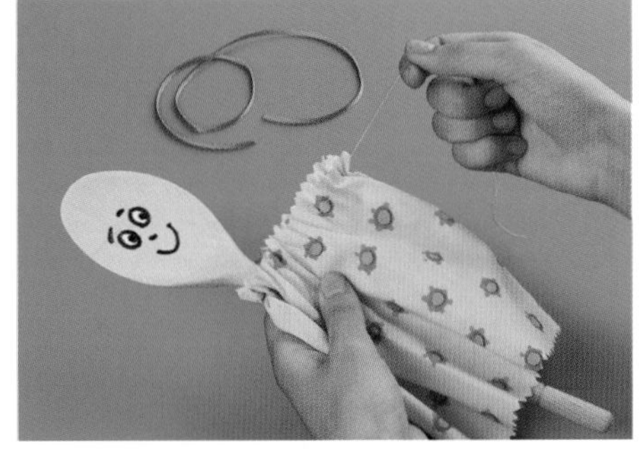

4 Pull the thread to gather the top of the fabric around the puppet's 'neck'. Wrap a length of ribbon around the top of the handle (a dab of glue will help to hold it in place) and tie in a bow.

5 For hair, make a bundle of yarn and tie in the middle to secure the yarn. Glue the bundle of tied yarn in place and trim with scissors.

string prints

With just a wooden block and a length of string, you can create your own printing block.

you will need

MATERIALS

- wooden block (building brick or wooden offcut)
- PVA glue
- length of string
- poster paints or acrylic paints
- paper

TOOLS

- scissors

LEARNING THROUGH PLAY

- Printing
- Creating repeat patterns

ADULT SUPERVISION

A certain amount of patience is needed while you wait for the glue to dry. You may prefer to make the printing blocks one day, then use them another day.

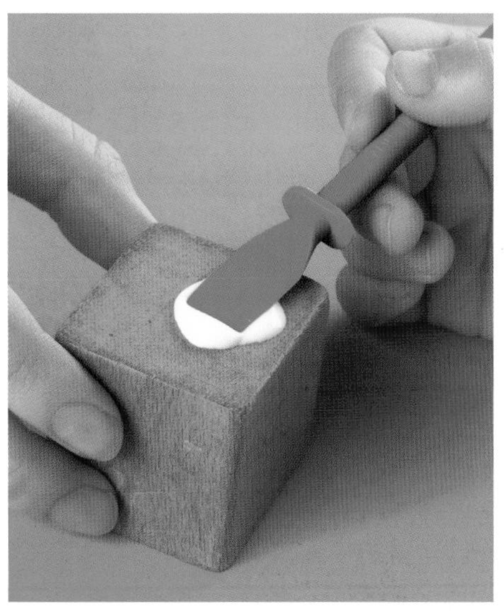

1 Coat one surface of the block with PVA glue.

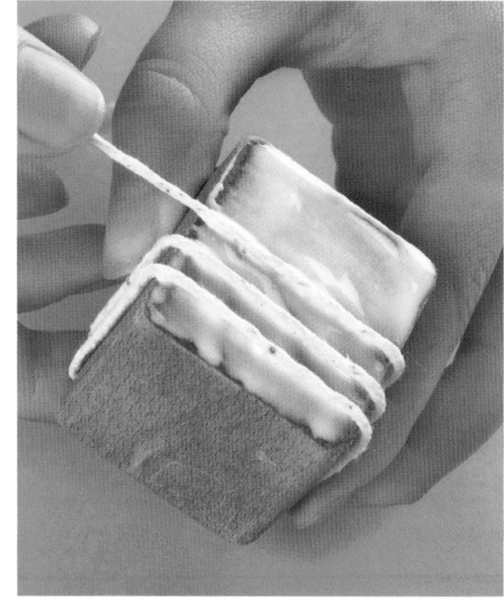

2 Wrap the block with string. You can create different patterns by cutting the string into suitable lengths before applying it to the block.

3 You must leave the prepared block until the glue has dried. Once dry, cut off excess string. Dip your printing block into paint then apply to the paper.

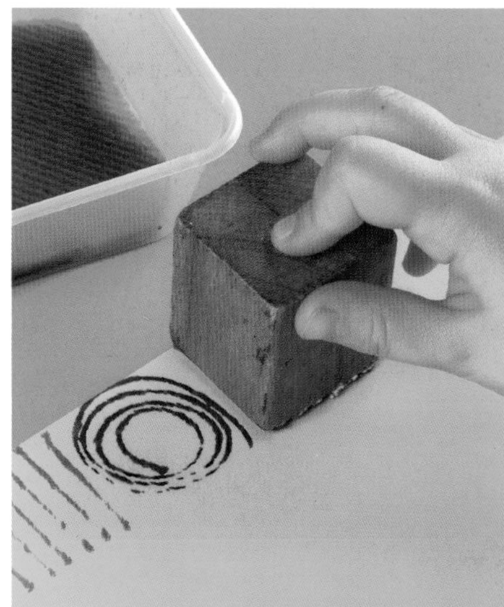

4 Keep dipping and printing until you are happy with the result. One print may be just right for a greetings card. By repeating the pattern on a large piece of paper, you can create your own gift wrap.

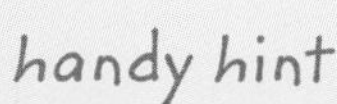

handy hint

Make sure the wooden block is smooth; if you are using an offcut, you may need to rub it with sandpaper before you begin.

painted china

Personalize a cup or plate – or even a whole set of china – with special paints.

you will need

MATERIALS

plain white china

ceramic paints

TOOLS

paintbrush

LEARNING THROUGH PLAY

- Choosing and mixing colours

ADULT SUPERVISION

To make the design permanent, the painted china has to be baked in a hot oven. Follow the manufacturer's instructions carefully.

handy hint

If you want to experiment with your designs or create a temporary decoration – on a vase, for example – do not 'set' the painted china in an oven. The design can then be washed off. Make sure, however, that paint that has not 'set' does not come into contact with food, as it may be harmful.

1 For round objects, such as cups or egg cups, use a wad of paper towels or rags to prevent it rolling around as you paint. Paint the first colour of your design – stripes are easy.

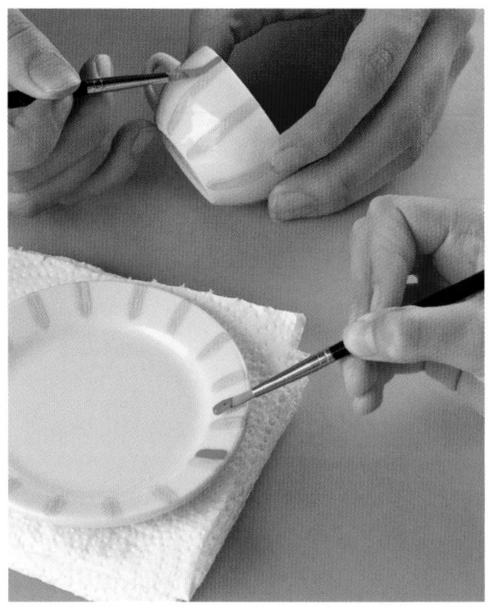

2 When the first colour is dry, add your second colour. If you make a mistake while painting, wipe it off immediately, using a damp cloth.

3 Add the third colour – and even a fourth, if you like – until you are pleased with the result

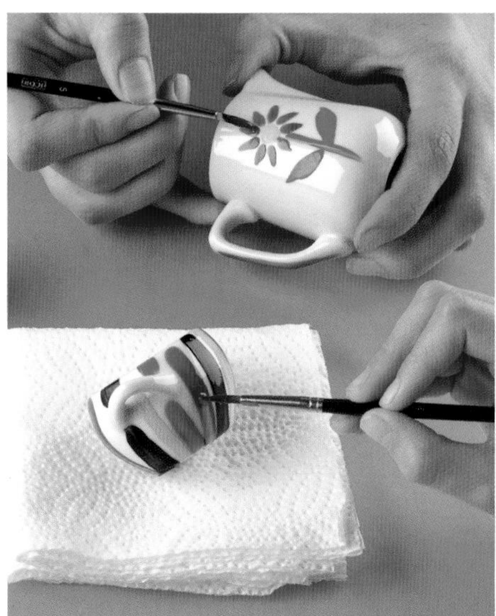

4 When you are confident you can try designs such as flowers. For spots, dip the blunt end of a pencil into paint.

spotty shoes

Decorate a plain pair of fabric shoes and you will have some really fancy footwear for parties and dressing up.

you will need

MATERIALS

- plain fabric shoes
- old newspapers or tissue
- fabric paints
- ribbons
- beads

TOOLS

- wooden stick or cotton buds

LEARNING THROUGH PLAY

- Painting
- Threading

ADULT SUPERVISION

To make the design permanent and weatherproof, you will need to 'set' the fabric paint. This is done with a hot iron – which is not easy on the undulating surface of a shoe, so you will need to use your ingenuity.

1 Remove the shoe laces and stuff the shoes with old newspaper or tissue paper.

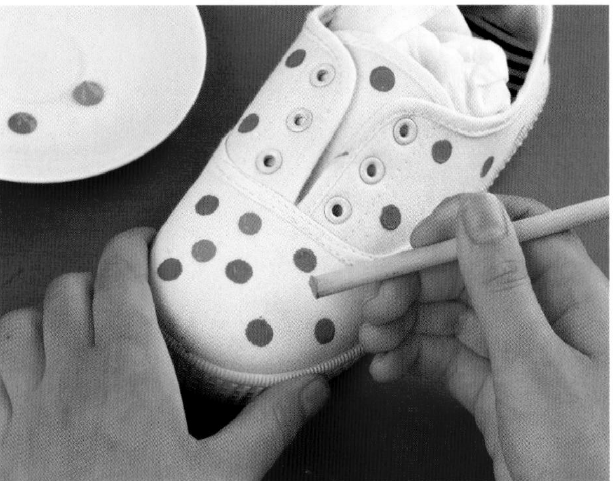

2 Dip your stick or cotton bud into fabric paint and apply to the shoe. Spots are an easy pattern to do but you can come up with your own design.

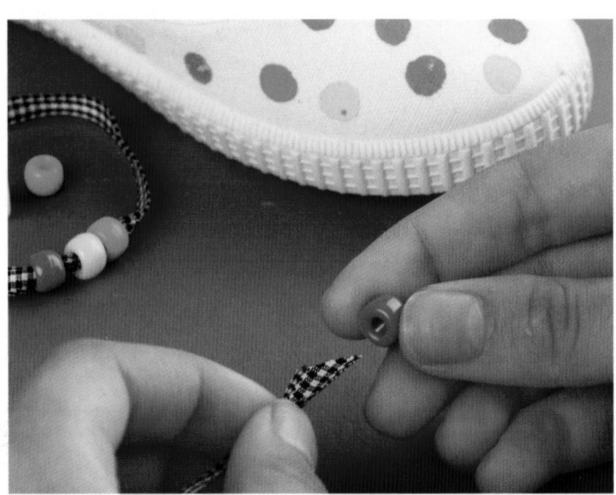

3 Leave the paint to dry thoroughly before replacing the laces. If you like, you can use ribbons instead of laces, adding a few beads before you thread the ribbons through the holes.

handy hint

If you are using ribbons to lace your shoes, bind the ends with sticky tape to prevent them from fraying. This also makes it easier to thread the ribbon through the holes.

tie-dye

Use cold water dyes to turn a plain vest into a colour explosion.

you will need

MATERIALS

- cotton vest or T-shirt
- string
- cold water dyes in yellow, pink and blue

TOOLS

- plastic sheet
- rubber gloves
- bucket
- scissors

LEARNING THROUGH PLAY

- Tying knots
- Mixing colours

ADULT SUPERVISION

Make up the dye according to the instructions on the packet; older children can help with this. Supervise all stages of the dying process. Help with tying strings and with cutting them, taking care not to snip the fabric.

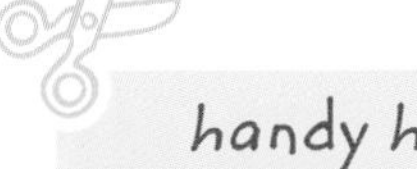

handy hint

When submerging only half of the garment in the dye, use a stick or wooden spoon balanced across the top of the bucket, to support the other half.

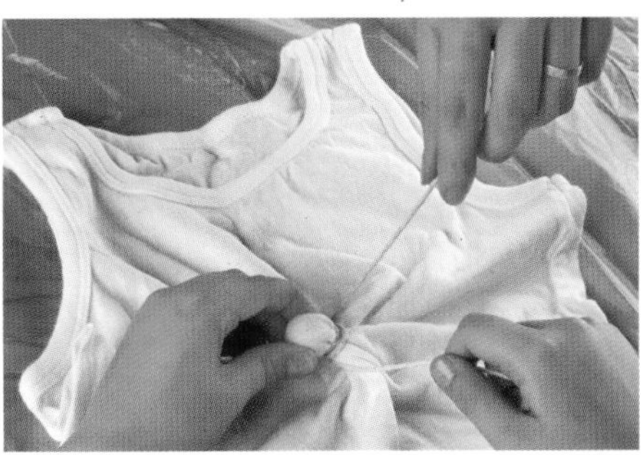

1 Wash the vest in soapy water, rinse thoroughly and wring out but leave damp. Protect your table with a plastic sheet. Find the centre of the vest and pinch both layers between your finger and thumb, then tie a piece of string around.

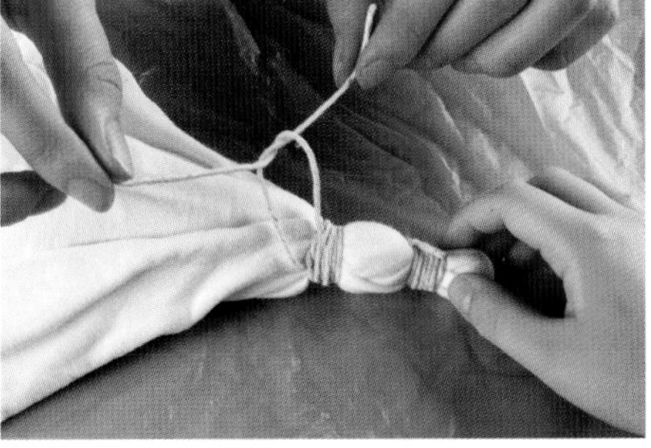

2 Take a second length of string and wrap it around, a few centimetres from the first. Repeat until you have tied a number of wraps.

3 Make up the yellow dye in the bucket, following the manufacturer's instructions. Wearing rubber gloves, place your bound-up vest in the dye bath and push down until it is submerged; leave for 1 hour, or according to instructions.

4 Remove some of the strings and add others in between.

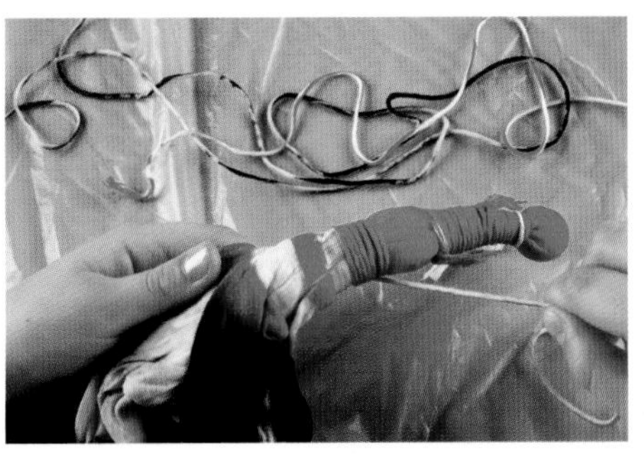

5 Now make up a bucket of pink dye and, wearing rubber gloves again, plunge one end of the vest in this. When the time is up, rinse, then dip the other end in a bucket of blue dye. Rinse, then wash thoroughly and remove all the strings before hanging up to dry.

painted butterflies

By folding paper, splodges of paint are transformed into butterflies, as if by magic.

you will need

MATERIALS

- thick paper
- water-based paints such as poster paints or acrylics
- felt tip pens (optional)

TOOLS

- paint brush or cotton buds
- scissors (optional)

LEARNING THROUGH PLAY

- Experimenting with paint
- Cutting out

ADULT SUPERVISION

Once they understand the principle, children can be allowed to unleash their creativity. For older children, try arranging wax crayon shavings on the unfolded paper, then folding and pressing with a hot iron, which will melt the wax.

handy hint

Once dry, the butterflies can be cut out and used in collages, stuck to a pinboard or the fridge door, or hung from threads to make a mobile.

1 Fold a piece of paper in half, then open out again.

2 Add splodges of paint, using either a brush or cotton buds; apply two or more colours and work quickly, so the paint doesn't have time to dry.

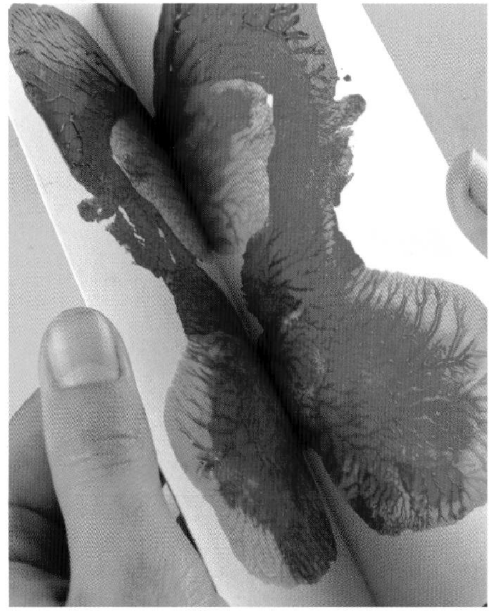

3 Fold the paper in half again and press down lightly. Open out to reveal your painted 'butterfly'.

4 Leave to dry completely, then add details such as antennae using either paints or felt tip pens.

needlecraft

materials

Once upon a time, children were taught to sew. Knitting too was a popular pastime and patchwork a practicality – for even when clothes were too worn out to be mended, scraps could be salvaged and sewn into a cosy quilt.

If taught the basics, children today can enjoy creating a whole range of lovely items. A few simple stitches can turn little scraps of felt into a fistful of finger puppets, squares of cotton into bean bag juggling balls or an old sweatshirt into a winter hat.

In order to have a good choice of materials ready, it is a good idea to start collecting remnants of fabric, knitting yarns, embroidery threads, ribbons, buttons and beads. Even plastic carrier bags can be magically transformed into a colourful garland with a few stitches (see page 100).

Needles are an essential piece of kit and you may wish to have several types at your disposal. For sewing, small fingers often find it easier to get to grips with a chunky needle with a large eye and these can be sharply pointed (darning and crewel needles) or blunt (tapestry needles). For embroidery threads and yarns, a large eye is essential to accommodate the thicker thread. It is also wise if adults supervise sewing activities, especially for younger children. Knitting needles are available in metal, plastic, wood or bamboo and in a range of

sizes. Though it may be tempting to buy the chunkiest ones available, needles of a medium thickness and a shortish length are probably the wisest choice for novice knitters.

checklist

- craft felt
- fabric scraps
- embroidery and sewing threads
- sewing needles
- knitting needles and yarn
- odd socks and gloves
- cross-stitch fabric
- embroidery hoop
- ribbons
- buttons and beads
- plastic carrier bags
- polyester toy stuffing

finger puppets

All you need to put on a puppet show are coloured felt scraps, a needle and some thread.

you will need

MATERIALS

coloured craft felt

embroidery thread

fabric glue (optional)

TOOLS

scissors

needle

LEARNING THROUGH PLAY

- Measuring
- Cutting
- Stitching

ADULT SUPERVISION

Cutting out shapes can be tricky for younger children, so why not cut out shapes for bodies, heads and other pattern pieces in advance? You will find a selection of alternative shapes on page 122, so you can make some of the puppets shown below right.

handy hint

Little fingers need practice to get to grips with needle and thread. To speed up the process, some parts of the puppet can be attached using fabric glue.

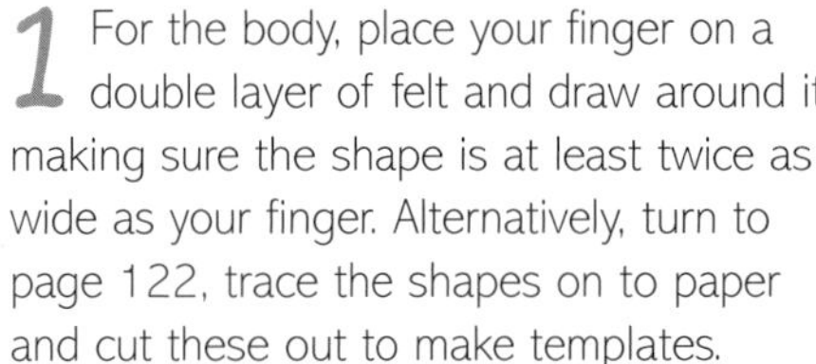

1 For the body, place your finger on a double layer of felt and draw around it, making sure the shape is at least twice as wide as your finger. Alternatively, turn to page 122, trace the shapes on to paper and cut these out to make templates.

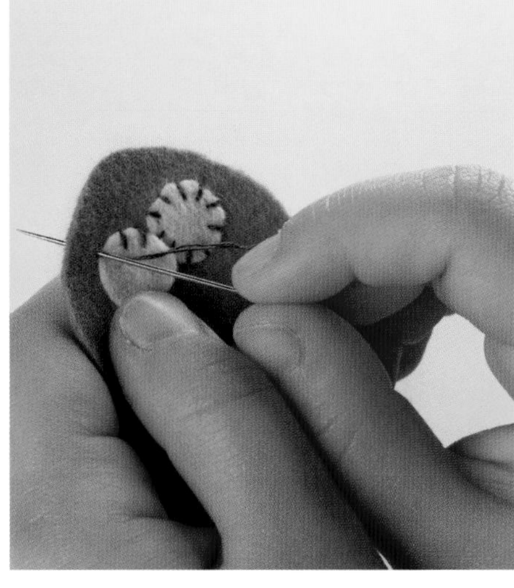

2 Cut out the felt pieces. Choose a piece for the front of the puppet and add circles for eyes. Stick or stitch these in place. Stitch eyes, mouth and other small details using embroidery thread.

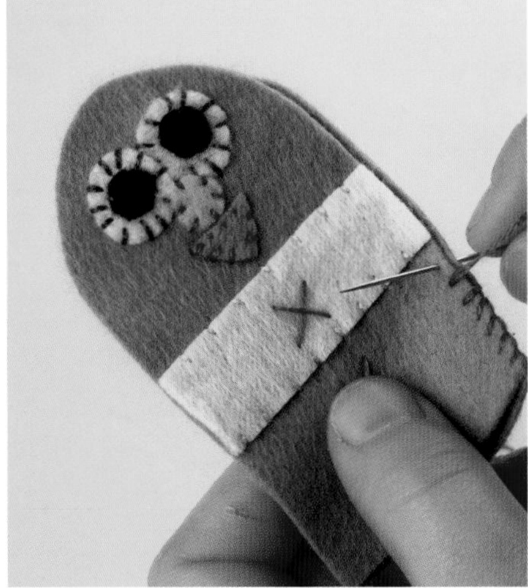

3 Now add other details such as clothes, cut from scraps of felt. Stitch the front and back of the finger puppet together. Do this by oversewing the sides or with a running stitch – whichever you find easier.

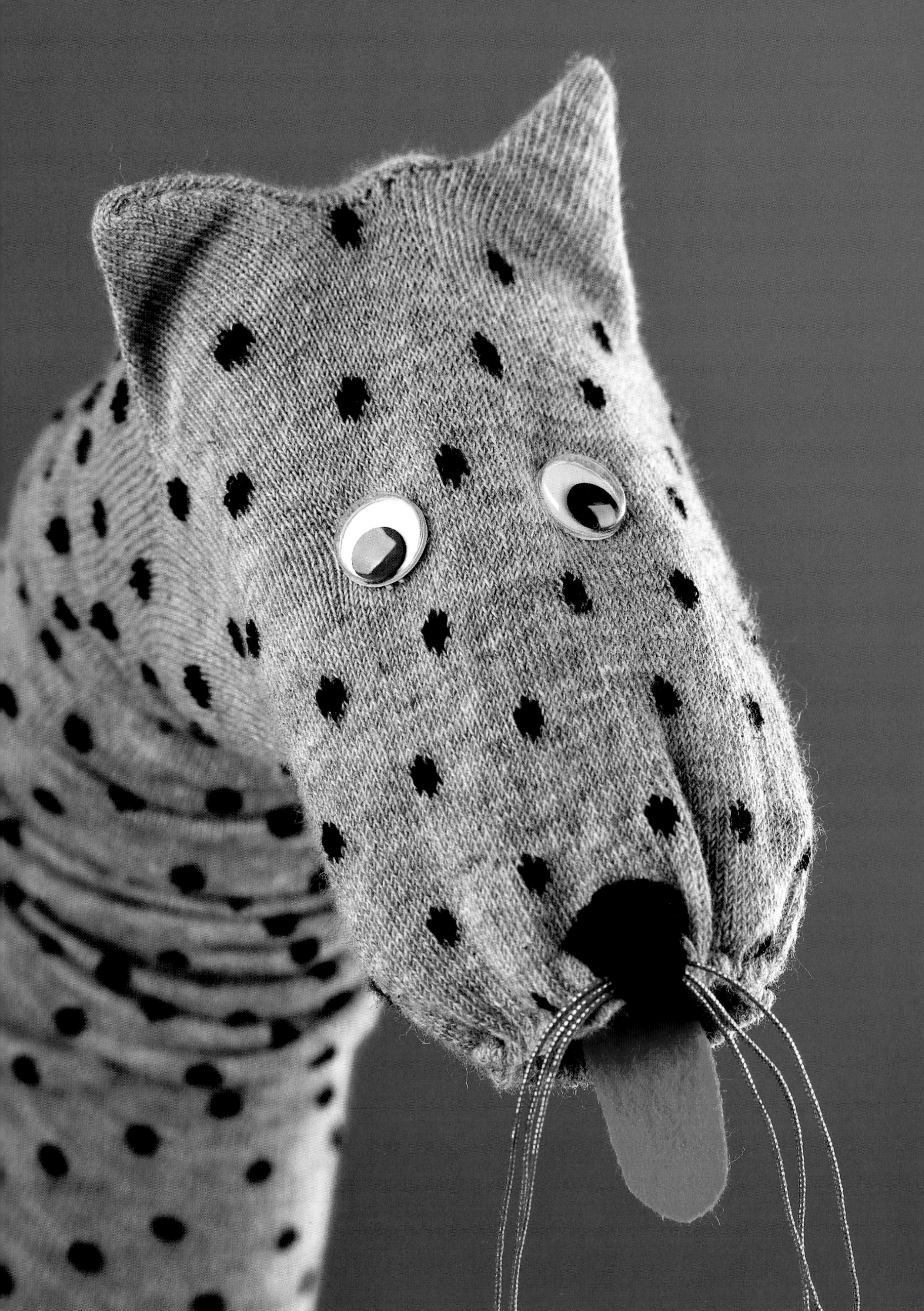

sock puppet

Is it a dog, a cat or a leopard? It all depends on the colour and pattern of the sock you use, or on your imagination!

you will need

MATERIALS

- long sock
- matching sewing thread
- 2 sew-on googly eyes
- few strands of fine cord
- small scraps of black and pink felt

TOOLS

- scissors
- sewing needle

LEARNING THROUGH PLAY

- Measuring
- Cutting
- Sewing

ADULT SUPERVISION

You will need to offer a lot of help, particularly to younger children, especially if they have limited experience of sewing.

1 Turn the sock inside out. Flatten out the heel and cut out a V-shape from the centre, then stitch up cut edges to form ears. Turn right sides out.

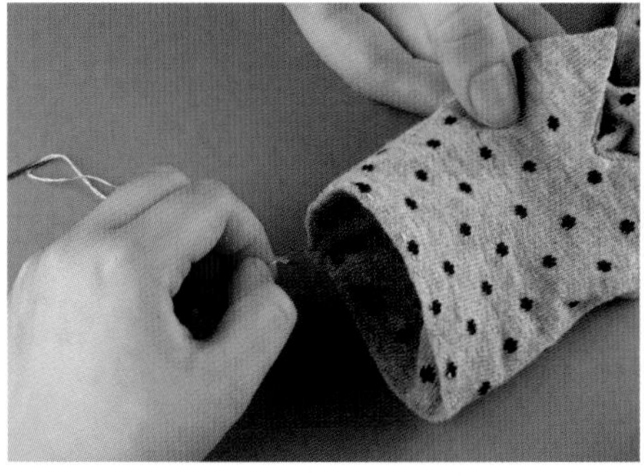

2 Push in the toe end, to form a mouth. Thread the needle with a double strand of sewing thread and sew a running stitch all round the folded edge and pull up to gather. Fasten off.

3 Sew on eyes, then cut a few lengths of cord to form whiskers and stitch these in place in the top centre of the mouth.

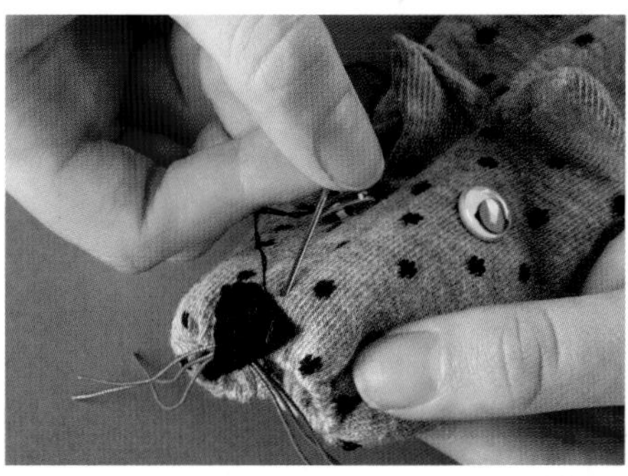

4 Cut a triangle of black felt and stitch on top of the place where the whiskers are attached, folding one point of the triangle over the folded edge of the mouth.

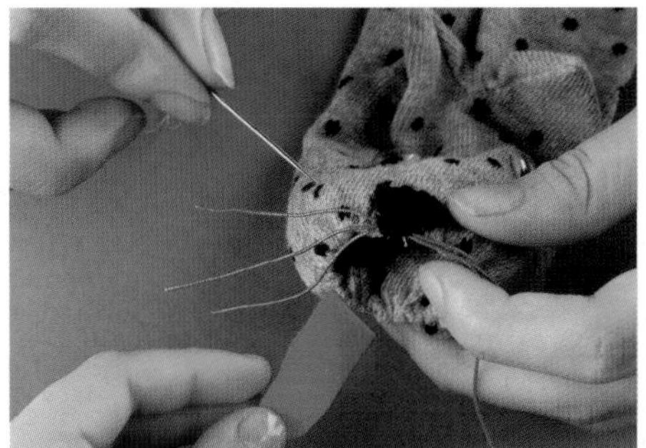

5 Cut a pink shape for a tongue and stitch in place inside the mouth.

handy hint

The character of the finished puppet depends on the sock. With a striped sock you could create a tiger or a zebra; with a grey sock you could make a mouse. Try to use your imagination.

snowman

With a couple of odd socks and basic sewing skills, you can make your own little snowman.

you will need

MATERIALS

- white sock
- scrap of heavy interfacing
- polyester toy filling
- white sewing thread
- scraps of orange and black felt
- striped sock
- scraps of knitting yarn

TOOLS

- scissors
- sewing needle
- knitting needles

LEARNING THROUGH PLAY

- ▸ Measuring
- ▸ Cutting
- ▸ Stitching
- ▸ Knitting
- ▸ Recycling

ADULT SUPERVISION

Children with limited experience of sewing or knitting will need plenty of guidance and instruction. Older children should quickly pick up the skills required.

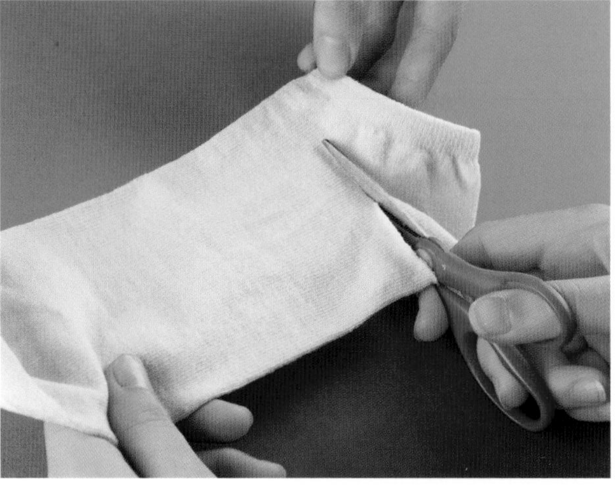

1 Cut across the top of the foot of the sock, just below the heel.

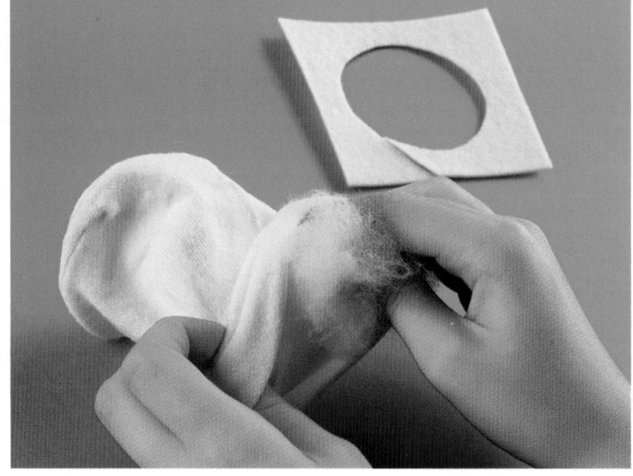

2 Cut a circle of interfacing, 6 cm (2½ in) in diameter, and push this into the toe of the sock, to form the base of the snowman. Stuff the body with polyester toy filling.

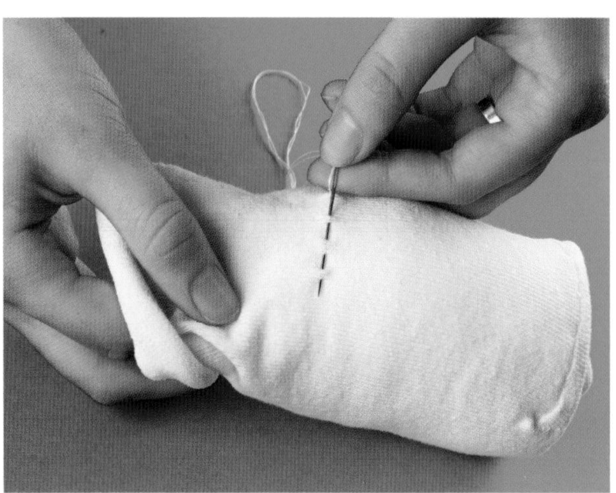

3 Thread the needle with two strands of white thread and attach the end of the thread to the sock, about 9 cm (3½ in) up from the base. Start to sew a running stitch.

continued overleaf

snowman

continued

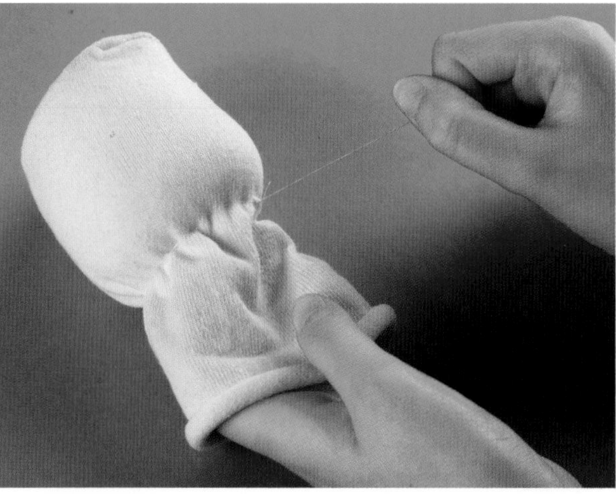

4 Sew the running stitch all around the sock and pull up to gather it; this forms the snowman's 'neck'.

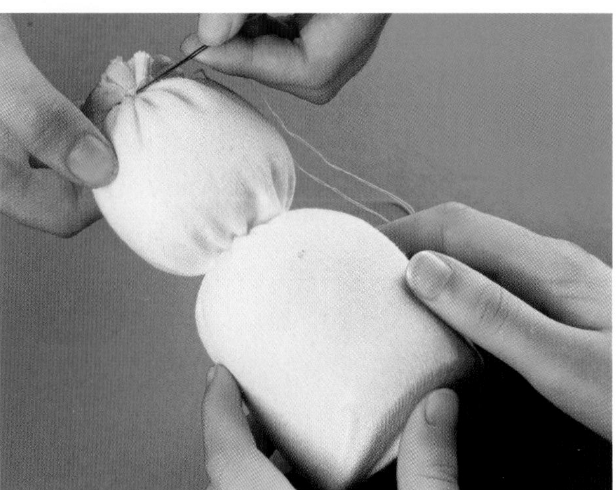

5 Stuff the head then sew another line of running stitch about 5 mm (¼ in) from the top and pull up tightly. Fasten off.

6 Cut a quarter-circle of orange felt. Roll it up into a cone and stitch to form a carrot nose.

7 Stitch the nose in place. Then cut small circles of black felt and stitch in place to form eyes, mouth and buttons.

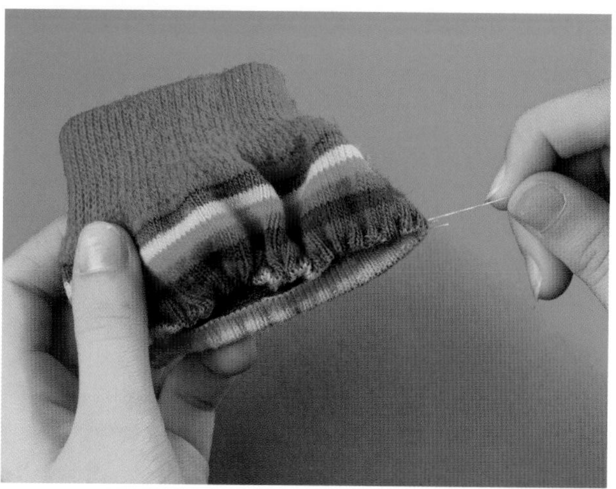

8 To make a hat, cut off the top of a striped sock, 8 cm (3¾ in) from the top of the ribbing. Fold under the cut edge and sew a running thread all round, pulling up tightly to gather, then secure.

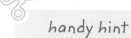

9 To make a scarf, cast on four stitches and knit until your work measures about 20 cm (8 in), then cast off. See page 93 for further instructions on how to knit.

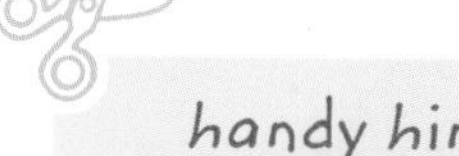

handy hint

Why not use coloured socks to make other characters, combining techniques from the glove rabbit project (see page 82), such as how to make arms.

glove rabbit

If you have an odd glove and an old sock lying around, transform them into a cuddly companion.

you will need

MATERIALS

- one glove
- sewing thread
- buttons
- one sock
- polyester toy stuffing

TOOLS

- scissors
- sewing needle

LEARNING THROUGH PLAY

- Cutting
- Stitching
- Stuffing
- Assembling

ADULT SUPERVISION

Guide children through the various stages, encouraging them to learn the processes of stitching, assembling and stuffing.

1 Turn the glove inside out and cut off the thumb and middle two fingers.

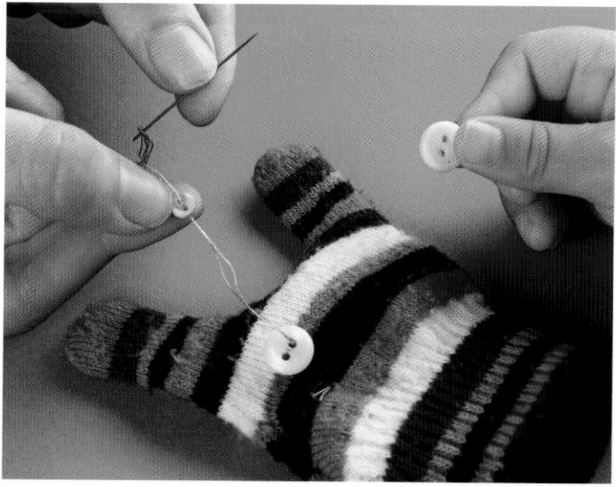

2 Sew up the gaps and turn right sides out. Sew on buttons for eyes.

3 Cut a 15 cm (6 in) length from the leg of the sock. Turn inside out. Make two 4 cm (2½ in) snips at one end, on opposite sides.

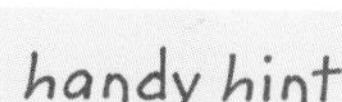

handy hint

When making this toy for a very small child, you may prefer not to use buttons as these can come off and become a swallowing hazard.

continued overleaf

glove rabbit

continued

4 Put a little bit of stuffing into the two fingers than were removed from the glove and place the cut edges in the slits, with the finger inside the sock. Stitch in place.

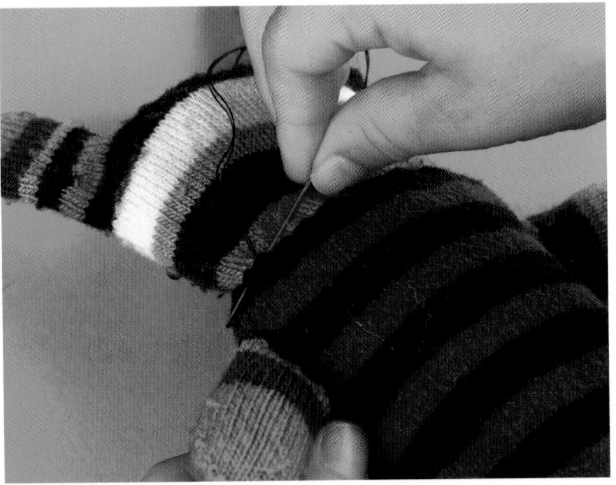

5 Turn right sides out and sew on buttons. Sew a gathering thread around the top of the 'body', draw up to gather slightly, slip neck (cuff of glove) inside and stitch together.

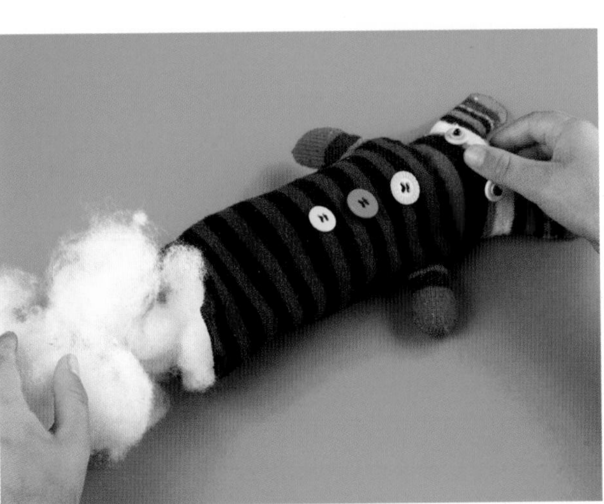

6 Stuff the head and body and stitch up the opening at the base.

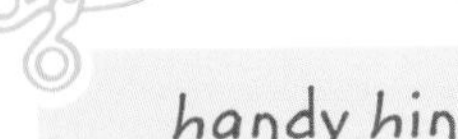

handy hint

The finished result will vary according to the sizes, shapes and colours of the glove and sock you have available, allowing plenty of scope for creativity.

9

fleece hat

Simply made from two squares of fleece, this hat is cosy to wear and is a good way of recycling old fabric.

you will need

MATERIALS

- fleece fabric

TOOLS

- ruler
- felt pen or ball-point pen
- scissors
- needle and thread

LEARNING THROUGH PLAY

- ▶ Measuring
- ▶ Cutting
- ▶ Stitching

ADULT SUPERVISION

Younger children may need help with stitching; older children may be able to use a sewing machine.

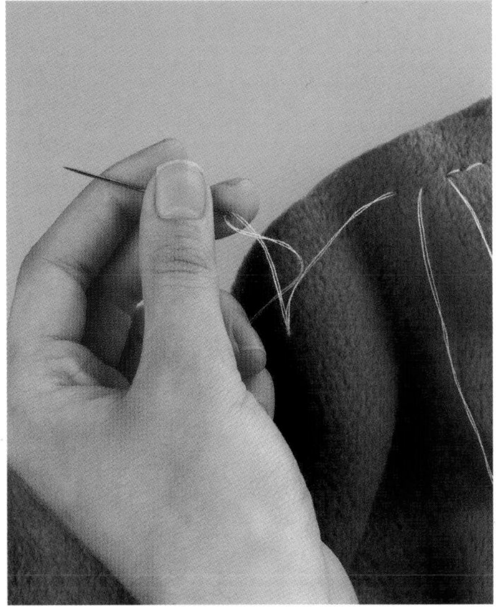

1 Cut two 30 cm (12 in) squares of fleece. Lay one on top of the other and stitch along three sides, about 1.5 cm (⅝ in) from edges.

2 Turn right sides out, so that the seams and hem are on the inside. Using a different-coloured fleece fabric, cut out a star shape (see page 123) and stitch in place.

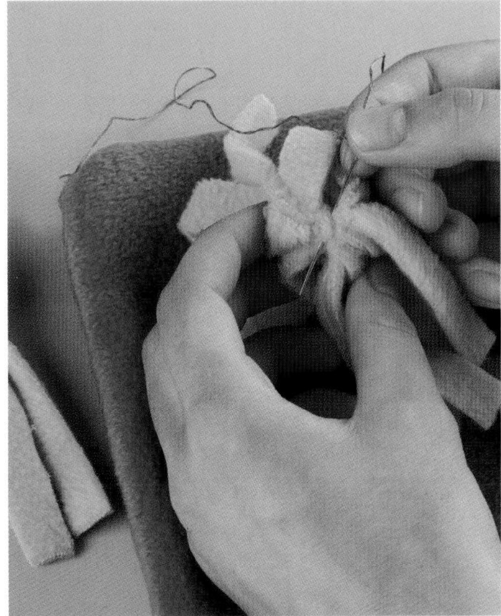

3 Cut strips and tie a bundle of these together to form a tassel. Stitch tassels to the corners of your hat.

4 Roll up the lower edge to form a brim.

handy hint

This hat is very versatile. You can pin or stitch the top corners together, or let them hang down. Use fabric recycled from old sweatshirts.

juggling bean bags

Unlike a ball, these fabric bean bags won't roll away. Use them for games of throwing and catching, or for learning to juggle.

you will need

MATERIALS

- fabric scraps
- sewing thread
- dried split peas, beans or lentils

TOOLS

- scissors
- needle

LEARNING THROUGH PLAY

- Measuring
- Cutting
- Stitching fabric
- Co-ordinating colours

ADULT SUPERVISION

Sewing can be tricky for small fingers, so offer to help. Younger children will enjoy choosing fabrics and filling the bags with beans.

1 Cut squares of fabric measuring 10 cm (4 in). Place two squares of fabric together, with right sides facing inwards.

2 Sew along three sides, about 1 cm (⅜ in) from the edge. Make sure stitches are firm and close together.

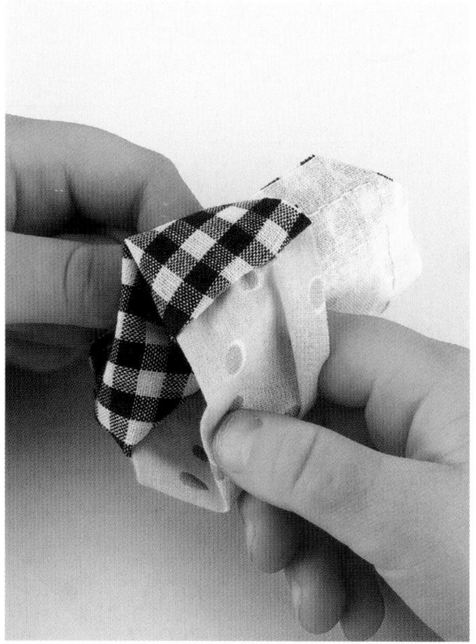

3 Snip off the corners and turn right sides out.

4 Fill about three-quarters full with dried peas, lentils or beans.

5 Fold raw edges to the inside. Place folded edges together, with the seams in the centre, then overstitch the opening.

handy hint

The stitching needs to be quite firm, without large gaps, or the dried beans will spill out. Older children might be able to use a sewing machine to stitch the seams.

rainbow flip-flops

Flip-flops are cheap and cheerful. Here's an idea for adding your own decoration to turn them into party sandals.

you will need

MATERIALS

- narrow sheer ribbon: 80 cm (32 in) of lilac and 60 cm (24 in) each of pink, green and blue
- 4 wooden beads
- 1 pair of rubber flip-flops

TOOLS

- scissors
- ruler

LEARNING THROUGH PLAY

- Measuring
- Cutting
- Threading beads
- Tying knots

ADULT SUPERVISION

Help younger children to measure and cut ribbon. Show them how to tie a reef knot.

handy hint

Instead of using exactly the same ribbons and beads shown here, use your own choice of materials.

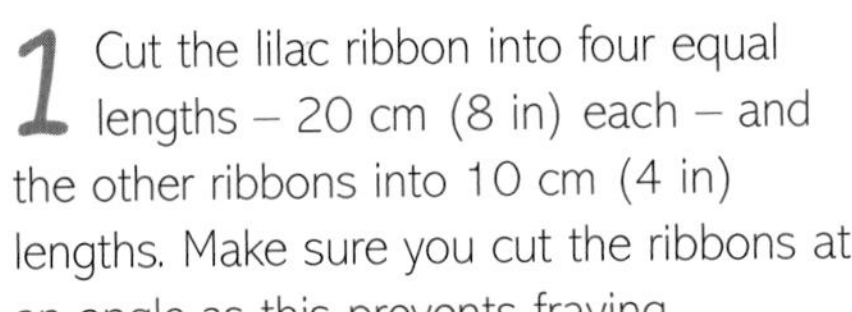

1 Cut the lilac ribbon into four equal lengths – 20 cm (8 in) each – and the other ribbons into 10 cm (4 in) lengths. Make sure you cut the ribbons at an angle as this prevents fraying.

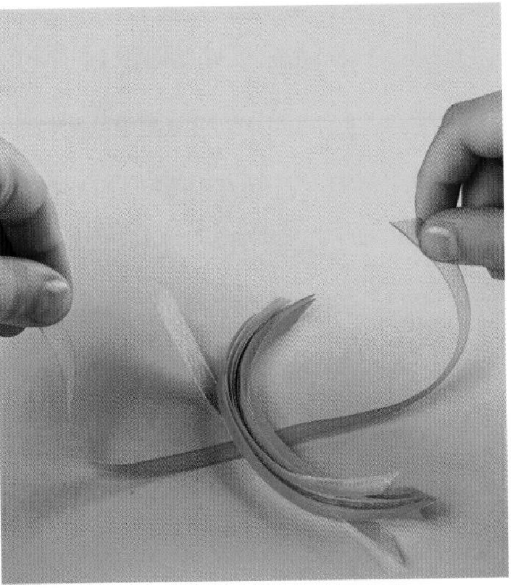

2 Lay a length of lilac ribbon on your work table, then lay three pieces each of pink, green and blue ribbon in a neat pile across it.

3 Tie the lilac ribbon around the other ribbons to form a tight bundle, then thread a bead on to the lilac ribbon and tie tightly.

4 Use the ends of a lilac ribbon to tie the bundle to the front of the flip-flop – round the top, to one side of the toe post – then thread a bead on to another lilac ribbon and tie this across the bundle, on the other side, using a reef knot.

knitted scarf

If you don't know how to knit, now is the time to learn. It is very satisfying wearing a scarf that you have made yourself.

you will need

MATERIALS

double knitting (sports weight) yarn, in different colours

TOOLS

scissors

darning needle

pair of knitting needles, size 5 mm (US 8)

LEARNING THROUGH PLAY

- Knitting

ADULT SUPERVISION

If you can knit, pass on your skills to your children. The instructions given here, for basic casting on, knit stitch and casting off, are enough to create a simple rectangle of knitting, suitable for making a scarf, a cushion cover, or squares that can be stitched together to make a quilt. The hat on page 86 can also be made from rectangles of knitting.

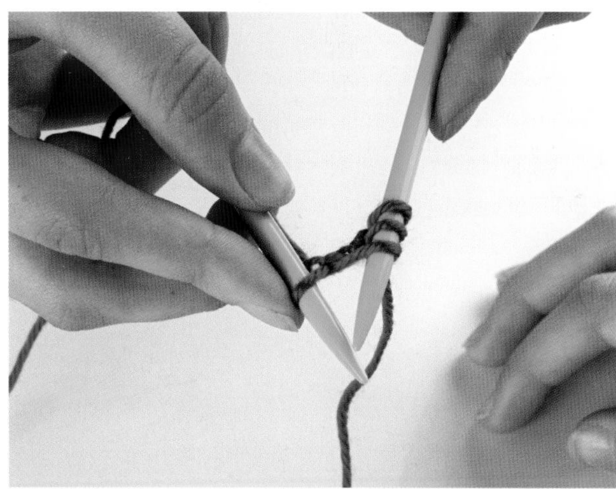

1 To cast on, make a slip knot in the yarn and slip the loop over a needle. Hold this needle in your left hand. Holding the other needle in your right hand, insert it into the loop, wind the yarn around this needle once, then slip the end of the needle under the yarn to pick up the loop, and transfer it to the left-hand needle. Repeat.

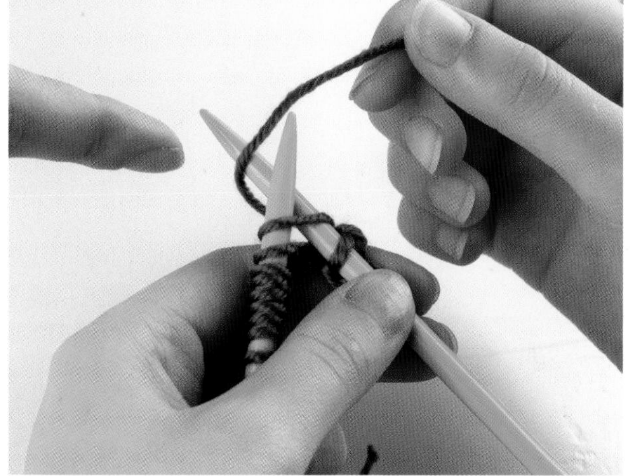

2 When you have 18 stitches on your left-hand needle start a new row. Slip the right-hand needle into the end stitch, wind the yarn around this needle once, then draw the yarn through the stitch using the point of the right-hand needle. Slip the loop off the left-hand needle; the new stitch is now on the right-hand needle.

3 Repeat step 2 until you get to the end of the row, then turn the work around and begin knitting the next row.

continued overleaf

knitted scarf

continued

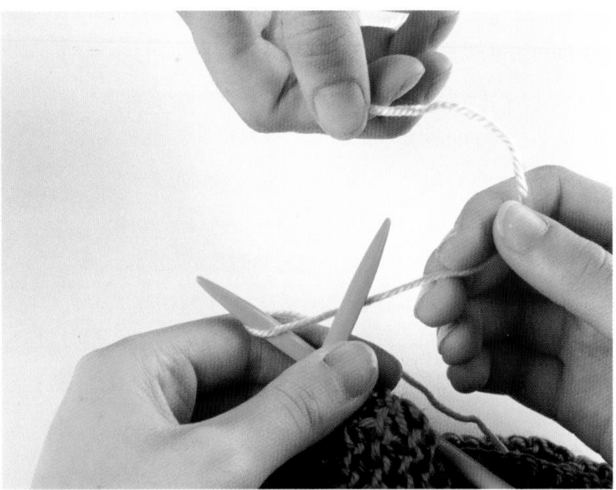

4 Carry on knitting until you think it's time to change colour, then, when you get to the end of a row, cut the yarn you have been using, leaving a tail, and start knitting with another colour. Knot the ends of the two yarns together.

5 Keep knitting, changing colours whenever you like to create lots of stripes. When your scarf is long enough, cast off. To do this, knit two stitches and, with the tip of your right-hand needle, lift the first stitch over the second. Knit another stitch and lift the previous stitch over the one you have just knitted, and so on until the end of the row.

6 The final step is to weave in the ends of yarn. Do not cut them off, or your scarf may fall apart. Instead, thread each end in turn into the eye of your darning needle and weave in and out of the first few stitches, then trim off any excess.

handy hint

Short plastic or bamboo needles, not too thin or thick, are ideal for children learning to knit. Though this project specifies 5 mm (US 8) needles, you could use smaller or bigger needles: the resulting piece of knitting will simply be slightly tighter or looser.

patchwork cushion

Make a colourful cushion from fabric scraps, to decorate your room.

you will need

MATERIALS

- scraps of cotton fabric
- sewing thread
- cushion pad, 24 cm (9½ in) square

TOOLS

- ruler
- scissors
- pencil
- sewing needle
- iron

LEARNING THROUGH PLAY

- ▶ Measuring and cutting
- ▶ Selecting and combining fabrics
- ▶ Stitching

ADULT SUPERVISION

Supervise the cutting and stitching. Press seams open using a hot iron. Older children may be able to use a sewing machine.

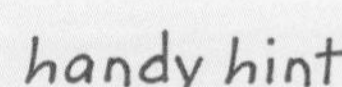

handy hint

Use cotton fabrics, which are washable. As the squares are only 10 cm (4 in), even small scraps can be incorporated into a project.

1 Cut out nine squares of fabric, each measuring 10 cm (4 in). Lay them out on your work table to decide where each one should be placed.

2 Place two of the squares together, with right sides of the fabric on the inside, then stitch a seam 1 cm (⅜ in) from the edge.

3 Add the third square from the row, stitching it to one of the other two squares.

continued overleaf

patchwork cushion

continued

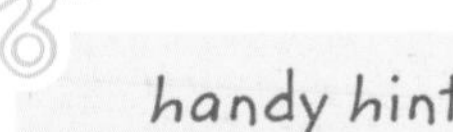

handy hint

To sew a strong seam, use backstitch; to stitch the opening closed, use slipstitch.

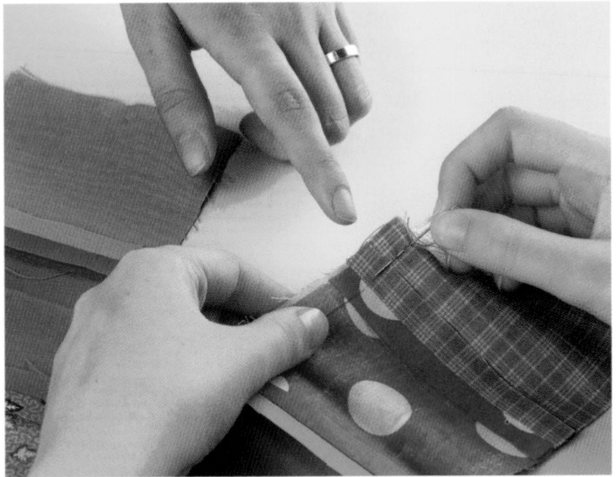

4 Stitch the remaining squares together in the same way, in strips of three. Press the seams with a hot iron. Now stitch two of the three strips together; then stitch the third strip. Press.

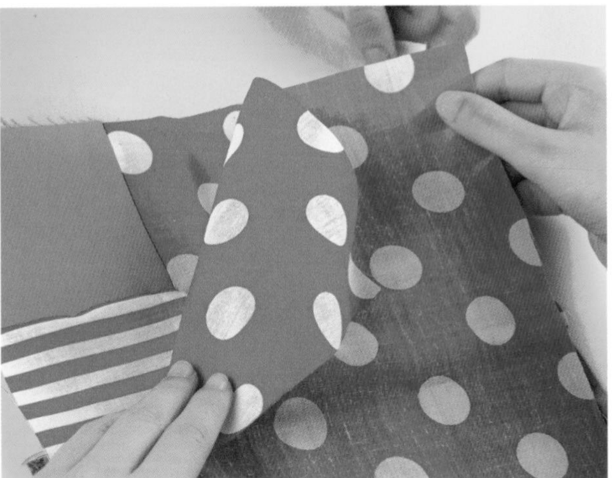

5 Cut a square of fabric measuring 26 cm (10¼ in), to make a back for the cushion. Place the patchwork and the backing together, right sides facing inwards, and stitch around three sides of the cushion, 1 cm (⅜ in) in from the edges.

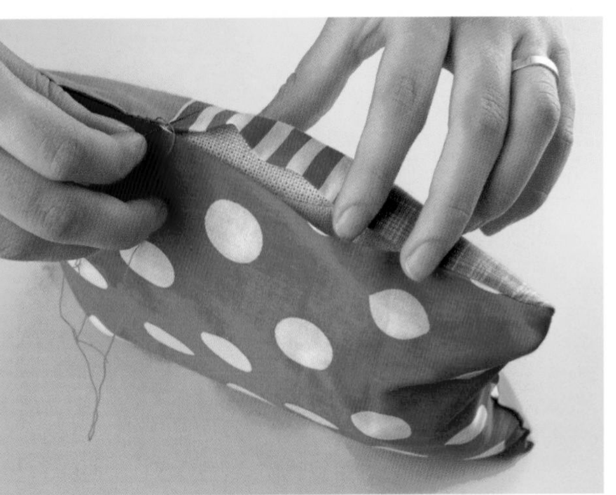

6 Turn the cover right sides out, put the cushion pad inside and slipstitch the open edges together.

cross-stitch picture

Cross-stitch is a great way to start learning to sew and it's easy to create your own designs.

you will need

MATERIALS

graph paper

felt tip pens

cross stitch fabric

embroidery thread

TOOLS

scissors

embroidery hoop

blunt sewing needle

LEARNING THROUGH PLAY

- Designing a motif
- Threading a needle
- Stitching
- Following a pattern

ADULT SUPERVISION

Show children the fundamental techniques of forming a stitch and following a chart.

handy hint

Cross-stitch fabric is available in various weights. For beginners, choose a coarse Aida, with 10 or 12 holes to 2.5 cm (1 in) or Binca, which is suitable for younger children.

1 Choose a design. You can use any of the charts on pages123–125 or create your own using graph paper: one square on the paper represents one cross stitch on the fabric.

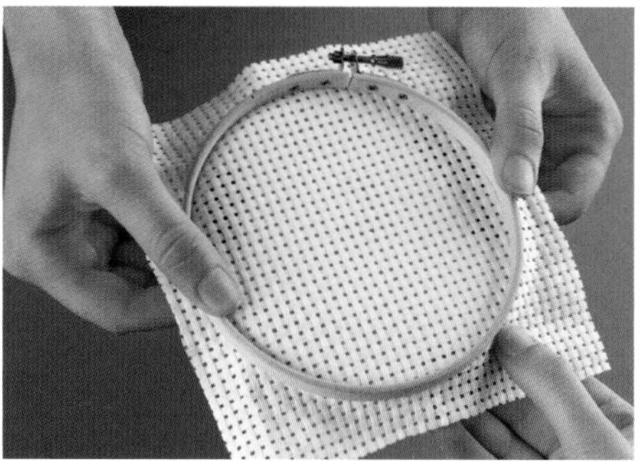

2 Stretch the fabric in an embroidery hoop; this makes it easier to hold and easier to stitch.

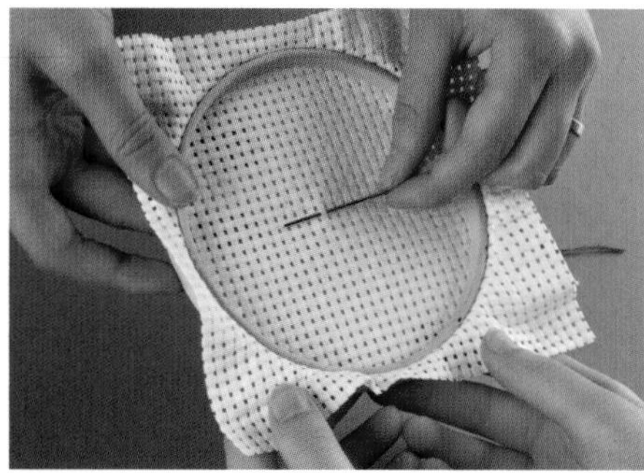

3 Thread your needle with two or three strands of thread (simply cut the thread and pull out the number of strands you need). At the back of the fabric, run the needle under a few threads to secure the end of your embroidery thread.

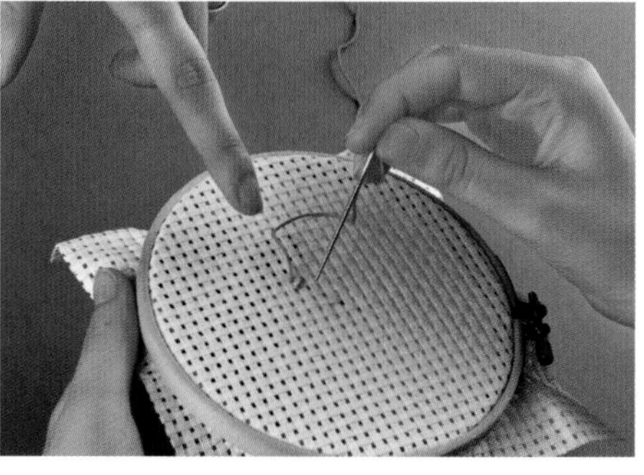

4 Bring the needle up through one of the holes in the fabric. To make a cross stitch, push the needle down through a hole diagonally opposite the one it has come up through, then make a second diagonal stitch across the first.

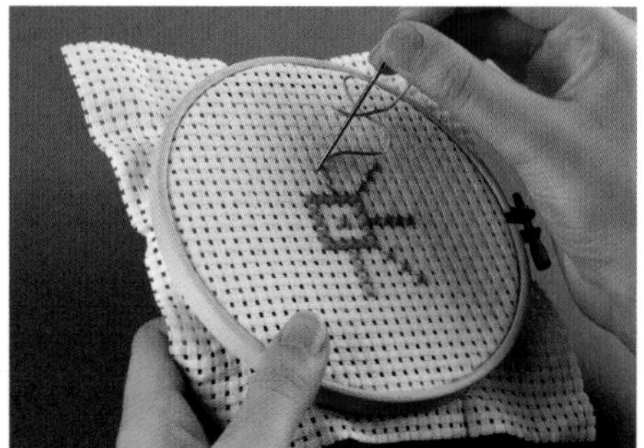

5 Follow your chosen design, making cross stitches to correspond with the ones on the graph.

hula-hula garland

Perfect for parties and dressing up, who would believe these garlands are made from recycled paper and plastic?

you will need

MATERIALS

- plastic carrier bags
- tissue paper
- sewing thread

TOOLS

- scissors
- sewing needle

LEARNING THROUGH PLAY

- ▶ Choosing and combining colours
- ▶ Sewing
- ▶ Cutting
- ▶ Dressing up

ADULT SUPERVISION

Younger children may need help with the stitching; older ones may be able to use a sewing machine, which will speed up the stitching process.

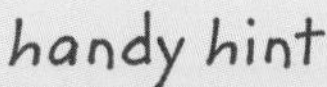

handy hint

Try to collect as many different coloured bags as you can and have fun combining different coloured plasic strips with different coloured tissue paper.

1 Cut strips 10 cm (4 in) wide and 80 cm (31½ in) long from tissue paper and from plastic carrier bags. If your strips are shorter than this, don't worry as you can join strips together.

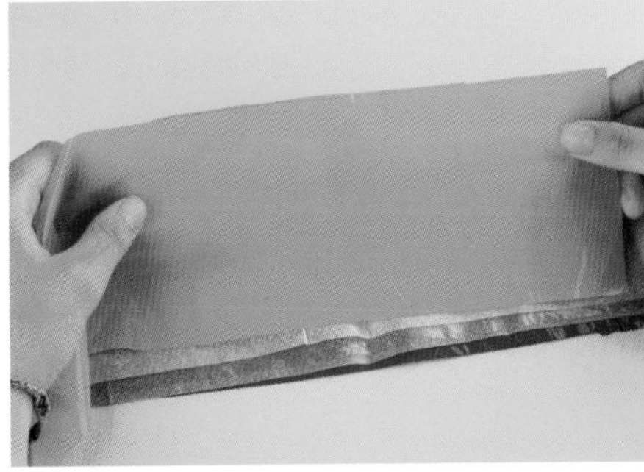

2 Layer strips of plastic and tissue on your work surface. Overlap ends by about 2 cm (¾ in), if necessary, to obtain the right length. Add more strips of plastic, and of tissue.

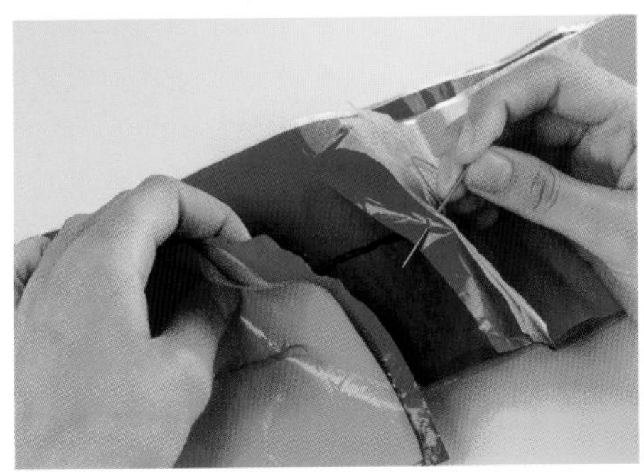

3 Using a needle and double strand of thread, stitch a line right along the centre, through all layers. Stitch a second line on top to make it really secure. Join the two ends by stitching firmly together.

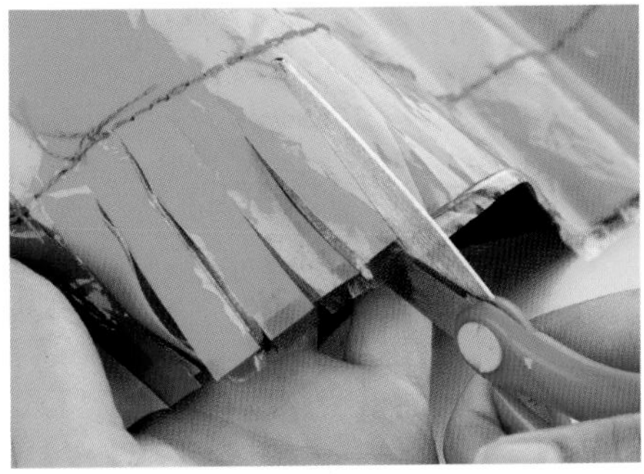

4 With scissors, make a series of cuts from the edge up to the line of stitching – but take care not to cut through the stitches. Repeat these cuts until you have a fringe on either side of stitching.

5 Now crumple up the garland in your hands. Really squeeze it, as this will create a nice ruffled effect. Now your garland is ready to wear.

NEXT

naturecraft

materials

When you are out and about, in the park, countryside or by the sea, it is fun to collect things like twigs, pebbles, seashells and driftwood.

You may also be lucky enough to have a garden, which is a great source of natural materials such as sticks and leaves and discarded items such as flowerpots.

Then, on days when it's too wet or cold to venture out of doors, you can use some of the stuff you have collected in your craft projects. Whether it is using a twig as the basis for a wind chime or rattle, or getting out your paints to make prints from a potato or some leaves, or to decorate a plant pot, some wooden lollipop (popsicle) sticks or an assortment of smooth pebbles, there is plenty in this chapter to keep you occupied whatever the weather.

The other things you'll need might be found in the tool shed, the garage, the cupboard under the stairs or the kitchen drawer, so have a good rummage before you embark on your chosen activity.

Some of the projects are designed to be displayed in the garden – or the balcony, patio or windowsill – and some would also make good presents.

checklist

- leaves
- clay flower pots
- twigs
- lollipop (popsicle) sticks
- string and elastic
- potatoes
- pebbles
- acrylic paints
- poster paints
- paint brush
- paper
- fabric paints

leaf prints

Celebrate the beautiful patterns of nature by using leaves to create simple prints.

you will need

MATERIALS

thick paper or thin card

fresh leaves

water-based paints: poster paints or acrylics

TOOLS

palette (such as saucer or plastic tray)

small roller or sponge

scissors

LEARNING THROUGH PLAY

- Applying paint
- Printing
- Creating repeat patterns

ADULT SUPERVISION

Help children select leaves suitable for printing. Fresh leaves are better than dry ones, which tend to crumble. One leaf should make several prints before it becomes too soggy.

handy hint

Use leaf prints to make greetings cards, pictures and gift wrap. Cut out individual leaf prints to make gift tags, or string them together on strong thread to make a decoration.

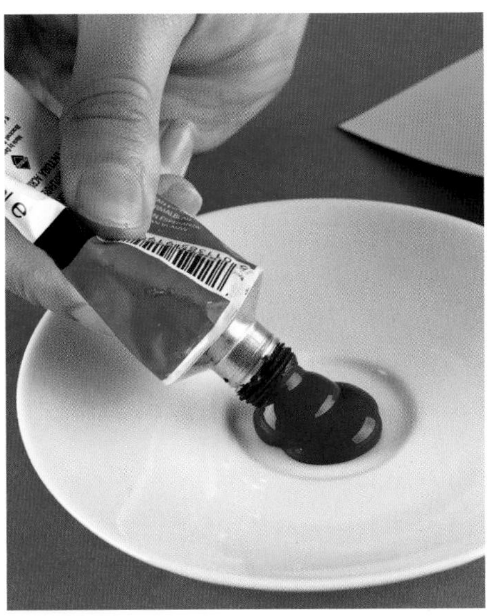

1 Fold a piece of card in half, to make a greetings card. Squeeze a little paint on to a saucer or similar flat surface.

2 For best results, choose a leaf with prominent veins. Coat the roller or sponge with a thin, even layer of paint and apply to the leaf.

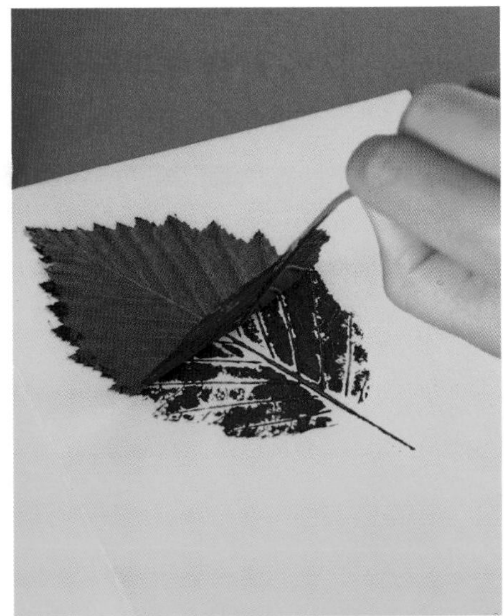

3 Press the leaf on to the front of the card and press down firmly; lift the leaf carefully to reveal the print.

4 You can use the same leaf to make up to six prints. Make a matching envelope by printing a leaf on the front or back flap.

painted flowerpot

Bright and beautiful pots can be planted with flowers and herbs to decorate a windowsill.

you will need

MATERIALS

terracotta flowerpot

white acrylic primer or emulsion paint

acrylic paints

TOOLS

paintbrush

LEARNING THROUGH PLAY

► Painting a three-dimensional object

► Being patient while paint dries

ADULT SUPERVISION

Painting the pot white to begin with will provide a good base for subsequent colours, making them appear bright. The paint will soak into the clay pot, speeding up drying times, so you will not have to wait long before applying the next colour.

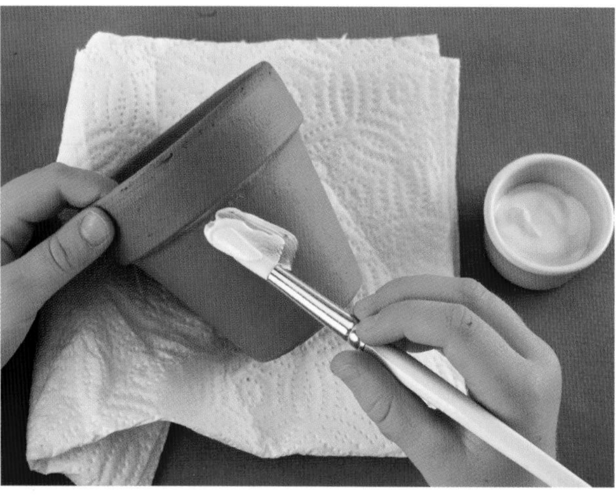

1 Paint the outside of the pot with white primer or emulsion paint. Leave to dry.

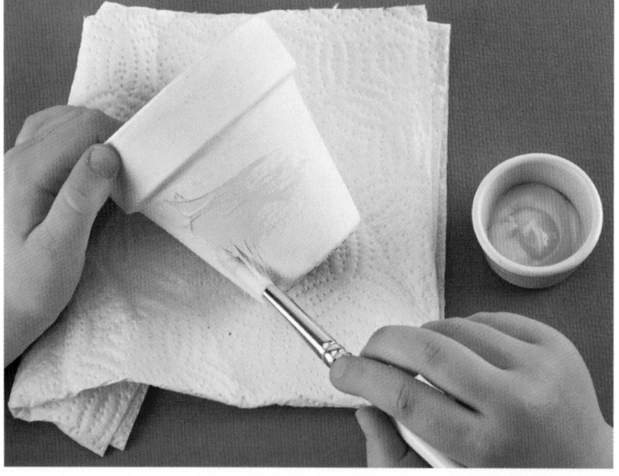

2 Now paint the pot in your choice of colours. Paint it the same colour all over, or paint the rim in a contrasting colour, if you like. Leave to dry.

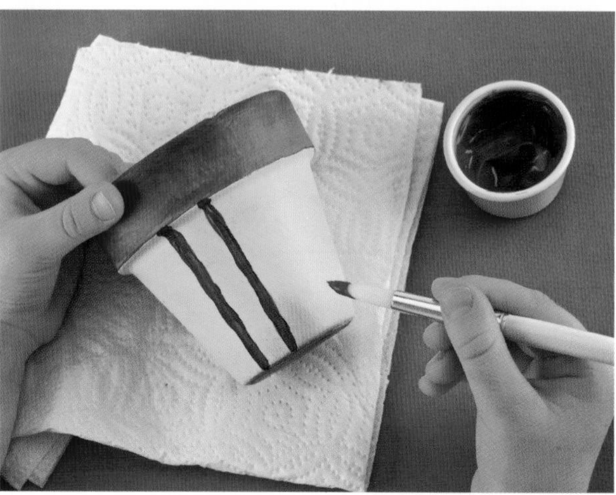

3 Now paint spots, stripes or other patterns on your pot, using any colours you like.

handy hint

Place newspaper on the table before you begin. Putting a pad of newspaper or kitchen paper under the pot as you paint will help to hold it steady.

lolly stick plant labels

Flat wooden lollipop (popsicle) sticks are ideal for labelling planted seeds and bulbs while you wait for them to grow.

you will need

MATERIALS

- wooden lollipop sticks
- acrylic paints
- permanent marker pen (optional)

TOOLS

- paintbrush

LEARNING THROUGH PLAY

- Painting
- Creating patterns
- Learning plant names

ADULT SUPERVISION

You may wish to prepare the sticks by painting them white in advance. You can use white gesso or emulsion paint for this. This initial coat prevents subsequent coats from soaking in to the wood and the white surface makes colours look brighter.

handy hint

These labels have a number of uses. When you sow seeds or plant bulbs in the garden or in a container, it helps to mark the position with a stick while you are waiting for the first shoots to appear.

1 Paint each stick, back and front, with white paint. Leave to dry.

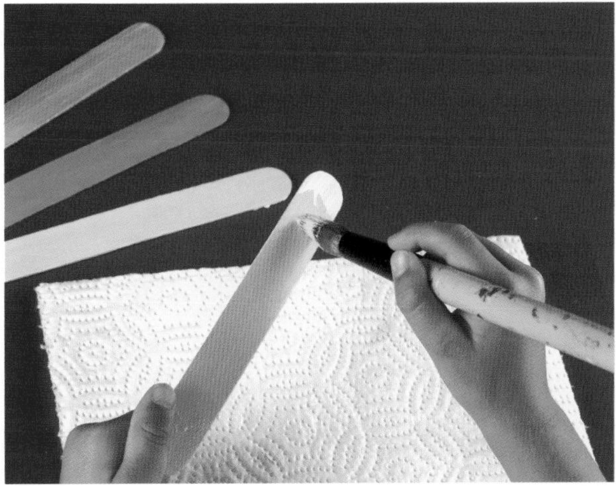

2 Use your choice of colours to paint both stides of each stick. Leave to dry.

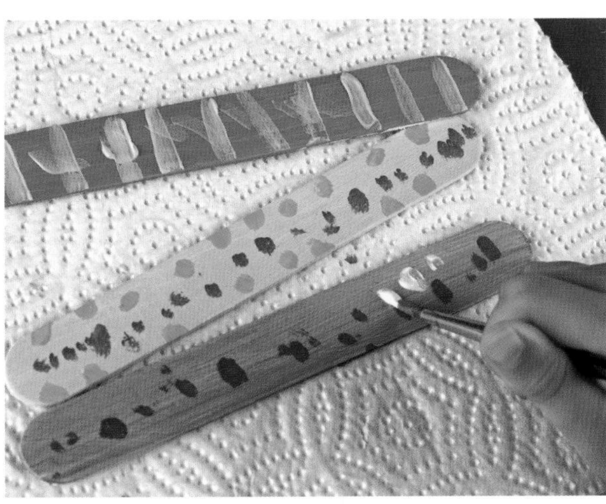

3 Paint your sticks with colourful patterns, on one or both sides. Use a permanent marker pen to write the name of the plant on the stick, if you like.

potato prints

Decorate a pillowcase with brightly coloured motifs – using a potato for a stamp!

you will need

MATERIALS

- potato
- absorbent paper
- acrylic paints, poster paints or fabric paints
- paper or fabric

TOOLS

- sharp knife
- paper plate
- brush, sponge or small roller

LEARNING THROUGH PLAY

- Printing

ADULT SUPERVISION

Cutting potatoes requires a sharp knife and this is best done by an adult.

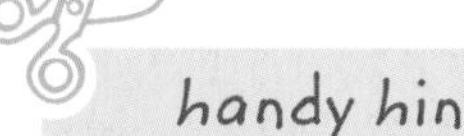

handy hint

You can make several different prints from a single potato – slice off the previous design to leave a new, flat surface. If you print on fabric, put newspaper underneath; for a T-shirt, place a thick wad of paper inside to prevent colour seeping from front to back. Use fabric paints, and follow the label's instructions to fix the colours.

1 Cut a potato in half. On the cut surface, draw a simple shape.

2 Cut around the outline of the shape using the tip of a small, sharp knife, then cut away excess potato around the shape. Wipe the surface of the potato to get rid of excess moisture.

3 Pour a little paint on to the paper plate. Use fabric paints for a pillowcase or t-shirt; acrylics or poster paint for paper. Use a brush, sponge or roller to spread a layer of paint on the potato.

4 Press the potato on to your fabric (or paper). Apply more paint to the potato and repeat. Use different shapes and colours to create a fun pattern.

twig rattle

Decorate a forked stick with found objects that will rattle when shaken – beads and bells are useful materials.

you will need

MATERIALS

- forked stick
- cord elastic
- wooden or plastic beads or other objects
- bells

TOOLS

- scissors

LEARNING THROUGH PLAY

▶ Threading and tying

ADULT SUPERVISION

Search for a suitable stick. You may have to prepare it so that it is nice and smooth: do this by peeling away the bark. You may also wish to rub it over with medium-grade sandpaper to make sure there are no splinters.

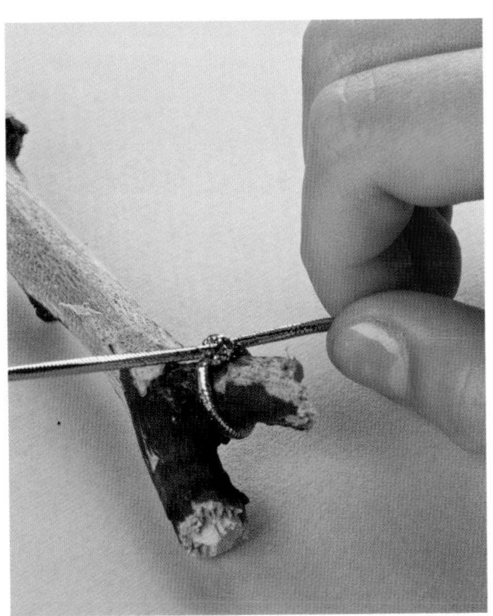

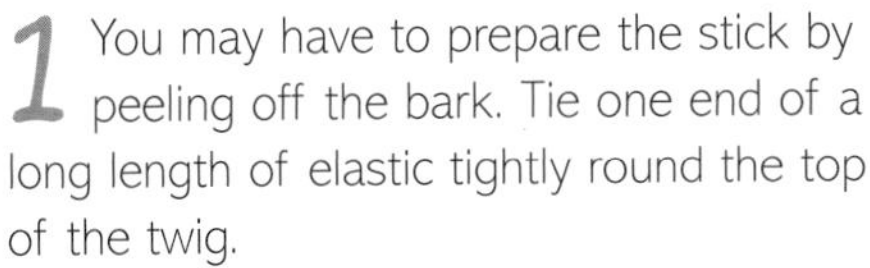

1 You may have to prepare the stick by peeling off the bark. Tie one end of a long length of elastic tightly round the top of the twig.

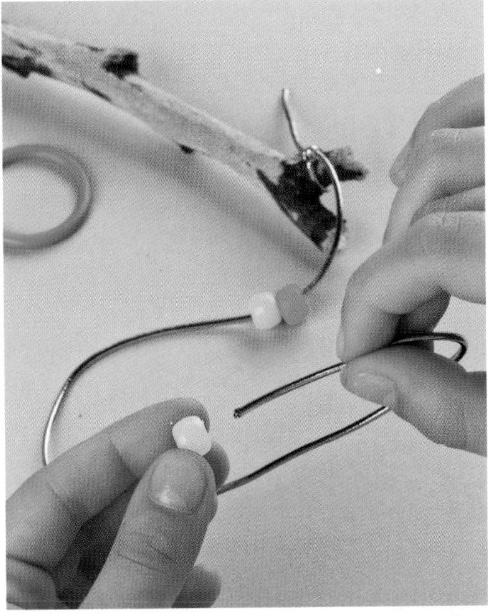

2 Thread some beads and bells on to the elastic.

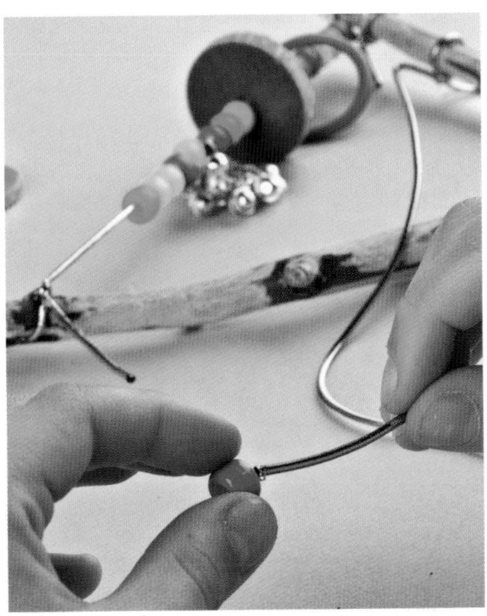

3 Tie the elastic to the other side of the twig and thread on some more beads.

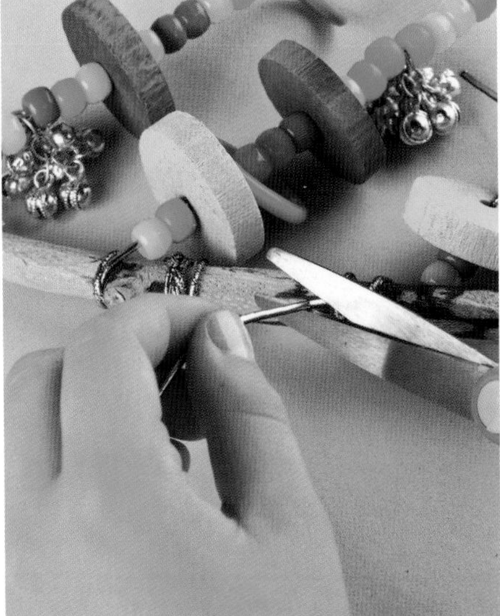

4 Keep going in this way until you have created several strings of beads and other objects, then tie off the end and trim off any excess elastic.

handy hint

Instead of a rattle, you could turn your stick into a bird scarer. Simply add strips of aluminium foil, in addition to the beads and other objects, then push the stick into the ground close to the plants you wish to protect.

painted pebbles

Smooth pebbles provide an ideal surface for creative painting and pattern-making.

you will need

MATERIALS

- pebbles
- white acrylic paint or emulsion paint
- coloured acrylic paints
- acrylic varnish (optional)

TOOLS

- medium paintbrush
- fine paintbrush

LEARNING THROUGH PLAY

- Painting
- Designing
- Choosing and mixing colours

ADULT SUPERVISION

Make sure work surfaces are protected with newspapers or plastic and clothes are protected with an old shirt or apron. Discuss ideas for painted designs.

handy hint

Finished pebbles can be displayed individually on a shelf or windowsill, or grouped in a basket or bowl. A coat of acrylic varnish will help to weatherproof painted pebbles that are to be left outside.

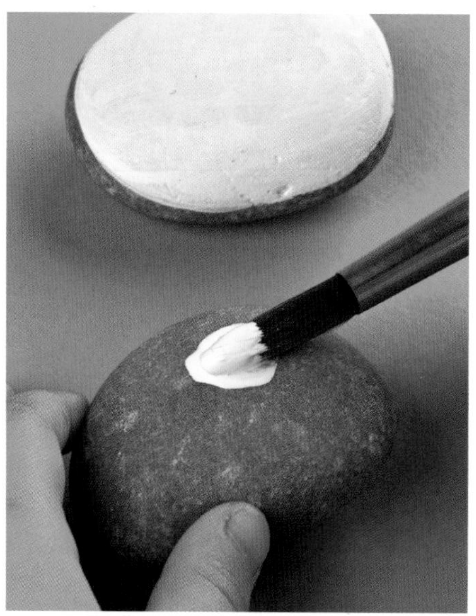

1 Paint pebbles with white primer or emulsion paint. Leave to dry.

2 To make a ladybird pebble, paint your pebble with red acrylic paint and leave it to dry.

3 With black paint and a fine brush, paint in details such as the head and spots. If you wish, protect the surface with a coat of varnish.

4 If you don't want to paint a ladybird, use your imagination and decorate your pebbles with whatever designs and colours you choose.

wind chime

Hung outside, or close to an open door or window, this will catch the breeze and create a pleasant sound.

you will need

MATERIALS

string

assortment of pebbles, shells and metal objects

sturdy twig

TOOLS

scissors

LEARNING THROUGH PLAY

- ▶ Selecting suitable objects
- ▶ Tying knots.

ADULT SUPERVISION

Organize a treasure hunt to find suitable objects: ones with holes in them. They could be natural things such as shells and pebbles; metal objects such as spools, cutlery and utensils; or plastic items such as buttons and small toys.

handy hint

As well as using this as a wind chime, you could use it as a bird scarer, to deter birds from eating seeds, fruit and young plants.

1 Tie a short length of string to one of your objects, using a firm knot.

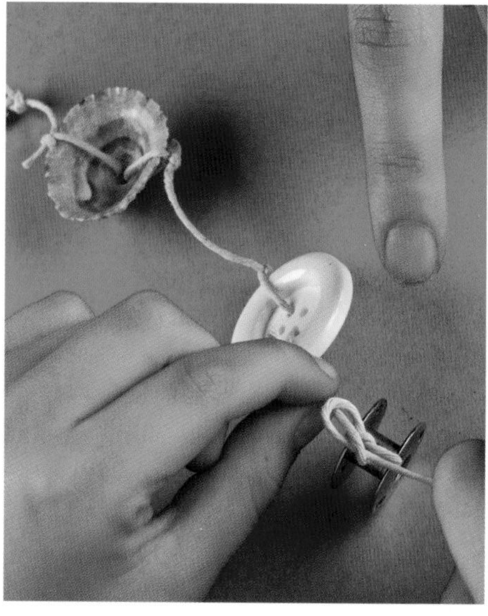

2 Tie the other end to a second object. Then attach a second length of string to this object and tie the other end to a third object.

3 Carry on in this way until you have created a string of objects. Then make three, four or five more strings.

4 Tie the strings to the twig, spacing them out evenly but keeping them quite close together. Then tie the ends of a length of string to either end of the twig.

templates

paper hearts
(page 22)

fishing game
(page 30)
magic wand
(page 42)

basic body

panda face

panda ear/eye

panda tummy

panda paw

hair

hair

body

T-shirt

shorts

tiger body

tiger face

tiger tail

tiger tummy

finger puppets (page 74)

fleece hat (page 86)

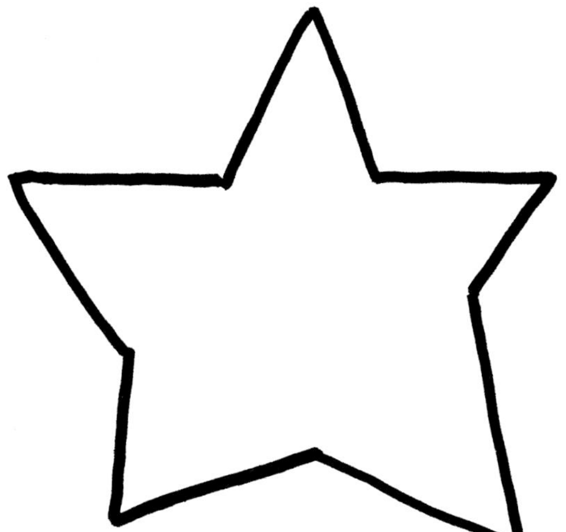

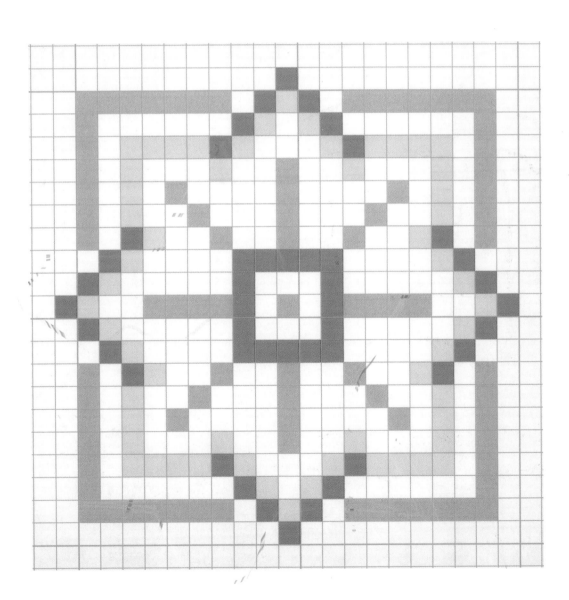

cross-stitch picture (page 98)

cross-stitch variations (page 98)

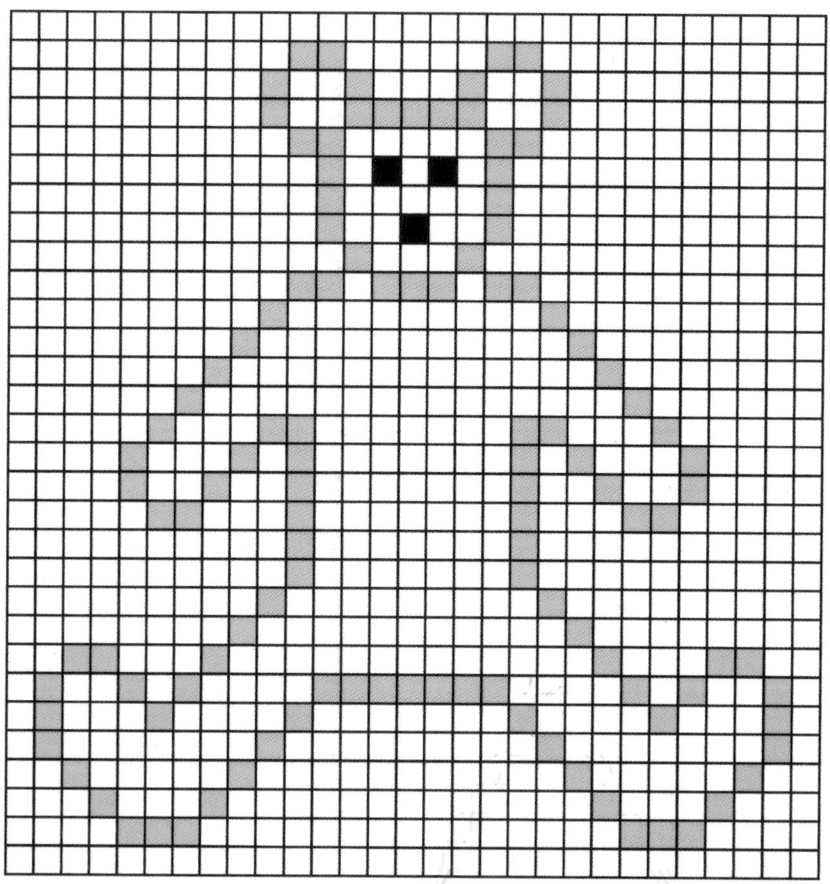

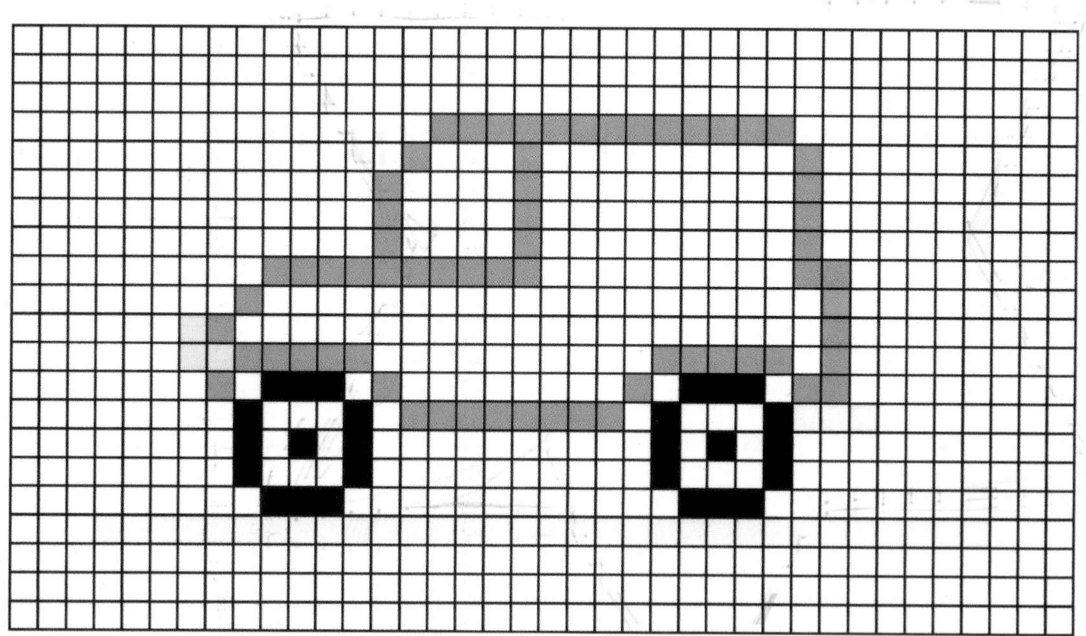

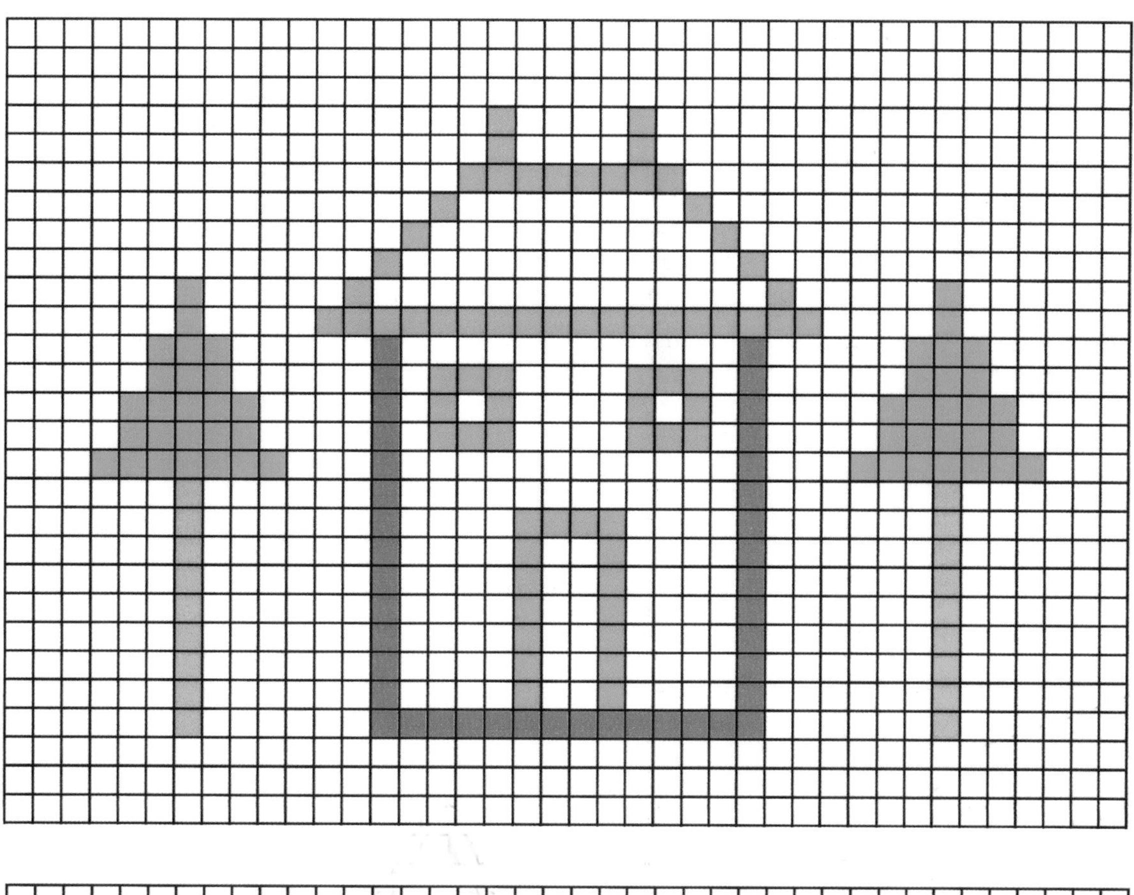

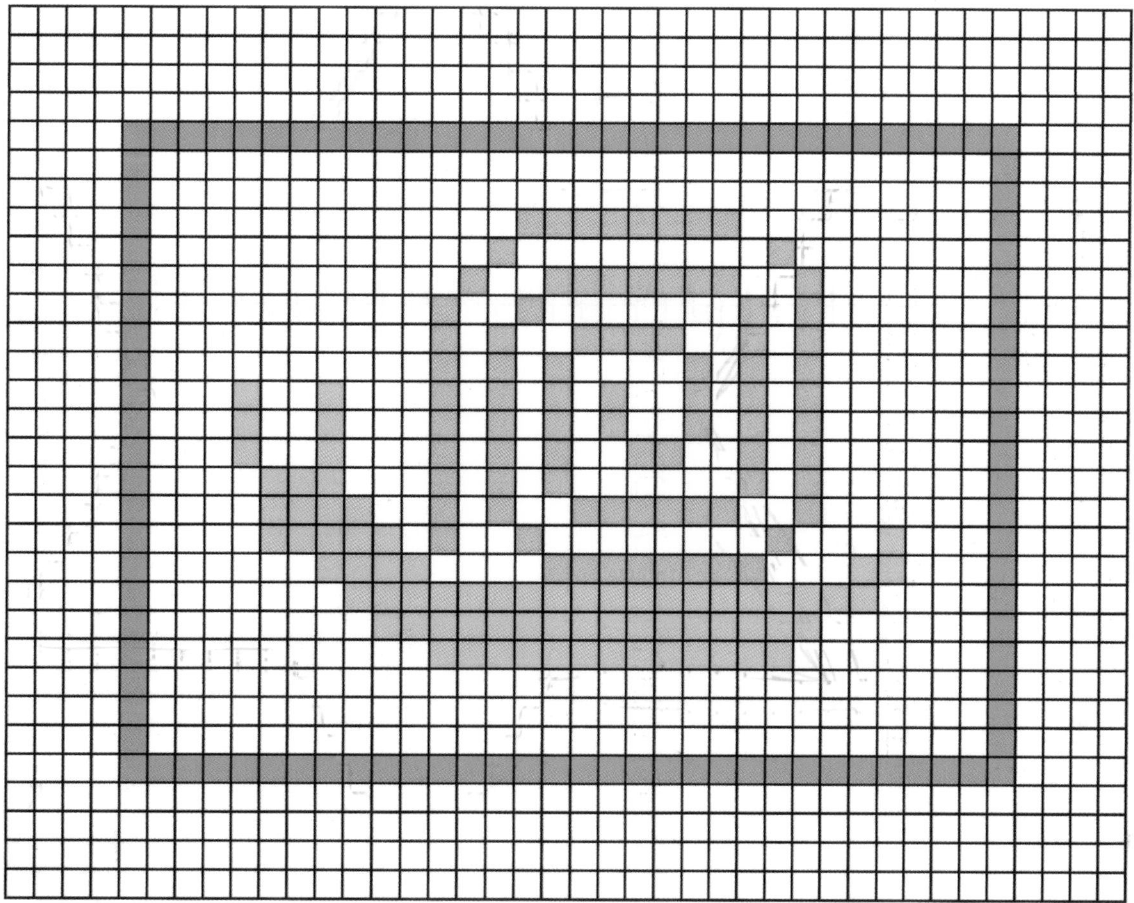

useful addresses

UNITED KINGDOM

The Art of Craft Limited
101 Lynchford Road
North Camp
Farnborough
Hampshire GU14 6ET
Tel: 01252 377677
Email: info@art-of-craft.co.uk
www.art-of-craft.co.uk
Craft supplies, tools and card-making materials.

Baker Ross Ltd
2-3 Forest Works
Forest Road
Walthamstow
London E17 6JF
Tel: 0844 576 8933
Email: enquiry@bakerross.co.uk
www.bakerross.co.uk
General craft supplier. Mail order only.

Craft Creations Limited
Ingersoll House
Delamare Road
Cheshunt
Hertfordshire EN8 9HD
Tel: 01992 781900
Email: enquiries@craftcreations.com
www.craftcreations.co.uk
General craft supplier. Mail order available.

Crayola
Tel: 01702 208170
www.crayola.co.uk
Crayons, markers, coloured pencils, modelling compounds and craft and activity products.

Dylon
Tel: 01737 742929
Email: info@dylon.co.uk
www.dylon.co.uk
Fabric dyes in a range of colours.

HobbyCraft
Unit 2A
Retail World, Team Valley
Gateshead NE11 0BD
Tel: 0800 027 2387
www.hobbycraft.co.uk
General crafts supplier. Call for your nearest outlet. Mail order available.

Homecrafts Direct
PO Box 38
Leicester LE1 9BU
Tel: 01162 697733
Email: info@homecrafts.co.uk
www.homecrafts.co.uk
Arts and crafts materials. Mail order only.

Paperchase
213-215 Tottenham Court Road
London W1T 7PS
Tel: 020 7467 6200
Stationery and art materials. Call for your nearest outlet.
Mail order: 0161 839 1500
Email: mailorder@paperchase.co.uk
www.paperchase.co.uk

AUSTRALIA

Funky Craft
Unit 2/31 Hume St
Huntingdale, VIC 3166
Tel: 9544 5525
Email: sales@funkycraft.com.au
www.funkycraft.com.au
Art materials and children's crafts.

Lincraft
www.lincraft.com.au
General craft supplier. Stores throughout Australia.

Spotlight
Tel: 1300 305 405
Email: service@spotlight.com.au
www.spotlight.com.au
General craft supplier. Stores nationwide. Mail order available.

SOUTH AFRICA

Art.Com
20 Reid St
Westdene
Bloemfontein 9301
Tel: 051 448 0499
Art materials.

Arts and Crafts 4 U
8 Flamingo Square
Blaauwberg Road
Table View
Tel: 021 556 1150
Email: info@artsandcrafts4u.co.za
www.artsandcrafts4u.co.za
Arts, crafts and haberdashery supplies.

Campbell Crafts
6 Dorman Street Gardens
8001 Cape Town
Tel: 021 686 6668
Email: campbellcrafts@netactive.co.za
Crafts supplier.

NEW ZEALAND

Archibald's Art Supplies
95 Main Street
Upper Hutt
Wellington
Tel: 939 2112
Email: archibaldsart@xtra.co.nz
www.archibaldsartsupplies.co.nz
Art materials and children's craft suppliers.

The Artshop
Devon St. East
New Plymouth
Tel: 06 758 0626
www.theartshop.co.nz
Art supplies. Mail order available.

Stationery Online
Tel: 0800 559 339
www.stationeryonline.co.nz
Mail order site with an Arts and Crafts section.

index

acknowledgements

A big 'thank you' to all the models – Jess, Josie, Olivia, Emma, Amber and Mia, Lucy, Amy, Katie and Anna, Charlotte, Noah, Oliver, Edith and Francesca – and to Lillie, whose beautiful hands appear in most of the step-by-step pictures; to Gavin and Roddy who took the photographs and to Jill, who booked the models and offered plenty of moral support. Thanks to to Emma Forbes for supplying DYLON Fabric Dyes and Geraldine Stewart for supplying Crayola products used throughout the book. Thanks also to Clare Sayer and Rosemary Wilkinson for asking me to do this book in the first place.

A CURIOUS BEGINNING

ALSO AVAILABLE FROM TITAN BOOKS

THE MADAME OF ESPIONAGE MYSTERIES
by CAROL K. CARR

India Black
India Black and the Widow Of Windsor
India Black and the Shadows Of Anarchy
India Black and the Gentleman Thief

THE PROFESSOR MORIARTY NOVELS
by MICHAEL KURLAND

The Infernal Device
Death By Gaslight
The Great Game
The Empress Of India
Who Thinks Evil

"You cannot mean to go friendless into the world and spurn the prospect of an excellent marriage to a man who will look past the indelible stain of your iniquities."

"I am quite determined to be mistress of my own fate, Mrs. Clutterthorpe, but I do sympathize with how strange it must sound to you. It is not your fault that you are entirely devoid of imagination. I blame your education."

Mrs. Clutterthorpe stood with her mouth agape, lips moving silently.

I stepped past her, then turned back as I reached the hall. "Oh, and you might tell your sources—it wasn't an American in Sicily. It was a Swede. The American was in Costa Rica."

TWO

As I walked down the path towards Wren Cottage, I found my step was very light indeed. I owed the Clutterthorpes a debt of gratitude, I reflected. I had been feeling a little dull after the long, gloomy months of Aunt Nell's decline, but the visit at the vicarage had cheered me greatly. I was always on my mettle when someone tried to thwart me—poor old Aunt Nell and Aunt Lucy had learned that through hard experience. I had been an obstinate child and a willful one too, and it did not escape me that it had cost these two spinster ladies a great deal of adjustment to make a place for me in their lives. It was for this reason, as I grew older, that I made every effort to curb my obstinacy and be cheerful and placid with them. And it was for this reason that I eventually made my escape, fleeing England whenever possible for tropical climes where I could indulge my passion for lepidoptery. It was not until my first butterflying expedition at the age of eighteen—a monthlong sojourn in Switzerland—that I discovered men could be just as interesting as moths.

It was perfectly reasonable that I should be curious about them. After all, I had been reared in a household composed exclusively of women. Friendships with the opposite sex were soundly discouraged, and the only men ever to darken our door were those who called in a professional capacity—doctors and vicars wearing rusty black coats and dour expressions. Village boys and strapping blacksmiths were strictly off-limits, and when a splendid specimen presented itself for closer inspection, I behaved as any good student of science would. My first kiss had been bestowed by a shepherd boy in the forest outside Geneva. I had hired him to guide me to an alpine meadow where I could ply my butterfly net to best effect. But while I pursued *Polyommatus damon*, he pursued me, and it was not long before the diversions of kissing took the place of butterflies. At least for the afternoon. I enjoyed the experience immensely, but I was deeply aware of the troubles I might encounter if I were not very careful indeed. Once back in England, I made a thorough study of my own biology, and—armed with the proper knowledge and precautions and a copy of Ovid's highly instructive *The Art of Love*—I enjoyed my second foray into formal lepidoptery and illicit pleasures even more.

Over time, I developed a set of rules from which I never deviated. Although I permitted myself dalliances during my travels, I never engaged in flirtations in England—or with Englishmen. I never permitted any liberties to gentlemen either married or betrothed, and I never corresponded with any of them once I returned home. Foreign bachelors were my trophies, collected for their charm and good looks as well as attentive manners. They were holiday romances, light and insubstantial as thistledown, but satisfying all the same. I enjoyed them enormously whilst abroad, and when I returned from each trip, I was rested and satiated and in excellent spirits. It was a program I would happily have recommended to any spinster of my acquaintance, but I knew too well the futility of it. What was to me nothing more than a bit of healthful exercise and sweet flirtation was the rankest sin to ladies like Mrs. Clutterthorpe, and the world was full of Mrs. Clutterthorpes.

But I would soon be past it all, I thought as I stooped to snap off a small sprig of common broom. Its petals glowed yellow, a cheerful reminder of the long, sunny summer to come—a summer I would not spend in England, I reflected with mingled emotions. At the start of each new journey I felt a pang of homesickness, sharp as a thorn. This trip would take me across the globe to the edge of the Pacific, no doubt for a very long time. I had passed the long, chilly spring months at Aunt Nell's bedside, spreading mustard plasters and reading aloud from improving novels while I dreamed of hot, steaming island jungles where butterflies as wide as my hand danced overhead.

My daydreams had been a welcome distraction from Aunt Nell's querulous moods. She had been by turns fretful and sullen, irritated that she was dying and disgusted that she was not quicker about it. The doctor had dosed her heavily with morphia, and she was seldom truly lucid. Many times I had caught her watching me, her lips parted as if to speak, but as soon as I lifted a brow in inquiry, she had snapped her mouth closed and waved me off. It was not until the last fit had come upon her, suddenly and without warning, that she had tried to speak and found she could not. Robbed of speech, she tried to write, but her hand was weak, stiff with the apoplexy that had stilled her tongue, and she died with something unsaid.

"No doubt it was a reminder to pay the milk," I said, tucking the broom into my buttonhole. But I had seen to the dairy bill as quickly and efficiently as I had done everything these past months. Accounts with the doctor, butcher, and baker had all been settled. The rent on the cottage was paid through the end of the quarter on Midsummer Day. Most of the furnishings had been carted away and sold, leaving the few pieces that had come with the cottage—a couple of chairs, a kitchen table, a grievously worn rug, and a poorly executed still life that looked as if it had been painted by someone with a grudge against fruit. All of the Harbottle personal effects and the last of my carefully mounted butterflies had been sold to fund my next expedition.

All that remained to be done was to take up my small carpetbag and leave the key under the mat, provided I could find the key, of course. Folk in the village were remarkably relaxed about things like keys—and waiting for invitations, I realized as I reached the doorstep. For the cottage door stood ajar, and I had little doubt one of the village matrons had availed herself of my absence to call with a cake or perhaps a meat pie for my supper. Aunt Nell had not been popular enough to warrant attendance at her funeral by the inhabitants of Little Byfield, but an eligible spinster would bring them all out en masse, bearing sponge cakes and consolation—or worse, unattached sons for my perusal. A daughter-in-law with competent nursing skills was a tremendous coup for an elderly widow, I reflected with a shudder. I pushed open the door, prepared to do my duty and offer tea, but the greeting died upon my lips. The front room of the cottage was a ruin, the carpet littered with broken bits from the wreckage of a cane chair. The only painting—the indifferent still life—had been slashed, its frame reduced to splinters, and the cushions of the window seat had been torn open, goose down still floating lazily upon the air.

My gaze fixed upon the drifting feathers and I realized that whoever had done this thing must have done so within the last few minutes. Just then, a slight scraping noise came from the kitchen. I was not alone.

Thoughts winged through my mind almost too quickly to grasp. The open door stood behind me. I had made no noise.

Escape would be a simple matter of turning on my heel and slipping silently out the way I had come. Instead, my hand reached out of its own accord to the umbrella stand and took up the sword stick I had purchased in Italy.

My heart surged in anticipation. The sword stick was a sturdy piece, made of good, stout hardwood. I pressed the button, releasing the sheath, and the blade came free with a silky murmur of protest. The edge of the blade was dull, for it had been some years since it had been sharpened or oiled, but I was pleased to see the end was still alarmingly pointed. *I must thrust rather than slash,* I reminded myself as I crept towards the kitchen.

A flurry of other noises told me that the intruder had not yet fled and, furthermore, had no notion of my presence. I had the element of surprise, and armed with that and my sword, I flung open the door, giving a very good impression of what I imagined a Maori battle scream might sound like.

Instantly, I realized my mistake. The fellow was enormous, and it occurred to me then that I had overlooked the essential precaution of taking the measure of one's opponent *before* launching an attack. He was well over six feet in height, and the breadth of his shoulders would have challenged the frame of any door. He wore a tweed cap pulled low over his features, but I discerned a gingery beard and an expression of displeasure at the interruption.

To my surprise, he did not use his size to his advantage to overpower me. Instead he turned to flee, upending the long deal table to throw a barrier between us. The most cautious course of action would of course have been to let him go, but caution held little charm for me. My rage was roused at the sight of the ruined cottage, and without any conscious decision on my part, I gave chase, vaulting over the table and following him down the garden path. His was the advantage of size, but mine was the advantage of terrain; I knew it and he did not. He followed the stone path to the bottom of the garden where the road passed by. I turned hard to the left and made straight for the hedge, plunging into a gap and emerging, breathless and beleafed, just as he passed by. I reached a hand and grasped him by the sleeve, yanking hard.

He whirled, his eyes wide with surprise—and panic. For a heartbeat he hesitated, and I lifted the sword stick.

"What is your business at Wren Cottage?" I demanded.

He darted a glance to the end of the road, where a carriage stood waiting. That glance at the conveyance seemed to decide him. I brandished the sword stick again, but he simply reached out, batting the blade aside with one thick hand while he grabbed my wrist with the other. He gave a sharp twist and I cried out, dropping the stick.

He began to drag me towards the carriage. I dug in my heels, but to no avail. My slender form, though athletic and supple enough for purposes of butterflying, was no match for this fellow's felonious intent. I lowered my head and applied my teeth to the meatiest part of his hand, just above the seat of the thumb. He howled in pain and rage, shaking his hand hard, but would not loose me. He put his other hand to my throat, tightening his grip as I bore down with my teeth like a terrier upon a rat.

"Unhand her at once!" commanded a voice from behind. I glanced over my shoulder to see the Continental gentleman from the lych-gate. He was older than I had thought; at this distance I could see the lines about his eyes and the heavy creases down each cheek, the left crossed with his dueling scars. But he drew no sword against this miscreant. Instead, he held a revolver in his hand, pointing it directly at the fellow.

"Devil take her!" the intruder growled, shoving me hard away from him and directly into the gentleman's arms. My newfound champion dropped the revolver to catch me, setting me on my feet again with care.

"Are you quite all right, Miss Speedwell?" the gentleman inquired anxiously.

I made a low sound of impatience as the villain reached the end of the road and vaulted into the waiting carriage. The horses were swiftly whipped up and the carriage sprang into motion as if the very hounds of hell were giving chase. "He is getting away!"

"I think perhaps this is a good thing," was my companion's gentle reply as he pocketed his revolver.

I turned to him, noticing for the first time that his brow was bleeding freely. "You are hurt," I said, nodding towards his head.

He put a tentative finger to the flow, then gave me a quick smile. "I am rather too old to be dashing through hedges," he said with a rueful compression of the lips. "But I think it is not so serious as my other hurts have been," he told me, and my gaze flicked to his dueling scars.

"Still, it ought to be cleaned." I took a handkerchief from my pocket, not one of those ridiculous flimsy scraps carried by fashionable females, but a proper square of good cambric, and pressed it to his face.

I smiled at him. "This was rather more adventure than I had expected in the village of Little Byfield. Thank you for your timely interference, sir. I was prepared to bite him to the bone, but I am glad it proved unnecessary. I did not much care for the taste of him," I added with a moue of displeasure.

"Miss Veronica Speedwell," he murmured in a voice thick with the accents of Mitteleuropa.

"I am. I believe you have the advantage of me, sir," I said.

"Forgive me for the informality of the introduction," he said. He produced a card. "I am the Baron Maximilian von Stauffenbach."

The card was heavy in my fingers. It bespoke wealth and good taste, and I ran my thumb over the thickly engraved crest. He clicked his heels together and made a graceful bow.

"I am sorry I cannot offer you a place to sit," I told him as we made our way into the kitchen. "Nor a cup of tea. As you saw, I seem to have been intruded upon."

The baron's eyes sharpened under his slender grey brows as he glanced about the wreckage of the room. "Has anything of importance been taken?"

I moved to the shelf where a tiny tin sewing box shaped like a pig usually stood in pride of place. It had been dashed to the floor and rolled to the corner. I was not surprised the housebreaker had overlooked it. Aunt Lucy had firmly believed in hiding one's money in plain sight, reasoning that most thieves were men and that a man would never think to look for money in so homely and domestic an article as a sewing box. I fetched it, crawling upon my hands and knees to do so. It customarily held all of the Harbottle wealth in the world, a few bank notes and some miscellaneous coins. I shook it and it rattled—a slightly less lively sound than it had given before I had paid the undertaker.

"No. That was the only thing of value and it seems to be untouched. Strange that he did not smash it open—perhaps he did not notice it in his haste. He has made a complete mess of the kitchen. I shall be ages clearing it up," I said peevishly.

The baron fell silent a moment, as if considering things carefully, then shook himself, muttering, "It is the only way."

"I beg your pardon, Baron?"

"Nothing, child," he said kindly. "I do not wish to alarm you, my dear, but I am afraid I must speak plainly now. You might be in danger."

"Danger! I assure you I am not. There is nothing worth stealing here, and that thief will hardly come again now he has been chased out by a sword stick and your revolver," I told him, but the baron's concerns were not eased.

He put a hand to my arm, and I was startled at the strength of the grip of those soft, elegant fingers. "I do not jest with you. I saw the notice in the newspaper about the death of your guardian, and I come to see you, only to find they have already found you. I am, almost, too late."

He bit off his words then, as if he had said more than he intended, but I seized upon his statement. "You said 'they.' You think this intruder has friends? Friends with malicious designs upon me?"

He shook his head. "You saw the carriage. What sort of burglar rides in a private conveyance? No, I cannot explain, child. I can only tell you that you must leave this place. Now. You have chased him away, but he will return and he will not come alone."

"You know him?"

His fingers gripped my arm still more desperately. "No! I do not, but I can guess. And your very life may depend upon my being able to persuade you that I am not some crazy man and that I speak the truth. And yet how am I to persuade you? You must believe! I am the Baron von Stauffenbach," he repeated helplessly, his voice thick with anguish. "Please, my dear child, if you will not accept my offer to take you to London, at least permit me to see you onto a train myself. You may ask to go anywhere in the world at my expense. But I must know that you are safe."

I had always followed the maxim that intuition should be one's guide, and so it was in this case. The gentleman's obvious distress was persuasive, but his willingness to permit me to choose my own destination decided me. O! There ought to have been a frisson of foreknowledge, a shiver of precognition that the choice to accompany the baron would prove the single most significant decision of my entire existence. And yet there was not. I was aware of a mild curiosity about his excitability and the natural lifting of the spirits that accompanies the beginning of any great journey. But above all this was the cool satisfaction at having saved myself the price of a ticket to London. It was to cause me great amusement later to reflect that my life turned on a penny that day.

He gestured towards the front door. "My carriage is outside and I will offer you every comfort."

"And once in London?"

He shook his head. "I will have to make plans as we go. I did not anticipate this." He fell to muttering again, this time in German, and I covered his hand with my own.

"I will come."

The years seemed to fall away from him. "Thank God for that!"

I detached myself gently. "I will fetch my bag."

He shook his head forcefully. "We cannot tarry, child. Time is of the greatest importance!"

I patted his arm consolingly. "My dear baron, I am already packed."

THREE

I WAS AS GOOD AS my word, and within ten minutes of agreeing to leave with the baron, I was in his carriage, my carpetbag and butterfly net perched on the seat beside me. I left the remains of the Harbottle treasury with a note for the landlord and considered the matter closed. I reasoned the sum should be sufficient to settle the damages. I had brought with me my own slender funds, tucked carefully into a clever pocket hidden in my jacket. I had changed from my mourning ensemble to a costume of my own design, and the baron regarded me curiously.

"You are not what I expected," he ventured at last, but his tone was not unkind and his eyes shone warmly.

I nodded. "I seldom am. I have tried, I assure you. I have been brought up to do good works and to conduct myself with propriety and decorum, and yet I am forever doing the unexpected. Something always gives me away for what I really am."

"And what are you, child?"

"A woman in search of adventure," I said gravely.

The baron sketched a gesture that encompassed me from

head to toe. "And these garments will help you to find one?"

I was quite proud of my ensemble. My boots were flat and laced almost to the knee to protect my lower limbs from thorns and branches whilst butterflying. I had modified my corset to a more athletic arrangement with light steel stays that might, in an hour of necessity, be used as weapons. I wore slim trousers tucked into the boots, and over it all a narrow skirt with a peculiar arrangement of buttons that permitted it to be raised to the knee or opened entirely to allow me to ride astride. There was a fitted jacket to match with an assortment of clever pockets, and into one I had tucked the good luck charm I was never without—a tiny mouse of grey velvet called Chester, the sole relic of my childhood.

My only jewelry was the small case compass pinned to my jacket, a present from Aunt Lucy to commemorate my first expedition—"So you will always find your way, child," she had told me, her eyes bright with unshed tears as I left home for the first time. I brought with me nothing of Aunt Nell's except an appreciation for a clean white shirtwaist. The fabric of this curious suit was a serviceable dark grey wool, but I had made one or two allowances for vanity. The grey wool was trimmed with scrolls of rather dapper black silk passementerie, while my hat was an absolute confection. Broad of brim, with a snug, deep crown, it was crafted of fine black straw and wound with a length of black silk tulle that could be lowered to veil my face should bees prove troublesome. A bouquet of deep scarlet silk roses clustered on one side, a splash of delectable color I had been powerless to resist. But even they had a purpose to serve in the field, being the perfect perch for delicate specimens with damp wings.

The hat was a stroke of inspiration, and I pointed this out to the baron. "You see, the fashion for narrow brims has made it necessary for ladies to carry a parasol as well, but that means the hands are never free. With this hat, I am entirely protected from the elements, yet my hands are unencumbered. I can lower the veil if I like to shield my face, and the hatpin is reinforced to make a very fine weapon." I gave a short laugh. "You needn't look so startled, Baron. I do not anticipate having need of it."

"Even after you find an intruder in your home?" he asked softly.

I folded my hands in my lap. "Yes, about that. I know you said you believe my life is in danger, but I must tell you I think you are quite wrong. No, the fellow was a lowly villain in search of easy pickings. Doubtless he, like you, read in the newspaper of poor Aunt Nell's passing and realized the cottage would be empty during the funeral. It is a common enough occurrence. The fellow was simply an opportunistic housebreaker, and I surprised him by coming home somewhat sooner than he expected. When I gave chase, he was alarmed at the thought of having a witness to his crimes and attempted to frighten me by making it seem as if he would carry me off. That is all."

The baron looked pained. "But if you do not truly believe yourself to be in danger, why have you come away with me?"

My tone was deliberately patient. "Because you were leaving Little Byfield. I was planning to depart this afternoon in any event, but you have very kindly saved me the cost of a ticket to London. I am obliged to you."

The baron clucked his tongue and muttered an imprecation in German. "And I thought I had persuaded you. Oh, child, what must I say to convince you of the dangers before you?"

"Surely it cannot be so bad as all that. I expect you are merely hungry. Things always look darkest when one is hungry or tired, I find." I reached for my carpetbag and unbuckled the straps. "I have some apples in here and some cheese. I regret there is no bread, but this will serve until we can stop for some refreshment."

I proffered an apple and a wedge of weeping Cheddar, and

the baron took them, turning them over in his hands. "The apple is a bit soft now, but it is from the orchard in Little Byfield and quite sweet, I promise," I told him.

The baron shook his head. "I do not require food, my dear."

"Spirits, then?" I rummaged in my bag until I found a flask, which I withdrew with a flourish. "It is a little something I acquired in South America, very good for restoring one's nerves."

He handed back the food but took the flask, swallowing a mouthful under my watchful eye before choking hard. "Very nice," he gasped.

I assessed his color. "You've a bit more pink in your cheeks, I am glad to say. You looked quite pale, you know. Have you difficulties with your health?"

"My heart," he told me, handing back the flask. "Sometimes the breath, it does not come easily; sometimes there is pain. But I have work yet unfinished."

"Work?" I replaced the flask carefully and tucked the food back into a clean cloth. "What sort of work?"

"To keep you safe," he said softly, and it was this gentleness that caught my attention. I peered at him closely, scrutinizing him from his aristocratic brow to the well-formed lips under the generous mustaches, the graceful hands that clasped his knees loosely, the watchful eyes that never left mine. "You have her eyes," he murmured at last. "Your mother's eyes."

My heart rose in my throat, threatening to choke me. I could not speak for a moment, and when I did, my usually low voice was quick and high. "You knew my mother! How very extraordinary. I must confess, I know nothing of her."

He hesitated. "She was the most beautiful creature I have ever seen," he said simply.

I gave him an arch smile. "I suspect I look nothing like her, then."

The baron protested, as I had expected he would.

"No woman can be so lovely and not know it," he told me firmly. He put a finger under my chin and tipped my head this way and that, studying me carefully. "You might be her twin. It is uncanny, as if I were looking into her face once more. The same lips, the same cheekbones. I told her once I could cut glass upon those cheekbones. And of course, the eyes. I have never seen eyes that color before or since."

"Aunt Nell used to say it was not decent to have violet eyes, that they were the telltale sign of a bad nature, like ginger hair or a hunchback. And village children used to tease me about being a bad fairy—a changeling child."

"Children can be very stupid," the baron said gravely.

"And dull, which is why I have no interest in becoming a mother of six," I told him. He lifted his brows.

"Six is a curiously specific number."

"I had a curiously specific offer today, but let us speak no more of that. Of course, I do not wish to be a paid companion or a daughter-in-law either. I have had quite enough of attending to elderly ladies," I finished absently.

"They were good to you, though?" he asked, his tone shaded with anxiety. "The Harbottle ladies? They treated you with kindness?"

"Oh yes. I was fed and clothed and I don't suppose I ever wanted for anything, not really. I had a new dress every season and new books to read. Of course, that was due to the lending library. We moved so often I could never keep books of my own. Aunt Lucy always bought a subscription to the library as soon as we settled in a new village. As I grew older, I pursued my own interests. I have traveled far and seen much of the world, and when the aunts had need of me, I returned to care for them. It was a pleasant enough life."

"Did you mind, all of this moving to and fro?"

I grinned. "If I am honest, I loathed it as a child. It always seemed that we moved just as I had amassed a good collection—eggs, frogs, beetles. I was forever leaving behind something I loved. The aunts were driven by their whims. One year we might live the whole twelvemonth in Lyme. The next they would have us move from town to town, four within the span of a year. I learned to accept it, as children do. And it taught me to travel lightly." I narrowed my gaze. "You said you knew them. I do not remember meeting friends of theirs. They kept so much to themselves. And I never knew my mother, not even her name. What can you tell me?"

The baron opened his mouth, his lips pursed. Then he closed it sharply and shook his head. "Nothing at this moment, child. The truth is not mine to speak. I must seek permission before I reveal to you what I know, but I promise you, I will seek it, and when the moment is right, I will tell you all."

I sighed. I was, truth be told, quite frustrated at the baron's obstinacy, but there was something steely in his manner that told me he would not be moved upon the point. "I suppose I will have to be satisfied with that."

The baron relaxed visibly then, but almost as soon as his expression eased, a shadow passed over his features again. "For now, the most important thing is to make certain that you are safe."

"You keep talking of my safety, but I cannot imagine why! I am the least interesting person in England, I assure you. No one could possibly want to harm me." That was not entirely true, I reflected. The last paper I had written for *The British Journal of Lepidoptery* had stirred quite a bit of controversy, but as I always published papers and conducted my butterfly sales under the anonymity of my first initial and surname alone, no ill will could be directed towards me personally. As strongly as I pointed out that publishing in scientific journals was a scholarly accomplishment, the aunts had protested just as vehemently that filling orders for Aurelian collectors was too near to trade to be permissible for a lady. They had compromised, albeit reluctantly, that I might continue my studies and work under the cognomen of V. Speedwell.

In the end, I had not minded, and it never failed to amuse me to receive letters that began with the salutation, "Dear Mr. Speedwell . . ." True, I had nipped the odd specimen out from under the nose of less diligent hunters, for I was indefatigable in my pursuit, but the very notion of some sort of lepidopterist cabal after my head was enough to make me laugh.

A wraithlike smile touched the baron's lips. "I will pray to God that you are right and that I am merely borrowing troubles that will not come to pass. In the meantime, until I am certain, you will be guided by me?"

I looked at him a long moment, holding his anxious gaze with mine. Then I nodded. "I will."

"Your trust in me is unexpected but most gratifying," he told me.

"I am a great believer in intuition, Baron. And my intuition tells me that you are a man upon whom I may rely." I did not add that he was the sole clue I had ever had to my mother's identity. I had no intention of permitting him to escape me until I had learned everything I could about my antecedents.

"From your lips to the ears of God," he said, and it struck me that when the baron mentioned God he did not do so flippantly. Whatever matter touched me, it concerned the baron deeply.

I leaned forward then, determined to press my luck as far as I could. "Will you answer one question for me? I promise to ask no others until you deem it fit."

"Very well."

I stated the question boldly, as I hoped he would wish.

"Are you my father?"

His kindly face creased in sorrow, but he did not look away. "No, child. I wish I were, but I am not."

A sharp and unexpected pang struck my heart. I had thought myself indifferent to the answer, but I was wrong. "Then we will merely be friends," I said. I put out my hand solemnly. Other men might have laughed. But the baron shook my hand, and having done so, he bowed over it and kissed it with courtly formality.

"We will be friends," he agreed. "And I will do everything in my power to make certain you learn what you wish to know."

"Thank you, Baron." I nodded towards his brow. "You are bleeding again. It is not a very hopeful omen, is it? A journey begun in bloodshed augurs ill, according to the ancients." I meant it as a jest, but the baron did not smile. And after a moment, neither did I.

The journey to London proved uneventful to the point of boredom, and I began to be a little sorry we had not taken the train. The baron insisted upon the precaution of ducking down various country lanes to make quite certain we were eluding any possible pursuers, with the result that the drive took twice as long as it ought. He also refused any suggestion of stopping for a meal, resorting instead to a selection of unappetizing sandwiches purchased at exorbitant cost from a roadside inn. I nibbled at mine as the baron continued to formulate a plan. He suggested and discarded a dozen options before throwing up his hands and applying himself to his own repast.

"We will think of something," he assured me. "But it is not good to deliberate upon such things when one is trying to eat. It disturbs the digestion. So we will talk of other matters.

Tell me, if you do not mean to be a governess or a companion, what sort of adventure do you wish to seek out?"

I wiped my mouth of crumbs and began to explain. "I am a student of natural history, all branches. I subscribe to all of the major journals on exploration and discovery. As you might deduce from my butterfly net, lepidoptery is my particular specialty. I hunt butterflies as a profession, filling orders for Aurelians who lack the means or the desire to hunt their own specimens," I added.

But the baron was not listening. An expression of wonder stole over his face, and he sat back, his mournful little sandwich untouched. "Of course," he murmured. "Stoker."

"I beg your pardon?"

He collected himself. "A very old and very dear friend of mine—Stoker. He is just the man to help us now. He will keep you safe, child."

My brow furrowed. "Baron, I realize I have been somewhat reckless in accepting your offer of transportation to London, and I have been quite cavalier in thinking that I must do as you bid me. But I do not believe I can countenance the notion of staying with this Mr. Stoker. He is even more a stranger to me than yourself. You must tell me something of him."

"Stoker is a complex fellow, but I have never known a man more honorable. He owes me a debt of gratitude, and his own conscience will not permit him to fail me if I call upon his aid. I would trust Stoker with the thing I hold most dear in the whole of the world," the baron said.

"You would trust him with your life?" I challenged.

"No, child. I would trust him with yours."

FOUR

IT WAS VERY LATE when we arrived in London—or very early, I suppose, for dawn was upon us, pale pearl grey light washing over the city as it began to wake.

"Only a few minutes more," the baron promised, and he sat upright in the carriage now. His shoulders had slumped with fatigue the last several hours, and I had managed to sleep a bit, curled over my traveling bag with the baron keeping watch on the road behind. But as we came into the city I rose, rubbing at my eyes and pinching my cheeks and pinning my hat more firmly upon my head. My previous visits to London had been brief ones en route to other lands, confined to stuffy train stations and unsavory cabs. The sight of the great sprawling gloom of the metropolis enthralled me.

"You like the city," the baron said with a twinkle in his eyes. "I should have thought a natural historian would prefer the country."

"I love it all," I told him somewhat breathlessly. "Every arrival in London is the beginning of a new story." I tore my gaze from the view of the city and gave him a smile. "I wonder if I shall divide my life scientifically into the periods B.B. and A.B.—before the Baron von Stauffenbach and after. Have you set me off on great adventures, then, Baron?" I teased.

But the baron made no reply. The carriage rocked to a stop and he instructed me to alight, taking my carpetbag himself as I carried my butterfly net. My grasp of London geography being tenuous at best, I had a notion we were somewhere east of the Tower on the north bank of the River Thames, but that was all I could determine. The neighborhood was in the heart of the docklands, filled with warehouses and cheap lodgings and people who looked—and smelled—distinctly unwashed. Gulls wheeled overhead, shrieking for food, and the heavy, greasy aroma of frying fish filled the air.

"Stoker's workshop is in the next street," the baron said, guiding me over the broken pavement with a hand under my elbow. "This is not the most salubrious quarter, but I did not think it wise to have my own carriage stop directly at his door."

We maneuvered through a narrow alley that debouched into the next street. The baron stopped at a nondescript door at the very end of an even more nondescript wall. It looked like any of a thousand other doors in London, and the building beyond seemed a sort of warehouse, with a high roof and plain, solid structure. "He lives here?"

The baron nodded. "It suits his work." He rapped sharply, more than once, but there was no answer, and I began to wonder if our adventure was destined to end as soon as it had begun.

To my surprise, the baron extracted a large ring of keys from his pocket and, after a moment's consideration, selected one. He fitted it to the lock and let himself in, motioning me to follow. He locked the door carefully behind us and replaced the keys in his pocket. We were in a small anteroom of sorts, and from the various empty packing cases scattered about the floor

I deduced it had once served as a shopfront for the warehouse behind. The baron beckoned me forward and we passed into the storage areas—a series of large rooms, each filthier and colder than the last, and all stuffed with rubbish. Windows ran along the south wall, revealing that the warehouse was built directly above the river. The dank odor of water was heavy in the air, and the floors were cold with damp.

Finally, we emerged into the warehouse itself, an immense cavern of a space, and I stifled a gasp.

"You have brought me to hell," I whispered in horrified delight, for the place was like something out of Dante's fevered imagination. The room was lit with the unholy crimson light of an enormous stove, and in its fiery glow I made out an endless assortment of shelves and hooks, each laden with something more grisly and disturbing than the last. Bones leered out from the gloom—long, knobby femurs and grinning, pointed skulls with great fanged teeth. Unspeakable things floated in specimen jars of ghoulish yellow fluids, and animal skins were pinned flat to the walls as if newly flayed from the flesh. A wide iron cauldron, large enough to boil a man, stood expectantly to one side, as if waiting for its next offering.

But none of these was as disturbing as the sight that met my eyes in the center of the room. There stood an enormous creature, rough flesh sculpted over a steel skeleton, pieces of wrinkled skin half-draped upon it, the rest hanging limp and lifeless to the floor like a discarded garment. Standing below it was a man, stripped to the waist, his naked torso covered in sweat and streaked with black, the smoky soot mingling with a collection of tattoos that spread across his back and down his arms. He wore old-fashioned breeches tucked into high boots and an apron fashioned of leather and fitted with pockets holding various tools that looked like instruments of torture. He was wrestling with the skin of the beast, the muscles of his back and shoulders corded against the strain, and he swore fluently as he worked.

I felt a smile rising to my lips, for this was no hell, no monster's den. It was, in fact, the lair of a taxidermist. The shelves along one wall were fitted with Wardian cases containing hundreds—*no, thousands*—of specimens, a veritable museum of natural history hidden away in a dingy warehouse on the north bank of the Thames. I longed to explore everything at once, but it was the man himself who claimed my attention.

"Stoker," the baron called.

The man whirled, his hands still gripping the animal's skin, his face imperfectly illuminated by the fire. He was half in shadow, and the shadow revealed him slowly. His left eye was covered by a black leather patch, and thin white scars raked his brow and the cheekbone below. They carried on, down the length of his neck, into the thick black beard, twisting under his collarbone and around his torso. They marred only the skin, I noted, for the muscles beneath were whole and strong, and the entire impression was one of great vitality and energy, strength unbridled. He looked like nothing so much as a fallen god working at a trade.

"Hephaestus at the forge," I murmured, recalling my mythology. The baron shot me a quick appraising glance.

"My dear?"

"Nothing," I said quickly, for the man had dropped his tools and was coming near. Just then he caught sight of me and paused, reaching for a shirt. To my regret, he pulled it on, obscuring his impressive form as he turned to the baron.

"Max, what the devil—"

The baron held up a hand. "I come to throw myself upon your mercy, Stoker. This young lady is Miss Speedwell. I must beg your help and ask you to keep her here. I cannot explain yet, but I must leave her with you."

Mr. Stoker turned the full force of his gaze upon me, scrutinizing me from my butterfly net to my neatly pinned hat, and shook his head. "Not bloody likely."

"Stoker, I know how you feel about your privacy, and I would not ask but I have no choice," the baron pressed, his voice low.

If I had had any sense of delicacy, I would have been acutely embarrassed by the situation. As it happened, I was merely bored with their discussion. I had little doubt the baron would prevail, and I was fairly itching to see what lurked amidst the collection Mr. Stoker had amassed. I wandered to the nearest shelf, where I peered at a specimen floating in a jar. It was a pretty little frog with enormous eyes and a faintly surprised expression.

I could hear them arguing in low voices behind me, the baron's aristocratic tones punctuated by Mr. Stoker's occasional profanity. I put out a hand and he called out sharply. "Do not touch that! It took me the better part of a year to find the damned thing and it cannot be replaced."

If he expected his harsh tone to cow me, he should learn differently right from the start, I decided. I picked up the jar and turned, setting a pleasant smile upon my lips. "Then you ought to have taken better care of it. Your seal is damaged, and the preservative solution is contaminated. The specimen looks to have been badly fixed as well. Pity, really, it's quite a fine little *Phyllomedusa tomopterna*."

His mouth tightened. "As the label quite plainly states, it is a *Phyllomedusa tarsius*."

"Yes, I see what the label states, but the label is wrong. You can tell by the coloration of its lower legs. These are very bright orange with pronounced tiger stripes. *Tarsius* has green legs. Really, I am quite surprised you did not see it for yourself. I should have thought so avid a collector would have noticed such a difference. Ah well, perhaps you have not had the chance to examine it closely."

Mr. Stoker's mouth gaped open until he closed it with an audible snap. "I assure you, Miss Speedwell, I am intimately familiar with that particular specimen, considering I collected it myself in the jungles of the Amazon."

I was enthralled. He had appalling manners and questionable hygiene considering the state of his hands, but any man who had been to the Amazon was worth talking to.

Evidently Mr. Stoker did not share my interest in conversation, for he turned back to the baron to remonstrate with him one last time. "I haven't time to mind strays for you, Max. I have to finish that bloody great elephant by next month or Lord Rosemorran will not pay me."

The baron put out his hand. "My dear friend, I would not ask if necessity did not demand it."

Mr. Stoker said nothing, and, doubtless sensing his advantage, the baron pressed it. "I ask you for this one thing in memory of the dangers we have known together."

Mr. Stoker's face flushed dark red. "It is a very genteel form of extortion to remind a man of his debts, Max. Very well, dammit. I am nothing if not a man of my word. You have it. I will keep the lady here until you come for her."

The baron put out his hand to clasp his friend by the shoulder. "You have repaid your debt in full with this."

"I cannot think how," Mr. Stoker protested. "Overbearing spinsters are not exactly your stock in trade."

I studiously ignored the insult as I replaced his *Phyllomedusa.* Within a few moments the baron was on his way, taking his leave of me with a bow over my hand and a smartly Teutonic click of the heels.

He hesitated, my hand still in his, his eyes searching my face. "I leave you in the best care—better than my own, child. I will send word soon."

"Please do," I replied with a touch of asperity as I flicked a glance at Mr. Stoker. He curled a lip by way of reply.

The baron hesitated. "You must know, if it were in my power to tell you everything . . ." he began. I held up a hand.

"I have come to know you a little in the course of our journey. I believe you to be a man of honor, Baron. It is plain that you are bound by strong loyalties. I must respect that."

"Respect it, but you do not like it," he finished with a kindly twinkle.

"And it is apparent you have come to know me a little too," I acknowledged. "I will bid you farewell in the German fashion then. Auf Wiedersehen, Baron."

He clicked his heels together a second time and pressed my hand. "God go with you, Miss Speedwell."

He left then, and Mr. Stoker saw him out, returning a moment later to find me studying his specimens again. "The baron did not tell me you were a taxidermist when he suggested I stay with you," I said pleasantly.

He returned to his elephant, taking up his tools. "I am a natural historian," he corrected. "Taxidermy is merely a part of what I do."

He offered neither a seat nor refreshment, but I was not prepared to stand on ceremony. I found a moth-eaten sofa lurking under a pile of skins and moved them aside enough to perch on the edge—carefully, for I noticed a leg of the sofa was missing, replaced with a decaying stack of volumes from the *Description de l'Égypte.* "It is very late—or very early. And yet you are at work."

He said nothing for a long moment, and I wondered if he meant to annoy me with his silence. But he was merely examining his glue, and as he began to apply it, he called over his shoulder. "I have not yet been to bed. I gather from Max that you traveled through the night. If you wish to sleep, shove the hides aside and take the sofa."

I sighed at this bit of churlishness, but fatigue won out over pride, and I began to move the hides. Suddenly, something in the bundle growled and I jumped back, nearly upsetting a case of fossilized eggs as I did so.

"For the love of God, watch what you're doing!" Mr. Stoker thundered. "'Tis only Huxley. He shan't hurt you."

I peeled away the hides to reveal a bulldog, squat and square, regarding me with statesmanlike solemnity. I slipped him a bit of cheese from my bag and he settled back happily, content to let me take the rest of the sofa. I curled behind him, feeling oddly contented with the warm, furry back of him pressed to my belly, and almost instantly I fell asleep.

FIVE

I WOKE SOME HOURS LATER, stiff and cold. The fire had burned down, but Mr. Stoker was once more working without his shirt, displaying his rather splendid musculature as well as his intriguing collection of tattoos. I regarded him through the veil of my lashes for some time as he labored, stretching a piece of elephant's skin tautly over its padded armature. It required finesse, I realized, for at times he was brutally strong, using the sheer mass of his muscles to force the weighty hide into position; at others he was gently coaxing, his hands as deft as a musician's. His language altered as well, for as he sweated and shoved, he swore like any common sailor, but as he persuaded, he murmured in a seductive whisper, enticing the beast to do his bidding. He looked younger then, less commanding, and I realized he was probably not so very many years older than myself, but something had hardened him. Only a certain softness at the mouth as it curved in pleasure at his work spoke of any gentleness in him. And the scars were commentary to his courage, for whatever animal he had faced seemed to have taken his eye and nearly his life. I wanted to hear the story, but I knew better than to ask. He did not seem inclined to confidences, and such a story must perforce be an intimate one.

So I yawned loudly, stretching my arms above my head and giving him time to resume his shirt before I sat up. Huxley nudged my hand and I gave him more cheese, scratching him soundly behind the ears.

"He is not a lapdog, for Christ's sake," his master growled. But Huxley merely rolled over onto his back and offered his belly. I scratched him thoroughly before I rose and went to look at the elephant.

"You have managed quite a lot. How long was I asleep?"

"Four hours, more or less."

"Very impressive that you accomplished so much in so little time," I told him.

"It is still a damned sight too slow," he lamented. He gestured towards the whole of the beast. "The trouble is securing this section without pulling the stitches there. The clamps are not holding as well as I would like."

"What is your plan for moving the specimen when it is finished?" I asked. "Surely you don't mean to haul it through the streets of London? It ought to have been assembled in situ."

He rolled his eyes heavenward. "Yes, I did think of that. I am not entirely devoid of intellect, no matter what you think of my *Phyllomedusa*." He had been working the back end of the beast and walked me around to see that the entire front half was missing. "You cannot mount an entire elephant in one go. The skin alone weighs more than a ton. It must be done in pieces, but no one has managed to do it properly, at least not yet. This one is simply an experiment, a chance to refine the process before I begin in earnest."

"For a patron? A lord, I believe you said?"

He nodded. "The Earl of Rosemorran, dilettante and

eccentric, but richer than Croesus. He acquired an enormous bull elephant—bones and hide—out of East Africa. I have done other mammal mounts to his satisfaction, so he agreed to let me practice on this smaller fellow to see if I can devise a better method before touching his prize."

"And he is paying you for this?" I asked with a dubious glance at the elephant's unfinished backside.

His lip curled. "Would I do this for my own amusement?"

I glanced meaningfully at the collected specimens in the workshop.

He sighed heavily. "These are not worth the sawdust they're stuffed with. They were mounted using old methods, and now they are crumbling to bits. I acquired most for next to nothing just so I could tear them apart and assess their imperfections. One cannot innovate new improvements without understanding old failures."

I poked the elephant experimentally. "And this one is proving a failure?"

"Thus far. I wanted to mount him on his own skeleton, but that won't serve. It will have to be two separate displays, one of just the bones reassembled into an articulated skeleton. The other will be a mount made to look lifelike with the skin properly stretched over a form sculpted to simulate the flesh. The difficulty is in the sheer bloody enormity of it." The fact that he did not apologize for his language made me like him better. "He must be pieced together, but I have not yet devised a method for doing so without making him look like Frankenstein's monster. He shall be nothing more than a grotesque if I don't work it out."

I noticed again the black streaks upon his arms—glue as well as soot, I realized, a hazard of his occupation. But the hair was simply a matter of being badly groomed, for it hung past his shoulders in unfashionably long, snarled dark locks that shone with a bluish tint in the late morning light. His beard was heavy and untrimmed, and with the eye patch and the slender gold ring glinting in his earlobe, it gave him the air of a rather impoverished pirate.

I moved past him to the section he had indicated, peering at the stitches. "You want another pair of hands," I said firmly. "Tell me where to hold so I do not mar the folds of the skin."

He hesitated, and I clucked at him impatiently. "Mr. Stoker, I am offering you my help. I am bored and likely to grow far more so in the coming hours. We do not know how long the baron means us to be thrown together, and we might as well pass the time in some useful fashion. You require extra hands. I have them. Now tell me where to put them."

He looked as if he wanted to argue, but in the end he merely pointed and I held the skin taut while he worked. "Hold it firm there," he barked. "Harder! A kitten could make a better job of it."

I tightened my grip and he grunted, the highest praise I was likely to receive, I understood. We worked for some hours, and at length it occurred to me that I was exceedingly hungry and thirsty. He must have sensed my flagging energy, or perhaps his own was dwindling. He brought out a loaf of bread and a suspicious-looking ham and hacked off wedges of both with a clasp knife. I produced a few soft apples from my carpetbag and we ate in silence.

When we had finished, he reached for a tin and withdrew a cigar, lighting it with a spill from the stove. He drew in great lungfuls of poisonously strong tobacco smoke, blowing it out in long exhalations.

He caught my stare and gave me a mocking glance. "Where are my manners? Would you like a puff?" he asked, extending the cigar.

I returned his gaze coolly. "No, thank you. I brought my

own." With that, I went to my carpetbag and drew out a packet of slim cigarillos, lighting one as he had done with a twist of paper at the stove. He stared at me in stupefaction until I blew out a perfect smoke ring, then gave a grudging laugh.

"Where did you acquire the habit?"

"Costa Rica," I told him. "And your cigar is inferior tobacco."

"Good tobacco is expensive and I am a pauper," he said lightly.

We smoked in silence, and as we did, my gaze fell to the scars that ran underneath his eye patch.

"Do not feel sorry for me," he ordered. The air around him fairly crackled with anger, and I regarded him coolly.

"I shouldn't dream of feeling sorry for you. You have two fine arms and two working legs and a strong back. You have a brain that seems more capacious than most, and as near as I can make out, your sight is otherwise unimpaired. What possible reason do you have to believe I would pity you?"

"You would not be the first," he said, his expression sullen.

I gave him a grim smile. "I am afraid you will have to try a great deal harder than that if you desire my sympathy. I have traveled widely in the world, and I have seen men with half as many functional limbs as you and twice the courtesy. If I pity you, it is only because you are so determined to be disagreeable."

His only response was a sort of growl, but I was finished with the discussion. I rose and dusted off my hands, grinding out the last of my cigarillo carefully on the sole of my boot.

"If we are to continue with the elephant, I must have an apron. I have only one other dress in my bag and it is silk." With that I moved to a pile of discarded cloths, finding at last a piece long enough and clean enough to serve my purposes. I tied it neatly about my waist and set to work again, testing the glue that rested in its pot near the stove.

"Is this warm enough?" I inquired, lifting the spatula and watching the amber threads pull like so much spun sugar.

"It wants a bit more heat," he said, and I noticed that his voice was marginally more cordial than it had been. He showed me how to move the glue closer to the heat to soften it and the proper method of applying it with the various spatulas while he stitched with enormous needles, setting small, precise stitches that would have put any needlewoman to shame.

We passed a long time busily engaged in our endeavors, working steadily until there was a noise at the door and a boy bounded in. He was a grubby child, no older than ten, but his eyes shone with intelligence and—when they lighted on me—curiosity.

"The post, Mr. S.," he said, proffering a single slender envelope. Mr. Stoker flicked a glance towards it and told him to throw it on the fire.

"Surely you will want to read it," I protested. He shrugged one heavy shoulder.

"Why should I? I know the contents well enough to say them off by heart. 'It is with deepest regret that we must write to inform you that your application to travel with the Royal Museum of Natural History on its forthcoming expedition to Peru has been denied.' Shall I go on? I know it word for word by now. If you like, I could probably set it to music, perhaps something moody and sad for a duet of oboe and bassoon."

He affected insouciance, but there was a bitter note underlying his tone.

"It mightn't be this time," I said reasonably.

"Oh, Christ preserve us, all of you butterfly chasers are the same—appalling optimists, always looking for the best, determined to find it."

I daubed glue at one of the gaping seams. "Precisely. You see, Mr. Stoker, one seldom finds something if one never actually looks for it. I should have thought an explorer would have a better grasp of that concept."

He snorted rudely and the boy stared from one to the other of us with rounded eyes. Mr. Stoker turned to him. "The coin is in the tin, Badger." The boy went to a shelf where a battered sweet tin sagged against a stack of teetering books. He emptied it of the single coin inside—so small as to be worth almost nothing—and thanked Mr. Stoker.

Mr. Stoker grunted by way of reply, and the boy tipped his cap to me, offering a winsome smile that shone in his dirty face. I grinned back at him and he bent to scratch Huxley behind the ears.

"Badger." The harsh voice brought the boy up sharply.

"Yes, Mr. Stoker?"

"The ham you brought yesterday gives me indigestion. Take it away, and tell the bloody butcher he is a criminal for passing that off as good meat."

The boy dove for the ham, wrapping it in a bit of sacking as carefully as one might a newborn babe. "I will tell him, Mr. S.," he promised, and scurried away, clutching his prize to his thin chest.

Mr. Stoker carried on with his work in silence, but his silence was a heavy thing and I was glad when he paused to brew cups of foul tea. He drank his from a tin that had once held peaches, but mine was in proper porcelain, albeit badly cracked and missing the handle. I held it carefully, watching as he stirred a horrifying amount of sugar into his with the handle of a paintbrush.

"Sugar if you want." He indicated with the paintbrush, and I refused politely. He bent to his tea and I studied him, noting the strong hands with broad palms, calloused and marked with scars, the noble brow, the proud nose. At length I shook my head, and Mr. Stoker, who had not been unaware of my scrutiny, I think, gave me a significant look.

"Do not tell me I disappoint you?" he challenged.

"Oh, indeed you do," I said evenly. "But probably not in the ways you expect."

"I already know you find me a boor. Rude and ill-mannered."

I shrugged. "That we have already established. Your frightful manners do not surprise me. The fact that you are a liar does."

He started, his complexion suffusing with a rush of angry color. But he mastered himself quickly, and when he spoke, it was with a deliberate attempt at lightness. "A liar. How clever of you to find me out."

"Not really. I saw how greedily you devoured the ham, and I saw that for several hours afterward, you worked quite comfortably. You have not coughed or swallowed overmuch or visited an unmentionable place in the yard—all signs of indigestion. In fact, you have worked with great enthusiasm and energy, a man in complete command of himself and perfect health."

The dull color receded and he looked away. "Yes, dammit, I lied to the boy."

"How many people is he trying to feed on his meager earnings?"

"Seven. Six brothers and sisters and an ailing mother," he said quietly.

"And the boy is too proud to take charity, I assume."

"Quite." The word was clipped.

"And you are too clever to offer it. I presume you have an understanding with the butcher not to take your messages sent through the boy too seriously?"

He hesitated, then burst out, "Yes, damn you, and he has a standing order to give them whatever offal and bones he has left over and put it on my account."

"An account I suspect you can ill afford to settle."

The proud nose twitched. "I manage to keep myself."

"But not well," I pointed out. "You eat scraps, preferring to spend your coin upon cheap tobacco, sugar, and—unless I am very much mistaken about the aroma emanating from your person—inferior gin. Yet you have ambition, Mr. Stoker, and great skill. I have learned more from watching you these past hours than in years of reading books and journals. You ought to be a university lecturer or a field explorer."

Somewhere in the depths of his tangled beard, his lips twisted. "You have seen my prospects, Miss Speedwell. I am rejected."

I flapped a hand. "By a second-rate institution run by charlatans and fools. Everyone knows the director was given his post because his aunt is the mistress of the chairman of the board of directors."

He choked on his tea, coughing mightily until I rose to strike him hard upon the back. He wiped his mouth on the back of his hand and regarded me with amazement.

"Miss Speedwell, I have hiked the length of the Amazon River. I have been accosted by native tribes and shot twice. I have nearly met my death by quicksand, snakebite, poisoned arrows, and one particularly fiendish jaguar. And I have never, until this moment, been quite so surprised by anything as I am by you."

"I shall take that as a fine compliment indeed, Mr. Stoker."

He tipped his head to study me for a moment.

"How do you know Max?"

"The baron? I do not know him. He simply appeared." I did not know how much the baron had related to him, so I confined my explanation to the barest facts. "I had been burying my late guardian, Miss Nell Harbottle, and the baron came to pay his respects. He kindly offered me transport to London."

"And you came away with him? Just like that?" He seemed to have forgot his tea. It grew cold and scummy in the cup as he listened to my curious tale.

"It was a sensible decision," I temporized. "There was a housebreaker in the vicinity. The baron had persuaded himself I was in danger."

"Yes, so he said. Life and death," Mr. Stoker said, his expression mocking. I might have told him the rest of the story, but I did not care for his tone. For the present, the villainous intruder would be a secret I shared only with the baron.

I shrugged. "An elderly gentleman's fancy. No doubt many ladies would be missish about staying alone in a rather remote country cottage with a possible criminal at large, but the prospect did not afright me. I might have remained at Wren Cottage, but it was my intention to leave anyway. By coming away with the baron, I saved myself the expense of the journey to London. I must be mindful of my money," I said. I looked deeply into my cup of tea.

He bristled. "You will have no call to spend it under my roof. Max has placed you in my protection. That means it is my responsibility to feed and shelter you until he returns," he told me, his tone aggressive.

"Really, Mr. Stoker, that is not necessary. I can pay my way," I began.

"I have the merest embers of pride left, Miss Speedwell. I beg you let me warm myself upon them," he said. He had spoken casually, but I knew instinctively that he was a man who had come down greatly in the world, and I had no wish to injure him further.

"Then I must thank you for your hospitality, Mr. Stoker. And you must grant me my pride as well. I should like to be of some use whilst I am here. Perhaps some tidying up would be in order,"

I suggested hopefully, regarding the chaos of his surroundings.

"Touch so much as a hair of a sloth's head, and I will have you shot," he said darkly. "But you may continue to help me mount the elephant. It is a bastard of a job for one man."

I ignored his profanity. I had grown accustomed to it in the previous hours, and if I was perfectly honest, it provided a bit of spice to conversation when one had spent so much time listening to the chatter of women.

"I wonder that you took it on without a proper assistant," I mused aloud.

"I have not the means to engage an assistant," he reminded me.

"Nor the common sense to decline the commission," I added. He started again, and I held up a hand against the tirade I could see building within him. "It was not a criticism, Mr. Stoker. There is no shame in a man's being ambitious. In fact, I find it rather necessary in this day and age. A gentleman cannot always depend upon his birthright to support him. Sometimes circumstances demand that he make his own way in the world, and I applaud such spirit."

His gaze narrowed. "What do you mean, 'gentleman'?"

"I mean that you are quite clearly a person who has suffered some reverses in the world. Whether they are unique to you or whether your entire family have suffered, I cannot say. But I know that you are not a man who was born to drink his tea from a peach tin or wear patched boots." I looked pointedly at his feet. "I happened to notice that your boots are from John Lobb. They are old and well-worn and patched with care, but they are of excellent make and extremely expensive. This speaks to a man who is not what he seems."

He stared at me in slack-jawed mystification. "How the bloody hell can you possibly know that?"

"I knew a charming young Belgian who insisted upon

ordering his boots from that establishment. He instructed me on the finer points of gentlemen's footwear. But it was you who betrayed your birth, I am afraid—by way of your vowels, Mr. Stoker. You are careful with them, as only a gentleman bred from the cradle can be. While your vocabulary may be colorful in the extreme, your diction is impeccable."

He said something thoroughly profane then, and I merely smiled into my cup. He subsided into nursing his tea, and we fell to an oddly restful silence before I spoke again.

"Why do you not fund your own expedition, Mr. Stoker?"

He gave me a nasty smile. "I believe we have discussed my financial affairs already, Miss Speedwell. You are conversant enough upon the matter to know the answer to that question."

I shook my head. "I suppose it was to be expected that you would lose your nerve."

"I beg your pardon?"

"You must believe me sympathetic. I quite understand, Mr. Stoker. Such experiences as you have suffered whilst on expedition would temper the sharpest enthusiasm. But we are scientists, are we not? We understand the difference between base and precious metals. Some things are purified and strengthened by trial, others destroyed."

He ground his teeth together against my compassion. "I assure you, your sympathies are quite misplaced. I have not lost my nerve, you insufferable woman. I am doing what I can with what I have."

I shook my head. "I think not. You have placed your trust in the Royal Museum of Natural History, an institution we both know to be corrupted both by ignorance and greed. And yet you appear to have collected their rejections with the same verve you collect your tragically flawed specimens. Tell me, how many times have they turned you down?"

"Two dozen," he ground out.

"Good heavens, Mr. Stoker. I am sorry to add pigheadedness to your list of faults, but I suppose I must. Why do you persist in applying to them to aid you when it ought to be the other way round?"

He had opened his mouth upon the insult, but my last sentence must have proved too intriguing to ignore. "Explain," he ordered.

I smiled. "I thought you would never ask."

SIX

I LAUNCHED INTO AN EXPLANATION—ALTHOUGH less charitable types might have been inclined to call it a lecture. "The Royal Museum of Natural History is dependent upon explorers to collect its specimens, to chart new and undiscovered lands, and to bring back new species. You are such a man, and yet they do not want you—doubtless because they are familiar with your uncertain temper and execrable personal habits. Nevertheless, you are a scientist of considerable gifts. One has only to give this place the most cursory glance to realize you have assembled a collection that is both thoughtful and instructive, no matter how wretched its condition. There is real brilliance here, Mr. Stoker. If you were to mount your own expedition, on your own terms, the museum would have no choice but to come to you, begging for the specimens you acquire. You have simply put the cart before the horse," I told him.

He shook his head as if to clear it. "I smoked opium once. It felt like listening to you, only rather more mundane."

I tipped my head thoughtfully. "I smoked it once as well. I must say I did not much care for the aroma. It smelled of flowers and gunpowder, which was not unpleasant, but there was something else, something more animalic. Sweaty horse, I think."

He drew me back to the subject at hand. "How, I beg you, Miss Speedwell, is a man of no fortune and fewer prospects supposed to fund such an expedition?"

I puffed out my lips with impatience. "Really, Mr. Stoker, your lack of imagination is sorely trying. You might apply to subscribers. Wealthy people are always looking to spend their money in ways they can boast of to their friends. For that matter, your patrons need not be wealthy. You could advertise and take very small subscriptions from prosperous merchants and other up-and-comers. Promise them their name on plaques or to call a species after them. People love to have things they don't understand named for them. And your expedition needn't be costly. Your skill at preparing and mounting your specimens is evident. Can you hunt them as well?"

He nodded his head towards a particularly vicious-looking mount of a hyena. "Through the heart at two hundred yards."

"There you are, then! You need only a few local guides to show you the way and some bearers to bring back your trophies and specimen cases."

For the first time, he gave me a faint but very real smile. "Miss Speedwell, expeditions are a bit more complex than that."

I flapped a hand. "They do not have to be. Expeditions are enormously expensive because they have to cart around everyone's self-importance. Most of the leaders of these undertakings are dilettantes, gentlemen scientists who insist upon touring in luxury, packing so much silver and linen they might imagine themselves in a London hotel. You are a resourceful man. Are you not familiar with the intrepid lady travelers? Women like Isabella Bird and Marianne North? They managed to go right round the world with little more than what they could fit into a saddlebag. I am persuaded you could travel quite easily with a single bag. I mean to."

I pointed to my carpetbag. "Except for my net, everything I have need of in the world is contained in that bag—including a second hat and a rather sizable jar of cold cream of roses. Do not tell me you couldn't travel with as little. I have faith that men can be as reasonable and logical as women if they but try."

He shook his head. "I cannot seem to formulate a clear thought in the face of such original thinking, Miss Speedwell. You have a high opinion of your sex."

I pursed my lips. "Not all of it. We are, as a gender, undereducated and infantilized to the point of idiocy. But those of us who have been given the benefit of learning and useful occupation, well, we are proof that the traditional notions of feminine delicacy and helplessness are the purest poppycock."

"You have large opinions for so small a person."

"I daresay they would be large opinions even for someone your size," I countered.

"And where did you form these opinions? Either your school was inordinately progressive or your governess was a Radical."

"I never went to school, nor did I have a governess. Books were my tutors, Mr. Stoker. Anything I wished to learn I taught myself."

"There are limits to an autodidactic education," he pointed out.

"Few that I have found. I was spared the prejudices of formal educators."

"And neither were you inspired by them. A good teacher can change the course of a life," he said thoughtfully.

"Perhaps. But I had complete intellectual freedom. I studied those subjects which interested me—to the point of obsession at times—and spent precious little time on things which did not."

"Such as?"

"Music and needlework. I am astonishingly lacking in traditional feminine accomplishments."

He cocked his head. "I am not entirely astonished." But his tone was mild, and I accepted the statement as nothing like an insult. In fact, it felt akin to a compliment.

"And I must confess that between Jane Austen and Fordyce's *Sermons*, I have developed a general antipathy for clergymen. And their wives," I added, thinking of Mrs. Clutterthorpe.

"Well, in that we may be agreed. Tell me, do you find many people to share your views?"

"Shockingly few," I admitted. "I presented my interpretations to a vicar in Hampshire once and he was fairly apoplectic upon the subject. I lost my position on the flower-arranging committee."

"A tragedy indeed," he said with his now familiar mockery.

"You've no idea. In a country village, one's standing is determined by committee appointments and good works. I was relegated to a convalescent hospital, and I must say, I was glad of the change. The men there were not half so tiresome as the ladies who arrange the flowers, I can assure you. I was quite disappointed to lose my position there within a month."

His lips twitched. "For what reason?"

I shifted a little. "Because I amputated a toe without permission."

"You are joking."

"I never joke about gangrene, Mr. Stoker. I was reading to one of the patients when he complained of a certain discomfort in the appendage in question. I examined him, and it was painfully obvious that the poor fellow was suffering from a gangrenous toe. It had to come off, and immediately, or septicemia would set in and the fellow would die."

"I don't suppose the convalescent hospital had someone more suited to the job of amputation—say, an actual physician?"

"Of course," I explained patiently, "but he was at luncheon."

"And you could not wait an hour for the fellow to come back?"

"One cannot play games with septicemia, Mr. Stoker. It was common knowledge that the doctor's Sunday luncheons were taken with a great deal of good Irish whiskey. He would not have been in a fit state to take off so much as a hangnail if I had waited for him. So I asked Archie if he would like for me to take matters into my own hands, as it were, and he said he would just as soon have me as the doctor, and between us we managed quite well."

"How is it that you were not brought up on charges?" he demanded. "Practicing medicine without the proper license is thoroughly illegal."

I pulled a face. "Really, Mr. Stoker, I should have thought that you would understand the notion of an action taken in extremis. And the doctor himself admitted it was very neatly done. Besides, if there had been any sort of inquiry, he would have been brought up on disciplinary actions for being an inebriate. I agreed to go quietly, and he agreed to forget the whole thing—quite sensible of us both, under the circumstances." I smoothed my skirts. "We seem to have digressed. You have not answered my point that one may travel with all the necessities of a comfortable life quite handily."

His gaze narrowed in suspicion. "Yes, well, if this is your way of angling for an invitation, you needn't think I will bring you along if I plan an expedition. I have no need of amateur lepidopterists."

"I am not an amateur," I replied tartly. "I have supplied specimens to some of the foremost collectors in this country and abroad."

"Indeed. And what are your rates? Asking as one professional to another," he said rudely.

"Three pounds for the average specimen. Naturally, I charge more for special orders."

"Three pounds! Do you dip the bloody things in gold first? That is highway robbery."

"It is the standard rate for quality specimens, and mine are the best," I retorted. "And fear not, Mr. Stoker. If I were to travel with a formal expedition, I should want a leader with a good deal more nerve and initiative than you seem to enjoy. Besides, I am well aware of the narrow-mindedness and lack of original thought demonstrated by most gentlemen explorers, and I could never bring myself to work under their direction. I am much better suited to my own devices. My own travels have always been undertaken at my own initiative. I go where I choose."

To my surprise, he did not take offense at my riposte.

"And where do you mean to go now, Miss Speedwell?"

I tipped my head, considering. "I had in mind the Malay Archipelago. I should like to try for a *Hypolimnas*, I think. The *bolina* in particular is quite striking, and I am certain I could find a buyer without difficulty. In fact, I should probably have to beat them off with a parasol if I am successful."

The efforts of the previous night and past day seemed to have caught him up at last, for he yawned broadly.

"You ought to rest," I told him, half wondering if he would refuse out of sheer mulishness. "I know you have been working almost continually upon the elephant, and a rest would enable you to return fresh to the fray. I would be very happy to pass the time in reading, if you would not mind the loan of your library," I added, nodding towards the shelves bowed by the weight of the ponderous volumes.

He opened his mouth—no doubt to protest—but I reached for his tea tin and took it firmly from his hand. "You really do look quite wretched, you know."

If I had been more timid, there is no question he would have cursed me and gone straight back to work. But I was dauntless, and he allowed me to take the tin from him as he stretched his limbs upon the sofa. Almost as soon as he was recumbent, his entire body succumbed to fatigue and he slept. Huxley puffed a sigh of indignation, for his master was far too large to permit him to share the sofa. He retreated under it to snore wetly as I roamed the workshop.

I moved to the specimen shelves to look over the Wardian cases, handsomely made, and each set with a small metal plaque incised with a series of letters—R.T.-V. I traced them idly with a fingertip, a growing suspicion beginning to take root in my mind. "R.T.-V.," I murmured. "Revelstoke Templeton-Vane. Now, this is a very interesting development indeed."

I dredged up all that I knew of the famed explorer and natural historian, but the facts were few and I had been on the other side of the world when his story had been splashed across English newspapers. The darling of the naturalists, he had established himself as a brilliant scholar with a series of papers reconciling Darwin's and Huxley's conflicting views of natural selection. But everything had been lost on a disastrous expedition to . . . Where was it? I cudgeled my brain and could not recall until I remembered Mr. Stoker's brief mention of hiking the Amazon. That was it, of course. He had headed a single expedition to South America, and that one trip had seen his career wrecked upon the shoals of infamy. I had heard only snatches of his ruin, but there had been vicious rumors, and he had all but disappeared from the scientific community for years.

But here were his Wardian cases, consigned to a derelict Thames-side warehouse. And then there was the matter of his name. It took little imagination to derive Stoker from Revelstoke. So, the once brilliant comet whose light had burned out so flamboyantly had come to rest in obscurity and poverty, I reflected as I looked about the dilapidated room.

I ran a finger over one of the cases and it came away black. I shuddered. It was unthinkable to sit idly by when I was surrounded by so much filth. As a scientist I rebelled against the disorder, and I had long since discovered that nothing thwarted the mental processes like clutter. While Mr. Stoker slumbered on, I swept the floor, dumping the sweepings into the dirt yard I found behind the workshop. I cleared out the ashes from the stove, putting them carefully aside in a pail and leaving a thick bed under the grate. This I polished and laid with a new fire, kindling it merrily as I rummaged about the meager stores for the makings of a soup. I scoured a wide pot and put it to the boil, hoping it had not held something unsavory in the recent past. I found a beef bone only a little past its prime and put it into the pot, adding a few limp carrots and their tops, and an onion with its sprouted green cap. In the dirt yard I discovered a struggling herb, etiolated as it was, and chopped it to add to the pot. There was salt in great quantities—he apparently used it in many of his preparations—and I did not think he would begrudge a little for the soup pot. I added this with crumbs of the loaf from the earlier repast to thicken the broth. As it bubbled away, I found spoons and took up the pail of ashes to polish them, rubbing them until they gleamed.

After this, I continued to tidy the workshop, dusting

the cases and straightening the books and wiping the sticky worktables of the worst of their grime. The endless stacks of newspapers, I was amused to see, had provided him with drawing paper, for most of the margins held small sketches—some faces or ships, others botanical specimens or animals. He was a gifted artist, I realized, capturing in a few strokes of pencil or charcoal the essence of what he intended to depict. I had attempted enough sketches and paintings of my butterflies to know true talent when I saw it. His technique was rough and hasty, but his talent was far beyond my own.

I tamped the newspapers into neat bundles without sorting them, skimming the headlines to see what I had missed in the years I had been abroad. The Irish question appeared often, as did the Mahdist War in the Sudan. The Prussians featured frequently, but that was no surprise. The Prussians were always up to something nefarious. And there had been an impressive number of gunfights in cities in the western United States. But that, too, was no great surprise. In my experience, Americans were very friendly and very fond of their firearms. I put these aside and moved on to the shelves holding bottles of chemicals. He had a collection of them, many potent, all flammable, and quite a few capable of producing nasty burns if permitted to touch bare skin. Most bottles contained preservatives in various dilutions, although one bore a label that crumbled at the tentative poke I gave it. I sniffed experimentally and was assaulted at once by the cloying pickled smell of formaldehyde. I gave it a wide berth and continued on, tidying until I had brought a reasonable semblance of order to the place. I was intrigued to find a florilegium of Romantic poetry tucked under a pot of hide glue and was just about to settle in to read when I heard a roar of outrage.

"Holy Christ, I told you not to touch anything." Mr. Stoker had come awake, wincing a little as he sat up and worked the stiffness from his muscles.

"I did not move anything," I assured him. "I merely stacked the books and correspondence so they would not fall over, and I cooked a meal. I would have replaced the preservative solution in some of those appalling jars, but it does not seem to be plain ethyl alcohol, and I did not wish to damage the specimens by changing the solution."

"At least you have that much sense," he said grudgingly. "The solution is of my own devising."

"And not very effective," I told him, pointing towards the jars of suckling pigs floating in scummy yellow fluid.

"Those were early efforts, designed to show me where the flaws were in the formula," he said nastily. "And if Your Highness would care to look at the specimens on *that* shelf, I think you will find the solution is clear as Irish crystal."

I did as he bade, nodding in approval. "Well-done. That is perhaps the finest preserving work I have seen. Did you use plain formaldehyde? No, of course, you will not tell me. I ought not to have asked. I should love to see you preserve something. I have only ever managed to fix butterflies, and of course, mounting Lepidoptera is nothing so difficult as mounting mammals."

He gave me a curious and not wholly friendly stare. "How did you come to be interested in butterflies? They are the usual province of the lady naturalist, but I am rather surprised you didn't find yourself studying something with teeth."

"Hm." I was examining another of his little pigs, marveling at the curl of its pink tail. "How extraordinary. One can almost hear it squealing." The specimen, one of his best, was so arrestingly lifelike I was not entirely certain it had not moved. Like my butterflies, it gave the impression of cessation, as if it had paused in whatever it was doing but only for a moment. Stillness coupled with expectancy; these are the qualities all good preparations must convey.

I shook myself free of my reverie. "What was that? Oh, butterflies. They afforded me the chance to get away from the villages where I grew up. Girls are not supposed to go roaming about the countryside without purpose. It is considered eccentric. So I bought a butterfly net and a killing jar, and that made it quite all right."

A ghost of a smile touched his lips. "That I can understand. I was always thought odd for stuffing my pockets with jars of frogspawn and dissecting rabbits instead of eating them."

I smiled at the notion of him as a boy with a pocketful of bottled tadpoles, but he suddenly tired of conversation. With an abruptness I had noted before in his manner, he gave me a cool look and picked up his pot of glue. "I think I will return to my elephant. I have wasted quite enough time already."

He strode back to his pachyderm, leaving me to amuse myself with Huxley. I did not mind. "Reclusive men are a good deal of work," I murmured to the dog. Mr. Stoker was not my first encounter with a fellow uncomfortable in the company of women, and would assuredly not be the last. He might have a pathological dislike of women in general, but with a certainty borne of experience, I put his thorniness down to a heartbreak in his tender youth. Some people never recovered from their early losses, I reflected. I ladled out bowls of soup for Huxley and myself, pointedly ignoring Mr. Stoker as he worked at the elephant. The fragrance of the soup rose in a steamy cloud, inviting and rich, and the dog and I sipped contentedly until Mr. Stoker threw down his spatula and stalked to the soup pot. "What is this, then?"

"Food for the dog," I said evenly.

He gave me a sour look and ladled up a portion. There were no other bowls, so he took his in a chipped porcelain basin that was clearly a piece of laboratory equipment.

"It is a miracle you have not poisoned yourself," I observed.

He shoveled a spoonful of soup into his mouth. "I would make a rather cutting remark about poisoning myself on your cooking, but I cannot. This is sublime. I can't think when the last time was I had hot food."

He ate three bowls, each more slowly than the last, until he scraped the final savory spoonful and gave a sigh of repletion.

"You do not take very good care of yourself," I said. It was an observation, not an accusation, and he seemed to take it as such.

He shrugged. "Too much work, too little time, and too little money. You were not wrong about my habits. I sleep when I can and grab the odd bit of food when I think of it to keep myself going. And there is always gin," he added with the jaded air of a practiced debauchee.

I said nothing but went to my bag and retrieved the flask. "Here. Something I picked up on my travels. I find it quite bracing."

He took it from my hand and swallowed deeply, then spluttered so hard he nearly choked. "Good God, what the devil is that?"

"South Americans have a specialty called cachaça, something like rum but made from sugarcane rather than molasses."

"I am familiar," he said with a rueful look. "I lost the better part of a year to the stuff in Brazil. But it was nothing like this."

I deliberately overlooked the reference to his past. If he had worked so diligently to conceal his true identity, it was not my place to unmask him. At least not yet. "When I was butterflying in Venezuela, my host was a gentleman with extensive sugarcane fields in Brazil. He finds cachaça to be a trifle tame for his tastes, so he distils it twice. This rather more potent aguardiente is the result."

He took a second swallow, this one more modest, and wiped the neck of the flask upon his sleeve as carefully as a lord. He blinked heavily. "I think I have gone blind. And I am quite certain I do not care."

I capped the flask and replaced it in my bag. He flipped up his eye patch, and to my astonishment, I saw that his eye was whole and unblemished as the other, aside from a narrow white scar crossing the lid. I noticed also they were blue, not the striking bright blue of a Morpho but the very dark blue of *Limenitis arthemis astyanax*, a Red-spotted Admiral I had hunted successfully in America. Compared to the frivolous Morpho, the Admiral was a very serious sort of butterfly.

"You have sight in that eye," I said, almost accusingly.

He nodded, pressing his knuckles into his eyes. "As much as in the other, believe it or not. But it fatigues easily, and when it does, my vision becomes blurred. I see two of everything instead of one. Then I've no option but the patch to rest it."

"Thereby fatiguing the other," I pointed out.

He replaced the patch and shook his head as if to clear it. "No help for it if I am to get that bloody elephant finished."

Just at that moment there came a scraping noise from the doorway.

"I've brought the evening papers, Mr. S.," Badger said brightly. "And your sweets."

He handed over the newspapers and a twist of peppermint humbugs to Mr. Stoker, who fell on them greedily. I turned to the boy. "I am so glad you've come. I have a bowl of soup that will go to waste if you don't eat it up, and if I give more to the dog he will be terribly sick. Would you mind?" I ladled out the soup into Mr. Stoker's basin and wiped off the spoon.

Badger washed neither his hands nor his face, applying himself directly to the food. He slurped as happily as Huxley had, finishing the bowl in minutes as Mr. Stoker flicked through the newspaper. Suddenly, he sat forward, every muscle in his body so still I knew something very bad indeed had happened.

"What is it?" I demanded.

He did not speak. He merely gripped the newspaper, his knuckles turning white. I came to stand behind him, reading over his shoulder.

"No!" I exclaimed, dismayed. "It cannot be."

The headline was sensational, but it was the details of the story that gripped my attention. A German gentleman, identified as the Baron von Stauffenbach, had been found dead in his study. The room had been ransacked and the police were treating the death as suspicious. There were no clues as to the identity of the assailant. It ended with a note that an inquest was to be held in two days' time.

"It cannot be," I repeated.

"It is," Mr. Stoker said flatly. "He must have been murdered just after he returned home."

"Murdered!" Badger looked up from his soup bowl. "Who's been killed, then?"

I glanced to Mr. Stoker, but he seemed unable to reply, his expression one of frozen horror. As I watched, the newspaper trembled slightly in his hand. Clearly he was in the grip of strong emotion, and in no fit state to react.

"A friend," I told the boy. "Perhaps you ought to go now, Badger."

He licked the last of the soup from his bowl and rose obediently. The action seemed to rouse Mr. Stoker, and he stood, flinging aside the newspaper.

"Not so fast, lad. I have telegrams to send." Having thrown off his torpor, he moved like one possessed, his actions swift and desperate. He tore a bit of paper from a scientific journal and scribbled in the margin. "You will send twelve copies of this wire—one to each of these twelve offices. Send them and wait for replies, do you hear? Most of them will be in the negative. You can throw those away. But the one that is in the affirmative, that one I will have." He scrawled another missive and handed it over. "This telegram only goes to Cornwall, to be delivered by the messenger directly into the hands of the addressee and no other," he instructed. He rummaged through a collection of tins and jars to cobble together a handful of coins. "More when you come back."

Badger pocketed the coins and ran to the door, saluting smartly. "You can rely upon me, Mr. S."

A heavy silence fell then, punctuated only by the crackling of the fire in the stove and Huxley's damp snores. I felt quite helpless in the face of Mr. Stoker's rage, for he was clearly angry, his lips thin, his color high, his hands working themselves into fists and loose again as he strode the length of the workshop and back. It was right that he should be angry, and grief and horror would have their parts to play as well. But as I watched him, I realized something else assailed him, driving him to pace like a caged lion—fear.

At length, he abandoned his pacing for action, moving swiftly to a decrepit old Gladstone bag, which he began to pack. He rummaged amidst the various trunks and shelves, extracting sundries that he threw into the bag, including the florilegium of Romantic poets and a stack of enormous scarlet handkerchiefs. After a moment's hesitation, he returned to one of the trunks. He made a grimace of distaste as he plunged his hand into it, and I could not see what he withdrew, but he tucked the item into the pocket of his trousers and slammed the lid of the trunk closed with vehemence. I went to him and put out my hand.

"Mr. Stoker, you have been very generous to extend your hospitality to me, but I am clearly intruding upon a time of quite personal grief. I will take my leave of you now and thank you."

He whirled on me, his anger as palpable as a lash. "Leave? Oh, I think not, my girl. You and I are bound together, at least until this is finished."

Appalled but sympathetic to his strong emotion, I strove for patience. "Mr. Stoker, I understand you are naturally distressed at the death of your dear friend, and I extend my deepest sympathies to you. I am clearly in the way and have no business here. I must leave you."

"You do not understand, do you?" His voice was frankly incredulous. "You *are* my business now."

"I? That is impossible."

He threw a rusty black suit into the moldering bag and strapped it shut. "Think again, Miss Speedwell."

"Mr. Stoker, again, I am sorry for your loss, but I must insist—"

He reached out and clasped my wrist. He was demanding, not coaxing, and I could feel the weight of his emotion to my bones.

"My dearest friend and mentor is dead, and as nearly as I can comprehend, you are the reason. Until I discover why, you do not stir an inch from my sight."

"Be reasonable, Mr. Stoker! How can I possibly be the cause of that poor man's death? I was with you from the time he left me here until he was killed. You must see that."

"The only thing I see is that he brought you here, convinced you were in mortal danger, and that was the last thing he ever did."

"I will not go with you," I said, pulling my wrist free and folding my arms over my chest.

"I think you will. Max told me to guard you—with my life if need be—and I do not intend to let him down. Now, whoever murdered him has almost twelve hours' advantage on us. We must leave as soon as Badger returns with replies to my telegrams. I am arranging for us to depart London and meet up with friends of mine who will provide us with a sort of refuge until the inquest is concluded and we have answers. At this moment, I am not certain if you are a victim or a villainess, but believe me, I will discover which."

"In that case, why not simply go to the authorities—" I began.

"No! That is not a possibility," he thundered, his features suffused with rage.

I adopted a patient tone of the sort nurses use with very small boys or deranged men. "I understand your distress, Mr. Stoker—"

"I do not think you do," he cut in swiftly. "But you will. Now, sit down and be quiet until Badger returns." He pushed me towards the sofa and I sat heavily.

"Mr. Stoker—" I began, rising to my feet.

He loomed over me as I pressed back against the sofa, bracing his arms on either side of my shoulders. "If you think I will not bind you hand and foot like a pig on a spit, I beg you—I *beg* you—to try me."

I subsided into silence, my bag on the floor at my feet, butterfly net resting atop. He resumed his pacing, and I sat with my hands folded, counting his steps. Clearly there was no arguing with him, seized as he was by his sentiments, and I decided to wait for a more propitious time. *You did long for a fresh adventure,* I reminded myself. And perhaps this was the beginning of one, I supposed, for I did not believe myself to be in any material danger from Mr. Stoker, no matter how filthy his temper. I relied upon my instincts, excellent as they were and sharply honed by years of travel among uncertain folk. Not everyone was content to let explorers traipse about their property in the pursuit of butterflies, and my excursions had brought me among some quite uncivil characters. A certain bandit chief in Corsica came to mind. But I had eluded his attempts either to murder me or make me his wife, and we had parted on excellent terms. In fact, he had even been gracious enough to give me a series of lessons on how to defend myself with some skill. I was entirely convinced I could enjoy similar success with Mr. Stoker. Besides, he clearly had very little experience in menacing women. He had not even thought to confiscate my hatpin.

So I resolved myself to be cooperative, and for several minutes Mr. Stoker busied himself about the workshop, rummaging through various boxes and tins to scrape together the remaining coins that comprised his modest treasury. He ruffled the pages of several books and a few banknotes of very small denominations fluttered free. He pocketed the money, then doused the lamps and the fire in the stove, leaving only one slender candle to banish the gloom. He slipped a knife into a leather sheath depending from a lanyard that he looped about his neck, buttoning it securely under his shirt. I might have raised an objection, but again came that instinctive certainty that no matter how angry, no matter how enraged he became, his fury—even armed—would never be directed in any meaningful way at me. I resumed counting as he walked. I had just reached six hundred and eighty-two when Badger returned, brandishing a pair of telegrams.

"I have them, Mr. S.!" Badger thrust the papers into Mr. Stoker's hand, and he read them over swiftly.

"Good lad." He handed over another palmful of coins. "There's a good fellow. I know I can rely upon you."

"Yes, sir, Mr. S.! And I will take care of Huxley, never fear." The boy coaxed the bulldog out from under the sofa and tied a bit of string to his collar for a lead. Mr. Stoker took up a slouchy, low-crowned hat, which he jammed upon his head before hefting his bag. He turned and gestured sharply to me.

"Come on, then."

I made a point of pausing to scratch the dog behind the ears before we left. It was better for Mr. Stoker to comprehend fully that I was no one's captive but my own.

SEVEN

Mr. Stoker chose not to share the details of where we were bound, and I knew better than to ask. Although I had remarked upon his loss, he was not yet grieving for the baron, I reflected. That would come later, after the finality of death sat with him during some long moment of quiet contemplation. Then, and only then, would it become real to him. For the present, Mr. Stoker was a man of action, propelled by his fear and his rage, moving ever forward and towing me ruthlessly in his wake. I saw no point in giving any impression other than peaceful compliance, so I purposefully took up my bag and net and accompanied him through the darkening streets. He walked swiftly, with the smooth-hipped, rolling gait of a man who has spent a great deal of time on horseback or at sea. He walked with his hand clamped to my arm, but he needn't have bothered. I had no thoughts of escape. The puzzle of the baron's untimely death was too intriguing to be ignored. And if, as Mr. Stoker assumed, there was anything I could possibly do to shed light upon the subject, I now realized it was my duty to do so. It had further occurred to me that in losing the baron, I had lost the one remaining connection to my mother. In finding the answers to his end, I might well find the answers to my beginning, although it would be the rankest of bad manners to admit so selfish a motive to Mr. Stoker in his time of bereavement.

I trotted on obediently, turning down this street and then that, following Mr. Stoker's guiding hand until we reached the looming enormity of Paddington Station. With its spacious arches and exuberant iron lacework, Mr. Brunel's pride and joy had persuaded me that in spite of their reputation for stodginess, engineers were in possession of truly flamboyant imaginations.

But Mr. Stoker had no eyes for this marvel of modern engineering. Instead he ducked into a shadowy corner and studied a timetable intently, peering up at the station clock as he made his calculations.

"Surely that was a circuitous route," I ventured, half expecting him to ignore me.

"A necessity. I wanted to make certain we were not followed."

Before I could ask him to elaborate, he nodded towards the ticket counter. "We have a quarter of an hour before our train leaves. Come along."

I did not move and he turned back, his expression darkening. I forestalled him. "You may purchase the tickets. I will avail myself of the ladies' accommodations while you do so."

He opened his mouth—to swear at me, I had no doubt—but I lifted a hand to silence him. "I have no intention of eluding you, even though you must see now how absurd it is to attempt to abduct a lady in a public place." I nodded towards the portly figure of a bobby striding into the station. To my astonishment, Mr. Stoker lifted the timetable as he pulled the brim of his hat lower, shielding his face.

Clearly he had no wish to attract the attention of the

constabulary, and I pressed my advantage. "Now, my dearest possession is my butterfly net," I told him. "It is the foundation of my profession and my most beloved tool. I will give it to you as a pledge that I will meet you on the platform before the train leaves."

He made a strangled sound, but I was already shoving the net into his hands. I walked briskly away, leaving him to secure the tickets. The lavatory was some distance, past the bookstall and confectionary stand, and I felt my stomach give a hungry little lurch as I strode past the refreshment rooms and the wafting scent of roast beef. I completed my errand quickly, emerging with clean hands and smoothed skirts. I was just tweaking my cuffs into place when a gentleman fell into step beside me. I was not unaccustomed to such approaches, and in my experience, a frosty look of gravest hauteur is the best method of discouragement.

But as I turned to give him my most withering glance, I faltered. The gentleman was a stranger to me; of that I was certain. Yet he regarded me with an expression akin to that of Moses beholding the Promised Land. I hesitated a mere second, and in that second, he had his opportunity. He took my elbow and whirled me to a stop behind the tobacconist's stand.

"Sir!" I protested, and instantly he dropped his hand.

"You must forgive my importunate approach, Miss Speedwell," he said, giving a swift glance around us. The milling travelers passed us by without a second look, and he stared at me, his gaze avid as it roved my face. "A thousand apologies. I had no wish to startle you," he said, his voice low and earnest and beautifully modulated. He was perhaps a few years above forty, well dressed, and smelling faintly of green spices. No grey yet threaded his black hair, and I wondered for a moment if he had resorted to boot black to retain an impression of youth.

But no. There might be a line or two at the corners of his eyes, and his jaw might have softened a touch beyond first youth, but his mouth curved into a smile of such dazzling charm, I knew this was a fellow who would retain his appeal well into old age.

"You have the advantage of me, sir," I replied coolly.

"Again, I can only ask your forgiveness," he said, but I marked he did not correct the omission. He raised his hands, sketching the outline of my form as he took me in from hat to hem. "Are you quite all right? I could scarcely breathe for thinking you might have been involved in this horrible business of murder."

"What do you know of it?" I demanded.

He shook his glossy head. "I only know the gallant old fellow did not deserve to die in such a terrible fashion. But you are here and unharmed, and that is all that matters now. It was clever of you to elude that ruffian," he added, no doubt referring to Mr. Stoker.

"The baron's death is nothing to do with me," I returned sharply. In spite of Mr. Stoker's suspicions to the contrary, I refused to countenance the notion that I was in any way connected with that foul deed, and I resented this gentleman for suggesting it. "Sir, you are speaking in riddles," I informed him.

He spread his hands, giving me another of his charming smiles. "Of course I am! I am half out of my mind with relief after so many frantic hours of worry about you. But you are safe now. I have come to take charge of you. The baron meant to deliver you into my care. That is why he brought you to London," he said simply.

I scrutinized his face, the handsome, even features, the guileless expression, and I did a rapid calculation. It was possible, just barely possible, that this fellow was my father if he had enjoyed a *very* indiscreet youth. There was something familiar in the sculpture of his bones that made me wonder if he might be. And I could not blame him for his reticence. Surely no gentleman would own such a truth in the mayhem of a London train station.

But something about his smile troubled me. Although he wielded it with practiced charm, it did not touch his eyes. And while he professed relief and joy at finding me, his gaze darted about us as his finger went to his collar. It was a minute thing, that tug upon his collar, but it was enough. He had delivered his lines with the smoothness of one who has often rehearsed, yet his own unconscious gesture had betrayed him.

"If you know my name," I told him evenly, "then you must know I am a natural historian."

"There is all the time in the world for us to become acquainted," he promised. "But we must go now."

He put his hand to my elbow, but I ignored the prompt.

"It is a pity you are not also a student of natural history," I said. "If you had read Duchenne's or Darwin's works on facial expressions, you would be a much better liar."

His eyes widened and his mouth fell open as a dark tide of red anger rose in his cheeks.

"There!" I said in some triumph. "Now you have it. Your expression accurately conveys your feelings—unlike a moment ago when you were lying. Your eyes gave you away then. And I feel I ought to make it quite clear that I do not appreciate being detained by men who ply me with falsehoods," I finished.

Instantly, my companion was contrite. "It seems I must ask your apology once more, Miss Speedwell," he said simply. "I have been too swift and I have frightened you, and I shall never forgive myself." He reached into his coat and withdrew a card case. It was a flashy thing, gold and set at each corner with gems so large I could only assume they were paste. He extracted a card and presented it to me. Unlike the baron's, this was of thin cardstock, the flimsiness of the paper betraying an attempt at economy.

"Edmund de Clare," I read aloud. Penciled beneath his name was the address of his lodgings in London—the Empress of India Hotel, a respectable but not fashionable establishment. He doffed his hat and swept me a theatrical bow.

"Your servant, Miss Speedwell."

"To what purpose, Mr. de Clare?" I asked.

"To the purpose of assisting you at what can only be a most difficult time. I understand your confusion," he pressed. "A young lady, alone in the world, without friend or family to offer succor. But I am here, ready and willing to offer my services and take on the mantle of protector so recently relinquished by the baron."

It was a pretty speech; I must credit him that. And a woman who had not learned self-preservation at the hands of a Corsican bandit might well have succumbed to his blandishments. But I was made of sterner stuff.

"How very kind of you, Mr. de Clare," I said, giving him a smile that would never have fooled Messrs. Duchenne or Darwin. "But I have business I must conclude before I place myself entirely in your care."

He did a masterful job of concealing his frustration, but the little tic at the corner of his mouth betrayed him. "My dear child, there is simply no time to spare!" he said, bringing his face close to mine, the scent of green spices heavier now, filling my nostrils. "Even now the peril approaches." He would have put a hand to my wrist, but I turned slightly to elude him.

"The peril?"

"From more than one source," he said grimly. "I do not wish to alarm you, Miss Speedwell, but the man you are with is no proper person to have the care of a lady. In fact, I must warn you that you are in the gravest danger from him."

"Indeed? Whatever has he done?" I asked, widening my eyes. I could fairly smell the frustration wafting from him.

"Things I cannot bring myself to speak of in your presence," he returned shortly. "But you are not safe with him, no matter what you believe. Now, will you come with me?"

I tipped my head and considered. "Very well," I told him.

The mask of concern dropped and I saw an instant of naked triumph in his eyes. "I am glad to hear it," he told me, and I did not doubt his sincerity. Whatever his ultimate purpose with me, he was thoroughly desperate to separate me from Mr. Stoker.

Just then I caught sight of a placard in the refreshment rooms advertising ham sandwiches, and my mind whipped back to the little scene between Mr. Stoker and his errand boy as he divested himself of the remains of the ham. A devilish stratagem proposed itself to me, and I accepted.

"A moment, sir, if you please. I find I am in need of the ladies' accommodation again," I told Mr. de Clare, lowering my lashes modestly. "A touch of alimentary distress," I murmured.

"Of course, of course," he said, his tone now soothing. Clearly nothing would be too much trouble for me now that I had capitulated.

"Would you be so kind as to procure me a little ginger beer from the refreshment rooms while I wait? My aunts always said there was no sounder cure for digestive troubles."

The jubilation he had been hard-pressed to conceal slipped a little. He did not care to let me out of his sight, but I had given him no choice. My confession of digestive upset was painfully banal—and something no lady would admit to a gentleman without urgent necessity. Every rule of custom and society dictated his response, and he did not disappoint. "Of course," he said again. "I shall go at once and wait for you directly outside the ladies' conveniences," he instructed. "Do not depart from there without me."

I gave him my assurances, and the second his back was turned as he made for the refreshment rooms, I bolted, plunging into the crowd of travelers. I took the stairs two at a time, heedless of the stares I attracted and the muttered complaints of those I jostled on my way to the platform. Mr. Stoker was there, striding about like a prowling tiger as he waited. The train stood upon the tracks, puffing out great clouds of black smoke as it began to ease forward.

"It's about bloody time," he burst out as he caught sight of me. "Where the devil have you been?"

I gave him a wintry smile. "I had a little difficulty with my hat. But it's quite all right now," I assured him as I slipped Mr. de Clare's card into my pocket.

Mr. Stoker grasped my hand and shoved me ahead of him, tossing me lightly onto the steps of the moving train. He followed, and as I turned to glance over his shoulder, I saw Mr. de Clare emerging onto the platform, his countenance ruddy with anger and thwarted purpose. I gave him a smile but resisted the urge to wave. It would have been unseemly.

We found an empty compartment and Mr. Stoker secured the door as I arranged myself comfortably. Now that I had leisure to consider my actions, I found it interesting that I had so instinctively thrown in my lot with Mr. Stoker rather than seizing the opportunity to elude him. It would have been the work of a moment to appeal to a passing policeman for aid or to accept Mr. de Clare's offer of assistance.

But to what end? My subconscious had understood what I finally had the chance to reason out logically: if I involved the authorities, our adventure was at an end. This impetuous flight from London would be over before it began. Clearly Mr. Stoker feared apprehension by them, for reasons I did not yet understand. His insistence upon playing a lone hand was no doubt dictated by sound purpose, and I longed to discover it. I was mindful, too, of the baron's implicit trust in him, a trust dictated by his own long acquaintance with the fellow. Well, I was up to the task of taking care of myself, I thought stoutly, but it seemed a good deal wiser to stay the course the baron had set me upon. He had apparently known Mr. de Clare and still chosen to deliver me to Mr. Stoker.

Why then did I refuse to share with Mr. Stoker the story of my meeting with Mr. de Clare in the station? I ought to have made a clean breast of things, but it nettled me that Mr. Stoker insisted upon such high-handed secrecy. He had not even confided where we were bound, and so long as he insisted upon secrets, I felt entitled to a few of my own. Besides, I reasoned, should Mr. Stoker prove a less than satisfactory partner in adventure, I now had a viable means of escape. I could afford to trust him until he gave me cause not to, and that was a comforting thought.

EIGHT

"I WISH I HAD KNOWN earlier we were embarking upon a train journey," I mused aloud as I rummaged in my bag. "I would have brought more food. And you needn't have bothered with first-class tickets, you know. I would have been perfectly comfortable in third. Indeed, the trains in certain remote regions of Eastern Europe make no marked distinction between the two."

Mr. Stoker, who had been watching the lights of the city with a decided intensity, relaxed as the metropolis fell away behind us. "There is no privacy in third class," he reminded me.

"Have we need of privacy?"

He did not reply. Silence lay between us then, heavy and unpleasant, and I thought I would run mad if it persisted for the duration of our journey. He had still declined to tell me exactly where we were bound, and the omission nettled me. My frustration demanded relief, and in my experience, men could often be goaded into speaking if one could only lay a hand upon the correct inducement. In Mr. Stoker's case, anger might well do the trick, I surmised, and I decided to prod his temper to discover any tender spots I might use to my advantage.

"I must say, this makes an improvement, Mr. Stoker. I thought you entirely incapable of initiative, but I am very glad to see that I was wrong. I think there is every possibility of your making a thorough success of yourself if you continue on in this vein. Of course, one could wish you would turn your energies to something more profitable and wholesome than felonious abduction, but it makes a start, does it not?"

I smiled pleasantly at him, and he glowered at me from his seat opposite. I was thoroughly satisfied with how swiftly he had turned to anger, and I made a note of it for future encounters.

"I cannot make out if you are the bravest woman I have ever met or the most ludicrous," he said in a stringent tone. "You ought to be frightened out of your mind, shrieking and swooning and sobbing upon the floor. Instead, you insult me."

"Not at all! I meant it as a most sincere compliment," I told him. "This act demonstrates considerable spirit and an unconventional mind, two qualities the great explorers have always united. And, more to the point, why should I be afraid? I have the consolation of a clear conscience, Mr. Stoker. I know I have in no way contributed to the baron's misfortunes, and I do not think you believe it either. This is merely a passing fever of the brain, a momentary whim. Your reason will restore itself in due course, and we will proceed from there. In the meantime, I believe the best strategy for me to adopt is one of peaceful compliance, just as one would do with a sleepwalker or a madman."

"You think me mad?"

"You did just abduct me," I pointed out reasonably. "I do not know that I should not call it madness, per se, but you must own it is a bit peculiar." I did not bother to explain that it could hardly be considered a proper abduction when I was clearly there of my own volition. I might have escaped him a dozen times, but it seemed unkind to raise the point when he thought he was doing such a masterful job of keeping me in tow.

I half expected a lecture of some sort, but he had said all he intended to say, and we fell into a sharp silence then. This time I did not attempt to rouse him from it. The hours slipped by, and the dusky purple twilight deepened to blackness. The stars emerged, shyly at first, and then winking brightly, and a lopsided, waxing moon rode above the trees as we journeyed further west into the countryside. Eventually he dozed, and I occupied myself by thinking of Mr. de Clare. Clearly he had things to tell me, but it was his misfortune that I had received such excellent instruction at the hands of my Corsican friend. An accomplished bandit, he had stressed to me the importance, at all times, of following one's intuition, no matter what logic might dictate. I had done so at Paddington when faced with the question of accompanying Mr. de Clare, and it was not until I had the leisure of the train journey that I reasoned out why my instincts had insisted upon Mr. Stoker as my companion at the expense of Mr. de Clare. I had not been conscious of the thought at the time, but I realized, as I listened to Mr. Stoker snoring softly in time with the train wheels, that whether or not the baron had indeed sent him to retrieve me from Mr. Stoker like a parcel, Mr. de Clare had chosen his approach with care. He had not spoken to me when Mr. Stoker was at hand, but the moment we were divided, Mr. de Clare had presented himself. Had he truly been a messenger sent from the baron, he would have had no compunction about announcing his purpose to both of us.

Unless. I looked at my sleeping companion, the features drawn by a creator in a harsh mood, with no softness to spare. The nose was aggressive, the sort of nose Alexander would have looked down as he conquered the world, and the cheekbones and brows matched it in sharply molded grandeur. The jaw, though shadowed by the beard, was obviously strong, and the upper lip, what was visible of it, was slender and hard. Only the gentle curve of the lower lip betrayed him as a sensualist. That lower lip told stories to which the rest of his face gave a lie, and I wondered which to believe. Taken together, this collection of features could be hero or villain, martyr or tyrant, and if Mr. de Clare believed him to be my captor, it made perfect sense that he should wait to make his approach until Mr. Stoker was absent. Had he viewed himself my deliverer from whatever menace Mr. Stoker offered? It was a chilling thought. But I remembered again my lessons in Corsica and shook my head stubbornly. I would not, could not believe that Mr. Stoker would be my doom.

It was only much later that I decided my Corsican friend had much to answer for.

We changed trains at Taunton and again at Exeter before alighting at last at Taviscombe Magna. Here we were the only passengers to leave the train, and I was not surprised there was no one to meet us. Mr. Stoker gestured impatiently. "The night air is cold here. Have you a coat? Put it on."

I retrieved a long striped coat from my bag and buttoned it securely. He merely slung an untidy old frock coat over his shoulders, wearing it as a cloak, and as we moved into the moonlight, I smiled.

"What is so bloody funny?" he demanded.

"You. I hope we do not meet with any superstitious countryfolk. They will take you for the ghost of a disheveled highwayman."

He muttered a curse and started off down the narrow lane that led from the village and into the countryside. The moonlight was our only means of illumination, and the going was difficult at times, the lane pitted and rough. We walked for some time without a word passing between us, but as the moon rose directly overhead, I stumbled and he put out a hand to steady me.

"Thank you."

He hesitated. "I suppose we could rest for a moment if you require it."

"Not at all," I returned briskly. "The walking is sufficient exercise to keep me quite comfortable. We should be chilled through if we stopped. But you might tell me where we are bound, so as to pass the time more easily."

"We are going to friends of mine. They are encamped nearby."

"Encamped! Are your friends Gypsies, then?"

"They are not. They are members of a traveling show."

I stumbled again and he swore softly. "Can you not keep your feet, woman?"

"You surprised me," I said by way of apology. "A traveling show? I am intrigued. What sort of traveling show?"

"You will see soon enough."

He fell to a moody silence again, but I would have none of it.

"Mr. Stoker, I understand that you are mightily put out with me, and I daresay if the circumstances were reversed, I should treat you with the same unfounded suspicion. But I would like to point out that I have been very cooperative for a victim of abduction, and the least you can do is make a little polite conversation."

He stopped then and faced me squarely in the moonlight, his face thrown into harsh shadows. "Victim? When, for all I know, you ordered the attack upon the baron?"

I gave him a pitying look. "I know you think it possible, but you are a man of science. You have been trained not to hypothesize until you have developed all of your data, is that not true? Therefore, you must also believe it possible that I am innocent. The baron himself entrusted me to your care. Would he have done so if he believed me to be a dangerous person? Did you yourself not say his precise charge was that I was to be guarded, *even at the cost of your own life*?"

He said nothing for a long moment, emotions warring upon his face. "He did," he ground out finally. "And yes, I will concede it is far likelier you are an innocent in all of this than a perpetrator. But you are the only possible connection I have to discovering what happened to Max." His voice held a note that in another man might have sounded like a plea.

"I understand that, and whether you want to believe it or not, I am deeply sorrowed by whatever calamity has befallen him. I knew him only for the duration of our journey to London, but I believe he was a kind man and he meant to help me, although I think if he could see you now he might question his own judgment at leaving me in your care."

His mouth opened, then snapped abruptly shut. I said nothing more. My arrow had flown true.

"I will entertain the notion of your possibly being an unwitting participant in this affair," he said, his voice chill with anger, "but you must understand that I will nurture suspicions against you until I am persuaded otherwise."

"So long as you give yourself the chance to be persuaded, I am content with that. And you must let me help you discover who did this terrible thing."

"Out of the question," he said flatly.

I strove for patience. "Mr. Stoker, I understand you must fear I will somehow turn the situation to my own advantage, but I promise you, I have every bit as powerful a motive as you for discovering the truth behind the baron's murder. After all, sir, you are not suspected of complicity."

To my astonishment, his features relaxed a little. Not quite a smile, but almost. "You are rather put out just now. Oh, you're doing a damned good job of hiding it, but it rankles that I will not accept your word for the matter."

"I am not accustomed to being doubted, Mr. Stoker. I have been accounted strange and unfeminine by many people, but my word is as good as any man's. I find it galling that the only remedy is to try to reason with you."

"What would you prefer? Pistols at dawn?" he mocked.

"If it would persuade you," I replied stoutly. "Although, if I am honest, I would prefer swords." My pursuit of the intruder at the cottage might have been fruitless, but it had given me a taste for bladed weaponry.

His gaze was piercing. "I think you actually mean that. You would be very happy to put a bullet in me just now."

"Or to take one if it cleared my name."

He shook his head. "The moonlight has addled your brain, Miss Speedwell. I have no intention of arming you, much less facing off in a duel."

I did not take the opportunity to instruct him on the lethal properties of a cunningly wielded hatpin. We resumed our walk then, but I fancied there was a trifle less coldness in his manner than there had been before.

"What will you tell your friends?" I asked suddenly. "They will want to know why we have come to them."

"You will be my newly wedded bride whose family do not approve. I will say we are in fear of being apprehended by your wicked guardian who was robbing you of your fortune and that we require a place of safety until we can secure the money for ourselves."

"That is a plot straight from a penny dreadful. No one could possibly believe it. More to the point, you and I could hardly masquerade as a couple joined in the harmonious state of matrimony. We seem distinctly unsuited."

He did not speak. Instead, he turned sharply on his heel and placed himself directly in front of me. It was like running straight into a mountain, I thought as I collided with him, dropping my bag and net to the road and putting out my hands to avoid a fall.

He reached into his trouser pocket and retrieved something—the item he had taken from his trunk, I realized. Before I knew what he was doing, he had taken up my left hand and stripped off my glove. He pushed something cold onto my finger.

"What is this?"

"A prop," he replied.

I stared at the slim gold band that rested on my finger. It was bent slightly, and the gold was scratched, as if it had been hurled in a fit of temper. "How is it that you happen to have a spare wedding ring in your possession, Mr. Stoker? Are you in the habit of abducting ladies and forcing them to pose as your wife?"

He snapped in response. "That is none of your concern. Now, you will answer to the name of Mrs. Stoker whilst we are among my friends. You may address me as Stoker or husband, I care not which."

"What about Lucifer?" I muttered under my breath.

He ignored me. "What is your Christian name?" he demanded.

"You may call me Mrs. Stoker," I instructed him, lifting my chin. His laugh was harsh and low.

"No one who knows me would believe for a moment I would engage in such formality with a woman to whom I was married. What is your Christian name?"

"Veronica," I said at last.

He gaped at me. "You mean like the plant veronica? The Plantaginales commonly known as speedwell? You are joking."

"I am not," I replied with some irritation. "My aunt Lucy was very fond of gardening."

"So she named you as a sort of botanical joke?"

"Veronica is a very useful plant," I pointed out. "It is also known as bird's eye and gypsyweed and it is the largest member of the family Plantaginaceae. It makes a very fine tea for the relief of catarrh."

"Christ, I suppose you ought to be grateful she didn't call you Gypsyweed. Haven't you a more familiar name? Something other children or a sweetheart called you?"

"I knew no other children, and my sweethearts, as you so vulgarly phrased it, are none of your concern."

He lifted a brow. "Sweet*hearts*? Plural? You are a dark horse, aren't you?" I said nothing more, and he sighed. "Very well. For the duration of our time here, you will be my darling Veronica." He tucked my hand into the crook of his arm, holding it there rather too firmly for comfort. "Now, put a smile on your face and gaze at me with adoration. We are here."

All was quiet save the skittering of night creatures and the occasional call of a nightingale. The camp itself, a motley collection of tents and farm wagons and Gypsy caravans, was slumbering. Here and there a lamp glimmered like a glowworm in the darkness, but only one spot betrayed that anyone might be wakeful. It was a sizable tent, striped in red and gold and hung with Chinese lanterns that bobbed in the light breeze. Mr. Stoker kept a hand tucked under my elbow as we picked our way through the camp. Each of the tents and caravans boasted a colorful sign, but we were moving too quickly for me to take them in. At last we reached the striped tent and paused outside, long enough for me to read the banner that stretched across the front of the tent, the letters spelling out in elegant scrolls: PROFESSOR PYGOPAGUS' TRAVELING CURIOSITY SHOW.

We had arrived.

NINE

BEFORE I COULD FORM a question, Mr. Stoker had reached out and twitched a small streamer of bells that hung outside the flap. From within, a stream of music issued, an odd, otherworldly sound of longing and wistfulness, almost painful to hear, it was so sharp with yearning. A voice rose above it.

"At last, Stoker—enter!"

Mr. Stoker lifted the flap and gestured for me to follow. What I stepped into was a scene straight out of a dream. The tent itself was hung with garish silks and more of the Chinese lanterns, its floor fashioned from a layer of thin Turkey carpets. But it was not the odd decor that caught my attention. The tent was full of people, and not one of them was like anyone I had encountered before. There was a woman so enormously fat that her chair was the size of three armchairs fitted together. She held a plate of cream cakes and was working her way through the lot, munching with diligent delicacy. Beside her stood a man with the face of a lion, his features obscured by a full growth of hair some four inches long, and wearing a full-dress military uniform with an astonishing array of medals and decorations. He rested his hand on the back of a rocking chair in which a very elderly lady seemed to be sleeping. Next to them stood the largest man I had ever seen, for if Mr. Stoker was a good six feet in height, this fellow was seven, with the sort of bulging muscles one seldom saw outside of caricature. Next to him sat two chairs almost back to back. There were no arms between the chairs, and I soon realized why. The pair of gentlemen seated in them was conjoined at the ribs and sat, rather like bookends, the back of one man's shoulder touching the back of his brother's. One of them held an accordion, the source of the strange music, while the other held only a slender cigarette in a holder a foot long. This he waved as we entered.

"Make way, make way, the bridegroom cometh!" he cried, waving his cigarette holder in a purely theatrical gesture.

Mr. Stoker moved to stand in front of him, pushing me along in front.

"Good evening, Professor," he said. "It has been a while."

"Two years almost to the day since you left us," the professor said silkily.

A muscle twitched in Mr. Stoker's jaw, and I understood then that he was wary of the reception he might find here. "I realize my leave-taking was a trifle sudden," he began, but the professor waved him to silence.

"And yet the prodigal always returns; is that not what the Bible teaches us? And meting out the just deserts. I seem to recall something about every man receiving just what he is owed," he remarked with a thin smile that did not reach his eyes. He shifted his gaze to me, giving me a curiously appraising look.

Mr. Stoker spoke. "May I present my bride, Veronica Stoker? Veronica, this is Professor Pygopagus."

To his credit, he did not stumble over either my name or the word "bride." He was watching me closely, and I had the strangest feeling that however I handled myself in the next few minutes would prove crucial to our future cordiality with one another.

I stepped forward and extended my hand. "How do you do, Professor?"

The professor clasped my hand and gave a little crow of delight. "Look, children—Stoker has brought us a bride! My dear, you are most welcome to our little family of curiosities," he said, but there was no real warmth in his voice. He held my hand in his, and I felt the skin slide over fleshless bones as he continued to speak. "Now, there are far more members in our traveling show than are gathered here, but you will appreciate that it is very late, and the others have retired. They require more beauty sleep than the rest of us," he added with a twist of his lips. "Permit me to introduce you."

He gestured to each of the others theatrically. "First, my dear Madame du Lait. Madame? Madame!" He clapped his hands together sharply. The elderly woman in the rocking chair started and lifted a brass ear trumpet as she cocked her head.

"What? Why do you disturb me?" she demanded irritably. She was swathed in half a dozen shawls and traveling rugs, and she peered out at the company with colorless eyes filmy with age.

"My dear Madame, I wish to present our newest arrival, Mrs. Stoker. Stoker has returned and brought his bride."

It took three more attempts to make her understand, but when she did, the withered old face pulled a frown. "Stoker!" she exclaimed. "I never liked him. Moody little devil."

"Ah, but I am certain you will find his wife charming," the professor instructed, his mouth twitching with a smile. I moved to shake her hand, but she had already fallen asleep again. The professor made a gesture of dismissal. "One must make allowances, my dear. She is one hundred and fifty-three years old. She was Napoleon's wet nurse."

From behind me, I heard Stoker murmur dryly, "And for an extra halfpenny, she'll show you the teat where she gave him suck."

Before I could respond, the professor had moved on, gesturing towards the tremendously obese woman. "This is our dear Tilly, the fattest lady in the land and the loveliest." He blew her a kiss and she simpered. She did have a beautiful complexion and a charming set of dimples. She waggled her cream-covered fingers at me and I smiled in return.

"Next to her is her husband, Leopold the Lion-Faced Lord. He isn't really a lord," the professor added, sotto voce, "but, again, one must make allowances."

The gentleman bowed—an elegant, almost regal gesture under the circumstances. "Welcome to our little family, Mrs. Stoker." His voice was surprisingly melodious, deep and resonant.

"Thank you . . . er . . ."

"Please, call me Leopold. We do not stand on ceremony here," he said kindly.

The professor spoke again. "This is Colosso," he informed me, pointing out the enormous fellow, who put out a hand to shake mine. His was more than twice the size, and I felt like a child as he carefully enfolded my fingers.

"Welcome," he said, his accent thick and unmistakably Italian. His greeting to me was cordial enough, but the look he gave Mr. Stoker was one of purest hatred.

Before I could determine why, another snippet of music began to play, a sinuous and inviting sound that coaxed and seduced, filling the ears with unseemly thoughts. The bells at the tent flap sounded softly, and a woman glided in. She wore a long silken robe of Oriental origin, its sleeves sweeping the ground as she moved. On her feet were tiny slippers of gilt leather, turned up at the toes. Her hair, black as my own, but woven into an intricate series of tiny braids, fell to her tightly sashed waist. Her eyes were dark and impenetrable, and her every gesture graceful. I felt very English at that particular moment, and deeply aware of the practicality of my own costume, becoming as it might be.

"Salome," said the professor softly.

I realized then that Mr. Stoker had turned a most surprising shade of puce, and I wondered if he was about to have a fit. I stepped briskly forward and put out my hand.

"Veronica Stoker," I said firmly.

A smile toyed with the corners of her mouth. She shook my hand gravely. "Yes, I heard that Stoker was returned to us. With a wife," she added. It was masterfully done. With that one sentence she managed to convey curiosity and disbelief, but so elegantly that it was quite clear she considered the matter a tremendous joke.

Mr. Stoker's hand closed tightly around my arm. "Salome," he said shortly.

She came forward and kissed me on both cheeks, leaving the scent of her musky perfume behind. It reminded me of decayed flowers, ripe and sensual and deeply narcotic. "Welcome, my dear."

A less clever woman would have kissed Mr. Stoker as well, but she did not. She merely darted him a glance to show that she had considered the gesture and dismissed it. Then she smiled brilliantly and withdrew, bowing gracefully at the tent flap. Stoker was perspiring freely.

"Our principal dancer," the professor explained. "And now you must meet my brother, Otto."

He waved a hand to the fellow conjoined to him, and again that soft, yearning line of melody he had played upon our arrival issued from the instrument in his hands. Otto left off playing then and gave me a polite bow from the neck. Then he resumed his instrument, moving into a pretty bit of Chopin.

I inclined my head. "How do you do, Otto?"

The professor made a gesture of impatience. "Pay him no attention, my dear. He is a singularly annoying fellow. He is a selective mute and communicates only through his music. You will learn to interpret it in time."

He turned to Mr. Stoker, who had wiped his brow with a handkerchief and seemed to have recovered himself. "Now, I understand from your rather urgent telegram that you wish to return to the show. When last you came to us, these souvenirs of your trip to the Amazon were fresh," he said with a graceful inclination of his head towards Stoker's scars and eye patch. "I remember the tale. You were lucky to escape with your life," the professor said softly. "I always said you had nine lives. How many do you have left? I wonder."

Stoker swallowed hard, but his tone was deliberately casual. "By my reckoning, this is probably the last."

The professor's mouth split into a wide grin at Stoker's display of bravado. "Then we had best make it count. You remember the rules. I keep only those who earn their way. If you do not work, you do not eat, and you most certainly do not stay. The last time you were with us, I was content to let you work as a conjuror."

I stared at Mr. Stoker in surprise, but he merely nodded towards the professor. This development was clearly something he had anticipated. "That should not present any difficulties."

"But this time I require something more," the professor told him. "I am in need of someone to take Rizzolo's place. He left us a few weeks ago, and the crowds since then have not been what they ought to be."

Stoker hesitated only a heartbeat. "Fine."

The professor's eyes narrowed, and for the first time, I detected cruelty in the set of his mouth. "Are you certain?

Perhaps your vision is impaired now."

"I will do the act. For Christ's sake, I taught Rizzolo."

"Too true! Too true. Of course, I cannot permit you to include any of my regular performers in the act," he added with an air of silky menace. "Far too dangerous."

"Fine," Stoker said, biting off the word sharply. His fingers flexed over mine.

The professor stroked his chin. "I expect your devoted bride would be only too happy to provide you with a partner."

He flicked his inscrutable gaze to me, and I drew myself up to my full height. I did not grasp the full measure of his insinuations, but I knew my loyalties must lie with Stoker.

"Whatever my husband asks of me, I will be only too happy to do," I said stoutly.

The professor's expression shifted to one of delight. "I am pleased to hear you say so," he told me. "As to accommodations, you and your bride may have Rizzolo's old caravan for your private use."

I opened my mouth to remonstrate, but Stoker tightened his grip on my hand, nearly crushing the bones, and I cursed myself for a fool. Of course we would share accommodations. That was what married people did, I reminded myself firmly.

"Thank you, Professor," Stoker said.

The professor turned his charming smile upon me. "And now, I am certain you would like to retire with your bride. You have had a long journey."

The words were gracious, but there was dismissal in the tone. It seemed to suit Stoker, for he gave a jerk of his head and nudged me out of the tent as I was still attempting to make my farewells.

"Pity we didn't stay longer. I quite fancied one of those cream cakes," I said wistfully. "We have not had a proper meal in quite some time."

"There are only a few hours left until breakfast. You will have to make do until then," he replied irritably.

"Stoker!" We whirled at the voice behind us. It was Colosso, following us on silent feet through the shadows of the camp. Beside me I felt Mr. Stoker tense, and with an instinct I am not certain he even realized, he took half a step forward, putting himself between me and the enormous fellow.

"Colosso," he returned coldly.

The other man came forward, and it was like watching the progress of a mountain. He moved slowly and with inexorable purpose, stopping only when he was toe to toe with Stoker, forcing him to bend his head back to look him in the eye.

"Do you mark what I promised you the last time?" Colosso demanded.

Somehow, even with his neck crooked at that impossible angle, staring up at this force of nature, Mr. Stoker managed to sound bored. "Something about fileting out my spine to play like a fiddle."

Colosso's gaze narrowed. "You think I forgot?"

"Well, it is possible. I imagine the air is rather thin up there," Mr. Stoker replied.

I stifled a laugh, for the expression on the giant's face was purest venom. "It is no joke to be the enemy of Colosso," he said. He leaned forward swiftly, forcing Mr. Stoker even further backward. "There will come a reckoning."

"Unless you mean to suffocate me with your halitosis, kindly step back and let me on my way," Mr. Stoker stated flatly.

Colosso smiled then, a gruesome thing, for the corners of his mouth turned down as he grinned, and several of his teeth were broken to the root. He put one stiff finger squarely into Mr. Stoker's chest. "The reckoning is coming. And soon."

He turned and moved away, slipping silently back into the shadows with a noiselessness that was frankly unnerving in so enormous a man.

"What the devil was that about?" I demanded.

Mr. Stoker slid a hand under my arm and propelled me forward. "Nothing. But let's go before he changes his mind and decides to have my liver on toast for his breakfast, shall we?"

He said nothing more until we reached the empty caravan. It stood at the end of the encampment, a little forlorn, for it was dark and unwelcoming. But Mr. Stoker soon lit the lamps and gestured for me to precede him, up the narrow stairs and into the bow-topped little wagon. It was as comfortably fitted as any ship's cabin, and I was quite pleased. The furnishings were rather meager, but it was clean and tidy. A table that could fold out had been latched to one wall, and a pair of small, cozy armchairs were pushed against a tiny stove whose hearth was cold to the touch. Against the back wall, a wide bed had been fitted, and to my relief, I saw it was spread with almost clean linen. And it was with enormous interest that I realized it did not have a twin.

I heard a groan from behind me. "Bloody hell," he muttered.

I guessed he had just noticed the sleeping arrangements, and I turned to him with an artless air. "I suppose you could always take the chairs if you are feeling bashful."

He eyed the upright armchairs.

"I haven't slept in a proper bed in six months. A night on those chairs might cripple me entirely."

"Then there is no alternative, I am afraid," I said cheerfully. "We shall have to share the bed."

His expression was dubious. "Miss Speedwell—"

I held up a hand in a gesture of mock severity. "It is Mrs. Stoker, but you may call me Veronica. If you don't want to give away our masquerade, you must practice calling me by my nom de guerre, even when we are alone."

"Very well. *Veronica.*" He hesitated, searching for words,

mining each one slowly and with care. "I suppose I may have been a trifle precipitate in coming here. I reacted badly to the news of Max's death and the possible consequences," he began. "I must confess I did not think the matter through as well as I ought. I realize now I have put you in an untenable position. I know you have traveled alone, but this is a very different situation for a lady. This entire charade could have devastating consequences for your reputation."

I gave a distinctly unfeminine snort. "And this only now occurred to you? My dear Mr. Stoker, I set myself beyond the pale the moment I put myself under the baron's protection. Surely you don't think polite society would approve of such an action? Or my remaining in a gentleman's quarters at all hours without a chaperone?"

"I did not think," he muttered.

"Then it is a very good thing you are not often called upon for the protection of ladies in distress," I returned. "But you need have no fear upon that score in our present situation. I daresay I have more experience of the world than you."

He gaped like a fish pulled from the water, and it was a moment before he found his tongue. "Surely you don't mean—"

"I do. And why not? The female of the species is just as prey to the passions of the flesh as the male, and with greater cause, as it is her responsibility to propagate. But I am tired and it is far too late to engage in a thorough discussion of Darwin versus Wallace, don't you think?"

I opened the windows of the caravan to let in a draft of fresh cool air, heavy with the scent of hedge roses and honeysuckle. "Ah, that is lovely!" I said, drawing in a great deep breath of it.

"It is bloody cold," he argued, but I would not be crossed. I gave him a cool stare.

"Mr. Stoker, I am prepared to suffer only one discomfort while sleeping. You may share the bed with the windows open or you may sleep on the chairs with the windows closed. It matters not in the slightest to me."

I reached for the top button on my coat and he licked his fingers, diving to snuff the lamp. I waited a moment for my eyes to adjust to the gloom, then removed my coat, jacket, shirtwaist, and skirt, folding them neatly and placing my hat tidily on top. My stockings were rolled into a bundle to fit under the crown of my hat, and my corset left under it all so as not to offend Mr. Stoker's delicate sensibilities. I slipped under the coverlet in my chemise, courteously moving to the far side. All the while I was conscious of him in the darkness, breathing softly as he heard the rustlings of my clothes coming free.

He did not relight the lamp. He undressed in the dark as I had and slid into the bed. The mattress dipped alarmingly, flinging me into him.

"Oh, for God's sake," he muttered, shoving me back against the wall. But I had been highly amused to discover that my face had brushed against his feet. He had observed the gentlemanly expedient of lying with his head opposite my own. It was a trifle disappointing—for all his hygienic defects, he had the potential to be a deliciously attractive fellow—but it was an unthinkable breach of my rules to contemplate indulging in the pleasures of the flesh with him. He was, after all, an Englishman, and I never trifled with my own countrymen.

Unfortunately, my mind was of another opinion entirely, for I was kept wakeful by a number of interesting thoughts regarding Mr. Stoker and his physique. I amused myself for a while thinking about his musculature and his intriguing tattoos, but as this brought me no closer to peaceful repose, I distracted myself with other questions. Mr. Stoker, it seemed, was similarly afflicted. I felt him turn over more than once, shaking the entire caravan as he did so.

"Why haven't you slept in a bed in six months?" I asked.

"Because I sold it to pay for supplies," he murmured, his voice thick with sleep.

"A foolish economy. A man can hardly work to his full potential when he is robbed of proper rest," I observed.

"And he cannot get proper rest if his bed has been seized by bailiffs because he did not work," he retorted.

"True enough. Does this mean you will lose the commission from Lord Rosemorran? Since you failed to finish the elephant, I mean?"

He groaned. "Damn it to hell. I didn't even think of that." He swore again.

"I am sorry to have pointed it out. Perhaps he will understand the delay if you explain to him."

He gave a bitter laugh. "Explain what? That my mentor died and I had to abduct his murderess?"

"Now, now. I am not a murderess. Furthermore, I think you know it."

"It did occur to me that you might have slipped out of my workshop when I was sleeping and done the deed yourself. Why are you so certain I am convinced of your innocence?"

"It would take an excessively stupid man to put himself in so vulnerable a position as yours with a woman he thinks capable of killing in cold blood," I pointed out reasonably as I put out a fingertip to touch his calf. He jumped, shaking the caravan again. Heaven only knew what the rest of the camp must have thought—no doubt they attributed the movements of the caravan to connubial exuberance.

He exhaled heavily. "Very well. You did not kill Max. But that does not mean you are entirely free of culpability."

It was my turn to sigh. "Your vacillations are enough to make a dervish dizzy. One moment you are willing to be reasonable, and the next you have persuaded yourself I am a villainess. But I understand your doubts. You do not know me well enough to understand that I am precisely what I appear to be. I am a lepidopterist with a penchant for handsome men and an otherwise entirely unremarkable life. What I present is no more and no less than exactly what I am. I have no protective coloration, Mr. Stoker. And you must believe me when I say I will do everything in my power to clear my name."

He groaned again. "That is what I am afraid of."

We were silent for a little while, and from a distance I heard the soft hooting of an owl.

"I am very sorry about the baron."

He grunted. "Go to sleep, Veronica. And if you snore, I shall tie a bell to your neck and throw you out like a meddlesome cat."

"I shan't snore," I promised him, but he made no reply. Sleep had crept in, and after a little while, she came for me too.

TEN

I AWOKE WITH A STARTLINGLY foul odor in my nostrils. It required little imagination to deduce the source. I opened my eyes to find Mr. Stoker turned on his side away from me, his feet resting on my pillow, a scant inch from my face.

I pinched his toe hard, eliciting a howl of outrage.

"What the devil was that for?" he demanded, coming instantly awake and sitting bolt upright. The bedclothes slipped to his waist, and I deliberately permitted my gaze to linger upon his bare torso, tracing a path from the anchor on one biceps to the serpent-twined staff upon the opposite forearm and everything in between. It was a delectable sight and the perfect compensation for having his malodorous feet inflicted upon me. After all, I might not intend to use him for a plaything, but I could still appreciate looking through the toy-shop window.

"Your feet. Were on my pillow," I informed him. "Kindly move them so I may rise and complete my morning ablutions."

"I am coming with you," he said, throwing back the covers

to reveal he had slept in his trousers. I sat up and made no attempt to cover myself, entirely aware that my chemise was thoroughly transparent in the strong morning light. He colored to the bottom of his beard and looked sharply away.

"You will not. I have put up with quite enough of your high-handed behavior, but I will draw the line precisely *here*, Mr. Stoker. I have never shared ablutions with a man, and I have no intention of beginning today. A lady ought to be able to wash herself in peace. Now, I shall take only what I require for this morning's toilette and leave the rest of my possessions in your care as a pledge of my good faith. Otherwise, I will scream this camp down and inform everyone that you have abducted me against my will."

"They would never believe you," he said, but his voice was shaded with doubt and I pressed home my advantage.

"But they might wonder. And in their wonder, the professor might well decide you are too much bother and turn us out. Where will you go then? You told me this was your only refuge."

He dropped his head into his hands. "Why must you argue before I have even had my tea? So many words."

Taking advantage of his inertia, I hopped nimbly over him and gathered up my things. I took a toothbrush, soap, and flannel, as well as a few other miscellaneous items and my clothes. I made an elaborate show of leaving behind the rest of my well-curated bag and wrapped myself in a quilt before stepping out of the caravan into the pink light of morning. It seemed impossible that so short a time had passed since my arrival in London with the baron. And equally impossible that the dear old gentleman was now dead, I reflected grimly.

A kindly fortune-teller pointed me to the necessary spot for performing my toilette—a washing tent had been erected and was mercifully empty—and when I was finished I returned to the caravan in twenty minutes, neatly attired and carrying two tin mugs of tea. But Mr. Stoker, still exhausted from his days of hard work upon the elephant mount, had fallen asleep again.

"What a wretched abductor you make," I said softly. I might have taken up my things and been halfway to Cardiff by the time he awoke. Instead, I applied myself to my tea and a book. I took from my bag my favorite novel and was halfway through the third chapter when he awoke.

I gestured towards his mug of tea. "It has gone cold now, but you ought to drink it anyway. Strong and with plenty of sugar, just as you like it."

He put out his hand for the tea and took a healthy swallow, then squinted at my book. "What are you reading?"

"*The Unlikely Adventures of Arcadia Brown, Lady Detective. Casebook One,*" I told him.

He snorted. "Cheap literature? You surprise me. All that blather about your scientific views, and that is what you choose for entertainment?"

"Arcadia Brown is a thoroughly modern woman. She is intelligent and intrepid and shrinks from nothing," I told him, peering over the cover to give him a severe look. "Her world is not confined by the limitations of either her sex or her society. She creates her own adventures and sees them through to the end with her faithful sidekick, Garvin. She has been my inspiration for some years now."

He shrugged. "She sounds deadly dull."

"Dull! My dear Mr. Stoker, clearly you have never had the unparalleled pleasure of reading one of her casebooks or you would understand the inaccuracy of that remark. One has only to follow in her footsteps for a single investigation, read a single instance of her cry of 'Excelsior!' as she takes up her parasol and leaps into the fray to unmask a villain, read a single syllable of Garvin's stalwart devotion—"

He held up a hand. “No, thank you. I still think any mind capable of grasping the subtle differences between sexually driven and societally driven natural selection would be embarrassed at such low amusement.”

I flicked him a glance. “My interests are varied. They include natural history, lady detectives, and good hygiene,” I said with a significant lift of the brows towards his feet.

“What in seven hells does that mean?” he demanded.

“It means that if you come to bed smelling like something from a barnyard again, I will scrub you myself with rose soap and a firm hand,” I threatened.

It was enough. He fled immediately, muttering obscenities and carrying all the accoutrements needed for a proper wash. In the interim, I decided to tidy up a bit in the interests of having a suitably comfortable space in which to live. I had faults I was prepared to own, but slovenliness was not one of them. Even in the most rudimentary hut in the South Pacific I had done my best to achieve a semblance of order—not from any misplaced domesticity but simply because I found I could think better if comfort and tidiness had been achieved.

Once this was done, I decided to pay the professor a visit—or, to be strictly correct, the professor and Otto. There was no such thing as a private conversation for either of them, I reflected. I could not imagine what it must be like to go the whole of a lifetime without a single moment’s privacy. The pleasures of solitude were denied them entirely, and I repressed a shudder as I approached the tent and jangled the bell outside to announce my presence.

“Enter!” I heard the familiar thread of melody that Otto had played the night before to herald my arrival.

“Ah, it is our dear Mrs. Stoker! I hope that you found everything in the caravan to your satisfaction.” The professor was holding a traveling desk on his knees, spread with ledgers and account books, both of which were marked with rather more red ink than black. Otto was tinkering with his accordion, his eyes closed.

"Yes, thank you. I was wondering if I might have a quick word about the act that Stoker and I will be performing," I began.

The professor gave me a singularly enigmatic smile. "But of course. He will be taking the place of Rizzolo, our resident knife thrower."

"Knife thrower?" I asked, my voice a trifle high.

"Indeed. Stoker learned the skill as a boy. I daresay it will come back to him," he said smoothly.

"Pity me if it doesn't," I murmured.

He threw back his head and laughed. "What a charming addition to our little family you have made. So, you did not realize your husband was an expert in the bladed arts?"

"I did not," I temporized. "Our acquaintance has not been of long duration. I daresay there is rather a lot we have yet to learn about one another." That much was entirely true, I thought ruefully. I managed a maidenly duck of the head as I imagined a shy new bride might give.

The professor reached out and patted my hand. "Console yourself, my dear. Stoker is one of the finest I have ever seen. He honed his skills in South America—where he added a few new ones to his repertoire," he said, his smile now decidedly feline. "He is the most dangerous man I have ever known." His features twisted into an expression of mocking sadness. "At least, he *was*. This was before his accident, you understand. I do hope the loss of the eye will not affect his marksmanship. His scars were still fresh the last time I saw him. Tell me, is there any sight at all left in his eye, or is it entirely gone?" He leaned forward, as if hungry to hear something to Mr. Stoker's disadvantage. The entire conversation was strange to me. I had the oddest sensation that we were fencing, but only one of us was armed. His resentment of Mr. Stoker was almost palpable, and I thought again of the brute Colosso and his warning of the evening before.

I chose to reply to the professor's question with the unvarnished truth. "He can see perfectly, but it sometimes grows fatigued and then his vision is compromised."

The thin silver brows steepled in a concern I felt certain was feigned. "Ah, well. We must presume the worst and hope for the best, must we not? It is my motto."

"Quite a sound one too," I said faintly.

"My dear, you are quite pale. You do not fear acting as your husband's assistant, do you? Really, I cannot permit him to use any of my other performers in case his aim is less than true," he told me. "But I have no doubt that love will guide his arm! He would not harm so much as a hair upon the head of his own true love," he finished with a grand theatrical gesture.

I returned his thin smile. "Love. Of course. I must rely upon his love to protect me."

The professor nodded. "Ah, my dear. How fortunate you are! Otto and I have never been blessed in that regard." Otto suddenly roused himself and played a mournful little dirge. "That is enough," the professor snapped. "I must apologize, my dear. Otto has a peculiar sense of humor."

"Not at all," I said.

"But we do enjoy hearing about the love stories of others," the professor said with studied blandness. "How did you meet our dear Stoker?"

I was not prepared for this, but I had always maintained that if one were to trade in lies, it was best to keep them as simple and near to the truth as possible. "We were introduced by a mutual friend. He thought we would get on because of our shared interest in natural history."

"Ah! Stoker's accomplishments in that field are well-known to me," he said with a twist of the lips.

"Indeed?"

He waved a hand. "He gave us an excellent demonstration of his skills when last he was here."

I waited for him to continue, but he did not, and Otto's melody changed to something suitably introspective.

"I quite enjoy your music," I said truthfully to him. Otto flicked me a glance. His expression did not change, but he began to play the odd little melody with which he had saluted me, this time embroidering the tune with a few Mozartian flourishes.

"How baroque," the professor commented dryly.

"It is a beautiful melody. I regret I am not musical. What is the piece?"

The professor shrugged. "It is of his own devising, a melody to conjure an image of you."

"Of me? How extraordinary."

"Not really. Otto develops such little tunes for everyone who travels with the show. It is his way of forming a connection, as it were."

"Then I must thank you, Otto," I said. He did not respond but merely began the tune over again, this time playing with the cadence of a military march.

"That means he wants you to go away. It is nothing personal, oh no!" he hastened to assure me, his watchful smile firmly in place again. "It is merely that he tires easily and does not care for my garrulous ways. If you leave, I will have no one to talk to and he will take a nap. Really, it's like having a lapdog attached to one at times."

I rose, but the professor put out a smoothly manicured hand and touched my wrist. "My dear, you must accept my best wishes for a successful debut in our little show. Kindly remind your husband of what I told him last night. If he fails, he will have to leave us. I cannot keep mouths to feed that will not keep themselves."

In spite of his silken tone, something faintly malicious glimmered in the depths of his eyes.

I lifted my chin. "Then I can promise he will. And I shall do everything in my power to ensure it."

"Spoken like a devoted wife," the professor said, releasing my arm.

I took my leave then, the last few notes of Otto's melody dying away as the tent flap dropped behind me.

I had just returned to the caravan and resumed adventuring with Arcadia Brown when Mr. Stoker burst in, soaking wet and covered in soapy lather. His hair was dripping rivulets onto the floor, and he had wrapped a bath sheet about himself like a toga. He loomed over me, drenched and panting, having obviously run all the way from the bath tent.

"You look like one of the less capable Roman emperors," I observed. "Go back and finish the job properly."

"I have a crow to pluck with you. It just occurred to me—"

"It just occurred to you that I was at liberty and might make my escape. Yes, I know. You are a wretched abductor, Mr. Stoker. I suggest you do not take up felonious activity as a career."

His expression was sullen. "You will have to make allowances. It is, after all, my first abduction." He drew the bath sheet about himself more tightly.

I put aside my book. "I am tired of this silly pretense that I am being held prisoner. Let us dispense with the absurdities."

"It is not absurd," he said, sounding slightly aggrieved. "I am keeping you captive until I learn the results of the inquest and discover the truth of what happened to Max."

"You are doing no such thing. I might have stabbed you forty times with a hatpin while you slept. I could have bolted the door to the caravan and set fire to it. I could have poisoned your tea. I could have thought of a dozen ways to have killed you and carried them out before sunrise. So let us stop pretending that you are my captor or that I am staying here out of anything other than my own irrepressible curiosity."

His nostrils flared like a bull's, and he seemed to grow even larger as he stood over me, hands flexing on his bath sheet. But when he spoke, his voice was controlled. "What do you mean 'curiosity'?"

"I mean that we have been so busy running hither and yon we have not considered the baron's murder properly. Murder is an act of chaos. It lies with us to bring order and method to the solution of the deed. We are scientists," I reminded him.

"I am a scientist. You are a dilettante," he returned with as much hauteur as a man in a bath sheet could manage.

"I am perfectly happy to stand my professional credentials against yours any day, my dear Mr. Stoker. But I am not the one dripping upon the carpet. Now, please go and finish your bath, and when you return we will proceed in an orderly fashion and prepare for the performance—a performance which you neglected to inform me would put my life in danger," I added with a narrowed gaze. I went on. "The professor has made it quite clear that if we do not have an act, we will not have a place here, and I quite agree with you—this traveling show offers an excellent chance to consider our options. So our first order of business is to formulate an act that will satisfy the professor and the punters. But not until you have finished your bath," I repeated. "And you will want to shave off that monstrous beard. At present you resemble one of the less domesticated varieties of yak."

He stroked his chin. "I rather like it," he said stubbornly.

"No, you don't. You are forever tugging at it and scratching. You wear it because you have been too distracted by your work to shave, but you have nothing like that excuse now. Besides, if anyone manages to follow us here, it will help to disguise you if you remove that atrocity."

He considered this for a moment.

"Very well. I will go and have a shave. And when I return, we can practice for the act."

"An excellent notion. Is there anything I ought to do to prepare?"

His smile was thoroughly nasty. "Yes. Paint a bull's-eye on your chest. I shall be throwing knives at you and I should hate to miss."

ELEVEN

Mr. Stoker returned in due course, hair untrimmed and dripping but smelling deliciously of fresh soap and clean male animal. He had not touched the beard as of yet, and I raised the point with him.

"I was about to take care of it when Leopold offered to shave me later. He is quite experienced, you know."

"I should have thought the one thing of which Leopold had no experience was shaving."

"In that case, you would be wrong. He accepts himself for what he is, but he has upon occasion shaved the whole of his face."

I paused, struck by the enormity of such a thing. "And those are the only times he has seen his own face. I cannot imagine it."

"Yes, well, faces change," he said softly. I did not look at his scars, but I knew he was thinking of them, for his features had taken on a faraway and tortured expression. Before I could ask, he caught sight of the garment in my hand. "In the name of bleeding Jesus, what are you sewing? Is that my shirt?"

"It is, and I must say, it is in a deplorable state. But at least the material is quite good and will stand up to proper mending. Unfortunately, mending is not one of my skills," I said, holding up the shirt. Somehow I had managed to attach it to my own skirt, and I took up scissors to snip it free. Mr. Stoker was not so patient. He grasped it and jerked it loose with a single wrench, the stitches popping as he brandished it at me.

"But this is the shirt from my bag. Where is the shirt I was wearing?"

"Hanging out to dry, along with your stockings. They were both filthy and smelled vile. I washed them and hung them out so I didn't have to smell them any longer. It is a lovely sunny day, so they ought to dry quickly. I found this in your bag and thought you could wear it today, but it wanted mending, so I was attempting it as a sop since I knew you would be outraged at my washing your things." I nodded towards his other garments. "Your suit is terribly rusty. I brushed it, but it looks as though you have put on quite a bit of weight since you bought it. I daresay the seams will have to be let out."

He fixed me with a venomous look. "Did you just call me fat? And did you clean the caravan?"

"I offered no observation upon your physique, but since you ask, if I were to make a comparison, Cabanel's *Fallen Angel* comes to mind."

His brow furrowed. "I am not familiar with it."

"Aren't you? You ought to look it up sometime. Quite his best work, I think. A trifle sullen, but I am sure you will see the resemblance," I said sweetly. Cabanel's Lucifer was indeed sulky, his painted eyes filled with tears of rage at his fall. But the rest of him . . . the memory of that long shapely thigh and beautifully muscled chest sent a delightful frisson down my spine. "And yes, I may have tidied up a little."

I had done a good deal more than that. I had moved the

chairs and plumped the cushions, cleaned out the stove and laid a fire, and picked a few sprigs of wild hyacinth to stand in a little jug upon the table. The windows sparkled, and the brass rails of the caravan gleamed. I was well pleased with my efforts.

He curled a lip. "What a lovely wife you make."

"How revolting. I didn't do any of this for you, you impossible man. I did it for myself. I prefer to be surrounded by order and cleanliness. And as a scientist, I can only say your penchant for filth is deplorable." He was still staring at the shirt in his hands. "It isn't the Shroud of Turin, Mr. Stoker. There are no religious mysteries to be found there. It is a shirt."

"It is a symbol of your interference," he said stubbornly. "I had no notion when I brought you away from London that you would be so . . . so *managerial*."

"You ought to have," I pointed out. "I did much the same in your workshop, and I would do the same at Buckingham Palace if I found arrangements did not suit me. I think better when I am in motion and things about me are orderly."

"And what do you have to think about?" he demanded.

"This business with the baron—" I began, but I had no chance to finish. A knock sounded at the door of the caravan. It was open, and the visitor had rapped at the doorjamb before putting her head inside.

"Good morning," said Salome. Her lips were twitching with amusement, and I wondered how much of our conversation she had overheard.

Mr. Stoker, still half-naked, promptly thrust his arms into his still-torn shirt.

"Good morning," I told her. "Do forgive my husband. He is being shy this morning. Won't you come in?"

"Thank you, but no," she said, lingering in the doorway. "I merely wanted to extend an invitation to you."

"To me? How very kind."

Mr. Stoker made a strangled sound.

"Not at all," Salome continued smoothly. "It occurred to me that you traveled only with a very small bag and likely do not have a costume for participating in Stoker's act. Come to my tent later. I will make certain you are properly attired." Her ebony gaze swept me from top to toe.

I thanked her warmly and offered her some refreshment, which she promptly declined. She left then, and I noticed the smell of her musky perfume lingered. I moved to open the windows further to let in a little of the freshening breeze and banish the heavy scent.

Mr. Stoker gave me a level look. "She wants something," he said. His voice was oddly flat and his color was once again high.

"Of course she does," I agreed. "No doubt she wants to have a nice cozy chat about you."

He blinked furiously. "What do you mean?"

I waved him out of the way and drew the curtains back to air them out.

"The lady is naturally curious about your bride, and one cannot blame her. Obviously there has been a relationship of some significance between you—and a decidedly carnal one unless I miss my guess."

He choked a little. "How can you possibly know that?"

I gave him a pitying glance. "For a natural historian, you know surprisingly little about the facial expressions of higher-order primates. Remind me to find a copy of Darwin's book upon the subject for you," I added, thinking of how useful the work had proven in my encounter with Mr. de Clare.

"I have read the bloody book," Mr. Stoker countered. "I simply did not realize you were studying me like some sort of specimen."

"I wasn't," I corrected. "I was studying her."

He had made a hash of putting on his shirt, so intent had

he been upon my observations. I gave the shirt a sharp tug and it fell into place. "That's better. I will leave you to finish dressing on your own, and then we must prepare for the act."

Mr. Stoker spent the rest of that morning sharpening the set of knives Rizzolo had left behind and practicing his aim by throwing them at an apple box. I did not watch. When he had finished plying his blades, he set to altering his black suit. He had indeed been a *much* smaller fellow when he had last worn it, and there was scarcely enough fabric in the seams to permit the alterations. The waist was largely unchanged, but it appeared he had developed the muscles of his back and thighs admirably. He ordered me about, instructing me to fix pins where he could not reach.

"The shirt is improved since you mended it, although I must say it is a bit tight across the back. Perhaps you ought not to throw knives in it. I daresay the extra effort will cause it to split. Have you a neckcloth?"

He rummaged in the pocket for a moment, then drew out a pathetic little scrap of black silk.

"I have pen wipers nicer than that. Never mind. I will attend to it."

"Help me out of this coat," he ordered. "I feel as if I were in the grip of a lethargic anaconda."

"Goodness, how you complain! Here, only be careful of the pins." The warning had come too late. In attempting to shrug off the coat, he had driven half a dozen pins directly into his shoulder, and he howled in outrage.

"Get it off!"

"Heavens, Androcles didn't have this much trouble with his lion. Very well—hold still!" I ordered. He opened his mouth to rage some more, but I stood toe to toe with him and he subsided, clamping his mouth shut. "Now, ease yourself down onto the chair, and I will be able to see what the trouble is."

He did as I bade, and I bent to extricate him. "The pins have gone all the way in. All I can see are the beads, so hold very still. I will be quick."

He said nothing, and I plucked a dozen pins from his shoulder. At the end of each trembled a drop of blood. Carefully, I pulled the coat away, extricating him from the rest of the pins. I removed the waistcoat as well, not surprised to find sizable spots of blood dotting the creamy white cambric of his shirt.

"Remove your shirt, please. I have just the thing."

I rummaged in my bag for my medical kit and extracted a small bottle.

"Oil of calendula. Frightfully old-fashioned, but Aunt Lucy swore by it," I pronounced. "It will stop any chance of infection from those filthy pins."

He had removed the shirt and was sitting gingerly—no doubt because the trousers were snugly pinned as well. I poured a little of the oil onto a handkerchief and applied it to the punctures and the few scratches I found. While I attended him, he amused himself by rummaging through the little collection of bottles, examining the various oils and tinctures. He said nothing, but his expression was thoughtful.

"I daresay you find this silly after what you have endured," I said with a nod to his scars.

He gave a tentative shrug. "Yes, but I will admit I prefer your ministrations. At least your preparations smell better. I think the Brazilian fellow who stitched up my wounds used dung to poultice them."

"Hold this," I instructed. He pressed the handkerchief to one of the pinholes whilst I bent to inspect his scars. One of them wrapped over the top of his shoulder, neatly clipping the head of the Chinese dragon tattooed upon his back.

"Rather remarkable," I murmured. "His poulticing may have been rudimentary, but his stitching was first-rate. Do you happen to know what size needle he used? I should think it was an embroidery needle rather than darning, but I should very much like to be sure."

Stoker gave me a sour look. "I believe it was the sharpened quill of a porcupine. Are you quite finished with your inspection?"

I straightened, brushing off my skirts. "I apologize, but you did introduce the subject yourself. You needn't hold the handkerchief there any longer. Unless you suffer from some sort of bleeding disorder, I suspect you have clotted by now."

He handed back the bloodied handkerchief and I slipped it into my pocket with the bottle of calendula oil. "All finished. I will leave you to remove yourself from the trousers as best you can. On second thought, I had best leave the calendula oil with you."

I gave him the oil and the handkerchief with a smile as I left.

Salome's tent was almost precisely as I could have imagined—a sensuous bower of draped silks heavily perfumed with incense. But I had not pictured the stockings hung up to dry or the litter of dirty handkerchiefs and soiled chemises. A gilt pasteboard box of bonbons stood open on a little divan, the sofa scattered with the remnants of the confections, here a shred of coconut, there a scrap of candied peel. She motioned me to sit, and I brushed them aside to settle next to a heap of crumpled fashion magazines. I was not surprised she harbored a tendresse for Mr. Stoker, I reflected grimly. Their personal habits were frighteningly similar.

She began to rummage through her trunks. "So, how do

you like the traveling life?" she asked. "It must make a change for you."

"How can you tell?"

She shrugged one languid shoulder. "One can always tell a newcomer to this life."

"It is interesting," I told her.

She lifted her head to give me a scornful look. "I should have known butter would not melt in your mouth. You are not the sort of woman to speak her mind, to speak with passion," she said, flinging her arms wide in a gesture that Bernhardt herself would have thought overdone.

I found her assessment of me amusing, but there was little point in disabusing her of it at this stage. I had discovered in my travels that people can seldom resist correcting those they believe to be less knowledgeable than themselves, and it occurred to me I might use this to my advantage to learn a little more about my erstwhile husband and his current predicament.

Salome was clearly relishing the role of tempestuous lover pitying the placid wife, and it seemed that pandering to her sense of self-importance would be a simple matter indeed.

"Oh, I beg you will not speak of passion," I murmured. "I should hardly know what to think."

For an instant I wondered if I had laid on the disingenuousness with too heavy a hand, but I was soon relieved upon that score. Salome flicked me another of her scornful glances and even managed to curl her lip. It was an impressive performance.

"That is because your blood is cold. I cannot believe Stoker has married a woman like you," she burst out. "A man like that, with so much fire in him, he is like a bull when he is roused, so proud, so sensual." Her eyes took on a nostalgic gleam, and I smothered a yawn. She was so utterly predictable, I found it impossible that Stoker had not tired of her histrionics within a fortnight.

But I merely dropped my gaze and darted an innocent glance up at her. "You have known him so much longer than I," I began modestly. "You must understand him much better than I could hope to."

"This is true," she said, fairly exuding triumph as she bent to rummage in her trunks again.

"Then you must know what grudge Colosso bears against him," I ventured, scarcely daring to hope she would take the bait.

But Salome could not resist the opportunity to flaunt her greater knowledge over me. She rose, one hand to her hip. "Of course I know! It is because of Baby Alice."

"Baby Alice?"

She rolled her eyes heavenward. "Truly, does your husband tell you nothing?" She heaved a sigh. "Stoker was with the show when he was a boy. For half a year he traveled, learning the knives and conjuring. Then he went away for a long time, but always he comes back to see us, particularly me," she said, giving me a lascivious grin. "The last time he came was four years ago. We had not seen him in a very long while, and when he came, he was so different, we almost did not know him. He was scarred from an accident in Brazil, and he did not know if he would keep his eye. And his spirit, it was broken. He did not even want to see me," she said, curling her lip. "He kept to himself, juggling Indian clubs and rigging the ropes in exchange for his keep only. He talked to no one except Baby Alice."

"Who was she?"

Salome flapped a hand in a dismissive gesture, a goddess brushing aside a flea. "She was a nobody—a freak born without legs from the knees down. The professor, he dresses her in infant's clothes and puts her in a pram, and she is billed as 'Baby Alice, the Adult Infant.' But Alice does not like this, and she complains to Stoker. One day, when he is fishing in the river, he has an idea. It took him months, but he created for her a tail, like a fish—all silver and green and pink. With it she can swim, she is free, like a mermaid."

"How intriguing. Did it work?"

"Of course it worked! Stoker has gifts in his hands," she said a trifle dreamily. She was lost for a moment—no doubt in a haze of indecent memories, an impulse I understood only too well.

I cleared my throat to bring her back to the subject at hand. "It must have changed Baby Alice's entire life," I surmised.

"It might, but the professor, he will not hear of it. Baby Alice makes too much money for him to consider losing her."

"What happened then?"

She shrugged. "Stoker helps her to leave. She finds a place in another show earning fifty pounds a week and even Mr. Barnum is interested in her. And the professor does not forget. He has been losing money ever since she left, and for this he blames Stoker."

She turned again to her trunks as I thought about her story.

"That does not explain Colosso's resentment."

"He loved Baby Alice," she said, her tone bored. Clearly other people's love affairs were of little interest compared to her own, and she left the conversation there. It was enough. I understood both the professor's resentment and Colosso's, and I marveled that Stoker had chosen to come here of all places, where enemies surrounded him.

Salome rose, her arms laden with garments, and began tossing the clothes onto my lap in a pretty heap of color.

"A blue costume—it ought to be purple with those eyes of yours, but blue will do well enough. And a dash of color for the train. Ah, here it is! Cherry," she said, emerging with an armful of taffeta. "So the color trails behind you when you move. Try it on."

She bustled me behind a screen, thrusting clothes at me. "What about this green? No? Perhaps green is not your color."

Green was most decidedly *not* my color, but I was too busy wrestling with the costume she had provided to discuss the matter. The blue garment was a sort of extended bodice that covered the essentials—barely. It joined between the legs to conceal one's modesty but left the limbs bare, and the neckline plunged dramatically, revealing the shoulders completely.

Salome was still sorting through costumes. "Scarlet?"

"I think the blue will do nicely," I told her, emerging from behind the screen.

Her eyes widened and she gave a nod. "It is good. The décolletage is perfect," she said, eyeing my bosom. She circled around me slowly, scrutinizing me from head to heel, her expression growing more sour by the second.

"You are a striking-looking woman," she pronounced finally, her eyes narrowing. "Tell me the truth. What are you doing with Stoker?"

I summoned a newly wedded simper and batted my lashes in a revolting display of sentimentality. "I love him."

She snorted by way of response. "No, you do not. Otherwise you would ask me about him, how well I know him. And I know him *very* well," she said, her expression dreamy.

"Stoker's past amours are of no interest to me," I told her.

"And that is how I know you do not love him!" she cried, striking at her chest. "A woman's heart is not satisfied without knowing such things."

I was not of a mind to debate with her on the subject, so I merely gave her a noncommittal smile and stroked the blue taffeta. It was spangled with silver sequins and finished with tiny blue and silver glass beads.

"This is pretty. Did you have it made in London?"

She gripped my arm suddenly. "You need not pretend with

me. I know it hurts your heart to think of him with me. You may ask me anything you like—anything at all. I will have no secrets from you because we are women together. And women must be strong against the ways of men. Let us share our secrets."

Her eyes burned with emotion, and her grip was starting to leave a mark upon my arm. I extricated it gently and gave her a pat. "You seem upset. Shall I bring you a cup of tea?"

She plunged her hands into her hair, tearing at it. "If I am upset it is because you do not wish to be friends. You reject me."

She looked suddenly forlorn, and I hastened to reassure her. "Not at all. I would be very happy to be your friend. But I think if we are to be friends, we should put aside the lies. To begin with, your name is not Salome, is it?"

She hesitated, then burst out laughing, dropping the Oriental accent and the portentous delivery in favor of an accent straight from the Chiltern Hills. "No. It's Sally."

"And where are you from, Sally?"

"Dunstable," she said, a trifle sullenly. "How did you know?"

I nodded towards her dressing table. "You have a letter there addressed to Sally Barnes in care of the traveling show. And, if you will pardon the observation, you were trying just a trifle too hard to feign exoticism."

"It is my bit in the show," she told me airily. "I am Salome, an Eastern princess driven by misfortune to make her way in the world by dancing for the public."

"And how much of your clothing do you take off?"

She gave me a bitter look and picked at a cuticle. "Just down to my drawers and a sort of chemisette. It's all gauzy and Turkish-like."

"Well, whatever the professor pays you, I hope it is enough," I told her.

"Pays me!" she snorted. "He hasn't paid me in a month. If

you ask me, he's on his last legs with this show. And then we'll all of us be out on our ear."

"I am sorry to hear that."

I made to change out of the costume, but she shook her head. "Keep it. You will need something for the act and blue makes me look bilious. It suits you," she said, her expression sulky.

"I meant what I said, you know. I should like to be friends."

Her gaze narrowed. "And you're really not jealous that I used to lie with Stoker?"

"No more than I am of the trousers he wears," I said cheerfully.

She was not certain if she ought to take offense at that, but it was to her credit that she chose not to. She shook her head. "If he were my husband, I'd want to slit the throat of any woman he'd been with."

"Then I suppose it's a rather good thing you are not married," I replied. "Remind me to send you some literature on the free love movement. I think you might find it illuminating."

She looked me over again. "You are an odd duck, missus. A face like that, you could be on the stage, making more money than you could count. You could have a duke, if you liked—or even that tubby Prince of Wales. What are you doing with Stoker?" she demanded again.

"I told you," I said gently, "I simply adore him. It was love at first sight."

She gave a sharp crack of laughter. "You lie worse than me. I'll find out what he is up to with you, missus. There aren't any secrets in this camp. Not from me."

"I shall consider that a warning."

TWELVE

In spite of our exchange of barbed words, Salome insisted upon giving me not only the blue costume, but also a cherry pink cape of sorts to go over it and a pair of tights that were more or less the color of my flesh. She also applied the necessary cosmetics. She powdered my face heavily with rice powder and wielded a kohl stick and lip paint with enthusiasm. Her skills were considerable, and I felt a completely different person as I made my way back to Mr. Stoker.

"What in the name of Christ happened to you?" he demanded. His eyes darted to the plunging neck of the costume and flared wide, the pupils quite black against the dark blue of his eyes.

If he found my costume and cosmetics a change, it was nothing to the alteration in his own appearance. Leopold had worked wonders upon him, shaving off the monstrous beard and mustaches, revealing a firm jaw that stood as counterpart to the proud nose and high cheekbones. The beard had, as I had noted before, hidden a perfectly delectable underlip, now entirely visible. His scar ran slim and pale down the landscape of his cheek, over his jaw, and beneath his collar. It sketched a parallel line to his jugular, perilously close to that region of mortality, and I marveled that he had come so close to death and fought his way free. It said a great deal about the character of the man, and I felt—not for the first time—that the fellow I had met was a shadow of what he had once been. The question remained, was the damage irreparable? Life had broken him, but could he be mended?

I nodded towards his freshly shaven chin. "That is quite a change."

He dragged his gaze up from my décolletage. "As is that."

"Salome," I replied dryly. "It is a bit much; you've no need to say it. But I did think this would further disguise me should we encounter the baron's murderer. Mr. Stoker, are you listening? You've gone quite glassy-eyed." I snapped my fingers sharply in his face, and he nodded.

"Yes, I heard you."

"Good. I suppose I might as well leave this nonsense on until the performance. Now, where are your knives? If I am to do this thing, I must have a bit of practice to make certain I do not lose my nerve in front of a paying crowd."

He recovered himself then and retrieved his knives, although I caught an unwilling glance or two directed towards my décolletage as we made our way to the little practice ground he had arranged. The cape had covered my legs, but I dropped it once we arrived, and Stoker made a sort of whimpering sound.

"Are you quite all right?" I asked.

"Entirely," he said, his voice suddenly hoarse. I hoped he would not find my bared limbs too distracting, but as soon as he bent to his task he seemed to forget me entirely as a person. He moved differently, his very form suffused with purpose and his attention focused with an intensity I had seen only when he was working at his elephant.

He positioned me in front of a large circular target, spreading my arms like the outstretched wings of a bird. He secured my wrists in a pair of soft leather restraints, giving me a brisk nod.

"These are mostly for appearance. You can pull out easily enough if you have a mind to, but they will serve to make it all the more dangerous in the eyes of the crowd. They are also a good reminder to hold still. If you do lose your nerve and flinch at the wrong moment, you could be badly hurt." He bent to secure another restraint at my feet, nudging my ankles far apart. His hands were warm even through my stockings, and I indulged in a delicious little shudder as he took his time about the buckles.

He strode some ten or twelve paces away and laid out the knives with a surgeon's precision. After a moment, he turned back to me, one knife resting lightly in his palm. He grasped it by the blade. "Do you want to know when I mean to throw it or shall I surprise you?"

"Just get on with it," I told him, my teeth gritted hard against the chattering that had set in. I was suddenly glad of the restraints, for I suspected my nerve might have failed me then, and I was certain my knees would have. I did not close my eyes. I merely waited, forcing myself to breathe slowly and evenly, a patient lamb waiting for the slaughter.

Suddenly, he stopped and dropped his arm. "You might stop muttering the Lord's Prayer, you know. It is thoroughly distracting."

"Oh, how curious—I did not realize I was. Odd, I am not even religious."

"Shall I pause whilst you sing out a few verses of 'Nearer, My God, to Thee' or do you want to move directly to committing your soul into the hands of Jesus? I can wait."

"I am ready," I said firmly.

He resumed his throwing stance again, and this time I did not have a chance to give way to my nerves. I felt a whisper next to my ear and a hard thud, and the next thing I knew, a blade quivered beside my head, a breath away from my face.

"Hm. A little too close. I ought to correct for that," he said blandly.

"That would be an excellent notion."

The next blade was on the other side of my head but a little further out, and the one that stuck in just above me was perfectly positioned. He placed a dozen knives about the outline of my body, most of them sitting precisely where he intended. He unfastened the restraints and gave me his hand. I stepped forward and felt my knees give way instantly.

His arms went tightly about me, holding me upright. My head was pressed into the hollow of his shoulder, and I could hear the slow, solid thud of his heart under my ear. It was exquisitely comfortable, but I swiftly regained my footing, pushing him firmly aside. "I am quite steady now, I assure you," I told him.

His features were stony. "Mind you don't do that tonight. Neither one of us can afford it."

He strode to the target, where he wrenched the knives free, then stalked away. I did not wonder at his sudden churlishness. We had been thrown together under difficult circumstances, and in spite of his casual air, I knew he was keenly aware of the fact that every time he hurled a blade, he held the power of life and death over me.

I thought of the baron then, and his assurance that he was trusting my life to Mr. Stoker's hands—and I wondered if he could ever have imagined how literal that promise would become.

A few hours later the camp stirred to life in preparation for the evening's performance, and I found myself unaccountably restless. I knew it could not be nerves, for I do not have a nervous temperament, but I decided a sip or two from the flask of aguardiente would not go amiss. I was still drinking from it when I heard Otto's accordion begin a seductively rousing song, beckoning the townsfolk to the show. I could hear the professor reciting his patter, charming and coaxing the local people, seducing them into parting with their money as they visited the various tents. He lauded the Herculean strength of Colosso, a hero straight from myth, and rhapsodized about the size and beauty of Tilly, the Fattest Woman in the World. Colosso's musculature was certainly impressive, but his long flesh-colored garments of an unmentionable nature and the furry loincloth he wore over them somewhat detracted from his Olympian appearance. And Tilly, while enormous indeed, was not quite as advertised, given that the professor promised she outweighed a steer. Only Madame du Lait lived up to her name, happily lifting her blouse for an extra copper to show the audience her ancient bosom.

The image was not a pleasant one, and I drank a little more to banish it. Just then Stoker appeared in his altered black suit, the seams straining dangerously and the shirt open at the collar.

"You need a *cratav*," I told him grandly.

"A what?"

"A *vacrat*. Wait, that isn't right either. You know, that thing, that cloth that ties about your neck," I explained helpfully.

"You mean a cravat?"

"Yes! Precisely. Oh, you are clever," I said. I brandished a bit of scarlet silk. "Salome gave me a castoff scarf. I think the scarlet will do quite well, don't you? It ought to hide the blood quite nicely if you miss."

He started at me, comprehension dawning slowly. "Holy

Christ, you're drunk as a lord!"

"I am not the slightest bit *incoxitated*! Really, Mr. Stoker, the very suggestion, the very idea. My aunts were on temperance committees."

He reached for the flask of aguardiente and took a healthy draft for himself. "Did you at least eat something?"

"Oh yes. The hairy fellow, looks like a lion. He brought me something to eat."

I was smiling broadly at him. For some unaccountable reason, I felt quite happy and very relaxed about the prospect of permitting him to throw knives at me, and I decided to tell him so.

"You know, Stoker, I am really quite content that you should throw knives at me. I have perfect faith in your *abitilies*."

"My *abitilies*? Yes, they are quite remarkable," he said. "Now, I want you to stay here. I have a quarter of an hour to sober you up and I guarantee you shall not like it. Do not move."

He disappeared and returned again before I could find my slippers. Salome had given me a pair of high-heeled satin mules beaded with crystals. I swayed on them as I walked, but I fancied that was rather the idea. "Mr. Stoker. I cannot seem to find my slippers."

"They are on your feet, you daft woman. Now, pay attention. I want you to drink this coffee. It is black as the devil and twice as strong. Drink it all." I did as he bade, pulling a face at the taste of it. "Good girl. Now, pull back your hair," he instructed as he placed a basin of water on the table in front of me.

I tried, but the locks kept slipping through my fingers. With a muttered curse, he strode behind me and gathered up the hair in his hands. There was no warning for what came next. He pushed me forward, holding my face under the cold water for a full ten seconds, then lifted me out. He did it twice more before I emerged, panting and a good deal more alert than I had been.

"I think that will do, Mr. Stoker. I am quite recovered," I assured him. He did not release me immediately. No doubt he wished to ascertain for himself whether I was in full possession of my faculties. He merely stood behind me, his hands heavy in my hair. I turned my head slightly, regretting it instantly, for the room moved a little as I did so. "Mr. Stoker?"

He stepped backward very quickly, removing his hands as if I had suddenly scalded him. He flung a towel at me and I dried my face and hands. "Thank you. I am a little giddy, but I am quite sure that, too, will pass."

"Good," he said sharply. "The next remedy was slapping you across the face, and I doubt you would have thanked me for it. Now, can you stand?"

I did so slowly and with great deliberation. "Perfectly."

He snorted. "Not by half, but it will have to do. I'll support you as we walk. I had thought to let you walk around as I did a bit of conjuring, but it won't do. I shall have to put you in restraints to begin with, so just stay there and smile mysteriously as if it were all part of the act. Whatever you do, do not say a word, do you understand?"

"Oh, perfectly." I smiled broadly and he muttered another curse before taking my hand and leading me from the caravan. Once outside he quickly tied the scarlet neckcloth and then put his arm firmly about my waist, holding me securely on my feet as we made our way to the tent where we would be performing. He guided me to a flap at the back, and from the front I could hear the professor explaining that the great Rizzolo had been called away and that in his place they were privileged to have Rizzolo's own mentor, the greatest of the greats, a man who held the secrets of magic within his fingertips, the astonishing

Stoker and his beautiful assistant. I giggled, and Mr. Stoker lifted his hand, his palm flat.

He said nothing, but I understood the warning implicit in the gesture and bit my tongue hard against another laugh that was bubbling up. After that, things began to happen quite quickly. The crowd hurried in, jostling and whispering, and then, with a final flourish of hyperbole, we made our way through the rear flap. I waved and smiled, and Mr. Stoker scowled, which suited his role as mysterious conjurer quite perfectly. He secured me in the restraints and I blew him a kiss, which seemed to distract him, but only for a moment. He turned but did not address the crowd. They fell silent with expectation, and still he said nothing. The moment stretched on, the tension peaking in exquisite torment, and only when they were at their most fevered and excited did he speak. It was masterfully done. They were spellbound, all eyes fixed upon him as he moved slowly in front of them. I realized then how exotic he must seem to these plain countryfolk. He was big as a farm lad, but he moved with a natural grace that would have done credit to any member of the genus *Panthera*. He was predatory as he stalked them, demanding their attention and respect, and they watched him in awe as he conjured items seemingly from thin air. He brought out silk handkerchiefs and velvet roses, a handful of golden coins, and from behind one boy's ear, a tiny mechanical bird that hopped when he held it on his palm. They were intoxicated with him, as much from the force of his personality as the tricks themselves.

He directed their attention to the arrangement of knives and made a great show of asking the village blacksmith to test my restraints and his own blades. The fellow agreed that all was as it should be and Mr. Stoker stepped to his mark, bouncing the first knife slightly on his palm. The crowd was hushed, their nerves taut as an archer's bowstring as they waited. Again he toyed with them, delaying the inevitable until he judged the moment was ripe. Then, in a motion so fast a cobra would envy him, he whipped the knife through the air, pinning it to the board beside my head. The crowd roared, and he did it again, eleven more times in quick succession until the knives were quivering around me. They cheered and he bowed. He made no sign of releasing me, so I merely smiled and inclined my head as they applauded. One of the lads had been appointed to pass his hat, so he made his way through the crowd collecting the coins they showered happily upon him.

At last he turned to me, saying nothing as he removed the blades. Then he moved to unbuckle the restraints. "Can you walk on your own?" he asked softly, his mouth grazing my ear.

"Doubtful," I admitted.

He sighed. "No matter." He released the restraints and scooped me up in the most undignified fashion possible, flinging me over his shoulder like a sack of grain and waving to the crowd. They roared in laughter and I suppressed the urge to kick him as he ducked out of the tent.

"Was that necessary?" I demanded of his backside.

"Entirely," he told me. "You said you cannot walk and I have no intention of throwing out my back simply because you cannot hold your drink. This is the easiest way to carry heavy loads."

I did kick him then, but I missed, for my foot swung at empty air and he merely clamped a large warm hand to my thigh. "Mr. Stoker, that is *most* inappropriate," I said, more for form's sake than out of any real objection. I had found the experience thoroughly stimulating. But we had reached the caravan by then and he set me on my feet.

"Thank you for the ride," I said cordially.

He leaned closer to me, and I realized the moon had risen, slightly fuller than the night before, shedding a romantic silver light upon the landscape. His dark hair was tumbled and the moon glinted upon his earring, giving him a mysterious air. In the distance I heard the music from Otto's accordion—some melody I had never heard, full of longing and promise and urgency. Even the roses had unfurled, wafting their heady fragrance into the night air to intoxicating effect. It was as if the entire world conspired to create an atmosphere so romantic only a poet might have done justice to it.

Mr. Stoker's gaze rested on mine, then moved down to my lips and back again. His lips parted, slowly, so slowly, and he spoke. "We can't repeat it, Veronica," he said, his voice oddly thick.

He leaned closer still, and the night seemed full of him. The clean male scent of him was in my nose, and I could feel the solid warmth of his flesh as he stood so very near to me. "No, we mustn't," I agreed. "Such proximity is dangerous."

Something warred in his face, dueling emotions he could not quite master. "Yes, quite dangerous," he said, moving closer still, almost unwillingly, his body seemingly drawn to mine against his wishes. It occurred to me then that he was dangerously close to doing something we would both regret—probably the instant it happened.

I gave him a cool smile.

"To begin with," I told him, stepping nimbly away, "I do not think your clothing could endure it."

"My clothing?" His head snapped back as if I had doused him with cold water. The dreamy expression was gone from his eyes as he stared down at me.

"You have just split the backside of your trousers with that demonstration of virility. I hardly think you can afford another."

I turned on my heel and went into the caravan under my own power, as steadily and smartly as I had ever done anything in my life.

THIRTEEN

I AWOKE THE NEXT MORNING to find Mr. Stoker up and dressed and thrusting a cup of tea under my nose. "You've five minutes to dress before we leave," he said coldly.

From a quick glance outside, I deduced he had not spoken in jest. The camp was full of activity—the various tents had all been dismantled and stowed, and I saw that enormous draft horses had been harnessed to each of the caravans. He had busied himself in stowing anything loose into the cupboards and making certain the furnishings were properly secured. He tossed me my bag and left without another word. I drank my tea hastily, scalding myself a little, for it was strong and hot, and dressed as quickly as I could. Having long experience with aguardiente and excellent recuperative powers, I suffered no ill effects from the previous evening and even whistled a little tune as I repacked my bag and tucked it into a cupboard before leaving the caravan.

"Good morning, missus," called a voice. I looked to the front of the caravan, where a groom was walking up with a pair of horses. His trousers were patched and his face half-hid beneath the shadow of his cap.

"Good morning. Are those for us?"

"Indeed they are, and no finer horseflesh will you find in this establishment," he assured me. He paused to let me greet them, holding them quite still while I stroked their velvety noses. "I've kept them back special for your caravan, missus."

He lifted his head and I saw then that he was a surprisingly comely fellow, with warm brown eyes that fairly danced. His mouth was merry as well, smiling almost as if it had a will of its own.

"That is very kind of you."

He shrugged. "Well, it takes a brave lady to let a fellow throw knives at her."

"Brave or entirely devoid of sense. Take your choice."

The grin deepened, and I noted that his cheeks were dimpled. I had seen the other grooms in passing, gnarled old fellows with skin like shoe leather. How they must have hated this delightful young man!

"I am Mornaday," he told me, extending his hand. I shook it, feeling a tiny rush of pleasure at the touch of his warm, smooth palm against mine. One of the horses tossed her head and gave a snort.

"Ah, all in good time, love," he told her soothingly. He gave me a nod. "Best get these ladies hitched. I'll see you later, missus," he promised.

I went to collect a roll and another cup of tea, and by the time I returned Mr. Stoker was already seated on the narrow bench behind the horses. He did not offer a hand as I climbed up beside him.

"Good morning," I said politely. "Where are we bound?"

"Ten miles down the road. Village called Butterleigh."

"Only ten miles? How curious. I should have thought we would go further."

"The horses can manage fourteen, but it isn't wise to push them so far every time." He picked up the reins, and at some unseen signal, the caravans all began to move forward. The professor and Otto rode in a curious conveyance, a landau of sorts padded in old velvet and shaped like a scallop shell. It was highly theatrical and the professor gave a jaunty wave as they passed us to take the lead on the road to Butterleigh.

I turned to Mr. Stoker, but he kept his gaze fixed forward and said nothing. I suspected I had pricked his pride the night before. Whether it was the moonlight or the euphoria of having got through the performance without maiming me, the flicker of interest I had seen from him was clearly the aberration of a moment, and a more logical fellow would have shaken my hand and thanked me for my firmness. Instead, Mr. Stoker was indulging in a first-class fit of pique, and had we not been thrown together on the road, I would have left him to it. However, I was not prepared to travel next to his stony silence, so I embarked upon conversation, certain he would not rebuff me—at least not for long.

"The professor likes to travel in style," I observed.

"It is his idea of free advertising," Mr. Stoker replied, thawing a little. "He knows every farmhand and small child we pass along the road will stare goggle-eyed and then tell half the county. So smile and nod as we pass. The more cash we can make for him, the more welcome we will be." He flicked me a glance. "You did rather well last night. I quite expected you to faint."

"I cannot think why." I bristled. "I am not prone to nervous attacks, and I do not know why you believe I might be. I am stalwart as a lion, Mr. Stoker. Stalwart as a lion."

He made a strange sound then, like a rusty squeezebox,

and then, as it warmed and lit his entire countenance, I realized he was laughing. I poked him firmly in the ribs.

"I do not appreciate being laughed at."

"Oh, I am not laughing at you, dear Veronica. I assure you. I am laughing at myself for being so foolish as to ever have doubted you," he assured me.

I was not entirely persuaded, but as he had unbent enough to laugh, I did not pursue the matter. Instead I turned to the scenery, drawing in great, deep drafts of the soft June air. All was fresh and green, the trees unfurling their tender leaves, the hedgerows budding in the gentle sunshine. The entire land was awash with newness, and in the air was the sharp tang of cool earth, newly turned by the plow to receive the seed. Something about the fragility of it all pierced me then, and when a bird began to sing sweetly in the trees, I felt overcome. I had no words to describe my feelings; I was no poet, and neither was Mr. Stoker. But he must have felt something of the same, for he let the reins rest slack in his hand and drew in a deep breath of that bewitched air and began to speak.

"'I stood tip-toe upon a little hill, / The air was cooling and so very still, / That the sweet buds which with a modest pride, / Pull droopingly, in slanting curve aside, / Their scantly leaved and finely tapering stems, / Had not yet lost those starry diadems, / Caught from the early sobbing of the morn,'" he recited. Then he gave me a glance, only a little self-conscious. "Keats."

"Yes, I know," I managed. "But you surprise me. I should have thought you would prefer autumn."

"Oh, you have the right of it—I do love the 'mists and mellow fruitfulness,' but I can summon enthusiasm enough for any season. As much as I want the rest of the world, there is some part of me so rooted in this island, I cannot shake the pull of it. For all the glories I have seen, the mountains and the seas and the horizon itself, stretching to the furthest reaches of the eye, there is nothing to touch an English morning in spring."

I could scarce speak for the emotion that rose within me—a tremendous longing for some unnameable thing I had never known and was terrified I should never find. I was struck with a bone-deep love for my native country, an affection so tender I could scarcely breathe, and I turned away.

"Veronica, are you weeping?" he asked suspiciously.

"Don't be ludicrous," I returned tartly. "I do not weep. It is a symptom of the rankest sentimentality, and I am never sentimental." I bent my head to study my compass. "West southwest."

His lips twitched in the semblance of a smile. "We are headed in the correct direction, Veronica. We have only to follow the tail of the horse in front of us."

"I like to know where I am bound," I replied. "Now, let us discuss the matter of money. How much will secure the professor's goodwill?"

We fell to talking of financial matters then, and Stoker explained to me that the coins collected for the price of admission were enough to keep the show itself traveling, but not sufficient to pay the performers. The acts were expected to supplement their own salaries, either by passing the hat or through the sale of the cartes visites, the photographic postcards each act had printed up at their own expense. Some of these were gruesome—such as the one that showed a painfully thin professor and Otto, bared to the waist and exposing the band of sinew and muscle that connected them. Others were faintly salacious. (It needs little imagination to understand that I am speaking of Salome here.)

"Unfortunately, there isn't much excitement to be had in a card depicting a conjuror," Mr. Stoker said ruefully. "And no time to have some made up with you bound to the target and knives scattered all around."

"Probably for the best," I reminded him. "Such cards would only advertise our presence when we are attempting to behave as discreetly as possible."

He quirked his brow at me. "We have gone about that in the most curious way, haven't we? Joining a traveling show. I must have been out of my mind."

"On the contrary," I said with some briskness. "I found it to be a stroke of inspiration. We will be the purloined letters, hiding in plain sight, just like the story by Mr. Poe."

"I do wish I shared your optimism."

His voice was uncharacteristically soft, and I turned to him sharply. "What is the matter with you? We have now agreed upon something. Furthermore, I said something courteous to you and you have not cursed at me in a full five minutes. Have you a fever? Are you delirious?"

I put a hand to his brow and he slapped it away.

"That is better," I said, satisfied.

"Hostility is exhausting to sustain," he admitted. "Particularly at such close quarters."

"Agreed."

"I do not say I will not find it again," he said in a warning tone. "But for the moment, I am rather more encouraged than I have felt in the past few days. We have shelter and food and a place of refuge, at least for a little while—long enough for me to discover the results of the inquest."

"How? I trust you made arrangements before we left London?"

He hesitated, then decided, perhaps in the spirit of our recent amity, to trust me a little. "I did. I have a friend who will forward the newspapers as soon as the verdict has been published."

"A friend! Why then did we not seek sanctuary there instead of with the show?"

"Because my friend is at present not in London." I waited for him to continue, but he had resumed his shuttered expression.

"Then how will your friend receive the newspapers?"

"They will be forwarded from London, obviously. In turn, they will be sent to me in care of the nearest post office with only a day's delay." I opened my mouth, but he cut me off. "Yes, I was cautious enough to direct that they be sent to me under an assumed name."

It was on the tip of my tongue to tell him about my encounter at Paddington Station with Mr. de Clare, but I did not. He might have unbent enough to share a little information with me, and I took this as an excellent sign that we were making progress in this strange working partnership we had undertaken. But I also knew that my snippet of information could prove either entirely worthless or enormously valuable—and I had no intention of tipping my hand until I knew the significance of the cards I held.

Turning back to the conversation at hand, I gave him a grudging nod. "It seems you have thought of everything. But you have forgotten the most important element of your plan—you have me for an ally," I reminded him. "And I vow I shall not leave your side until we discover the truth of what happened to the baron."

He swore fluently then, cursing until the birds stopped singing. I did not mind. In fact, I had rather missed his irascibility, and I found myself smiling as we made our way down the country lane towards Butterleigh. I knew we ought to be devising a strategy, deciding upon a course of action. But fleeing London, while securing our safety, had also removed us from any meaningful involvement in the developments. We were hampered by geography, and I decided in the inviting warmth of that late spring morning that this was not an entirely undesirable situation. The tumultuous events of the past few days and the exotic atmosphere of the traveling show had conspired to create a curious effect upon me. I felt entirely relaxed for the first time since I had arrived back in England to nurse Aunt Nell.

I had not realized what a toll those cold, dreary months had taken. I was not meant for sickrooms and poultices; I was fashioned of the stern stuff of adventurers. I had not the temperament for nurturing, and the tedium of Little Byfield had leached me of my natural vitality. I felt in this new adventure I was rousing to life again. I was a butterfly, newly emerged from the chrysalis, damp winged and trembling with expectation. I had witnessed the process often enough on my hunts, and I made a point never to net such tender beauties. I left them to stand upon a branch, opening their soft wings for the first time to the sun, letting its rays warm and revive them until they were strong enough to fly. There would be time enough for my own flight, I decided.

For now I was content to sit upon my branch and restore myself. Besides, I considered, for all we knew, the baron's murderer had already been apprehended. Even now he might be sitting in jail, awaiting justice. And if that were the case, it would serve us nothing to form a plan. No, far better to make our way quietly along with the traveling show for a few days while we let the police do their necessary work. In a larger town, it would be a small matter to secure a newspaper and see what new developments had arisen. If the miscreant had been taken, Mr. Stoker and I would have nothing further to fear, and we could return to London and thence go our separate ways. Satisfied with my reflections, I closed my eyes and turned my face to the sun. If I had known it was to be my last truly peaceful moment for some time to come, I should have made a point of enjoying it more.

* * *

The journey was a pleasant one, and by afternoon we were comfortably ensconced in a river meadow, the caravans and tents arranged much as they had been before. A number of grooms I had not yet met busied themselves unhitching the horses and securing them in a makeshift paddock a little distance away. Soon, cooking fires were kindled and chairs and tables appeared and the campsite took on its customary air of pleasant busyness.

In contrast to my excellent mood, Mr. Stoker had sunk into a gloom from which he seemed determined not to stir. We quarreled loudly about leaving the windows of the caravan open, a fight that seemed far more about him taking advantage of the opportunity to shout than any real opinion on the state of the windows. I shouted back because I enjoyed the exercise, and in the end I threw my flask of aguardiente at him and told him to marinate in the stuff if it would sweeten his temper. I left him sulking in the caravan and took my net to pursue what winged prey I might find in the river meadow. I seldom hunted properly in England as my clients all preferred more exotic species, but the chase kept my skills sharply honed, and I prepared for this expedition as carefully as for any other. I fished out a selection of minuten—the tiny headless entomological pins used for display—and worked them into my cuffs. It was a clever trick I had learned to keep them upon my person and save the trouble of carrying a box. It also served to discourage unwanted suitors from attempting to hold my hand—a not uncommon occurrence upon my travels. I slipped a small jar for common specimens into my pocket, but anything exotic demanded something more exacting.

The lush red roses of my hat had been specially ordered and were lined with cork, the perfect repository for such specimens. Any truly rare finds could be swiftly dispatched with a careful pinch to the thorax and then pinned to the roses, out of the way and in no danger of damage from a jar or box. It was my own technique and one I had not seen duplicated anywhere except by a rather eccentric fellow from Belgium who appeared one day on a meadow path in the Rocky Mountains with a cloud of Hoary Commas—*Polygonia gracilis* with its splendid escalloped orange wings—quivering upon his sola topee. He looked like a madman, but I realized instantly that as a woman I could employ the habit to much better effect. My ensemble was completed with the addition of my compass, the one piece of equipment essential to any explorer. I made a note of the direction of north and picked up my net.

No sooner had I stepped from the caravan than I nearly collided with the attractive groom, Mornaday. He extended a hand full of fruit.

"Pear, missus?" he asked with a bob of the head. "I was collecting fruit for the horses. They do like a bit of a treat. The pears are only a little green. Will you have one?"

I thanked him and took it, more to be polite than out of any real desire to eat it. I bit into it and was surprised to find it ripe, the juices bursting forth from the snowy flesh and over my hands.

"Ah, you've a good one there!" he said with a chuckle. He brandished a striped handkerchief and I took it gratefully, laughing as the juice dripped from my chin. "That's better," he said, glancing at my butterfly net. "I say, missus, if you're after butterflies, I saw a blue one, a Morpho, I think it's called. Just down this way. I can show you, if you like."

Taking my arm, he guided me down the riverbank quite some distance, through a watery meadow and to a secluded little copse, singing all the while. He had a very pleasant tenor, and his rendition of "Early One Morning" would not have disgraced the public stage. When we at last reached the clearing, I turned to him with an air of expectation.

"How very kind of you to guide me. A Morpho, you say?"

He gave me a broad smile. "It were bright blue, with black teardrops at the bottom of its wings," he said promptly.

"I am afraid that is no Morpho, Mornaday. You have just described *Papilio ulysses*, a Blue Swallowtail indigenous to Australasia. Hardly to be found in Devonshire. Which leads me to conclude you did not see a Blue Swallowtail in this copse."

He opened his mouth and I held up a hand. "Nor did you see a Morpho, my dear fellow. The Morpho habitat is strictly limited to Central and South America." While he continued to gape, I gave him an extended lecture upon the species differences between the two most common Morphos, *menelau*s and *peleides*, and the Blue Swallowtail, *Papilio ulysses*. For good measure I discoursed at length upon instars and imagos, enjoying every moment of his glassy-eyed incomprehension. After half an hour or so, I took pity upon him and concluded my remarks. "And that brings me to the obvious question, Mornaday. Why did you create a pretext to see me alone?"

He hesitated, then grinned, and when he spoke, his voice was somehow more cultured than it had been before. The accent was smoother, and his vocabulary was no longer quite so limited, and his air of diffidence melted away under a more authoritative mien.

"I beg your pardon, Mrs. Stoker. I ought to have realized that such methods would not deceive an expert lepidopterist."

"But how did you know I was an expert? I might be the most casual hobbyist."

He nodded towards the net. "My father was a collector. I know an expensive ring net when I see one."

"That still does not explain your purpose in bringing me here."

He stepped closer and I saw that the brown eyes were flecked with gold and amber. "Does a fellow need a reason when the lady in question is so enchanting?"

He had pitched his voice low and husky, and he had to stand quite near to me in order to be audible, by design, I suspected. I shook my head. "No, Mornaday. It will not do. You have seen Mr. Stoker. He is a large fellow. He throws knives with astounding accuracy. You would not dare bring me here for mere flirtation."

He hesitated, then reached forward suddenly to take my hand. "I brought you here because I was afraid for you."

"Afraid for me? My dear fellow, whatever for?"

His expression was grave, the flirtatious note quite absent now from his delivery. He was as sincere and plainspoken as a parson. "As you say, Mr. Stoker is a large fellow and he throws knives. That quarrel sounded dangerous."

"If you heard that, then you know I gave just as good as I got. Rest easy, my gallant. I can assure you I am utterly safe with him. He would sooner cut off his own arm than harm a hair of my head."

"Can you be certain of that? I understand you have known him only a short while. Such limited acquaintance can be deceiving."

I sighed. "You are correct, of course. One may be entirely mistaken in one's assessment of a character if it is taken too quickly. But that goes for the ordinary person, Mornaday. And I am no ordinary person. I have traveled the world and made extensive acquaintance from the tip of South America to the Swiss Alps. I am thoroughly skilled at taking the measure of a man quickly. And I can tell you that I am content to remain in his care."

The narrow gaze did not soften. "It is a strange life for a lady, this traveling show. Are you certain he does not coerce you to be here? You have chosen it of your own free will?"

"As much as anyone chooses anything," I promised him.

"How long have you been acquainted?" he asked.

"Long enough," I returned tartly. This was an interrogation, not a seduction, I reflected with no little irritation. I had no intention of succumbing to his blandishments, but it was a trifle insulting that he had not made a better job of offering any. "Your concern is very kind, but I think this discussion is at an end."

He sketched a slight bow. "Forgive me if I have been indiscreet. But it is important that you know you may rely upon me should you ever have need of a friend. Remember that."

I smiled. "Very kind indeed. Now if you will hand me that butterfly net, I mean to be off. I think I spy a *Lasiommata* lurking beyond that stream and I mean to have it."

Fresh with purpose, I returned from an hour in the meadow with a pair of pretty captives in a jar. They were nothing special, and certainly not worth the trouble of killing, but appealing nonetheless. I carried them back only to admire them. I would set them free, entirely unharmed, after a few hours.

Mr. Stoker was pacing in front of the caravan when I arrived. "Aren't they lovely?" I asked, brandishing the jar. "I saw a lovely *Lasiommata*, but it eluded me, and I had to settle for these two as compensation. This is merely a common *Vanessa atalanta,* but I do think it charming. And here is *Gonepteryx rhamni.* I quite prefer the common name of Brimstone butterfly, don't you?"

"Where in the name of the oozing wounds of Christ have you been?" he demanded.

"In the meadow, as you can plainly see."

He took me firmly by the elbow and thrust me up the stairs and into the caravan. There he pushed me into one of the armchairs and positioned himself directly in front of me.

"You are not to do that again," he said severely. "I was

half out of my mind. If you mean to go off, you must tell me."

I considered this a moment, then shook my head. "I do not think so," I said politely.

"What the bloody hell do you mean you don't think so? I just gave you an order."

I smothered the urge to laugh. It would have been very rude, and I had little doubt it would have inflamed his temper even further. I adopted a deliberately soothing tone.

"I am sorry you were worried, Mr. Stoker, but I am quite capable of looking after myself in a meadow. I went hunting for butterflies. You do recall that I am a lepidopterist?"

"Yes," he ground out between clenched teeth. "But you must not go haring off on your own. It is not safe."

"How absurd you are! Not safe indeed. What could be safer than a meadow? Do you know what you will find in a meadow? Cows. There are cows in a meadow. Cows and wildflowers and butterflies."

He dropped his head into his hands. "You are the most impossible woman I have ever known," he said, his voice muffled.

"Am I? I cannot think why. I am entirely reasonable and thoroughly logical."

"That is what makes you impossible." He lifted his head. "Very well. I will appeal to your sense of logic. If I do not know you are gone and where you are bound, how will I know if you are in distress?"

"Should I be in distress? In a meadow? You mean if the cows organize some sort of attack? I have extensive experience with cows. They almost never do that."

"Forget the bloody cows," he said, clearly making an effort to hold on to his temper. "The baron was killed, murdered in cold blood, or have you forgot that?"

"Of course I haven't. But that has nothing to do with my

going off on a butterfly hunt."

"It has everything to do with it!" he roared back.

"Heavens, you're a stubborn man! No wonder no woman will live with you." As soon as the words were out of my mouth, I wished them back. His gaze fell to the slender gold band upon my left hand and he rose without a word and left the caravan, slamming the door hard behind him.

I slid the ring from my finger and held it to the light. It had not been worn for long, I realized, for the gold was still bright and the edges unworn, although it had been badly damaged at one time. An inscription had been engraved inside, and I turned it to the light to read it. *For C.M. from R.T.-V. Sept. 1882.* I did not know the identity of C.M., but it required little imagination to determine that the tender bridegroom had been Revelstoke Templeton-Vane, and that in September of 1882 he had taken a wife. The question was, what had he done with her?

I looked at the inscription again. No poetry, then, I thought, and for some reason, I was surprised. A man who loved the Romantic poets ought to have fairly covered the thing in verse. But there were only the initials, inscribed coldly into the gold, and nothing more. I slipped the ring back onto my finger and took up my reading, applying myself once more to the adventures of Arcadia Brown, Lady Detective, but my attention wandered. I had the beginning of a violent headache, and the vague feeling of a storm gathering. There were no clouds to be seen, and I was not often given to fancies, but I put a hand into my pocket and drew out my little velvet mouse and held him tightly in my palm as I waited for what was to come.

FOURTEEN

Mr. Stoker nursed his resentment for the better part of that day, for I did not see him again until it was time for us to perform. That is not to say that I did not hear him. Shortly before we were to begin the act, I made my way to the tent, slipping through the shadowy areas behind, where few of the paying customers ventured. One had to be quite careful here, as the ropes and tent pegs were difficult to see, so I was picking my way slowly when I heard my name in conversation. It was Salome speaking, and I soon realized to whom.

"Why did you marry Veronica? Is she with child?" The voice was teasing, and the reply was brutal and swift.

"God, no!" Too late, he must have remembered that we were supposed to be devotedly in love, for he hastened to repair the damage. "That is to say, it is far too soon for that sort of thing. I would like some time with my bride all to myself before I have to share her with a child."

Salome laughed, a velvety, seductive sound, and I knew instinctively that she would be standing quite close to him in the darkness.

"Oh, Stoker, why do you think you can deceive me? After what we have been together? Tell me the truth now. Do you really prefer her to me?"

I heard the rustle of fabric and a decidedly masculine gasp. "That's really quite an inappropriate question under the circumstances, don't you think? You oughtn't—that is, I am a married man, Salome."

"Are you? You don't seem married to me." After this came more rustling and another groan.

"Leave me be, Salome. I am quite devoted to Veronica," he said, his voice strangled.

"I don't believe that," she murmured. "Tell me why you like her. Tell me why you married her."

There was a moment of imperfect silence between them, for I heard still more rustling and then, quite abruptly, a ragged growl and another laugh from Salome, this one sharp and unpleasant.

"You think you can push me aside? You think you can forget me? For her?" Salome caught her breath suddenly. "Let go of my arm. You're hurting me."

"And I will do a good deal more if you try any more of your sly tricks, either on me or on Veronica. You're not to go near her, do you understand me?"

"A little late for you to suddenly play the protective husband, don't you think? Why did you do it? Tell me why you married her."

"I mean it, Salome, and if you think I don't, I beg you to give me the chance to prove it. Leave her be. And me as well."

He must have stalked off then, for she cursed as she came around the corner. She brought herself up with an exaggerated start when she saw me.

"Oh, Veronica! I did not know you were there."

"Really, somehow I think otherwise."

She gave me an appraising look followed by a shrug. "I was the first woman to know him. You will understand why I am curious about you. We are very different." She stepped nearer. "How did you meet him? What do you speak of together?"

I tipped my head. "Such interesting questions. But really, you ought to ask Stoker if you want them answered. Oh, but I am forgetting. You already did."

With that she flicked her hair and walked away, swinging her hips as she moved. Out of the shadows I saw a figure sidle up to her, and I was interested to recognize the form of the flirtatious groom, Mornaday. Having halfheartedly tried his luck with me and found it wanting, he had no doubt decided to cast his line in likelier waters, I reflected. I wished him joy of her, but it did seem a trifle much that we should now share two men.

I proceeded on to the tent and found Mr. Stoker pacing by the back flap.

"Finally! Where in the name of hell have you been?"

"Eavesdropping," I said with deliberate sweetness.

He stopped and stared at me. "What—"

I reached up and applied my handkerchief to his face, scrubbing vigorously. "You have lip rouge on your mouth."

He had the grace to blush. "Yes, well, that was—"

"That was none of my business, but you look quite ludicrous. *Quite* ludicrous indeed. If you mean to exchange favors with Salome, I would only ask that you attempt a little discretion. We must give the appearance of content married life if the masquerade is to be credible, must we not?"

He snatched the handkerchief out of my hand. "Give me that! You've rubbed my skin raw."

I gave him a look of mock contrition. "Oh, I do apologize. It is such a garish shade, it is quite difficult to remove."

He scrubbed at his own face. "Better?"

"Yes, although there is some on your collar. And you might want to attend to the top button on your trousers."

He muttered a curse, but I gave him a brilliant smile. "It sounds like a very full house tonight."

"Veronica, about Salome—"

I placed a hand on his sleeve. "Really, Mr. Stoker, you needn't bother. I assure you she does not trouble me in the least. If you decide to pay a call upon her, I shan't wait up. I will just leave the bolt on the caravan door undone. You can let yourself in—only do be quiet getting into bed, won't you? I am quite tired this evening and would so hate to be awakened."

He stared at me openmouthed, then snapped his jaw shut and took me hard by the wrist, half dragging me to the flap.

I smiled to myself that I had provoked him to such a fine display of temper, but I was by no means finished. I had not even begun.

We stood outside the tent, listening to the incoming crowd, a thin layer of canvas providing us with a modest bit of privacy. "They sound keen," I remarked. "Almost as keen as you in the arms of the delicious Salome."

He whirled on me. "That is enough," he growled. "I swear to the devil, Veronica, if you vex me further, I will not be responsible for my actions."

"Oh, come now, Mr. Stoker. You will have to do better than that if you mean to make me afraid of you. I have been menaced more effectively by poodles."

"God, you have a vicious tongue," he retorted. "But I am no more afraid of you than you are of me. I have little doubt your bark is worse than your bite."

"How do you know, Mr. Stoker? I haven't bitten you yet."

I leaned close and snapped my teeth, a whisper away from his nose. He bent to me and my lips parted of their own volition. My fingers crept to his shirtfront and I could feel the pounding of his heart under my palms. His hands were curled into fists, and he held them at his sides, as if fighting the urge to touch me with every particle of his being. His mouth was a breath away from mine, and yet he did not move closer. He did not *finish* it. He simply stood, as perfectly still as one of the mounts in his own workshop, captured in a moment that stretched tautly into an eternity.

I was conscious of a curious buzzing in my ears and realized it was my own excitement fizzing in my blood. I understood then what a significant miscalculation I had made. I had thought to toy with him and instead had managed to rouse myself to a fever pitch. Whatever pleasant dalliances I had enjoyed in the past, those interludes would be drops in the ocean compared to the tidal wave of this man. And the knowledge of that shook my composure to the core—a composure I would not, *could not*, afford to lose. Worse still, I had used my trick of prodding his temper to provoke something entirely different, and it felt suddenly shabby and mean to have done so.

I stepped sharply backward, letting my hands fall, empty, to my sides.

"How uncivil of me," I told him, forcing my tone to lightness. "I do apologize."

He ignored the apology. "We are on," he told me, turning to enter the tent. He did not look back to see if I would follow.

For the whole of the act, something was off about Mr. Stoker. His patter was forced, his conjuring sloppy, and the crowd was restless. Without the dulling effects of the aguardiente, I noticed the pungent smell of the tent, the mingled aromas of sweat and sawdust, and the sharp odor of excitement. I noticed the faces with their avid eyes and ruddy cheeks, countryfolk bent on a little harmless entertainment. I heard their murmurs and whispers, the titters of anticipation as he moved to the knives. He buckled the restraints, his hands tight upon my limbs, his movements ungentle. He was clearly still disturbed by the scenes behind the tents, and I could not imagine why. I had given him carte blanche to visit Salome and he had responded with irritation and a fine display of temper. I should never understand men, I reflected, even if I devoted myself to the study of them as I had lepidoptery. To begin with, I should need a considerably larger net, I decided with a private smile.

But if he was not himself, I must in fairness own that neither was I. I had been aware of a dullness settling upon me, an ache in the bones that usually presaged fever. I shook it off, forcing myself to smile at the crowd and play the devoted assistant, all the while longing for my bed and the sweet release of sleep.

He finished his work at the restraints and invited a local fellow, this time the dispensing chemist, to test them. He did so, and Mr. Stoker took up the first blade. He held it a bit longer than was his custom, and when it flew through the air, I felt it divide the hair at the top of my head. The crowd gasped. Mr. Stoker went rather pale, but the second blade was true, striking precisely where it ought. I gave him a brief nod of encouragement, and with the slight movement, pain shot through my head like a bolt of lightning.

"Not now," I muttered through gritted teeth. But the body is a treacherous thing, and I felt the swoon coming upon me as a creeping blackness advancing from the edges of my vision. My knees gave way and my body sagged against the leather restraints just as the knife left his hand. I opened my mouth to cry a warning, but of course it was too late. Instead of the dull thud of the knife hitting the wood, there was the soft whisper of blade on flesh, and the horrified gasp of the crowd was the last thing I heard as I slipped into unconsciousness.

* * *

The swoon lasted only a few seconds. I revived swiftly enough to find that I was still confined by the restraints and that the edge of the blade was still resting solidly in my arm.

Mr. Stoker was at my side, staring at me in nearly incoherent horror. "For Christ's sake, Veronica, I wish you'd stayed unconscious. You will not enjoy this."

A bubble of hysterical laughter rose within me. "Neither will you," I observed.

He wrenched off his neckcloth and tied it on my arm, knotting it firmly above the quivering blade. It was agony, and I gave a little groan, causing his hand to tremble for a moment.

He gathered hold of his nerves then, and when he spoke it was with calm authority. "I have to remove the blade now. When I do, it will bleed. Quite a lot. Try not to move. And do not hold your breath. It will only make the pain worse."

I obeyed him and nodded, never taking my eyes from his pale face. He did not hesitate. He reached for the blade and pulled it free in a slow, steady motion. The blood flowed freely then, a scarlet ribbon spilling over the spangled blue taffeta of my costume. I heard a woman scream, but I stood, immobile as stone. The crowd pressed around us, gasping. They made no move to leave but edged closer still, and he cursed them.

"God damn you, get back! She needs air. Move back, I said, or I'll gut the lot of you!" He wrenched me free of the restraints and caught me before I slid to the ground.

I motioned to the makeshift tourniquet he had fashioned. "Too tight," I murmured. "It hurts."

"Better that than losing the blood," he snapped. He gathered me into his arms, as gently as one might take up a babe, and stood. He kicked and cursed his way out of the tent and carried me straight back to the caravan. He tore the place apart as he looked for needle and thread and the other assorted oddments he would require.

"You needn't be so untidy," I said drowsily. "I will only have to clean up after you."

"Shut up," he growled. "I can't find the needles. Why in the name of hell can't I find the needles?"

"You are holding them," I pointed out helpfully.

Just then there came a jangling of the bells at the door and Leopold put his head inside. "I have come to help. Salome is bringing hot water and Tilly is brewing up tea for after. I told her to make it very sweet and add a full measure of brandy. What can I do?"

Mr. Stoker threaded the needle, and I noticed his jaw was set tightly.

"Perhaps you ought to do the sewing," I said helpfully to Leopold. "Mr. Stoker seems a trifle upset."

"I will stitch it myself," Mr. Stoker contradicted. "Now, be quiet."

I faded away again, slipping into unconsciousness, but it was the pain that brought me back again. I opened my eyes to see him with a needle in his hand, and when I tried to protest, he ordered Leopold to hold me fast as he worked. By then I had grown delirious and only ever remembered pieces of that night—the awful pain in my head, the fever that rose, higher and hotter, as Mr. Stoker worked over me, forcing open my mouth and pouring in a foul and familiar remedy.

There were pleasanter things too, a cold compress upon my brow and a murmur of reassurance when I fretted and tossed. I thought at one point that I was on board a ship—a ship that sailed on endlessly with no shore in sight, tossed upon a black, raging sea of pain that would not let me go. I wanted to drown in it, to slip overboard and let the deep carry me down, but every time I stepped towards the beckoning waves, something called me back, some sense of business left undone. At length I slept and the sea was quiet at last.

When I woke, my head still hurt but the pain was milder now, a dull discomfort instead of a hot knife into my temples. I moved a little, surprised at the stiffness and ache in my arm until I saw the bandage, white and neat as a nun's habit, and the memory of it all washed over me like a crashing wave. The caravan was dim and I sighed in relief. It had been a short bout, then.

"You have been unconscious for two days," Mr. Stoker informed me.

I looked to the little armchair where he sprawled. His eyes were sunk in exhaustion and ringed with grey shadows. "You look a fright," I told him.

"Yes, well, I still look better than you. Could you take some soup? There is a little on the hob and you ought to have some nourishment."

I nodded and he busied himself, returning in a moment with a battered tin cup and a spoon. The steam from the cup was fragrant and my stomach growled in anticipation. Stoker nodded. "That is a good sign."

Tenderly as a mother hen, he spooned soup into my mouth until the cup was empty.

"More?" I asked hopefully.

"Not just yet. Let that sit awhile, and if you manage to keep it down, you can have more in an hour."

I turned my head to the windowsill to see that my jar was empty. "Where are my butterflies? The *Vanessa* and the *Gonepteryx*?" I demanded.

"I let them go. They were drooping and I felt sorry for them. Now, be still."

He felt my brow then, impersonally, and when he had finished reached for my hand. He kept his finger on the pulse at my wrist for some seconds, then settled back with an air of satisfaction.

"How long have you had malaria?" he asked in a conversational tone. He was clearly pleased with himself for making the diagnosis, and for that he deserved the truth.

"Three years. How long have you been a doctor?" I wanted a little truth of my own.

He gave me a smile that was no less charming for his obvious fatigue. "Considerably longer than three years. And strictly speaking, I am not a doctor. I am a surgeon. How did you know?"

I gestured towards his right arm. "Your tattoo. The asklepian—a serpent twined around the staff of Asclepius. No one but a medical man would suffer to get that. And given the anchor upon your other arm and the Chinese dragon upon your back, I would say you were once a navy man as well."

"Surgeon's mate aboard the HMS *Luna*. We sailed the tropics mostly, although I saw a bit of everywhere."

"And that is how you recognized the symptoms of malaria."

"I noticed the bottle of Warburg's Tincture in your bag when you took out the oil of calendula. Bitter stuff, that. Most commonly used for tropical fevers—and the most common tropical fever is malaria. I have been watching for the symptoms ever since I found the bottle among your things."

"Yes, well, I have had no recurrence for almost a year. I had rather hoped I was finished. The tincture was simply a precaution."

"Pity you didn't take a few more precautions," he said meaningfully.

"You mean like telling you," I countered. "It's very simple, really. I didn't want you fussing over me. I wanted to be treated as an equal."

"And it never occurred to you that you might begin by treating *me* as an equal? Veronica, you cannot expect confidences if you will not give them."

I closed my mouth, struck by the truth of it. I gave him a

nod. "A palpable hit, Mr. Stoker. Very well, I will trade you confidences, tit for tat."

"All right. What do you want to know?"

"Why do you hide your identity?" I asked.

His face went quite still, as immobile as marble under a sculptor's hand—and just as pale. For a long moment he did not speak, but then he gave a gusty sigh and the fight seemed to go out of him. "How did you know?"

"The letters on the Wardian cases in your workshop. There are few natural historians with the initials R.T.-V. For Revelstoke Templeton-Vane. The cases were from an expedition, were they not?"

"If you know my name, you already know the answer to that." His voice was clipped and cold. Our exchange of confidences was clearly not proceeding as he had anticipated, but I thought I would push my luck just a bit further.

"The Templeton-Vane Expedition to Amazonia: 1882 to 1883. For the purpose of cataloging the wildlife of the Amazonian rain forest," I recited from memory.

"How noble you make it sound!" he mocked. "That's what the newspapers and scientific journals called it. Really we were after hunting jaguars. As you can see, I found one," he added with a flourish towards the scar upon his face.

I attempted a different tack. "Why do you no longer use the name Templeton-Vane?"

He gave me a smile that was half a snarl. "If you know the name Templeton-Vane, no doubt you know the answer to that question as well."

I smoothed the bedcovers, pushing back the memories that threatened to engulf me. "I was on an expedition of my own at the time—in Java. You will understand why my grasp of news from the rest of the world is somewhat faulty."

His brows lifted in astonishment, some of his bitterness

falling away. "Java? Good God. You were there? When Krakatoa erupted?"

"Yes. I had the good sense to get as far away as Sumatra, but as it happens it was not nearly far enough. Things were . . . difficult."

"I can only imagine."

"No," I said reasonably. "You cannot. No one can. I certainly couldn't. That sort of horror is unimaginable, even for the most morbid of us. In a curious way, it proved Aristotle correct—'In all natural things there is somewhat of the marvelous.' If you use 'marvelous' in the strictest sense, as describing something that causes astonishment. I have never been so little, nor the wonders of the world so vast, as in those hours when the whole of the earth seemed to crack open." I paused, then resumed my discourse with an air of brisk detachment I did not feel, could never feel about that time. "News from home was scarce. It was months before I saw an English newspaper. I only ever heard that your expedition was unsuccessful and that you disappeared for some time into the jungle."

"And that is all that you heard?" he asked, his eyes bright with interest.

"I told you, I was familiar with the name and that you undertook an expedition to the Amazon which was not a triumph. Beyond that, I know nothing."

"Well, that explains why you remained in my care even though you knew who I was. Anyone else would have run as if they had seven devils on their heels."

I gave him a jocular smile. "Come now, how bad can it be?"

"As it happens," he said, not returning the smile, "very bad indeed. I lost my marriage, my honor, and damned near my eye as well. The newspapers called me villain and scoundrel and monster and printed a hundred stories of the evil I have done."

I shrugged. "You know what newspapers are. They forever make mistakes."

His gaze was dark and fathomless as a midnight sea. "Yes, they do. In my case, they did not tell the half of it."

FIFTEEN

After his dramatic pronouncement, I was silent a moment, then shook my head.

"I do not believe it. I should like to hear the truth. From your own lips."

He spoke slowly, as if chipping each word out of ice. "The truth is a hard mirror, and I am in no mood to look upon my reflection."

"I can well understand that, but you would do better to remember the story out of Plutarch about the Spartan boy and the fox."

"The Spartan boy and the fox?"

"Yes, the lad stole a fox pup but the Spartans had very strict rules against thievery. He hid the animal in his cloak, and rather than allow his misdeed to be found out, he let it gnaw out his vitals while he kept his silence."

"And your point is?" he asked acidly.

"That truth is like that fox pup. If you suffer its ill effects in silence, it can do irreparable harm. Perhaps even kill you."

He opened his mouth, and I waited for the blast of temper. But it did not come. Instead, he gave me a level, appraising look, and I thought of Keats' description of Cortez staring at the Pacific "with eagle eyes." He had eagle eyes, sharp and perceptive. "I know. But not yet. Just not yet."

It was more than I had dared to hope for. It was enough—for the present.

The thought of Keats sparked a memory and I smiled at him suddenly.

"What?" he asked, his tone suspicious.

"I have just remembered that Keats was a medical student. I am no longer surprised at your fondness for him. You walk common ground, Stoker." For the first time, I dropped the honorific and addressed him familiarly. It seemed we had come that far at least.

He gave me a tired smile. "Common ground indeed, but with rather less consumption on my part," he returned.

"Give it time."

The next few days were pleasant enough. I went for walks, building my stamina, and Tilly had taken it upon herself to "feed me up." She was forever sending over pies and hams and other assorted treats, and by the third day, I was feeling very much my old self.

But the more I seemed to gain in health, the more bedeviled Stoker seemed. I attempted more than once to shake the truth out of him, but he withdrew even further, until I was forced to go behind his back and sleuth out his troubles on my own. The first clue came when we were sitting companionably in the caravan. He was on the steps, smoking one of his wretched cigars, while Salome read aloud to me from the casebook of Arcadia Brown. It was a sore trial to listen to her—she stumbled over every other word—but her sluggish pace made it easy for me to let my mind wander. It was in the course of my mental perambulations that I noticed Leopold approach bearing a wooden box. He paused at the steps to exchange brief words with Stoker. I caught only snippets of their conversation, but it was clear to me that Leopold was troubled by his errand, an instinct confirmed by his repeated and fervent apologies.

He left the box with Stoker, hurrying away under Stoker's baleful gaze. I expected him to open it, but he did not. After a long moment, he extinguished his cigar and rose, putting the box to the side. He strode after Leopold, in the direction of the professor's tent, his shoulders set, his hands working themselves into fists.

"Salome," I interrupted. "Please be so good as to bring me that box."

She laid aside the book and did as I asked. The box was polished wood, nearly two feet long. I put a hand to the clasp, and Salome gave me a reproachful look.

"It is private."

"It is not locked," I pointed out. "Furthermore, if he didn't wish me to open it, he ought not to have left it lying around."

She could make no argument to that, and since she was as curious as I, she said nothing further as I turned again to the clasp. It gave way easily.

"How curious," I said, reaching into the box. I extracted an item the likes of which I had not seen since I had left South America.

Salome peered at it. "It is a whip."

"Specifically, it is a *rebenque*," I told her. "Used by gauchos. Cowboys," I explained, seeing her look of perplexity. "It is for the enthusiastic encouragement of livestock, usually cattle and horses."

I ran my fingers over the *rebenque*. It was a rather fine

specimen of its maker's art. Designed for discipline rather than damage, it was not as long or as vicious as a coachman's whip. But anyone who had seen one used on a man would know better than to discount its ability to deliver pain. The handle of this one was perhaps a foot and a half long, covered in rawhide. From it depended a single thong, also of rawhide, two inches in width and some eighteen inches long. The end was not tapered, for it was not meant to draw blood but to deliver a stinging slap. I gave it a single flick and it responded with a sharp crack.

"Stoker is no keeper of livestock," Salome pointed out. "What need does he have of this?"

"What need indeed?" I echoed grimly.

I put the whip back into its box and sent Salome away. I blew out the lamp before Stoker returned, and when he did, I turned my face to the wall and pretended to sleep. For a long while Stoker lay wakeful in the dark, and at length I could bear it no longer.

"That is a rather fine *rebenque*," I began.

He made a noise that was a cross between a growl and a sigh of exasperation. "Leave it, Veronica."

"I shan't ask you to explain. I already know," I said.

"The devil you do," he said sleepily.

"You think I am bluffing merely to draw you out?"

"That is precisely what I think. Now, go to sleep."

"Very well. I will not explain that I am familiar with the *rebenque* because of my own travels in South America. There is also no point in my sharing with you that I am well aware the professor will not let us remain here if you cannot earn our keep. With no target for the knife-throwing act, you would be forced to acquiesce to whatever scheme he devises—even something as torturous as a public fight for pay with a *rebenque*."

It was a long moment before he spoke. "Well, I am glad

you did not explain all of that. It would have been boring in the extreme."

"Would it also bore you to know that I have deduced he means you to fight Colosso?"

He remained silent and I went on. "You, I have little doubt, are skilled with the whip, but Colosso is a full head taller than you and outweighs you by an hundredweight. The *rebenque* is the only way to create a semblance of a fair fight. Have I got it right?"

"Yes," he sighed.

"When is it to be?"

"Tomorrow night."

"Good. I should hate to miss it."

And to his credit, Stoker laughed.

In the interest of further restoring my strength with fresh air and a little fortifying exercise—as well as providing a distraction for Stoker—I insisted upon walking out the next afternoon, thrusting a hamper of sandwiches at Stoker as I took up my net. We passed through the village so he might call in at the post office to see if his friend in Cornwall had sent along the latest London newspaper. He emerged a moment later, his hands empty, but his air was one of deep satisfaction, and I noted the edge of a thin parcel peeping from the top of his pocket.

"Come along," he said, taking my elbow. "I know just the spot where we shan't be overheard." We walked some distance out of the village, passing a few prosperous farms and an aggressively ugly Norman church before crossing the churchyard and into the copse beyond. I stopped short as he closed the gate behind us.

"A bluebell wood!" I exclaimed. "How lucky we are to

find them in bloom so late. Is there anything so lovely?" A river of bluebells flowed through the trees, carpeting the ground and filling the air with sweet, subtle perfume.

I spread a rug in a patch of gilded sunlight and stretched out, watching a pretty little *Hipparchia janira*—a common Meadow Brown butterfly—flap slowly amid the milkwort and oxeye daisies. Stoker took out his knife and applied himself to a pair of apples, removing the peel from each in a single long russet curl.

"That must serve you well as a taxidermist," I noted, taking a healthy bite of the apple. "It takes real skill to have the skin off in one unbroken strip."

"A thoroughly unladylike observation," he returned.

"Yes, well, being a lady is a crashing bore, or hadn't you noticed?"

He shrugged. "You seem to enjoy it."

"As you pointed out, I am not exactly a lady."

"You are when it suits you. You are fortunate that in our world those ladylike trappings provide you with a bit of protective coloration to hide what you really are."

I tipped my head thoughtfully. "And what am I really?"

"Damn me if I know," he replied. "I have been attempting to discover that since the moment you dropped into my lap, but you are as elusive as those wretched butterflies you hunt."

"I am an open book," I assured him.

He gave a snort of derision and rummaged for the parcel he had retrieved from the post office. He extracted a newspaper and a letter—a note from his friend, no doubt.

As he read, I reclined against a tree, twisting a curl of apple peel around my fingers. The air in that perfumed field was intoxicating, and it roused instincts within me that I seldom permitted myself to let slip the lead—at least not in England. I had no intention of acting upon them; that was strictly forbidden under the rules I had set and of which I reminded myself sternly and often. But it was pleasant to ponder the possibilities. "That groom, Mornaday, is rather handsome, wouldn't you say?" I said, thinking aloud.

He peered at me over the newspaper. "Bloody hell," he muttered. "Veronica, I realize you are accustomed to exercising your affections with a certain degree of freedom, but you cannot go about the countryside seducing assorted strangers. We are attempting to preserve the fiction of a happily married couple."

"Piffle. We gave a poor picture of it when you permitted Salome to—well, perhaps we had best draw a veil over that incident," I said, arching a brow at him. "And you have no fear I will misbehave with Mornaday. I only ever indulge my baser requirements when I am abroad. But if I did, Mornaday would serve quite nicely. He is a perfectly attractive fellow. He has lovely hands."

Stoker refused to rise to the bait. He resumed his newspaper, turning the pages with an outraged snap.

"Too lovely," I said slowly, sitting up.

"Hm?" He was busy reading again and paying me scant attention.

"For a groom, Mornaday has very soft skin. I noticed it when we first shook hands. His palms were very smooth, free of calluses. Have you ever known a man who works with horses to have tender hands?"

"No, they have hands like shoe leather," he said, peering intently at the newspaper.

"Then what is he playing at in taking a job as a groom? He claims it is his regular employment, but that must be a lie."

"We have more considerable problems than the softness of Mornaday's hands," he said tightly. He thrust the newspaper into my hands. "Read."

I skimmed the article, horror mounting in a cold wave. I

read it again, slowly this time, but the facts did not change. The verdict in the inquest had been murder by person or persons unknown. That much we had expected. We knew the baron had been murdered, and it had been an unlikely hope that the authorities had already apprehended his murderer. But the rest of the article revealed a far greater calamity. Besides reporting the verdict—and the fact that the baron had instructed via his will that he was to be privately interred with no formal ceremony—the newspaper seemed to relish relating that in a related matter, the Honorable Revelstoke Templeton-Vane, youngest son of Lord Templeton-Vane, was currently being sought by the Metropolitan Police to assist them with their inquiries into the murder of the Baron von Stauffenbach.

"Stoker, they cannot possibly mean—"

"They do," he said grimly.

He was right, of course; there was only one possible interpretation to the article: I was traveling with a man wanted for murder.

I skimmed the rest of the article, but it gave few details. "How do you think they came to connect you to the baron?"

He thrust his hands into his hair. "I rented the warehouse from him. There would be a record of the payments in his ledgers."

"You mean the baron owned the warehouse where you live?" He nodded in the affirmative, and I carried on. "The police would have discovered this when they looked through his papers. They must have called upon you only to find you missing." He groaned, and I knew I was on the right path. "Naturally, it would seem suspicious to them that you should disappear at the same time the baron was murdered. And with the inquest verdict of 'murder by person or persons unknown,' they have settled upon you as the likeliest candidate. This article gives only your name, but it is simply a matter of time before they circulate your photograph and description."

He lifted his head, his expression one of abject misery. "Why? Why did I not think of this when I left London?"

"Not to be critical at a difficult moment," I put in hesitantly, "but why did you not seek out the police as soon as the baron was murdered? It does seem the most logical course of action, doesn't it?"

"Not helpful," he said sharply.

"You did not answer my question then, but I should very much like an answer now."

He paused, and I realized he was making up his mind whether to trust me at last.

"Because in the eyes of polite society and no doubt those of Scotland Yard, I am already a murderer."

I stared at him, and he gave me a bitter smile. "Well, well. I have managed to render you speechless at last. I should think that calls for a drink."

He reached into the basket for my flask of aguardiente and took a deep draft. I held out my hand and took a hearty swallow of my own.

Then I gave him a level look. "Why do they believe you to be a murderer?"

He did not flinch. "Because I am."

It was a long moment before I could speak again. "I suppose I ought to thank you for being so forthright. As a matter of curiosity, whom exactly did you kill?" I thought for an instant of the wedding band I wore—a ring that had once graced the hand of his wife. He had mentioned his marriage as one of the casualties of his disastrous expedition. Had she been the victim of a homicidal impulse? I found that impossible to believe.

"A man who deserved it, and I would do it again, and that is all you need know," he said flatly. Not his wife, then, I reflected, but I was no less intrigued by the possibilities that remained.

Had she had a lover Stoker had revenged himself upon? Was it a business arrangement gone terribly wrong? Unpaid gambling debts? He went on. "The police in this country cannot touch me for it, but they know my name well enough. I am sorry to say that my first thought when I learned of Max's death was not for the loss of my friend, but the certainty that they would eventually settle on me as the likeliest culprit. And it appears I am correct," he added with a nod to the newspaper.

"You can hardly blame them," I said mildly. "You are a policeman's very dream, are you not? Connected to the baron by ties of business and friendship and burdened by an unsavory reputation. It would not be difficult to draw inference of motive somehow. A lazy policeman would be your undoing."

I meant to continue on in that vein, but he was staring at me, his expression one of frank disbelief.

"Stoker, you look like a carp. Whatever is the matter with you?"

"I just admitted to you that I am a murderer. I have taken a man's life, and you have nothing more to say upon the subject?"

"You have no wish to elaborate, and I have no wish to make you. What would you have me do, pry confidences from you like pulling teeth from a horse's mouth? Besides, I am not entirely blameless in the matter of withholding information."

His gaze narrowed. "What are you talking about?"

Swiftly and with clinical efficiency, I related my experience with Mr. de Clare at Paddington Station. All the while, his expression never altered from one of dispassionate assessment.

"And is that all?" he asked coolly when I had finished.

"Yes. I ought to be contrite, but I don't think I can manage it. You have kept your secrets; I have kept mine."

"But my secrets won't get you hanged for a murder you didn't commit," he countered, his color high.

"Oh, don't let's start this again," I protested. "We might

work very well together, you know, if only we could bring ourselves to trust each other. I have believed this from the first minutes in your workshop when I saw your sweet little *Phyllomedusa tomopterna.*"

"It is a *tarsius* with a genetic mutation," he corrected. "Now, do shut up and let me think."

"No. From this minute forward, we will work together, cooperatively, to solve this murder as it ought to be solved in order to clear you of suspicion and bring the baron's killer to justice," I told him firmly. "One ought to employ order and method to a murder investigation just as one should to a scientific investigation." I looked at him closely. "Perhaps this is why you are a failure. You are far too impulsive and lacking in discipline. Oh, do not fuss. You will give yourself an apoplexy. It was simply an observation."

He had started to storm at me but shut his mouth again on a hard snap of the teeth. When he spoke, the words were ground out between them. "This is never going to work if you insist on enraging me upon no provocation whatsoever."

"I wouldn't say *no* provocation. You did stab me," I pointed out helpfully.

"That was an accident, but you can be bloody certain the next time I do it, it will be with complete deliberation."

"Oh, fustian. You may bluster and storm, but we both know there shall not be a next time. I saw your face, Stoker. You were utterly horrified that I was injured and spared no time in coming to my aid. In fact, I am beginning to think your quickness is one of your finer qualities, in spite of the complications into which it has led us." He spluttered a little at this, but I studiously ignored him. "Now, if we take the excellent example of Arcadia Brown, Lady Detective, as our model, we must proceed in an orderly and rational fashion. Method must be our watchword, and in that case, I think we ought to focus our attentions on the baron himself. After all, the victim is the logical place to begin our investigation, is it not?"

"What qualities?" he asked with a suddenness that confused me.

"I beg your pardon?"

"You said I have fine qualities. What are they?"

"It is not nice to put someone on the spot, Stoker," I told him primly.

"Very well. We have established I am not nice. What am I, then?"

I tipped my head, thinking hard. "You are enthusiastic. I admire that. You have a curious mind, which is an excellent thing in a scientist. And you are, notwithstanding the recent unfortunate occurrence, rather good with knives and conjuring tricks. Now, about the baron—"

"That is all? The list in its entirety? I am enthusiastic and curious and I can pull a rabbit from a hat?"

"Oh, can you? I haven't seen that, but it sounds like great fun." I smiled kindly to show him that I meant it, but he replied with a curl of his upper lip.

"That is really what you think of me," he said, his tone one of mystification. "You have just described a seven-year-old boy."

I shrugged. "Some folk mature earlier than others, Stoker. It is no fault of your own."

"I am above thirty years of age. I have led, not accompanied, but *led* expeditions to Amazonia and the Galapagos. I have discovered forty-two species of animal never before named in the known world. I have seen active combat in naval battles. And you have reduced me to a moronic child who asks questions and performs coin tricks."

"I did not mean to hurt your feelings," I began, but he waved me off with a dismissive gesture.

"You never really know how others see you," he said. "But thank you for that illuminating description."

"It is simply what I have experienced of you," I pointed out. "You must admit your lesser qualities have been far more to the fore than your noble ones. Aside from your expert medical care of me—involving a situation for which you were at least in part responsible—you have been churlish and impatient, quick to anger, impulsive, suspicious, and frequently rude."

"Well, thank God I am not the sensitive sort," he said lightly. "Else I might think you didn't like me."

"I like you in spite of those qualities," I assured him. "I do not like people who are easy to get along with. I would far rather keep company with the hedgehog than the squirrel."

"Don't you mind the prickles?" he asked, and I had the oddest sensation he was laughing at me.

"Prickles don't frighten me," I returned stoutly. "Not even yours."

"I shall make a note of that," he said soberly.

SIXTEEN

IT HAD BEEN ON the tip of my tongue to tell Stoker about the ransacking of Wren Cottage, but his reaction to learning about Mr. de Clare had been so unguarded, I could not bring myself to shatter his peace twice in one afternoon. The story would keep, and I consoled myself with the thought that it would give him a fresh opportunity to rage at me when I did get around to telling him—an activity he clearly enjoyed. Besides, he had the *rebenque* fight to prepare for, and I believed it could not help his chances to have additional distractions. He insisted upon extracting a promise from me that I would go straight to bed and not tax my strength further.

I gave it to him because, in my experience, it is far better to tell a man what he wants to hear and then do as you please than attempt to reason with him. I counted to one hundred after he left, then slipped out of the caravan. The crowd was gathering as it did every night, but I noticed the change immediately. There was something extra in the air, some new hum of anticipation, and I realized with a sickening twist of my stomach that it was bloodlust. They were here to see something extraordinary, and the professor had done all in his power to ensure folk knew about it. A dozen of the riggers and acrobats had been pressed into service, distributing handbills, and I snatched one as I passed. I skimmed it hastily, then read it again in mounting horror.

I dashed as quickly as I could to the small tent where Stoker was preparing.

I found him removing his coat and waistcoat with studied resignation and brandished the handbill at him. "Have you seen this?"

"Veronica, you gave me your word that you would rest," he said, his expression thunderous.

"I lied, and we can discuss that to whatever length you wish, but later. Have you seen this?" I demanded.

He did not take it. "I have."

"Did you know the professor meant to use your real name when he advertised the fight?"

"No." His voice was clipped. "I knew he was angry with me over an incident that happened a few years ago, but I thought we were past it."

"You mean the departure of Baby Alice—Sirena as she came to be, thanks to your efforts."

"You have been busy," he said, taking up his *rebenque*.

"I had the story from Salome. I know he blamed you when Alice left."

"Yes, well, I never realized quite how far the professor was willing to carry a grudge."

I looked down at the smudged letters on the handbill. THE FIGHT OF THE CENTURY. ACCUSED MURDERER TEMPLETON-VANE TO CROSS WHIPS WITH THE LARGEST MAN ON EARTH! It was the tawdriest piece of sensationalism I had ever seen. I screwed the paper into a ball and threw it aside.

"Stoker, he has exposed you. It is only a matter of time before someone at this fight realizes you are wanted by Scotland Yard."

"I understand that," he said coolly. "It means we must leave this place as soon as the fight is over."

"No, we ought to leave now! What possible reason is there to stay?"

He gave me a long, level look. "Which one would you like? Pride? Obligation? After all, I do owe him for the past few days' keep. He has been kind enough to present me with a bill. If I don't work it off, he can send the bailiffs after us. And I already have quite enough people interested in my whereabouts."

He tested the weight of the *rebenque*'s handle, flipping it lightly from one hand to the other.

"This is my fault," I began.

He paused long enough to take me by the shoulders. "No, it isn't. The choice to do this is mine."

"Are you quite certain . . . that is, a fight of this sort requires a particular state of mind, I should imagine."

He gave me a look that was almost pitying, and when he smiled it was the smile of a vengeful god. "My dear Veronica, I am surprised you have not already learned—everyone has a capacity for cruelty. Not everyone gets the chance to exercise it."

He pushed me gently away. "Now, go back to the caravan and pack your bag. We will leave when this is finished."

Naturally, I did no such thing. I circled around the exhibition tent to the front and slipped behind Mornaday, who was one of the fellows manning the entrance. He gave me a nod as I slid inside, careful to keep to the back and out of the way of the jostling crowd. The air smelled of tobacco and sweat and the noise was indescribable. I glanced idly at the fellow next to me. I recognized him as one of the riggers, the men whose job it was to secure the many ropes that supported the various tents. Their main responsibilities were upon setting and striking the campsites, and in the meantime, the professor often set them to odd jobs. This one seemed bent upon his task, and I realized with a start he was holding a *rebenque*. He hunched over it, as if to shield it from view, but I was close enough to watch him about his business. He removed the handle of the whip, unscrewing the end to reveal the hollow cavity inside. Carefully, he filled it with iron weights, packing the iron with bits of sacking so it made no noise. He reassembled the handle so that it looked precisely the same, only now it weighed significantly more, I realized. And with a rush of outrage, I knew exactly where that *rebenque* was bound. The men shouted as they laid wagers upon the outcome, and I was not surprised to find the odds were laid heavily in Colosso's favor.

He was an utter beast of a man, and when he entered the tent, a great roar fairly shook the ground. He was stripped to the waist—the better to display his musculature—and his body had been coated with a thin film of oil. His head and face were shaven, apart from his vast mustaches, which were waxed to curl at the end, giving him the look of a diabolical ram. He smiled, showing a mouth full of brown and broken teeth, as he lifted his arms to goad the crowd to louder cheers.

Suddenly, the spectators fell silent. Stoker had entered, also stripped to the waist, to prevent his opponent from grasping his shirt. While his physique was impressive on its own merit, in comparison to Colosso's bulk it seemed slight as thistledown. I might have prayed then, but I was too engrossed in the battle at hand. The professor himself deigned to introduce them, sitting to the side of the ring in a padded chair, Otto beside him playing a rousing tune. The ring was marked out in chalk, and the center of it was beaten earth covered in sawdust, the better to soak up the blood, I realized. For one terrible moment, my vision swam, but I kept to my feet, digging my nails into my palms for stimulation.

The professor gave his little speech, his eyes bright with malice. Colosso's name elicited cheers from the crowd, a hectic adoration he accepted with an exaggerated bow. But when the professor said Stoker's name, a harsh murmur descended, and I heard one or two brave souls mutter, "Murderer!"

The professor stated the rules of the fight. Each man would be equipped with a *rebenque*. Striking with any other weapon or with the bare hand was not permitted. Neither was kicking or any sort of grappling hold. The first man to leave the circle would forfeit the fight.

Otto's music slid into something approaching a fanfare. "And now," the professor intoned, "let us commence with this contest of brute strength and cunning!"

Stoker already held his *rebenque*, but Colosso turned to take his from the rigger I had seen. Unlike Stoker's unadulterated weapon, the one Colosso held now carried a significant advantage, and my gaze darted wildly about the tent as I tried to determine how best to warn Stoker.

The professor gave a flourish of his hand and the two men advanced. Each now held a *rebenque* in his right hand, and to my horror, I saw them grip each other by the left forearm. At such enforced proximity, it would be impossible for Stoker to escape Colosso's blows, blows unfairly multiplied by the iron in his handle. I opened my mouth to scream a warning but instantly thought better of it. In that crowd, gripped as it was by bloodlust, we would be torn to pieces for disappointing them. Instead, I stepped forward, holding my breath as the combatants raised their arms. Instinctively, I reached into my pocket and stroked Chester's tiny velvet head. But there was no comfort to be had, no matter how small.

Stoker struck first, and the sharp crack of that whip was

a sound I would never forget. There was something primal about the collision of rawhide upon human flesh, and Colosso took a large step backward as the *rebenque* connected with his cheek.

But he recovered his footing, coming back to give Stoker a smile as he spat out a mouthful of his own blood. Stoker circled, attempting to keep him off his balance, an excellent strategy given the larger man's bulk. But there was nothing he could do against the strength of his blows, and Colosso landed four of them in quick succession, whip cracks against Stoker's torso, each leaving a smart red weal across his chest.

It was then that I realized Colosso was merely toying with him. The first blows were not intended to do anything other than let Stoker know that he could hit him whenever he liked—and that the blows to come would bring pain unlike anything he had ever known.

"Do it quickly," I muttered, knowing the futility of it. Barring a miracle, Stoker was going to get badly beaten, perhaps even killed, and I could do nothing to stop it.

But then the miracle happened. Colosso struck him with the handle of his *rebenque*, just once, but the blow to his cheek was enough. Stoker staggered back, still gripping Colosso's forearm in his own as blood streamed from his face. I saw him shake his head as if to clear it, his gaze coming to rest upon Colosso's weapon. He understood then, from the force of that blow, that the weight was not what it should have been. And the knowledge that Colosso had taken unfair advantage of him was as a red flag to a bull.

Folk talk of the berserker rages of the Vikings, of the chaotic fury of the woad-painted Celt, and these must have been fearsome sights to behold. But no heated anger could ever match Stoker's cold dismantling of Colosso. He made no moves out of blind wrath; each was as deliberate and calculated as a battlefield strategy, and each designed to deliver the most pain he could possibly inflict.

First, he tossed aside his own, lighter *rebenque*. With a speed so quick I could not follow it, he reached for Colosso's weapon, wrapping the rawhide thong around his broad palm. It took only a single lightning flick of his strong wrist to wrest the thing from Colosso's grasp. He flipped it once into the air, catching it on the descent. The weighted handle fit neatly into his fist, and he used it to break the larger man's jaw in two places. It took a surgeon to know exactly where to hit and a born fighter to land the blows, but there was no mistaking the sharp crack of splintering bone and the howls of pain as the jaw shattered under Stoker's assault. Colosso staggered to his knees, and Stoker brought the *rebenque* down one last time, sharply under his ear, sending him neatly into unconsciousness. With slow, deliberate precision, he lifted the larger man, his arms shuddering with strain as he hoisted Colosso over his head. He stepped to the edge of the circle, and with one last great effort, he dropped Colosso over the chalk mark and out of the ring.

The crowd roared its outrage, angered that the fight had been so short and they had lost so much, for few of them had wagered upon Stoker. Heedless of their dismay, he dropped the *rebenque* on Colosso's recumbent form and ostentatiously dusted off his hands as he gave the professor a long look of purest hatred. Then he turned on his heel to leave, and the crowd parted for him like the Red Sea before Moses, not a single man daring to stand in his way.

I scuttled out, hurrying to catch up to him as he strode to the caravan. He carried his shirt and coat but made no attempt to put them on. His skin was hot to the touch, as if he were fevered, and I saw as he whipped around to face me that the cool detachment I had witnessed in the tent was merely a façade for a rage so volcanic, he could scarcely contain it.

He opened his mouth, but no words came.

"I know," I told him simply. "I just wish you had broken his skull as well."

He managed a thin smile as I led him into the caravan. I thrust the flask of aguardiente into his hands. He was trembling now, as a horse will tremble after a long race.

"Drink it," I ordered. He did, and when he had taken two long drafts, I packed the flask and hurried him into his clothes, pausing just long enough to daub the blood from his cheek. Luckily, the wound was small, although I suspected it would bruise in spectacular fashion.

"I had forgot," he said when he could manage to speak.

"What?" I asked, thrusting our few belongings into our bags.

"What it feels like to want to take someone apart. I have not felt that sort of anger in years. It leaves one spent."

I could well believe it. The champion of the *rebenque* ring was sweating freely, perspiration darkening his hair and dampening his shirt. His hands were still unsteady, and I did not like his color.

"We cannot stay here," I warned. "Not now that your name is known. Every man in that tent knows who you are. We will have to walk some distance to make our way to the train station undetected. Do you think you can manage?"

He gave me a brilliant smile. "My dear Veronica, if I had to, I could fly."

SEVENTEEN

STOKER WAS AS GOOD as his word. All through the long night of walking, he supported me, weakened as I still was by my recent bout of malaria. He permitted me to lean upon his arm when I grew tired and guided me across streams and over gates. Slipping away from the traveling show was a simple matter. We avoided the horse lines and the late-night carousers, following the edge of the river as it wound downstream towards the town of Clackton. We might have easily caught the train in Butterleigh, but as I pointed out to Stoker, anyone bent on finding us would presume we had taken the most direct route. Stoker had purloined a few shabby coats from inattentive traveling folk, and with these buttoned over our own clothes, we boarded the third-class carriage at Greycott and rode as far as Old Ashton before disembarking. Stoker had kept his eye patch firmly in his pocket, and I had, with a little difficulty, managed to stuff my orchidaceous rose hat into my carpetbag. In our attempts to blend in with other travelers, we could afford as few distinctions as possible. We washed our faces and hands carefully and left the decrepit garments in the public lavatories, each of us emerging with a far more respectable appearance than we had previously presented. We breakfasted heartily at the local inn, finishing just in time to catch the next train. Stoker dipped into his slender funds to purchase a packet of boiled sweets and tickets—first-class this time, as much to muddle any would-be pursuers as to afford us a bit of privacy.

Alone at last, I fixed Stoker with a curious look. "You are the most complex and contradictory man I have ever known," I told him.

He unwrapped a boiled sweet and stuffed it into his mouth. "Shall I take that as a compliment or condemnation?"

"Neither. It is merely a statement of fact. You survived a brutal jaguar attack and spent what I can only imagine was a long and demanding period in the Royal Navy. You have willingly submitted to the extremely painful process of tattooing—not once, but upon multiple occasions. And you entered a *rebenque* fight with a man so fearsome, he ought to have picked his teeth with your femurs. All of this with perfect resignation and fortitude. And yet when a dressmaker's pin stuck you in the shoulder, you roared like a wounded lion."

He considered that a moment, rolling the sweet over his tongue. "There are times when it is entirely safe to show one's vulnerability, to roll over and reveal the soft underbelly beneath. But there are other times when pain must be borne without a murmur, when the pain is so consuming that if you give in to it, even in the slightest, you have lost everything."

"I suppose one might say the same of mental and emotional pain as well as physical," I mused. "One simply gets on with what must be done because if one paused and looked at it full in the face—"

"Then one would never find the strength to go on," he

finished, cracking the sweet between his strong white teeth.

"As Arcadia Brown would say, 'Excelsior!' Ever upward, ever forward."

I expected him to disparage my taste in popular literature again, but he merely inclined his head. "Excelsior," he agreed quietly.

"Your cheek is bleeding again," I told him. He rummaged for a handkerchief, and I realized how handy it was of him to carry scarlet ones. He always seemed to be mopping up blood with them.

"Pity if it scars," he said lightly. "The bastard would wound me on my good side."

"I don't know about that," I replied deliberately. "Both sides look entirely appealing to me."

His hand stilled, his expression inscrutable. "Veronica," he began. But I put up a hand.

"You needn't fear any predation on my part, Stoker. That was not a prelude to seduction. I was merely making an observation. You think those scars are off-putting, and to a woman with a feeble imagination, they might be. But for any woman who appreciates valor and courage, they are more attractive than any perfect profile or unblemished cheek."

For once he was speechless, and I took the opportunity to make myself more comfortable. "I mean to sleep now, Stoker. I advise you to do the same."

I closed my eyes then, as he rested his thoughtful gaze upon me. And in time, I slept.

I roused myself as we drew near to London and woke refreshed, if somewhat stiff. I poked Stoker from his snores.

"Bloody hell, what?" he demanded with all the grace of a bear roused from hibernation.

"We have nearly reached London. Where do we go from here? We cannot return to your workshop if there is a connection betwixt you and the baron. I wonder if we ought to seek out that Mr. de Clare. He was cryptic, to be sure, but he knows something of this business, and he might be able to offer us aid."

Stoker blinked, then rubbed his eyes, pressing hard for a moment. He gave a jaw-cracking yawn and stretched. When he was fully roused, he spoke, his tone stern. "Look here, Veronica, I know you mean to ferret about in this business, but I do not think I can let you do that. Max did entrust me with your safety, remember, and there is no call for you to be exposed to further danger. We don't know what this de Clare fellow is about. Let me see you back to your cottage, and I will find him."

"You! Haring about London when the Metropolitan Police are combing the streets for you? Not bloody likely."

He sighed. "I admit it is a plan not without its difficulties, but I think you will be safe at your cottage."

"It is not my cottage," I reminded him. "I gave it up, and no doubt it has already been let again. Besides, I do not think I would be any better off there than with you." The time had come, and so, drawing in a deep breath, I launched into an explanation of the circumstances under which the baron had found me.

When I finished, a muscle was twitching in his jaw, and when he spoke, it was through clenched teeth. "And did it not occur to you to mention this sooner?"

"We have not been in the habit of sharing confidences," I reminded him. "Besides, the ransacking of the cottage was simply the act of an opportunistic thief who got away with nothing."

"Was it?" He thrust his hands into his hair. "How can you

not see it?"

"I assumed the fellow who broke into my cottage was simply looking to steal whatever was at hand. It is a common enough occurrence during funerals."

"What did he take?"

"Nothing! He got away when I chased him into the garden. He grabbed my arm as if he meant to carry me off, but I do not believe that was his original intention. The baron helped me elude him, and when the fellow ran away, the baron seemed quite overcome. He insisted I was in some sort of danger and that I must go at once with him to London."

"Where he tells me that he is engaged in a matter of life and death and that I must protect you, even at the cost of my own life," Stoker finished.

"Yes, well, that was a bit melodramatic, I admit." I paused. "You look very much as if you're restraining yourself from shaking me."

"Maximilian von Stauffenbach was not melodramatic a day in his life. He was a pragmatist. If he said it was a matter of life and death, it was," he said, fairly spitting the words in his rage.

"And now you think that my thief is the one who broke into the baron's house as well and murdered him?"

"I do not believe in coincidences," he said. "Now tell me everything again. From the beginning."

I did as he bade me, beginning with the funeral and tea with the Clutterthorpes and ending with my arrival upon his doorstep. He shook his head, thrusting his hands again through his unkempt hair. He was beginning to resemble one of the more disheveled Greek gods after a particularly trying day of warfare with the Trojans.

"Why in the name of God didn't he tell me more?" he murmured. He lifted his head, and his expression was grave.

"I ought to have demanded more from him. Instead I allowed him to leave you there with no explanation, only a promise to look after you. Why didn't he tell me?"

I smoothed my skirts. "No doubt he expected to at some future time."

"That is it," he said, comprehension breaking across his face. "He expected to tell me because he did not observe a threat to himself, only to you. He was not the intended target of this murder. *You were*."

I blinked at him. "That is preposterous. I mean it, Stoker. I think you have finally taken leave of your senses."

"I am fully in command of them, I assure you," he replied coldly. "And if you would pause for the merest moment and consider what I am saying, you would see it too. Max did not come back to London alone, Veronica. He brought you. He did not take you to his home, but to mine, a place where no one would think to look for you. Good God, woman, he even told you he believed you were in danger! Why is it so difficult for you to believe someone killed Max in order to get to you?"

"Because I am not that interesting," I told him.

"Someone wanted to get to you," he went on. "They wanted you so badly they broke into your cottage. They followed you to London and they killed Max." He softened his voice marginally. "Veronica, who would want to kill you?"

"No one! You have known me for a handful of days, and yet I would wager you know me better than anyone else now living. I am as you see me. There are no mysteries here, Stoker," I said, almost regretfully. "I wish that I could rend the veil and expose some great secret that would justify what has been done to the baron, but I cannot. I am a spinster reared in a collection of uninteresting villages scattered across England. I write papers about natural history and I collect butterflies and I indulge in harmless love affairs with unattached foreign gentlemen. I know no one; I am no one. Perhaps it was a case of mistaken identity," I added helpfully.

"There was no mistake," he returned, his mouth tightening a little. "Someone wanted to harm you—so badly that they were willing to bludgeon an old man for the privilege. You know something."

"I know nothing," I insisted, but even I could not deny that whatever had befallen the baron seemed to touch upon me, albeit tangentially. "He did say he knew my mother," I told Stoker. It was a slender offering of peace, but it was all I had to give.

"Who was your mother?"

I spread my hands. "I have no idea. But if you and I are going to get to the bottom of this, we must stop playing at distrusting one another."

He curled a lip. "That's rather like a horse thief lecturing the farmer on locking the barn door, is it not? I have come to a conclusion. You insist that you know nothing. I do not believe you. There is a possibility we may both be correct."

"Go on."

"It is just possible that you know something you do not realize you know."

He turned his head, and I noticed the way the lamplight burnished his hair. It had a blue gleam in this light, coal black but with something glimmering in the depths. It was a shame that such hair should be wasted on a man, I thought idly. Any fashionable woman would have given fifty pounds for a wig made of it.

"Veronica?" He waved a hand in front of my face. "Pay attention when I am lecturing you. You can woolgather later."

"Very well. I admit, I have been less than forthcoming. I am done with it. Ask me what you like. I will tell you whatever you wish to know. I ask only the same courtesy in return." He opened his mouth, but before he could protest, I went on swiftly. "And I promise to ask only questions that may be pertinent to the investigation. You may keep your own secrets. Are we agreed?"

I put out my hand, and after a long, agonizing moment, he took it.

"Agreed. And as a pledge of good faith, you will take the first turn. He made no effort to find you after your first guardian, Miss Lucy Harbottle, died. It was only after her sister died and left you quite alone that he took the trouble to come to you. That begs the obvious question, what changed with Miss Nell Harbottle's death?"

I considered a moment. "Well, it left me finally and irrevocably alone in the world. I planned to leave Wren Cottage and begin my travels anew. But he could not have known it. I told no one save the vicar, and that only minutes before the baron arrived."

"Something else, then," he prompted. "What of your inheritance? Did Miss Nell leave you money?"

I smothered a laugh. "Hardly. There were a few notes and coins in her household box, but I left those behind to compensate the landlord for the damages."

"Bank accounts? Investments? Jewelry?"

I shook my head at each of these. "The sole household account was in both of our names and has a current balance of sixteen shillings. I have a little money of my own for traveling, but I keep it in a separate account. As to investments, there were none, and Nell did not wear jewelry save a cross that I buried with her. She had never left it off as long as I had known her and it did not seem right to bury her without it."

His gaze was bright and inquisitive as a monkey's. "Was it valuable?"

I shrugged. "Not in the least."

Stoker gave a gusty sigh. "What else? What could have brought them together?" He seemed to put the question more to himself than to me, so I sat quietly, letting him think.

He was silent some minutes as he pondered, then began to fire questions at me. "How did your aunts live? If there was no money in the bank, where did they acquire the funds to run the household? Did they have other friends? Did they correspond with anyone? Did they have peculiar habits?"

I put up a hand. "One question at a time if we are to be rational about this. First, the money. I do not know from where it came. A sum was paid into the account every quarter. Aunt Nell was quite discreet upon the subject, but she did indicate it was a family legacy. And before you ask, no, I know nothing of her family save that she and Aunt Lucy were born and bred in London. Aunt Lucy did say once they two were the only ones left, so I presume the money was an annuity to be paid for the duration of their lives. As to friends and correspondence, I can tell you quite certainly they had none of either. They were perfectly content with their own society and went out very seldom. They attended church and occasionally served on committees, but they did not go out of their way to make friends. And once we left a village, they did not engage in correspondence with those we had left behind. What else?"

"Peculiar habits," he commented. "Anything that struck you at the time as curious."

"The only habit I can recall is that they insisted upon purchasing a newspaper every day and it had to be the *Times*. They liked to keep current on affairs of the world. Aunt Nell was quite serious, always preoccupied with needlework and the Bible. The only present she ever made me was a motto for my bedroom: 'The Wages of Sin Is Death,'" I told him with a shudder.

"Christ," he said.

"Exactly. But Aunt Lucy made up for it. She was lively and kind, a great gardener. She did not like my traveling, but she understood it. My first butterfly net was a present from her, and she gave me a compass to mark my first expedition," I said, touching the little instrument pinned to my bodice. If I closed my eyes, I could still see her, with her cloud of fluffy white hair and her gentle hands, pressing it into my palm. "So you will always find your way home again, child," she had said, her eyes bright with unshed tears.

Stoker had fallen into a reverie, but he roused himself then, like an opium dreamer slowly emerging from a fugue. "I think I have it," he said. "Your aunts were hiding out after committing a crime."

"Stoker, you astonish me. I cannot believe that your imagination could lead you so far astray as to suggest that those two harmless old women were criminals!"

"Think of it," he insisted. "It is the only logical solution. They have money, enough to live comfortably, but they will not divulge its source. They do not encourage friendships or correspondence. They move from village to village. It makes perfect sense," he finished, sitting back with an air of satisfaction.

"I can think of a dozen explanations just as likely, and none of them involving felonious old women," I returned.

"You cannot name one."

I opened my mouth, then shut it abruptly. "Very well," I said after a moment. "I cannot think of one at present, but I have no doubt I could, and something just as outlandish as you propose. Tell me, Stoker, since you are so persuaded as to their guilt, what crime do you think they committed?"

My voice was sharp with sarcasm, but Stoker's was triumphant. "Kidnapping."

"I beg your pardon?"

"I think they stole you, Veronica. You did not belong to either of them. Where did you come from? They must have taken you. Perhaps your nursemaid was inattentive or your mother very young. You were left in a pram somewhere, no doubt in a park or on a village green, and in a moment of inattention, the Harbottle ladies snatched you up and carried you off."

"Stoker, in spite of your protests to the contrary, I can only assume that your taste in literature tends towards the sensationalist and absurd. The Harbottle ladies did not carry me off. I was a foundling."

"Ah, and where, precisely, were you found?"

"Oh, for heaven's sake, I cannot say! I never asked and they never told me. They were very close about their past. We did not speak of such things."

"What did you talk about?"

I puffed out a sigh. "I told you—gardening with Aunt Lucy, needlework and sin with Aunt Nell. Those were their sole interests and comprised the bulk of their conversation. Aunt Nell also supervised the cooking; Aunt Lucy taught me the rudiments of nursing. I read aloud to them in the evenings. That is the whole of it."

"It sounds a dreary life," he said suddenly.

"Of course it was dreary, but it was all I knew, and that made it bearable—at least until I discovered butterflying and the freedom it provided. When I was eighteen, I left on my first expedition to Switzerland in search of Alpine varieties. I sold the specimens to collectors and made enough money to fund another expedition, this one further afield, and that is how matters progressed for the next several years. The aunts did not like it, but the money was my own, and so they could not prevent me. I traveled, I came home for visits, and I nursed

Aunt Lucy and later Aunt Nell."

"Tell me about your aunt Nell's death."

I sighed. "A series of apoplexies. Her first was some months ago, a little after Christmas. It was quite a severe one, robbing her of much movement and most of her speech. The doctor wrote to me in Costa Rica and I organized my passage home. I found her much altered from the woman I had always known. The doctor dosed her heavily with morphia to keep her calm and quiet. A few months after her first attack, she suffered another apoplexy, much more violent than the first, and when she regained consciousness, it became clear she had entirely lost the power of speech. She tried to write, but that, too, was beyond her abilities, and the doctor said it was kinder to keep her under the spell of morphia until she passed. When she died, I will confess, it was a relief to me. I did not like to see her thus. She had always been a person of great energy and purpose, and it was difficult to see her reduced to so little."

"I can understand," he said softly. I did not much care for his sympathy in that moment, and I hurried on. "Surely even you must see that this line of inquiry is a dead end. The baron's past is a far likelier vein than mine. Let us begin with the poor gentleman himself. Had he enemies?"

Stoker shook his head. "None of which I am aware."

"He was a foreigner. Do you know whence he came?"

"Coburg. He studied in Brussels for a time and then attended university in Bonn."

"Excellent. And when did he come to this country?"

"Early in the '40s. He was a childhood friend of Prince Albert. After the Prince Consort married Queen Victoria he had some trouble settling in, and he asked Max if he would come and make his home in England. Max had no ties of his own left in Germany. His parents were dead and he had no siblings, so he came."

"Did he see the prince often?"

"Not very. The queen was a demanding wife," Stoker added with a ghost of a smile. "But when she could spare him, the two men had the occasional dinner or ride together. Most often they corresponded by letter. I suspect the prince simply felt more at ease for having one of his own countrymen close at hand."

"No doubt," I mused. "But as interesting as his connection with the prince might be, Prince Albert has been dead for decades and, as far as we know, the baron lived unmolested. If there was any sort of motive to harm him from his friendship with the prince, surely it would have caused some villain to act long ago."

"Agreed. So if the motive is not to be found in his friendship with the Prince Consort, we must look to his more recent past."

"How did you meet him?" I inquired.

"He was a guest lecturer when I was at university. We had common interests, and he was kind enough to act as mentor to me when I had few friends. Later, much later, he saved me," he finished simply.

"Was that the debt you both spoke of when he left me with you? The reason you felt you owed it to him to protect me?"

He nodded, and I thought that would be an end of it, but he spoke, each word as slow and heavy as if he were hewing them from a burial place—a burial place deep within himself. "When I was injured in Brazil, what followed was for me a very dark time. I do not speak of it. I do not even let myself think of it. But there are depths to which a man can sink, and I have plumbed them all. I could not bring myself out of it. I was content to stay there and to die there. My wounds had healed, but my body was in a far better state than the rest," he recalled with a bitter twist of his mouth. "Max sailed halfway around the world to bring me home. If he had not made it his business to search me out, I would have stayed, rotting in a prison I had made for myself, too sunk in despair to find my way out again. It was Max who found me, who cleaned me up and brought me back to England."

I said nothing, and he went on, speaking in a strangely detached voice, as if in a dream. "I did not appreciate it, not at the time. He wanted me to stay with him in London, but I was still too angry, too lost in my own misery. So I left him and went to the traveling show, running away from the truest friend I ever had. He let me go, at least for a while. Eventually, he found me again and asked me to come back to London. By then I was ready to accept the hand he extended. I took the warehouse for my workshop; I resumed my work. But still I resisted his efforts to rehabilitate me completely. It was as if, having once fallen out of the habit of civilized life, I could no longer find it again. Yet Max never gave up on me. He never stopped believing I could pull myself out of this abyss into which I had stumbled." He paused and gave a sharp laugh. "It's funny, really. Do you know what his specialty was? Restoration. He loved nothing more than to take old paintings—pieces damaged by neglect or time or war—and make them whole again. Pity he never finished with me."

He looked suddenly away, and I realized he must be feeling the baron's loss far more keenly than I had suspected.

"You said he owns—owned," I corrected sadly, "the building where you reside."

"Yes, I took it from him at a peppercorn rent when I left the traveling show. I . . . wanted a place where I could work in solitude." His eyes were shadowed, and I suspected the memories he tried so valiantly to keep at bay were wrestling their way in.

"How long ago was that?"

"Two years."

"And you have lived there since?"

"Yes. Max was generous to a fault. He came round once a month to collect the rent himself and we went to dinner—I suspect more for him to ensure I was having a proper meal than to get his money."

"He was a good friend," I said softly.

Stoker said nothing, just nodded. Impulsively, I touched his hand and he gripped it hard before turning loose of it. "Get on with the questions."

"Did he form any other close attachments that you know of?"

"None. He knew many people, but distantly. Max was more comfortable in his solitude than any person I have ever known. He was entirely happy alone. He had his books and his music and his specimens, and that was all he required. He also carried on a wide correspondence. His friends were far-flung across the globe, but none of them intimate. I probably knew him as well as anyone."

"What of his servants? Did anyone live in?" I asked.

"His housekeeper of twenty years, Mrs. Latham. She looked after him with the help of a succession of rather stupid maids, none of whom lived in. Mrs. Latham broke her leg last year, and Max held her post for her. He even paid the doctor's bills. She has never forgot that. Poor old hen would probably have died for him if she had caught the intruder who killed him."

"Just as well she never got the chance," I said soberly. "If the blackguard showed no compunction at killing the baron, he would have easily murdered her as well. Would she have profited by the baron's death?"

He shrugged. "A small legacy, but Max and I talked once and he told me he intended to leave his fortune—modest as it was—to various museums. Nothing for the servants to tempt them to murder."

"No, and even if they had, that would not explain the ransacking of his study," I said, thinking aloud.

"Unless they were attempting to cover up the crime."

"What a morbid imagination you have," I told him admiringly.

"Veronica, I spend my days up to my elbows in the gore of dead animals. And that is the *least* gruesome occupation I have had."

His mouth had twisted into something like a smile, and I found myself smiling back. The moment caught and held, and in that fleeting connection, something between us shifted. He reached out suddenly and took my hand in his, and when he spoke, there was nothing of the harshness he wore as armor. His voice was low, his eyes pleading.

"Let me go to the police. Whatever happens, you will be safe then."

I felt a hot flicker of anger. "That is not possible. They might—*might*—put me in some sort of protective custody if they believe our story. But it is far likelier they will not. And what happens to you if that is the case? If we take the risk and we're wrong, it is the hangman's noose for you."

"Veronica—" he began.

"I will not gamble with your life!" His gaze held mine, and I wanted so desperately to look away. But I did not, and in the end, he released my hand.

"Very well. I was afraid you would be obstinate, so I made arrangements with my Cornish friend. There is a property in London at our disposal, but only if we are very discreet. There is a skeleton staff in the house at present, and we must keep out of the way."

"What house?"

"Bishop's Folly. It belongs to Lord Rosemorran, the client who owns that bloody elephant. In Marylebone—not the fashionable part, which is all to the good for our purposes. The house itself is massive, but there is another structure on the property, the Belvedere. It was built as a sort of ballroom, but Rosemorran has stuffed it to the rafters with specimens from his travels. With a great deal of luck, we just might manage."

"Very well. We will throw in with Lord Rosemorran and hope for the best," I replied.

Stoker looked as if he wanted to say something else, but instead he merely turned and looked out the window at the passing view and said no more.

EIGHTEEN

SOME HALF AN HOUR later the train arrived and we disembarked amid the bustle of late morning London going about its business. My inclination was to hurry, particularly when I spied a bobby about his rounds, but Stoker held my elbow, restraining my pace. He pointed out, quite rightly, that undue haste might attract unwelcome attention, and so we strolled, for hours it seemed, until we came to our destination. A high brick wall separated us from what I had begun to think of as the Promised Land, but Stoker made no effort to enter by the main gates. Instead he led me to a smaller gate accessible only to those on foot.

"Why are we going in this way?" I asked.

"Because the main gate is always busy. Servants, tradesmen, the family—everyone sees what happens in the main court. This entrance is hardly ever used, and my friend has left us a key."

The brick wall was thickly tapestried in ivy, and Stoker began to burrow behind the fall of greenery, testing the bricks for a loose one.

"That was kind of Lord Rosemorran," I remarked.

"I was not speaking of Lord Rosemorran," he said, removing a brick and brandishing the key that had lain behind.

Before I could ask whom he meant, the gate swung open, and a slender figure clad in black stepped out.

"Cordelia!" Stoker exclaimed.

The lady in question smiled faintly as she beckoned us inside. "Hello, Stoker. Keep the key," she instructed. "You will need it to come and go."

Stoker did as he was bade and we slipped inside the gate while the lady locked up carefully behind.

"Cordelia, you were supposed to be in Cornwall. What are you doing here?" Stoker demanded. He looked none too happy to see her, but it did not seem to distress the lady.

She turned to me, her gaze as forthright as it was welcoming. I must have presented quite a sight, travel-stained and weary, but she was as courteous to me as if I had been a duchess. "You must be Miss Speedwell. I am Lady Cordelia Beauclerk. My brother is Lord Rosemorran and this is his home, Bishop's Folly."

We shook hands, behaving for all the world as politely as two acquaintances at a tea party while Stoker fairly vibrated with impatience. When the niceties had been observed, she turned to him.

"I was in Cornwall, but I decided I could be of more use to you if I were close at hand. I've only just arrived back."

Stoker began to speak, but Lady Cordelia shook her head. "Not here. Come."

She turned and we followed. This part of the Rosemorran estate was a sort of pretty wilderness, thick with trees and laced with paths. She led the way down one and then another, twisting us around to the heart of the property. Dotted here and there were the most fantastical buildings I'd ever seen—a miniature Parthenon, a small Gothic chapel, and even a

Chinese pagoda. These she sped past, but when we came to a little pond overlooked by a small cottage joined to a miller's tower, she paused.

"Is that—"

She looked at me and smiled. "A replica of Marie Antoinette's toy village? Yes. My great-grandfather was a trifle eccentric. He collected miniature buildings for his amusement. They're mostly crumbling to bits. Fortunately, the Belvedere is quite a different matter. It is utterly enormous and in somewhat better shape, although it is not luxurious," she warned.

"Fear not, Lady Cordelia," I said. "I have lived rough everywhere from the slopes of a Sicilian volcano to an island in the Andaman Sea."

She smiled. "The Belvedere has another advantage. We shan't be disturbed there."

Another bend in the path led to the Belvedere, and I stopped in my tracks, overcome with delighted surprise. The building was far larger than I had imagined, but it was not the size that charmed—it was the complete hodgepodge of architectural styles. A combination of Chambord, Castle Howard, and its namesake in Vienna, this Belvedere was an expanse of honeyed stone capped with lacy towers and a small, elegant dome. Somehow the effect was harmonious even though upon closer inspection it was clear that the place had been imperfectly cared for. One of the towers was crumbling a little, and the windows were overgrown with tendrils of ivy reaching to clasp each other across the panes of glass.

I realized then that Lady Cordelia had paused for my reaction. "It is spectacular," I told her truthfully.

She smiled. "You may not be so generous after you have seen the inside." She made to enter, but just as her hand came to rest upon the latch, there was a noise behind us, the scrape of a shoe upon gravel, and the three of us whirled as one.

A servant stood there, a lady's maid judging from her sober silk gown and elaborate lace cap. Her expression was avid as she looked from Stoker to me to Lady Cordelia. She held in her hands a taffeta evening slipper.

"I beg pardon, milady, but I have only discovered your slipper is torn. If you wish to wear it tonight, I must mend it now, but there is the unpacking to do. Which shall I do first?"

The question was the rankest pretense for snooping—that much was apparent even to me. She must have smelled an intrigue and followed her mistress to discover what she was about. But the intrusion did not seem to ruffle Lady Cordelia, who merely inclined her head.

"Ask Mrs. Bascombe for the loan of one of the parlormaids to help you unpack, Sidonie," she instructed. "When that is finished, you will have plenty of time to mend the slipper. And please tell Cook I shall want a cold luncheon but I intend to dine out tonight."

The maid was well trained. She asked no questions, merely bobbed a curtsy and turned to do her mistress's bidding, but her eyes were curious, and they lingered on Stoker with real warmth. She darted a glance over her shoulder at him as she walked away, but if Lady Cordelia noticed, she pretended not to. For his part, Stoker appeared acutely uncomfortable, and he hurried inside the Belvedere as soon as the door was open.

I followed, and for a few moments, while my eyes adjusted to the gloom, I saw nothing but monstrous shapes lurking in the darkness. The ivy at the windows provided a shifting, aqueous light, but Lady Cordelia lit a series of lamps, bringing warmth and life to the place. I moved into the heart of the Belvedere. Beyond the entrance lay an absolute wonderland, a paradise the likes of which I could never have imagined existed on earth. To call it a room was to make a new definition for that word; it was larger and grander than any room ever to claim the name. The ceiling was so high I could scarcely make it out. It soared nearly sixty feet overhead—alternating panels of painted plaster and wood with enormous skylights, the whole of it culminating in a dome painted with images of the nine Muses.

Two galleries circled the perimeter of the room, one atop the other, joined by a series of staircases, no two alike. The galleries were lined with bookshelves and display cases, each more crowded than the last with specimens. On the ground floor, cases and cabinets and plinths displayed what seemed at first impression to be a microcosm of the world itself. Art, nature, artifact—all were gathered there, as if to pay homage to the accomplishments of man and universe. A stuffed pangolin peered inquisitively at an Egyptian sarcophagus while a Leonardo sketch kept vigil over a mask from the Inuit people of the polar regions. A statue of Hermes, naked and muscular, skimmed past a pair of nesting dodos on his winged feet. Just behind him, a collection of corals fanned out in fiery precision, a flaming backdrop to a tortoiseshell some four feet across. And these were merely the treasures I could see. The rest of the vast room stretched before us, populated with thousands of such specimens.

I turned to Stoker and he gave me an unaccustomed grin. "Go on."

I followed Lady Cordelia as she wove her way through the great hall, pointing out her brother's prizes, each more astonishing than the last.

"This is from Pompeii," she told me, drawing my attention to a recumbent form. It was a dog, curled protectively into death, and I stared at Lady Cordelia, aghast.

"Oh, do not be alarmed, Miss Speedwell, it is not the real thing, I assure you. It is a plaster model acquired by my grandfather on his Grand Tour. That is the trouble with the

Beauclerk men. They are acquisitive as magpies. They see something they like and crate it up and bring it home, no matter the impracticality." She sighed. "And the result is that they have stuffed both houses—this one and the country seat in Cornwall—to the rafters. I have many times suggested that his lordship open it to the public, charge admission, and let people enjoy these treasures. It hardly seems fair to permit these things to molder away in here with only a handful of people ever seeing them."

I turned slowly, taking in the enormity of the room and its many treasures. "A generous impulse."

Her expression was rueful. "One that may be left to my nephew. There is so much work here, one hardly knows where to begin."

She nodded towards the lower of the two upper galleries. "There is a snug of sorts up there—a stove and a few sofas, even a campaign bed that once belonged to the Duke of Wellington. I think we ought to make some tea and hold a council of war," she said decisively.

I followed her up the stairs, turning once to look back to Stoker. "I have only myself to blame," he muttered, and I smiled to myself, thinking that he did indeed seem to be beset by managerial females.

In spite of her lofty rank, Lady Cordelia lit the stove and set to making tea, and I was able to observe her at my leisure. She was taller than I, and slender, although I suspected she owed this more to art than to nature. Her complexion was purest English rose, a gentle flush of pale pink upon an alabaster cheek, and her hair was dark gold, waving against her temple becomingly. In her first youth, she must have been extraordinarily pretty, but now—approaching thirty I guessed—she was handsome, the sort of comeliness that owes everything to elegant bones and serenity. She moved quietly and calmly, and it was this very tranquility I found so appealing. I aspired to such sangfroid, but I had found it impossible to reconcile detachment with passionate fervor. One may be elegant or enthusiastic, but seldom both.

If she was aware of my scrutiny, it did not offend her, and in a very short time we were comfortably ensconced with a tin of shortbread. She handed me a cup and smiled. "Napoleon's wedding china," she told me.

"Rather different from Stoker's notion of hospitality," I remarked.

She looked to him and they exchanged smiles. Their friendship was a comfortable thing, and no doubt of long duration to make them so easy with one another.

He put down his cup. "Lady C.," he began.

"Do not think to scold me," she remonstrated softly. "I read the newspapers before I sent them on. I could not stay away and do nothing to help. I know how black things are against you at present."

"All the more reason for you to have stayed in Cornwall," he argued. "If this all goes south, you might have at least been able to persuade the authorities that you had no notion we were here. Now—"

"Now I shall be able to offer you and Miss Speedwell proper assistance," she finished. Her smooth brow furrowed slightly. "It is unfortunate that Sidonie saw you. She is a terrible gossip, but if I explain the danger properly," she said to Stoker, "she will hold her tongue. You know how she feels about you."

I tipped my head. "How does she feel about you?" I asked Stoker pleasantly.

He flushed a dull red, but it was Lady Cordelia who replied. "My maid has conceived a tendresse for Stoker. Somehow she got it into her head that he is a proper buccaneer and she has never quite recovered. The French can be very suggestible," she added. I was beginning to like Lady Cordelia.

She turned to Stoker. "You must know it never entered my mind that you might be guilty," she said quietly.

"Bless you for that."

Her smile was tinged with sadness. "I know how much the baron loved you. You would never have repaid that affection with violence."

I interjected. "You, too, knew the baron, Lady Cordelia?"

She nodded. "Through my brother. His lordship collects, well, everything, really, as you can see," she said with a gesture that encompassed the whole of the Belvedere. "And the baron enjoyed art. My brother first made his acquaintance a decade ago. They attended an auction, both of them bent on acquiring a painting of lovebirds rumored to have belonged to Catherine the Great. The bidding was furious, and in the end, both of them were outbid. They consoled each other by way of a rather splendid bottle of port."

"Friendships have been built upon less solid foundations," I mused.

Her smile deepened. "Indeed. In any event, they became quite good friends. It was through the baron that we met Stoker. We were deeply saddened to hear of the baron's murder," she added with a pensive look.

"How did you learn of it?" I asked.

"Veronica," Stoker said, a warning edge to his voice. "What are you implying?"

"Nothing. I merely wanted to know his lordship's reaction." It was a lie of omission. Naturally, I was curious about the earl's reaction to his friend's death, but it also occurred to me that the Beauclerk family was the common ground between Stoker and the baron. Perhaps they knew more than they ought.

Stoker guessed my thoughts and disabused me of them swiftly. "His lordship and Lady Cordelia would be as likely to bludgeon Max to death as the queen would to ride naked in

Trafalgar Square," he said brutally.

To her credit, Lady Cordelia was not offended. She lifted a graceful hand against my quick apology. "Please, do not trouble yourself. It is the most natural thing to wonder, and I should have doubted your intelligence if you hadn't. The truth, as it so often is, Miss Speedwell, is quite prosaic. The baron was a friend who came to dinner two or three times a year. He and my brother occasionally met for lunch or attended art lectures together, but that is the whole of it. We did not know his friends, save Stoker, and we had no motive to harm him. I give you my word."

Her word could have been a lie, but I would have staked my own life upon that smooth, guileless brow. Lady Cordelia was that rarest of things—a creature without malice. She reminded me of a statue I had seen once in Sicily of a placid Madonna, above worldly cares and sweetly indulgent of those below her.

She went on. "As for my brother, the best way to explain Ambrose is to say he is vague and oblivious. It isn't his fault, of course, but he spends nearly all his time with his collections. He takes almost no notice of the world around him. That is why I have the management of his household. I keep his account books; I organize his staff. I even oversee the rearing of his children since the death of his countess."

I must have looked surprised, for she paused, and when she spoke again her voice was softer. "I love my brother dearly, Miss Speedwell, but I am not blind to his faults. He would be less than useless at murder. He has no stomach for the gritty realities of life. He couldn't even bring himself to talk about the baron's death with me. One of the advantages of being a lady," she said with a sudden wry twist of her pretty mouth. "Gentlemen seldom like to discuss unseemly things with us."

"But unseemly things are often the most interesting," I pointed out.

"Indeed." She gave a sudden smile, illuminating her face like a rainbow after a storm. "But we have more pressing matters to speak of than my brother. Is it possible to prove that you were not at the baron's house on the night of his murder?" she asked Stoker.

"Well," he said, tugging a bit at his collar, "in point of fact, I was with someone."

"Excellent!" she said, but almost as soon as the word fell from her lips, she followed Stoker's glance to me and gave a little sigh. "If you spent that evening together unchaperoned, I am afraid the damage to Miss Speedwell's reputation will render her a less than desirable witness to your whereabouts."

"Oh, that is the least of our troubles," I told her with a wave of the hand. I outlined—as briefly and delicately as clarity would permit—my previous romantic entanglements. "So you see," I finished, "the Queen's Counsel would label me a harlot and discount entirely any alibi I could provide. Also, I suspect leaving Little Byfield in the company of a gentleman I had only just met and spending the night with him in the privacy of his carriage would not be received at all well."

True to the maxim that a lady never betrayed shock, Lady Cordelia merely inclined her head. "Is there anything else?" she inquired pleasantly.

Stoker covered his face with his hands. "For the last several days we have been living as man and wife in a traveling show," he said, his words muffled.

Lady Cordelia gave a brisk sigh. "Well, I don't suppose you could have managed things much worse unless you had actually been found standing over his body with the fossil in hand."

Stoker winced, dropping his hands. "Is that what killed him? A fossil? The newspaper gave no details."

Lady Cordelia's sympathy was very nearly palpable. "I

sent only the edition with the briefest account. I thought it might be less painful for you to hear the details from a friend rather than read about them in some sensationalist story." They exchanged a look of understanding. "But I will tell you whatever you need to know. As far as the murder weapon is concerned, the investigators established it was a rather heavy piece of something—a shell, I think it was."

"An ammonite," he said flatly. "It was a fossilized shell. I know the one. He always kept it on his desk. What was it, then? A crime of opportunity?"

She shrugged. "The inquest determined it was murder by person or persons unknown. Signs of a brief struggle, and immediate flight when the housekeeper, Mrs. Latham, came to investigate."

"Was she harmed?"

"She was pushed down quite roughly and hit her head. She remembers nothing, only an impression of darkness and pounding feet. But she will be all right. She has gone to stay with her sister in Brighton," she said in the same distracted tone. She fell silent a moment, then roused herself, her manner suddenly brisk. "I think it best if we do not apprise his lordship of your presence here just yet. He returned from Cornwall with me and is locked in his study, wrestling with a rather thorny paper he is writing for the *Journal of Antiquity*. He would not thank me for the interruption. We will hope that by the time he is finished, the matter will be resolved. In the interim, you must stay here in the Belvedere."

"Are you certain we will not disturb his lordship?" I asked.

"My dear Miss Speedwell, when my brother is engaged in his writing, you could walk into his study unclothed and take a nap upon his desk and he would not notice. Besides, we cannot hope to hide you from him forever. Merely until we can choose a propitious time to tell him. Now, I shall require a scarf or glove. Some piece of raiment that I may use to introduce your scent to the dog."

I unwrapped the bit of scarlet silk I had worn at my throat and handed it over.

"That will do nicely. If you happen to see a creature that looks like an overgrown bear roaming about, that is Betty. Once she has your scent, she will not harm you."

"Betty?"

"Short for Betony," Stoker informed me. "His lordship's sheepdog from the Caucasus. Two hundredweight on a lean day."

"Heavens," I murmured.

Stoker turned to Lady Cordelia. "What about the gardeners? And the children?"

"The children are away," she told him. "The late countess's family like to have them for a few weeks at the end of spring each year. The younger ones, that is. Hugo and Casper are at school. As for the gardeners, so long as you take the path back through the shrubbery to the little gate, you should not be seen. They are busy planting an herb knot near the kitchens and the work is exacting." She gestured to a narrow door in the paneled wall. "Various earls through the centuries have used this as a sort of sanctum, a place to escape the family. They fitted it out with various comforts. You will find the necessary domestic offices in there, a sink and . . . and, er, other plumbing conveniences. The Medici cabinet by the stove has a few tins of cake and tea and other things to eat. Please help yourselves, and I will bring more provisions later. In the meantime, rest and make yourselves at home among the collections. I think you will enjoy them, Miss Speedwell, and Stoker has always longed for the chance to have a good rummage."

"You have thought of everything," Stoker said quietly.

A touch of rose blossomed on her cheeks at the compliment.

"I try." She stood and extended her hand to me. "Miss Speedwell, a moment?"

I took her hand and walked with her to the door, where we were just out of Stoker's earshot.

"Miss Speedwell, it is not my place to say this, nor your responsibility to respond, but I hope you will do your best to keep him occupied."

"I am afraid I don't take your meaning, my lady," I began.

She gave me a thoughtful look. "Then let me speak plainly. By whatever means necessary, I hope you will keep him from boredom. It is the demon that torments him and drives him to drink. It will destroy him if he lets it. And we who are his friends must not permit that to happen."

I nodded. "I will do what I can, Lady Cordelia."

She squeezed my hand and slipped away, graceful as a fawn as she departed.

I returned to the snug and fixed him with a challenging eye. "You have heard what Lady Cordelia suggests. That we hide out here in safety until the police have found the culprit."

"I did," he said in a perfectly reasonable tone.

"And you agree that this would be the most logical, sensible course of action?"

"I do."

"And you understand I mean to do precisely the opposite?"

His mouth curved into a slow smile. "I do. Where shall we begin?"

I returned the smile with one of my own. "At the beginning, of course."

NINETEEN

OVER TEA AND A tin of shortbread we plotted our strategy.

"Let us establish a working hypothesis upon which we both can agree," I began.

"The trouble is, we have bloody few facts upon which we can hypothesize," he grumbled.

I waved a hand. "A trifling matter. We shall turn our attention to the fact at hand. The baron was murdered in his own study. Not by either of us," I added firmly. "Further, we may infer that the crime was one of passion and not the culmination of some monstrous scheme."

"And how may we infer that?"

"The lack of a weapon. The murderer seized a paperweight, which you have identified as an ammonite belonging to the baron, a piece that rested upon his desk. It was the perfect weapon of opportunity for a careless villain who had brought no weapon of his own."

"Or a clever villain who would rather use a weapon belonging to the victim than something which can be traced to him," he pointed out.

I frowned. "I like my theory better."

"I had little doubt you would," he conceded graciously. "Carry on."

"In either event, the man—I think we can agree it was a man?"

He nodded. "Max was tall. I should think a woman would have to be uncommonly strong to have wielded that ammonite to such effect." An expression of singular distaste had settled upon his mouth and I hurried on.

"So our man was either a creature of sudden temper who quarreled with the baron and seized the nearest weapon at hand or a cool fellow with a cunning brain who plotted this out."

"Without knowing which, it will be difficult to track him," Stoker mused.

"Why so?"

He shrugged. "Tracking is my stock in trade, a skill I learned as a boy and perfected as a man. One must understand one's prey. I can track a jaguar through a jungle for forty miles and never lose him, but this—"

He looked suddenly tired then, and I realized what the past days had cost him. He had borne the loss of a beloved friend—one of the few he could claim. He had held my life in his hands, and he had confronted the ghosts of his past at every turn.

I thought of Lady Cordelia's parting words. Deliberately, I reached into my bag and withdrew the flask of aguardiente. I poured a measure into his teacup and handed it over.

He drank it slowly, the color coming back into his face as he sipped. I could almost see the warmth passing through him, kindling his blood where it had run cold and slow.

"Now," I said with an air of command, "try again. If you were to track the baron's murderer, where would you begin?"

"In the baron's study," he said promptly. "It is the last

place we know the fellow has been."

"But surely the police—"

"The police are only as good as the men they send. They are a motley crew, composed of respectable tradesmen's sons and vagabonds, liars, and clerks. Some are no better than the filth they arrest."

"You have no cause to think well of them," I observed.

"I do not." His mouth was a thin, hard, bitter line. "If they sent a blackguard who walks a beat to collect protection money and harass the prostitutes, the killer could have left a case full of calling cards and they still would not have found him. If they sent one of their best, then the place will have been gone over thoroughly. Even then, something may have been missed."

"Very well. We shall begin at the baron's. You will apply yourself to seeking out the spoor of this particular leopard," I said with some relish.

"And what will you be doing?" he demanded.

"I will be attempting to discover what the fellow was after."

"After?"

"Yes. He must have come for something. What was it? A quarrel over property? A personal misunderstanding? A lady?"

He shook his head slowly. "Max had no romantic attachments, not in all the years I have known him. He never spoke of anyone, at least. I always had the sense that he had no interest in love affairs."

"Really? I formed quite the opposite impression. I think he was a great deal in love with my mother."

"Why?"

"I haven't the faintest. But during our journey to London, he mentioned something about how I looked exactly like her. Something in his manner, the soft way he spoke of her. It was quite moving."

He sat back in his chair, his mouth now slack with disbelief.

"I could smother you with that tea cozy and no one would blame me," he said in a voice thick with emotion.

"Whyever should you want to?"

"Because, you daft, impossible woman, you have been concealing a possible motive from me for the whole of the time we have been together!"

"What motive? I merely said he seemed attached to my mother."

"And I am telling you, he had no love affairs. If he loved her, it was *the* love affair of his life. Something possibly worth his life, even."

"Rubbish," I said stoutly. "He told me nothing at all about her save that I look like her and that he would explain everything to me when he had the chance."

"A chance that never came," Stoker observed. "Rotten luck for you. I am sorry."

I shrugged. "At least I know a little more now than I once did. The baron knew her, and that is a place to begin."

"Indeed."

"So how do we get into the baron's house? The poor misused housekeeper is gone to Brighton," I reminded him.

"Another point for your argument that the killer has not a cool and cunning brain," he told me. "He was interrupted in searching the study. A more experienced fiend would have simply killed Mrs. Latham as well and carried on. He hurried out, giving her a knock instead."

"Searching the study," I began.

He lifted his eyes to mine. "Like your cottage."

"The same fellow?"

"Possibly. But what can he be looking for?"

"That is what we must ascertain. I presume a spot of housebreaking is in order?"

He grinned, a smile of rare and devilish charm. He dipped

into his pocket with his fingertips. "No need. I have a key."

"Then we need only wait for nightfall," I said. "What shall we do with ourselves in the meantime?"

His gaze brightened, but before he could speak, Lady Cordelia returned carrying a basket. "I have brought food—enough for tonight and tomorrow morning. I thought it best if I did not come down here every time. It might arouse suspicion."

I peered into the basket and saw a large cheese, a few roasted fowls, some cold potatoes, wedges of game pie, a loaf of bread, and the remains of a small saddle of beef. There was butter and jam and even a jar of chutney jostling for space with crisp apples.

"Bless you, Lady Cordelia. We shall feast like princes."

Stoker's gaze slid away from hers, and she tipped her head thoughtfully. "I presume from your guilty air that you intend to ignore my good advice and go out?"

Stoker looked abashed, but I refused to be cowed. "We do."

"To the baron's, no doubt?"

"Indeed," I said, willing Stoker to silence. I had the unshakable feeling he would try to apologize for our plan, perhaps even be talked out of it, and I had no intention of permitting that to happen.

"Of course you do. I ought to have suspected it. No creature of feeling and spirit would be content to sit by and let matters take their course. All nature would rebel against it," she acknowledged. I gave her a gracious nod, pleased she saw things my way.

She sighed. "In that case, here is a revolver," she said, handing over a small weapon perfectly sized for a lady's hand. "Make certain you leave after eleven. That is when Betony is taken out for her evening patrol of the grounds."

She left us then, and I realized Stoker had not said a word for the duration of her visit. "What ails you, Stoker? Cat got your tongue?"

He stroked his chin thoughtfully as he stared at the revolver. "I was merely thinking that it may have been a very grave mistake to introduce you to Lady C. If the pair of you ever put your minds to it, you could probably topple governments together."

I smiled as I pocketed the weapon. "One thing at a time, dear Stoker. One thing at a time."

Some hours later—after a cold meal of Lady Cordelia's offerings and several games of two-handed whist during which Stoker collected a sizable IOU from me—we ventured forth. I dithered a moment over my hat but in the end opted to lay my favorite rose-bedecked chapeau aside for my second-best, a much smaller and less obtrusive affair decorated with a lush cluster of violets.

Stoker peered at my carpetbag in stupefaction. "How much have you packed in there? It is a veritable Aladdin's cave."

I held up my hatpin to the light, admiring the slender strength of the steel. "Packing a bag efficiently is simply a matter of spatial understanding," I told him. I thrust the point of the pin home, skewering the hat neatly to my loose Psyche knot. He eyed the unguarded tip warily, but I noticed in addition to the blade he usually kept in his lanyard, he slid a second into his boot.

"Good heavens, how much trouble are you expecting?" I demanded.

He blew out the candle. "In my experience it is the trouble you do not anticipate that is the most dangerous." We stood in the darkness for several minutes to let our eyes adjust, saying nothing, scant inches apart. I could hear him breathing, long slow breaths, and smiled to myself. He was calm—almost unnaturally so, and this was precisely what I required in a partner in adventure. At my signal we moved to the door, slipping into the night. He took my hand and led the way through the grounds of Bishop's Folly, following the path we had taken earlier in the day. I expected he would drop my hand once we left the property, but he kept it clasped in his, even as we eased out of the gate and through the darkened streets.

He chose alleyways and quiet parks rather than the well-lighted thoroughfares crammed with the vehicles of the fashionable. We crept across silent squares and ducked into areas thick with shadows. Whilst society went about its business in the broad roads we skirted, the creatures we passed in the shadows were those who made their living by their wits—prostitutes and vagabonds, thieves and blackguards, bent upon their degradations. Once, when we heard the sharp step of a constable upon his rounds, Stoker whisked me into the dark corner of a tradesman's yard, pushing me up against the brick wall as his arms came firmly about me. I hitched my leg around his waist and twined my arms about his neck, knotting my fingers in his hair as he pressed his face into my neck, nuzzling the delicate skin of my ear. The bobby's light flashed our way, illuminating a stocking-clad leg and a glimpse of thigh tight in Stoker's grip. The bobby chuckled, no doubt taking us for a wayward maidservant and her panting swain, and went about his business. We waited a moment, clinging to each other as his footsteps faded into the distance.

Stoker pulled away just enough for me to see his eyes gleaming in the shadows. "He is gone," he said hoarsely.

But his hand still rested upon my thigh and my hands were still knotted in his hair. "In that case, we ought to let go of each other," I said evenly.

He sprang away from me, smoothing his hair as I straightened my skirts. "I must apologize—" he began.

I waved an airy hand. "Think nothing of it. Your quick thinking under the circumstances was commendable," I told him.

He slanted me a curious look but said nothing more.

Arm in arm, we proceeded on our way. After a rather uneventful passage across Hyde Park—we inadvertently disturbed a pair of male lovers entwined beneath a tree who cursed us roundly—we emerged near Curzon Street. Another several minutes saw us safely into the baron's street, a quiet but respectable address, and Stoker led me down to the area, where we gained entrance through the tradesman's door.

There is a stillness to empty houses, and this house was quieter still. It was as if nothing had ever moved there, no one had ever walked its echoing passages. Stoker had dropped my hand when we entered the basement, but as we crept upstairs to the main floor, I reached for his, suddenly very much in need of his warmth. The curtains had been drawn in the front of the house, but not the rear, and the shadows shifted as we walked, as though our very presence stirred something that had been resting only lightly.

"Do you think the baron haunts it?" I whispered.

He whirled on me, nearly upsetting an elephant's foot stuffed with an assortment of walking sticks. "Haunts? Don't be daft."

"It isn't daft. Some of the greatest scientific minds of our time believe in ghosts."

He squeezed my hand with a trifle more pressure than necessary. "This is no time to debate the mental shortcomings of Alfred Russel Wallace," he said in an acid tone. His hand was suddenly cold, and I realized that for him, the notion of the baron's ghost might not be entirely academic. If the old fellow haunted the place, the appearance of his specter would be far more upsetting for Stoker than for me. I returned the squeeze and drew him back a little.

"What are you doing?"

"I am going into the study first. If he is haunting the place, you shan't want to see that. I shall get rid of him."

"How? By menacing him with your hatpin?"

"You needn't resort to sarcasm, Stoker. I am certain I will think of something. In the meantime, behind me, if you please."

He muttered something profane but did as I bade him. I opened the door he indicated, pausing a moment to register my impressions.

"Well?" he asked nastily. "Any lingering ectoplasm, or are we free to proceed?"

I stepped forward. "Quite free," I replied, my tone distracted. Quick to sense a change in mood, Stoker put a hand to my shoulder.

"What is it?"

I sniffed. "I don't know. There is something here. I cannot place it. It certainly is no ghost. Do you think we might risk a light?"

He drifted away for a moment and I heard the creak of shutters being folded into place. After that there was the sharp rasp of a match, and then a little bud of light blossomed. He lit a candle. "We dare not light more than this. The window overlooks a small garden with a high wall. We should be safe enough."

He took a breath, steeling himself, I thought, then moved to the desk.

"What are you looking for?"

He frowned at the piles of papers and books, the upset inkstand, the scattered pens. "Anything amiss. The trouble is, Max was as tidy as they come. All of this is amiss."

I left him to it and wandered the room, hunting for the elusive scent that had tickled my nose when I had first opened the sealed room. I sniffed the chairs and the rugs, much to Stoker's amusement.

"You look like a demented bloodhound. What on earth are you doing?" he demanded, his brow furrowed as he moved to the baron's bookshelf.

I ignored him for a moment, putting my nose so near to the rug that the silk nub brushed the tip of my nose. Eureka! I peered into the pile of the rug and saw it—a tiny seed, greenish brown in color, and lightly curved. It appeared to be striped, but as I held it to the light of our solitary candle, I saw that it was actually ridged. I gave another sniff and detected a strong odor reminiscent of aniseed.

"Stoker, was the baron in the habit of chewing caraway seeds?"

"Caraway? No. He loathed the stuff."

"How do you know?"

He said nothing for a long moment as he traced a row of books, his fingers trailing along the spines. I waited, and finally he answered, his hand resting on a thick volume bound in green kid.

"He hated seedcake. Why?"

I withdrew a handkerchief and wrapped the seed carefully before returning it to my pocket.

"I think it might be a clue."

He snorted. "A caraway seed? Well, perhaps. But I doubt it is as good as this," he said, tapping the wide green book.

"What have you there?"

He slid it carefully from the shelf. "The only book in the entire study written in Italian."

"And is that significant?" I asked, coming to peer around his shoulder as he carried it to the desk.

"Only if you know that Max did not read Italian." He opened the book carefully, and for the first few pages, it seemed we were doomed to disappointment. It was some sort of treatise with colored plates upon the subject of mollusks, boring in the extreme, but Stoker riffled through the pages, and the secret of the book was revealed—a hollow space, neatly cleared out of the big book to leave just enough room for a packet of papers folded and bound with a violet silk ribbon.

I reached for it with greedy fingers, but before I could touch it, there was the sound of breaking glass.

Instantly, Stoker doused the candle with his bare fingers while I scooped the packet out of the book and shoved it into my pocket. Stoker's lips brushed my ear. "That came from the kitchen. Someone's had the same idea we did, only without a key."

"Housebreaker?" I whispered.

I felt his head give a shake in the negative under my mouth. "Housebreaker wouldn't make noise. He will be on his way here."

The thought ought to have filled me with fear; instead I was conscious of a rising excitement. I put a hand to my hatpin, and Stoker's closed over it.

"Easy. No need to seek trouble before it finds you. We shall use the adjoining door into the dining room, circle around him, and go out the way we came. He will be none the wiser."

I nodded and he led me swiftly through the connecting door, easing it closed just as footsteps trod heavily down the hall towards the study door. We crept into the hall, but just as it seemed we were about to gain the stairs in safety, disaster struck. In his haste, Stoker brushed against the elephant's foot, upsetting it and all of the walking sticks. The crash of them against the polished boards echoed throughout the house with all the drama of a cannon shot.

"Run!" Stoker commanded, pushing me. We fled, down the stairs and through the kitchen, broken glass crunching underfoot as we ran. Footsteps pounded behind us, and I caught a glimpse of a broad black shadow, darker than the darkness itself, bent upon catching us. Stoker wrenched open the door to the area, and just as I went to pass through it, a hand grasped for my shoulder. I shrugged away, kicking backward like a mule.

There was a muffled curse as my foot connected with something soft and fleshy, and that moment's delay was enough. I reached for Stoker's hand and he half hauled me up the stairs. But our malefactor had made quick work of his recovery. No sooner had we gained the pavement than I felt the weight of his hand upon my shoulder.

Stoker had me by one arm, the blackguard by the other, and I gave a gasp as the intruder's hand tightened upon my newly stitched limb. Stoker either heard me or felt the sudden drag as I came to a halt, for he stopped and turned, raising his fist, but before he could strike the fellow, a gunshot rang out. I heard the whine of the bullet as it passed some distance away, chipping a piece of stone from the façade of the baron's house. The malefactor had understood the warning. Instantly, the grip upon my arm released, and he fled, a shadow slipping down the street. A second shadow detached itself from across the street and gave chase, the pair of them disappearing into the night.

Stoker did not release my hand. "Are you all right?"

"I think so," I lied. There was a hot lick of pain along my newly stitched wound, but there was little point in alarming Stoker before we had reached safety.

"Come on," he ordered. He hurried me to the corner, where he hailed a hansom and gave an address not terribly far from Bishop's Folly. It was indiscreet, but it would save us an hour's walk, and I could have wept with gratitude.

"Did you get a look at the fellow?" he asked, pitching his voice low so the driver should not overhear.

"No. Did you?"

"Not at all."

"But I know who he is," I said grimly.

Stoker gave a start. "The devil you do! Who was it?"

"I cannot say for certain, but I believe it was my importunate friend from Paddington Station, Mr. de Clare."

"What makes you think so?"

"When we spoke at the station, I noticed a peculiar scent, something green and spicy. I thought it a sort of toilet water, but when I found the seed in the baron's study I recognized it."

"Caraway," he finished.

"Indeed. I believe Mr. de Clare has made another attempt to get my attention."

"Unless . . ." he began slowly.

"Yes?" I prompted.

"Unless he was keeping watch across the street in case we should appear."

I gaped at him. "You think Mr. de Clare was our savior instead? You think *he* fired the shot that drove the housebreaker away?"

"It is possible."

"Then how did the seed come to be in the study *before* we arrived?"

"Mr. de Clare and Max clearly had some connection. Perhaps it is as Mr. de Clare said and they were in league together. You must admit, it is also an explanation which fits the facts."

I nibbled at my lower lip for a moment, considering. "I suppose you are correct," I admitted. "It is possible that Mr. de Clare was telling the truth at Paddington. He might have had my welfare at heart, and he may be entirely innocent of any wrongdoing. But whether he was our housebreaker or our savior, why did he not declare himself?"

"He hardly had the chance," Stoker pointed out reasonably. "I didn't even have time to draw a knife. We fled from the intruder as soon as he appeared, and the fellow across the street was clearly more determined to give chase to the housebreaker than speak with us."

"So either Mr. de Clare was standing watch across the street and has just prevented us from being accosted by the intruder, or Mr. de Clare *was* the intruder," I summarized. "But what purpose did the intruder have in breaking into the baron's study?"

"Perhaps he was looking for that," Stoker suggested, gesturing to the pocket where I had secured the purloined packet . "If it was Mr. de Clare, perhaps the baron meant to entrust it to him at some point—presumably Mr. de Clare knew of its existence but not its precise whereabouts. With Max dead, the fellow would have no choice but to search on his own for it. He might have lost that bit of caraway seed at any time. Or perhaps he was looking for you." I said nothing, and Stoker went on, warming to his theme. "Yes, I like this idea quite a lot. What if Mr. de Clare knows something about you, something truly important?"

"Such as?"

"Oh, it could be anything. You say the aunts told you that you were a foundling, but what if my kidnapping theory is correct? You could have parents alive somewhere who have been searching for you for a quarter of a century."

"I told you the aunts would never do such a thing," I reminded him with considerable coldness.

"Very well," he amended. "Perhaps you really are an orphan but you were left something—something valuable like an inheritance. It might be a bit of money or some jewels. Max had the papers that can prove your claim, but with him dead and no clue of where to find the papers or you, Mr. de Clare has no choice save to return to Max's house to search for the packet—and keep watch, hoping eventually you will make an appearance."

"That is a tale straight from one of Mrs. Radcliffe's thrillers, Stoker. I expected better from you."

"It is a perfectly logical hypothesis," he returned. "Now, do shut up and stop interrupting whilst I'm being interesting. Where did I leave off?"

"Mr. de Clare is sitting watchfully every night, waiting for me to show myself."

"And tonight, finally, you do. But before he can reveal himself to you, we are attacked by the murderous fellow who broke in tonight. The vigilant Mr. de Clare sees him off with a shot and gives chase."

"So you like Mr. de Clare for savior whilst I like him for the villain. I suppose only time will reveal which of us has the right of it. I only hope when we do discover the truth, it is worth bleeding for," I said dryly.

"Why do you say that?"

"Because I think it is a propitious time to warn you—my stitches seem to have come undone."

He swore fluently and reached for my arm, sliding his fingers underneath my jacket. He brought his hand away and held it up to the fitful light of a passing streetlamp. It was dark and shone wetly. "Your sleeve is soaked in blood. Do you feel faint?"

"Not in the slightest," I lied as I pitched forward into darkness.

TWENTY

When I came to, I was lying on a sofa in the snug of the Belvedere. How he managed to get me out of the hansom and through the gardens without attracting attention I could not imagine.

"Quite simple, really. I told the cabman you were an inebriate," he informed me. He sat me up and wrenched my jacket aside. Next came my shirtwaist, leaving me in my corset cover. I snorted.

"What?" he demanded.

"I was just imagining poor Lady Cordelia's face if she were to see us now. We do seem to be very frequently thrown together in various states of undress."

He thrust my flask of aguardiente at me. "Drink this and hush. I shall have to clean it before I can tell how badly you've undone my handiwork."

The next few minutes were not pleasant, but he was quick and thorough, and as I had observed before, unfailingly gentle. As it happened, I had lost only a stitch or two, and he repaired my torn flesh, fussing all the while.

"Why the devil do I waste my skills upon you when you persist in rushing headlong into peril?" he remonstrated.

That particular remark was so blatantly unfair, it did not even merit a response, so I let it pass. I was too busy puzzling over the events of the evening.

"Do you think the fellow who shot tonight—whether Mr. de Clare or not—meant to do us a good turn? Or was he after the baron's murderer and we were simply the unwitting beneficiaries of his attack upon the assassin?"

"I do not know, and I care less," he muttered, clipping the end of the silk thread neatly. "It will certainly scar now," he warned me. "Don't you dare tell anyone that is my work. I used to be famous for the delicacy of my stitching, but now you've gone and ruined it."

I surveyed the line of tiny, precise stitches and shrugged, wincing only slightly. "I shall consider it a badge of honor, a souvenir of our adventures when I am in my dotage and no one believes I once pursued a murderer."

He opened his mouth to speak then but thought better of it. He tidied away the tools of his trade as I took up my shawl. I did not bother to re-dress, and he put my shirtwaist to soak in the little domestic office Lady Cordelia had mentioned. He came to sit beside me when he had finished. The packet lay in my lap, and I touched the violet silk ribbon.

"Why do you hesitate?" he asked.

"I suppose I have a keen appreciation for anticipation," I said lightly. "But I do not expect you to understand."

"Oh, it isn't that difficult," he replied. "Before you open that packet all things are possible. It might contain any secret at all. It might be the Casket Letters, or the baron's laundry list, or the revelation that your mother was a Russian princess."

"Precisely," I said with a small smile.

He rummaged in my bag a moment and returned with two of my slender cigarillos. He lit them from the fire and passed one to me. "Then let us enjoy our moment of anticipation to the fullest," he said.

"Thank you for not lighting your appalling cigars," I told him as I savored the sweet smoke.

He grunted by way of response and we sat for a little while in companionable silence.

"Sometimes it is better not to know," he said suddenly. He lifted his gaze to mine. "Sometimes it is better for secrets to be left alone."

"If I am not mistaken, that is the voice of experience."

"It is." He dropped his gaze to his hands, the cigarillo clasped lightly in his fingers. A slender stream of blue smoke rose, curling sinuously. He fell silent then, and I did not have the heart to pry.

"We do not even know this packet has information about me," I pointed out. "It might be something else altogether."

"Quite," he told me. He reached forward and ground out the last of his cigarillo on the stove. He took mine and did the same. "Very well. As Arcadia Brown would say, 'Excelsior!'" he proclaimed, lifting a mocking brow.

The ribbon seemed to protest at being untied. It hesitated a moment, then gave way under my insistent fingers. There was a drift of papers onto my lap, letters and newspaper cuttings, and I plucked one at random. It was from an American newspaper, a photograph with a small notice.

I read aloud, my voice suddenly hoarse. CELEBRATED IRISH ACTRESS LILY ASHBOURNE BEGINS AMERICAN TOUR, the headline ran. I read the rest of the piece, a brief description of her triumphs on the English stage, and studied the photograph. I handed it to Stoker without comment, but his was brief and to the point.

"Bloody hell."

"This cutting is from 1860. I was born in 1862. Twenty-first of June, to be precise. She must be my mother," I said, my voice tight. "Don't you think?"

A fleeting smile touched his mouth. "She couldn't be more like you if you had been twins," he assured me. I looked again at the elegantly resolute face, the ripple of black hair, the eyes with their curious expression of challenge.

"There is something audacious about her," I said.

"I should imagine so," he agreed. "Stage actresses are not known for their reticence."

I picked up another piece of paper. "This looks like a letter to the baron—it is addressed to 'Dearest Max.'"

"What does it say?"

I skimmed the prose quickly, noting the looping scrawl of the handwriting, the pale violet ink, the heavily underscored words. "It is from Lily. And—oh God."

He put out his hand and I gave him the letter.

"'Dearest Max, I hardly have the words to *thank you* for your kindnesses to me and to Baby. I was *so low* when you came to see us, and your assurances have revived my spirits. You know he will not receive my letters; my *only hope* lies with you. You *must* make him see his duty to me—and to our child. I shudder to think what will become of us if he persists in casting us off so completely. And you must not think I care about money or anything else. I want *him*, Max. I know he loved me once, and I believe he loves me *still*, in his heart of hearts. If only he would come to see me, to see his child, I know he would find the strength to defy his family. If he goes through with this marriage, I do not know what I will do. He *cannot* marry her, Max—he must not. It will be my destruction, and he will carry that for the rest of his life.'"

He broke off. "The letter is dated 20 February 1863."

"I was eight months old," I calculated.

"And your father was not doing his duty, either by you or your mother."

"So Max was acting as intermediary, consoling my mother and reminding my father of his obligations even as he planned to marry another woman. I wonder if he went through with his wedding."

Stoker had picked up another cutting, and as he read it, his face paled. "I suspect so."

"What is that?"

His expression was apologetic. "Your mother's obituary. Dated 20 March 1863."

"Less than a month after sending Max that letter saying she did not know what she would do if my father married another woman." I did not take the cutting from him. "Stoker, did she—"

He shook his head. "I cannot imagine how. Not if she was buried in this cemetery," he said, reading off the name. "Our Lady of Grace. In Dublin."

I blinked in surprise. "She was Catholic."

He nodded gravely. "Apparently. There is a mention of the priest who presided over her funeral, a Father Burke. Look here, it is his obituary. He died six years after your mother and according to this was the parish priest of Greymount in Dublin. Veronica, he would never have let her be buried in holy ground if she had taken her own life."

"Still," I persisted. "It is too coincidental. Unless she simply *willed* herself to die. Is that even possible?"

He shrugged. "I have seen stranger."

"So, my mother was an Irish Catholic actress. I suppose Ashbourne was a stage name. I wonder if there is any way of tracing her through the burial records to find her real name."

"No need," he said, producing another cutting. "Her real name was Mary Katherine de Clare."

"De Clare?" I took the cutting. Another piece from her triumphant American tour of 1860, but this one went into great depth about her past. "She ran away from home," I told him. "Born to a respectable Irish family and they disowned her when she went on the stage. Here is a photograph of her with her brother," I said, pointing to the cutting. "Edmund de Clare, as a boy of fifteen."

Stoker scrutinized the photograph. "Is this the fellow who accosted you at Paddington?"

I nodded and he handed back the cutting. The photograph was taken some years before Mary Katherine de Clare had changed her name and taken her place on the stage. She was dressed in a suitably girlish frock, standing behind her seated brother, serious in his town suit, but with the same elegant bones and graceful demeanor as his sister.

"Why didn't he tell me?" I murmured.

Stoker shrugged. "Perhaps he felt revealing himself as your uncle was too private a matter for a crowded train station."

"Perhaps."

I read on, learning more about my mother. Famed as a gifted tragedienne, she had built her career upon the death scenes of Juliet and Ophelia. But she had been best known for the role of Pháedra in an English adaptation of Racine's *Phèdre*. There was a photograph of her, dressed in purest white, poison vial held aloft as she contemplated her fate. I raised my eyes briefly. "I presume you have noticed all her best roles were suicides?"

His expression was skeptical. "That proves nothing."

"I suppose not," I conceded. I burrowed through the rest of the papers—a motley collection of obituaries, notices from her plays, and two photographs. "My God," I breathed. "Stoker, look."

I handed him a photograph of Lily Ashbourne holding an

infant. He read, "'Me with Baby. December 1862.' You were six months old."

I had been a plump infant, sitting upright in my mother's lap for the photograph. I must have moved, for my face was faintly blurred at the edge. But Lily's face was perfectly immobile, the moment captured forever, like a birdwing butterfly pinned to a card in all its brilliance. It had been nearly twenty-five years, but Lily Ashbourne's beauty was undimmed so long as that photograph existed to give truth to it. I peered closer and saw clutched in my chubby fist a tiny velvet mouse. Chester.

Wordlessly, Stoker handed me one of his great scarlet handkerchiefs to wipe my eyes. I moved on to the second photograph. Another photograph of me, clearly from the same sitting, for my white petticoats, stiff with embroidery, were unchanged. But Lily was missing. Instead, I was held by two women, their expressions wooden. Lily had contrived to look natural for the camera, as at ease as she might have been with a portrait painter. But these two were unaccustomed to having their pictures taken. Their chins were sharp, their mouths pursed in expressions of wariness. But even so, I knew them.

"It is Aunt Nell and Aunt Lucy!" I exclaimed. "The Harbottle sisters. I always thought they took me from a foundling home, but they must have known my mother."

I turned over the photographs. Scribbled in the same hand as the other, in a scrawl of violet ink: "Baby with Ellie and Nan." "I don't understand. Who are Ellie and Nan?"

Together we sorted through the papers until Stoker brandished one, triumphant. "I have it. A mention in this notice about her American tour that Miss Ashbourne will be traveling with her dresser, Nan Williams, and her maid, Ellie Williams, sisters."

I sat back, my mind working furiously. "It makes no sense. Why would Nan and Ellie Williams change their names to

Lucy and Nell Harbottle? And given me the name Veronica Speedwell? You notice there is no indication of what my mother called me, only 'Baby.' What does it mean?"

We searched through the rest of the papers, but there was nothing more to be learned.

Finally, we gave up, assembling the papers in a rough chronological order before tying them up again. I poured more of the aguardiente and we drank in silence, as comfortably as brothers in arms, as our thoughts ran ahead.

"It is possible," Stoker said finally, stretching out his booted legs, "that your father had much to lose by your birth."

"What do you mean?"

"That letter from your mother to Max. She insists that she does not want money from your father. That means he must have had it to give. And he is refusing, for the sake of his family, to acknowledge your birth. Whatever relationship he enjoyed with your mother, it was finished by the time you were a few months old—possibly because of his engagement to another woman."

"And Lily was disconsolate." I picked up the thread of his idea. "She even threatened suicide, albeit obliquely, in her letter. What if she was more explicit in her communications to my father? He had a family to think of, money, reputation. He was at the very least from a wealthy merchant family."

Stoker shook his head. "I would lay money on aristocracy. Gentry at least."

"You really think so?"

He curled a handsome lip in scorn. "If there is one thing I can smell, it is the stink of my own kind trying to cover their hypocrisy. Besides, she was a famous beauty, a successful actress, the sort of woman who would not favor a poor nobody with her attentions. No, to attract her notice he would have to be someone with a name, connections."

"That makes her sound rather mercenary," I protested.

"Love affairs often are," he returned easily. "They are an exchange of goods. He brought money to the liaison; she clearly brought beauty."

"I don't think so. She mentioned in her letter to the baron that she had loved him, and he her."

"It is possible. But at the beginning, to be noticed amidst all those other wealthy stage-door Johnnies, he must have had something quite special. Either he was very, very rich, or very, very handsome."

"And very, very ruthless," I added. "Imagine, courting Lily Ashbourne, the loveliest actress of her time, and then leaving her so coldly when she got with child. She was clearly devastated."

Stoker's voice was thick with constraint. "He might have been as well, you know. If she was correct, then he did love her, at least for a while. Perhaps his family made him marry this other woman."

"And so he cut off Lily—and his own child—without a word? That does not sound like the action of a feeling man."

"Sometimes the deeper a man's feelings, the less able he is to act upon them," he said hoarsely. "Or speak of them."

I finished off my share of the aguardiente. "I shall not ask about your devils, Stoker."

He gave a shrug and poured more of the liquor for himself. "They have been my closest companions for five years now. We're old friends, the devils and me."

I looked at the packet of papers still sitting upon my lap. "It looks as if I have devils of my own now."

"Do you?"

I nodded. "Yes. Because everything in that packet shows that it is entirely possible my father murdered my mother."

"Veronica—"

"No, hear me out, I beg you. He wanted free of her and of me. She wasn't going quietly. There were letters to Max—perhaps more than this one. Perhaps she made threats even. She was well-known. The newspapers would have trumpeted this story to the skies if they had got hold of it. We know he had a new wife to shield, a name to protect. We know my mother died very suddenly when she was scarcely twenty. And we know she could not have been a suicide, as she was buried in hallowed ground. Tell me it is not at least possible that my father murdered her."

Stoker gave me an even stare. "It is possible," he said finally.

"Could you at least pretend not to agree? I find myself in need of a devil's advocate."

He moved as if to touch my hand, then seemed to think better of it. "You have never struck me as the sort of woman to give way in the face of something difficult. Don't tell me I have misjudged you."

"Of course not," I said, squaring my shoulders.

"It is a terrible thing to believe your father capable of such a thing. But there is another fact which points to some difficulty from your father: your aunts were afraid, deeply so, if they changed their names and left Ireland."

"It explains so much," I mused. "We moved so many times when I was a child—and never for any good reason that I could discover. I would go off hunting, chasing after my butterflies, and when I came home, the aunts would have us half-packed and that would be the end of it."

"It must have been difficult to make friends."

"I wish you and I had met as children," I told him suddenly.

"I don't. You would have dragged me behind the nearest hedgerow and had your way with me before I sprouted hairs on my chin."

I smiled at him and he almost, very nearly, smiled back. "I think I should like to sleep now," I told him.

He rose then and tugged my feet until I was stretched upon the sofa. He tucked a blanket around me and bent to stoke the fire. When he had finished, he took another blanket and made a makeshift pallet upon the rug, taking the flask of aguardiente with him.

"There is always Wellington's campaign bed," I reminded him.

"I would rather be near to the fire."

"In the interests of propriety, you ought to be at least on another floor of the Belvedere," I teased.

"I do not care. I am staying with you until this business is finished."

"Lady Cordelia will think—"

"To the devil with what Lady C. thinks." He settled himself heavily onto the blanket and removed his boots. He took no pillow but folded his arms behind his head and closed his eyes, taking the occasional deep draft from the flask. "I like Cordelia but I shall bloody well be damned if I do anything just because she might have thoughts she oughtn't."

I smiled into the silence that followed this pronouncement.

"Veronica?"

"Yes, Stoker?"

"I know you are resilient as India rubber, but when the lot of this hits you, it will come like a brickbat. Trust me."

I thought of the secrets he carried, the pain that bedeviled him—pain of which he could not yet bring himself to speak. "And what should I do when that happens?"

"Do not keep it to yourself. Someone reminded me of the story of the Spartan boy and the fox. Someone who ought to take her own advice."

With that he fell silent, and soon his breathing was deep

and even and he slept, while I lay wakeful long into the night, thinking of all we had learned.

TWENTY-ONE

THE NEXT MORNING I woke to find Stoker had risen and gone, the flask of aguardiente entirely empty. He must have wakened some time in the night and finished it off, but I did not mind.

" 'Take it,' " I muttered, thinking of Sir Philip Sidney, " 'thy necessity is greater than mine.' " I refilled the flask with plain whiskey from the store cupboard—not half as potent, but useful in a pinch, I decided—and still there was no sign of Stoker. The little room for washing was empty, so he must have already attended to his ablutions. I did the same, pleased to find that my arm was stiff but there was no sign of incipient infection. Whatever his professional faults, he was a gifted doctor. I dressed myself with a little difficulty and opened the door upon a June morning dazzling enough to lift the dourest spirits. Flowers bloomed around the door of the Belvedere, and drifts of early rambling roses were just unfurling their petals, filling the morning with their fragrance. I stood upon the step, drawing in great lungfuls of the air, as good as any to be found in London.

Just then I heard a wet snuffling sound as the bushes gave an ominous rustle. Before I could whisk myself back into the Belvedere, the beast was upon me. A massive creature of bunched muscle and long fur hurled itself aloft, knocking me squarely to the ground before coming to sit firmly upon my chest. A wet, lolloping tongue caressed my cheek, and hot breath redolent of meat blew into my face. I thanked heaven for the thickness of my Psyche knot, which had taken the force of the creature's violent affections and softened my landing. Doubtless it had saved me from a nasty blow to the back of the head.

"Betty! I say, Betty, come back here!" A man broke through the bushes and stopped short. "My dear lady, I am most heartily sorry. Betty! Betony, desist this instant!" He accompanied his order with a sharp tug to the beast's collar, and she withdrew from my person, sitting next to me with an adoring expression.

The man came forward to help me up, and I saw then he was a gentleman, dressed in a country suit of rugged tweeds. I took his hand and got slowly to my feet.

"I must apologize again. I do hope Betony has not hurt you. She is a puppy, really, and poorly trained."

"She is charming," I said, almost meaning it. I patted my head. "And I think my hair took the worst of it." I felt for my pins, but they were secure, and I dusted my skirts, wincing only a little as my arm gave a sudden throb of protest.

"You are hurt," he said. "We must determine how extensive the injury is."

"It is nothing," I assured him. "At least nothing that the dog has done, I promise you, my lord. You *are* Lord Rosemorran?"

He blinked several times, as if trying to recall something. "Rosemorran? Oh yes. That's me. I say, have we met?"

"I am afraid not. My name is Veronica Speedwell, and I am trespassing."

"Trespassing? How very original. We do get the odd vagrant creeping about the place from time to time, but never a woman, at least not a clean woman with good vowels who could spot a lord at five paces. Any particular reason for trespassing here?"

"It is my fault, milord," came a voice from behind him. Lord Rosemorran turned just as Bet launched herself again, this time at Stoker. "Down, *down*, you ridiculous creature," Stoker ordered, his affectionate tone belying the command. Bet ignored it, planting her hind feet upon the ground and resting her front paws on Stoker's shoulders. In spite of his height of some six feet, she topped him by inches, and he ruffled her ears, earning himself several long licks for his pains.

"Stoker? Good to see you. How is my elephant coming along?"

"Not very well," Stoker said, his voice muffled by the dog's thick fur. I noticed he had resumed his eye patch and his voice was rough. He looked every inch the ruffian, no doubt the aftereffects of too much aguardiente.

"Stoker is in hiding from the Metropolitan Police," I volunteered.

"Indeed? What do they want with him?" Lord Rosemorran was as unflappable as his sister, it seemed, and I decided to tell him the truth.

"It has to do with Baron von Stauffenbach's murder."

"Ah yes. Dreadful business, that. Frightful shame. He was a good fellow, the baron. One of the best. Borrowed my Thucydides. Suppose it's gone forever now," he said, his tone abstracted. He fell silent a moment, his expression vacant, then collected himself. "So, what do the police think he had to do with the murder?"

"They think he might have killed the baron, which of course he did not. I know this for a fact," I assured him.

"No one would ever believe he did," he replied stoutly, and

I decided in that moment that I liked him. He was younger than I had expected, barely clearing forty, I should have guessed, and though his appearance was somewhat untidy in the manner of all distracted scholars, his manners were gentle and his face surprisingly attractive. He had his sister's kindly dark eyes and a twist to his mouth that spoke of good humor.

"Yes, well, the police do not see it that way, at least not yet," Stoker told him, pushing the dog firmly to the ground. She gave a low groan, as if sulking, but sat at his feet and he dropped a hand to her head. "I should like very much to prove it. In the meantime, I have taken refuge in the Belvedere without your leave—so unsporting, no apology could possibly suffice."

I noted his careful omission of Lady Cordelia's role in securing our bolt-hole, and he flicked me a quick glance to warn me to give nothing away as his lordship began to speak.

"Well, but if Miss—er, I am sorry, I have forgot your name." Lord Rosemorran looked to me.

"Speedwell."

"Speedwell. Like the plant? Charming. If Miss Speedwell can provide you with an alibi, then surely you are in the clear."

"It is entirely likely that the police will not be satisfied with my assurances," I said.

"Ah well, that is a pity. Surely it will all come right in the end," he said, cheering himself with his platitude. "And you're quite welcome to stay here as long as you like. You shan't be in anyone's way. Now, let us go into the Belvedere. I've had a rather good idea for the elephant's trunk, Stoker . . ."

I marveled at his lordship's easy acceptance of a fugitive finding sanctuary on his property, but he seemed entirely unruffled as he led the way into his collections, tossing questions behind him with little expectation of replies. "Have you found it comfortable in here? I must say, I shouldn't like the notion of sleeping amidst all of this death and decay. Of course, we've never had talk of ghosts in this part of Bishop's Folly, but one never knows. Have you seen ghosts since you have been here? No, of course not. Do hope you've had a good rootle around the old collections. Miss Speedwell, is there anything in particular here you would like to take a closer look at whilst Stoker and I talk?"

Stoker spoke up. "Miss Speedwell is a lepidopterist."

"A lepidopterist! Why didn't you say so? You'll want the Butterfly Cabinet," he said, changing course as erratically as a bee. He plunged down one aisle between his collections to make for an enormous piece of furniture that had been built to fit snugly between two of the great columns of the room. It was securely locked, but the key was hanging from a tassel that had been slung over a ram's horn nearby. His lordship opened the cabinet and stood back.

"Not a bad little collection," he began.

He said other things after that, but I did not hear him. From the tail of my eye I had seen it, beckoning, shimmering just at the edge of my vision. I moved on sleepwalking feet, ignoring my host entirely. He and Stoker must have fallen into conversation, for I heard the rise and fall of their voices, but I had no care for anything but *him*.

I stopped a scant inch from the glass and put out a finger. I heard a low moan and realized it had come from my own throat.

"Miss Speedwell? Is everything quite all right?"

"*Trogonoptera brookiana,*" I said reverently. "Rajah Brooke's Birdwing."

His lordship came to stand at my elbow. "Ah yes. Lovely, isn't it?"

It was stunning. Seven inches across and shimmering with light, the creature had wings as black as night blazed across with a streak of emerald green richer than any jewel in the queen's possession. A neat ruby head surmounted it all, and from this sprouted a pair of slender black antennae, curved as delicately as lace. The green slash ended in points, like feathers, and the vivid color was threaded with black capillaries, as though someone had drawn them in ink with the finest nib. It was this spectacular butterfly that had driven me to Sumatra in spite of the rumblings of Krakatoa. Such a small and fragile thing to have changed my life, I reflected.

I paid homage to his stilled beauty while his lordship went on. "From Sumatra, you know. Alfred Russel Wallace."

"Yes, he discovered and named it in 1855," I told him.

"Yes, I think my father acquired it from him in 1860 or thereabouts."

I turned slowly to face him. "You mean *this* specimen—"

"Came from Sumatra with Wallace, yes. Wallace brought a few home with him, and my father bought one. Capital fellow, isn't he?"

His voice was blandly cheerful, but when I flicked a glance to Stoker, I saw from his expression that he understood. The Earl of Rosemorran was a kindly man and perhaps even a devoted scholar, but he had not the slightest comprehension of the magnitude of his collection. I turned again to the butterfly, realizing with a start that it was merely one of a few hundred pinned specimens. They were mounted with Continental pins, my own preference, for the longer pin permitted a more thorough label to be attached, although the next to catch my attention was sadly anonymous.

"*Lycaena dispar,*" I said, my voice somewhat strangled. "The Large Copper. This butterfly has been extinct for the better part of thirty years."

"Has it indeed?" his lordship asked. "I'm afraid many of the labels have come off, and I don't know much about them. Interested in butterflies, are you, Miss Speedwell?"

Stoker took pity upon my nearly speechless state. "Miss

Speedwell is a lepidopterist by profession," he reminded the earl.

His lordship's brows lifted. "Yes, I recall now you said so. Why, that is most intriguing. A lady scientist," he said in a tone of wonderment. "What will they think of next?"

"There have been ladies interested in science since before Mary Shelley," said a slightly astringent voice behind us. We turned as one to find Lady Cordelia, her expression carefully neutral. Only the sharpness of her tone betrayed any impatience. But it was an impatience tempered with real affection as she looked at her brother. "I see you have discovered my guests, Ambrose."

"Your guests? They didn't say. Miss Speedwell told me they were trespassing."

"Miss Speedwell no doubt thought to shield me from the consequences of harboring a fugitive from justice," she said with a touch of her previous warmth. "But she and Stoker are here at my invitation."

"And mine now," her brother returned. "D'ye know, Cordelia, Miss Speedwell knows butterflies. That might be handy. We have said for ages we needed to catalog these fellows," he added with a nod to the lepidoptery collection.

Lady Cordelia inclined her head. "It would indeed be kind of Miss Speedwell to lend her expertise, but I am afraid there are more pressing matters to contend with, Ambrose. You see, Stoker—"

"Is wanted by the police to help with their inquiries," he finished irritably. "I know that. Damned insolent of them, if you'll pardon the language, Miss Speedwell."

"Certainly. And I agree. Insolent indeed. But the police will pursue him until they find him. They are convinced of his involvement in the baron's murder."

"Did you find anything in his house?" Lady Cordelia asked.

I opened my mouth, but before I could reply, Stoker

responded. "Nothing of note," he said flatly.

She clucked her tongue. "Pity. I had high hopes that you might discover something that would implicate another or at least provide a motive for his murder."

Stoker did not elaborate, and if his lordship wondered what we had been doing in the house of a murdered man, he did not ask.

"Well," Lady Cordelia said briskly, "as the secret of your presence here is out, you are welcome to remove your things to the guest rooms in the main house. We have plenty of space."

Stoker held up a hand. "Very kind of you, my lady. But I think Miss Speedwell and I would be more comfortable remaining here."

"Of course," she conceded gracefully.

"So long as his lordship approves," I put in quickly.

The earl gave a nod, clearly uninterested in mundane arrangements, and after a lengthy discussion about his enormous elephant trophy, he took his leave to return to his study while Lady Cordelia pleaded domestic responsibilities. I turned to Stoker.

"What was your purpose in that?"

"Hm?"

"Lying to Lady Cordelia about what we found in the baron's study."

His brow was furrowed. "Too soon to share. We have made no sense of it yet. All we have discovered is that you are the daughter of an actress—"

"And illegitimate," I threw in.

"It is not gentlemanly of me to stress the point, but yes, illegitimate to boot. And we know that somehow the baron was involved in acting as go-between in this liaison. We further know that at some point your mother died, possibly by your father's hand, possibly not. But her death left you in the care of the Harbottles, women who were so afraid that they changed your name and moved you from place to place." He tipped his head thoughtfully. "Do you suppose they killed your mother in order to keep you for their own?"

I narrowed my gaze into my severest look. "Do not be daft. Those gentle old women—it's unthinkable. And neither do I believe the baron's involvement in covering up my birth was a motive to murder him. It is all quite ancient history, after all. It happened a quarter of a century ago."

"Max's murder didn't," he replied.

"No, of course not. But to think that that heinous act was somehow connected to my birth is a tremendous stretch. Surely you see that."

"What about your uncle?"

"What about him?" I demanded.

"You don't find it just a little coincidental that he should make an appearance now, right when Max is killed? Your birth *must* be tied to Max's death."

"Must? That's a dangerous hypothesis," I told him. "There might be a dozen equally likely explanations."

He turned and fixed me with a roguish look. "Would you care to make a wager upon the point?"

"A wager?"

"I'll wager there is a connection between your birth and Max's murder, and I'll further wager that your uncle is involved somehow."

"Fine," I said, extending my hand. "A guinea."

"A guinea! Have a heart. I am a poor man," he said, clutching his pocket.

"A guinea," I repeated.

He shook my hand with ill grace. "Very well. A guinea. And when I win it, make it a nice, shiny new coin. I'll not have one that's dull and worn."

"They spend the same, Stoker."

"I shan't spend it. I shall hang it from my watch chain and wear it with pride."

"You would try the patience of one of the most forbearing of saints," I told him. "But you are my best hope of unraveling this tangled skein. Where do you think we should proceed from here?"

He tipped his head. "The sweet shop."

"To pursue the caraway seed we found at the baron's? But a sweet shop wouldn't sell caraway seeds."

"No, the sweet shop because I am out of humbugs," he said, turning out his pocket.

"I must congratulate you. I didn't think you had the power to surprise me any longer, Stoker, but I am continually astonished at your ability to consume sweets. It is a wonder you have a tooth left in your head."

He bared his strong white teeth and snapped them soundly. "Saint Apollonia be praised."

I tucked my arm through his, careful not to jar my wound. "Come on, then. Humbugs it is, and when we've bought them, we shall hold a council of war and decide our next move."

TWENTY-TWO

STOKER PROVED A TRUE connoisseur of sweets, selecting not only humbugs but bull's-eyes and acid drops and a bar of mint cake. He tucked them into various pockets, looking far happier than I had yet seen him.

Without discussion, we turned our steps south, towards the river, and after a long walk reached the Embankment. The day continued fine, and we could see pleasure boaters plying their craft along the waters of the Thames, the bellies of the sails swelling with a soft late spring breeze.

"One feels quite removed here from the bustle of the city," I observed.

"Hm," Stoker agreed, his teeth no doubt stuck together by one of the atrocities he had just purchased.

I turned to remonstrate with him, but just as I did, I heard the footsteps, running hard. Sensing the danger, Stoker reached for my hand, but it was too late. They were upon us, a gang of ruffians bent upon seizing the pair of us. I kicked and clawed and cursed them roundly as they shoved my head into a sack.

I don't know what Stoker did, but I could hear the sounds of a struggle and words that chilled me to my marrow.

"We only have need of her. If he keeps fighting, do what you must," instructed a low voice. I went still, straining my ears to hear more. I was held, quite tightly, but one of my arms had been caught up near my head, the hand trapped in the sack. I wriggled my fingers until I reached my hatpin, slipping it free. I had one chance, and I grasped it, driving the hatpin straight into the arm that pinioned me.

There was a great howl of pain and surprise, and I was hoisted unceremoniously into the air and flung over a solid shoulder.

I heard a blow and a low groan that was unmistakably Stoker. I only hoped he had the wit to stop resisting and acquiesce to our abductors. I could not tell how many men it took to subdue him, but I could distinguish a number of footsteps, first on pavement, then on wood, the dull thud of the planks and the plashing of little wavelets making it apparent they had taken us onto the river. There was a moment of struggle, as if my abductor found it challenging to keep his balance, and the world began to rock. We were on a boat, and the fact that they had snatched us in broad daylight spoke volumes about their desperation.

I was set down hard upon my bottom—upon a sort of bench, I thought, and my assailant put a hand firmly to my shoulder. "Do not move," he ordered. He made no attempt to bind me, but I did as he commanded, biding my time.

I heard the rough sound of an engine being started and from the abrupt shifting of the boat deduced it was a small one, every motion of our captors setting it to rocking. There was a flurry of orders and our little craft was under way. I strained my ears to detect any sign of Stoker's presence, but I heard nothing apart from the hurried whispers of the villainous wretches who had seized us.

No one approached me for a long while—no doubt they were too bent upon getting right away, but if they expected me to beg for information or release, they would be mightily disappointed, I vowed. I sat with perfect composure, hands tucked into my pockets, and waited for something to happen.

It took an exceedingly long time before something did. I amused myself by reciting poetry under my breath—not Keats; I found Byron to be much more appropriate for an abduction. At length, something over an hour later given how long it took me to remember "The Giaour," the sacking was plucked from my head and I emerged, dazed and blinking, into the afternoon light to face my captor.

"Hello, Mr. de Clare," I said courteously. "I presumed you were my abductor, but I hated to rob you of your dramatic flourish."

Mr. de Clare gave a rueful shake of the head. "Miss Speedwell, I regret the necessity for this more than you know. But I am afraid you have forced my hand."

I seized the opportunity to look about and take stock of my situation. The weather had turned for the worse, and in place of the bright sunlight, a cover of grey cloud had descended. The boat, as I had guessed, was a small thing—a pleasure yacht of minute proportions and little power, although it was bowling along handsomely under sail. The engine was still ticking on, and the tide was running out, so it was apparent that Mr. de Clare was putting as much distance as possible between us and London proper. I was not altogether familiar with the Thames or its environs, but just then a sight hove into view that would have gladdened the heart of any Englishwoman. It needed only a moment's glance at the long, elegant façade to recognize that we were almost upon the Royal Naval College at Greenwich.

Having established our whereabouts, I made a quick

inventory of the boat. On the deck, stretched out on his back, Stoker lay perfectly still. His head was still hidden by a sack, but his chest rose in deep, even breaths, and I saw no visible injury.

"Well, at least you haven't murdered anyone yet," I said pleasantly. I looked again to Stoker, whose breath began to alter strangely. His chest began to twitch in an odd pattern, and he looked for all the world as if he were going to have a fit of some sort. I stared hard at him, and after a moment, I turned my attention to the other occupants of the boat.

Besides Mr. de Clare, there were four other men—of the working classes from the look of their clothes. And one of them was remarkably tall. The other three were indistinguishable, dressed in serviceable plain clothes with unremarkable features. I doubted if their wives even bothered to tell them apart. As for me, I was far more interested in the large fellow who turned just then so that I saw his face.

"You!" I exclaimed.

Mr. de Clare smiled thinly. "Yes, you have already made the acquaintance of Silent John. I regret the muddle he made of things at your cottage. He is deplorably incapable at times," he added with a scornful glance at his colleague. Silent John merely stood, his booted feet a yard apart on the deck, his expression blank. "You see?" Mr. de Clare turned to me. "Incapable. He must be told what to do in very specific terms, and when you came upon him at your cottage, he was thrown into a quandary."

"He tried to abduct me," I returned icily. "As you just have."

"Abduction is a strong word," he remonstrated. "You have not been bound or injured. I have merely taken steps to ensure that we can speak without interference. You have left me no choice. I have much to tell you, Miss Speedwell."

I wondered whether to acknowledge that I knew my

mother's identity—or that I surmised he was my uncle. But before I could make up my mind upon the point, he glanced to Stoker's recumbent form.

Stoker had begun to have a fit, his legs kicking as his hands tightened into fists that drummed rhythmically against the deck. Mr. de Clare signaled to Silent John, who pulled the sack from Stoker's head. His eyes were rolled back into his head and his lips were drawn back in a snarl as he foamed a little at the mouth.

"We have no need of him and he has proven an encumbrance," Mr. de Clare said with an expression of distaste. He flicked his gaze to Silent John. "We must complete Miss Speedwell's liberation from this fellow. Drop him overboard."

If I had any doubts as to his villainy, that decided me. Without hesitation, Silent John lifted Stoker as if he weighed no more than thistledown and dropped him over the side of the boat. He made a hefty splash as he went in, and I jumped to my feet.

"Calm yourself, Miss Speedwell," Mr. de Clare instructed. "I do not know precisely how far he has exercised control over you, but you need fear nothing. He is gone, and we are here to protect you." He took a step closer to me, but I had chosen my moment well. I took my hand from my pocket, brandishing the tiny revolver Lady Cordelia had given me.

"Stand back," I commanded.

Mr. de Clare stopped, raising his hands in astonishment. "There is no need for this, my dear. Now, put the revolver down and let us talk."

"I am quite finished talking to you," I told him.

He jerked his head to Silent John, who began to advance upon me. I sighed. I had no wish to shoot the fellow in spite of what he had done to Stoker. I lifted my hand and pulled my hatpin free. The wind snatched at my violet-trimmed hat and carried it off just as Silent John reached for my revolver. I let him take it, luring him near, and as his fingers closed over the weapon, I drove the hatpin into his arm, pushing hard until I felt it strike bone.

He gave a deep cry of animal anguish and stumbled backward, but I already had one foot upon the rail. I gave my uncle a quick salute and dove overboard, letting the noisome green water of the Thames close over my head.

The river was far colder than I expected, the shock of it driving the air straight out of my lungs. I kicked to the surface, or at least I meant to, but my skirts, heavy with water, dragged me back again. I realized then that I had miscalculated my strength as a swimmer when fully clothed. I had just begun to consider the very real possibility of death by drowning when I felt something hard clasp me about the waist. The water was far too murky to see, but I knew that arm. It settled firmly around me, urging me backward on a hard male torso, and I relaxed against him. He pulled us calmly and easily to the surface. I glanced up to see we were just behind the stern of the boat.

Stoker, perfectly restored to health and sense, put a finger to his lips and held me up as I gulped in several deep breaths. Above us but looking in entirely the wrong direction, Edmund de Clare and his henchmen searched the river frantically. Stoker pointed to the steps of the Naval College a little distance away, and held up three fingers. I breathed in, and he held up two. I took one last precious lungful of air and he pulled me below the water again. With complete calm he towed me silently towards the steps of the college. I willed him on, painfully aware of how slender a chance we had of success. It would be but a matter of seconds before Mr. de Clare realized there was only one direction we could have gone.

Halfway to the steps, I felt a burning in my chest, my

lungs stale and empty. I pushed at Stoker, and he led me to the surface of the water. I looked back as I sputtered and gasped to find I had underestimated my uncle. He was already in pursuit, ordering his men to turn the boat and give chase. The worsening weather had driven the pleasure boaters from the river. There were few craft about, and none it seemed within hailing distance.

"We cannot make it," I burbled to Stoker. "At least you cannot if you are burdened with me. Go on. He shall not harm me, but if he gets his hands on you again, he will surely kill you."

Stoker's response was something entirely unprintable, but it warmed my heart to see how offended he was at the notion he should leave me behind. He gave me just enough time to take another breath before plunging us both underwater again, this time kicking with all his might as he pulled with his free hand, shuttling us through the dank green river like a son of Poseidon. The effort must have exhausted him, for the next time we surfaced it was at his behest, his chest heaving. I looked up to see Edmund de Clare's boat coming hard, and turned again to offer Stoker a chance at escape.

Before I could form the words, a swift little yacht, as slim and fast as a dolphin, swooped in to slide gracefully between us and Edmund de Clare. A hand reached over the side of the yacht, and above the hand loomed a handsome, grinning face I had last seen only two days previously.

"Would you like to come aboard?" asked Mornaday, the groom.

Without further ado, he hoisted me aboard the yacht, turning back to offer Stoker an arm. We flopped onto the deck in floods of brackish river water, breathing hard as Mornaday turned to the skipper of the craft.

"Back upriver, Tolly. And be quick about it."

The boat came nimbly about, nipping past the prow

of Edmund de Clare's boat. I saw him, his handsome face contorted in fury as he ordered his men to flee, pushing the boat hard downriver. Whatever he wanted with me, he wanted still less to attract the attention of anyone else, and I was as grateful as I was mystified by the turn of events.

Mornaday brought blankets and a flask of good Irish whiskey, which he urged upon us. He gave a nod to the Naval College as we sailed past, noting the bunting that had already been hung in honor of the queen's Jubilee.

"All of London will turn out to watch her ride past," Mornaday remarked. "A plump German housewife with little intellect and smaller understanding, and yet the whole world will pause to pay tribute to her longevity."

His broad accents were entirely absent now, as was his usually cheerful demeanor. This Mornaday was altogether more serious a fellow, focused and attentive to the business at hand.

"Are you a republican?" I asked politely.

He smiled, baring his lovely teeth. "I am an Englishman. I serve my country first, queen second. All that matters to me is England."

"And in what capacity do you serve England?" Stoker inquired.

"Policeman. Inspector Mornaday, at your service," he said, sweeping us a bow. He made it sound as if he were a lowly bobby, but I knew at an instant he was far more highly placed than that.

"Have you been investigating the baron's murder?" I demanded.

"Not officially, but yes. And I have been doing my utmost to keep you from danger, although you seem determined to thwart me," he added dryly.

"But why would the baron's murderer be dangerous to me?"

"I cannot tell you." He held up a hand at my exclamation

of dismay. "It will do you no good to remonstrate with me. It is more than my position at Scotland Yard is worth to even be with you now."

"But why would your position at Scotland Yard be put at risk by aiding us?"

"Because he is concealing the whereabouts of a man who is wanted to help the police with their inquiries," Stoker supplied.

Mornaday inclined his head gravely. "As you say. My duty is to bring you to my superiors and let them question you. But I have put another consideration first."

"What consideration?" I asked.

"Your safety. I believe that Mr. Stoker, while most assuredly *not* your husband, is the man best positioned to ensure your continued good health."

"That is rather generous of you, considering the fact that you have come to our aid twice," I said in an acid tone.

The grin flashed again. "Yes, I was the one who chased Mr. de Clare away outside the baron's residence. And if I were a better shot in near darkness, I might have brought this whole matter to an end then," he added ruefully. I did not glance at Stoker, but I knew he would be entirely smug about having been right as to Mr. de Clare's villainy. I had been wrong to give him the benefit of the doubt, and it stung—almost as much as the guinea I should most likely have to part with if our wager was settled in Stoker's favor. Mornaday went on. "I have better reason than most to know Mr. Stoker would have acquitted himself more than adequately without my intervention. However, given his family history, I am not entirely certain he would have done so without unnecessary bloodshed, something I wish to avoid."

"What family history?" I asked.

"I believe Mr. Stoker is better suited to explain that than I am."

Beside me, Stoker had gone very still, his hands resting loosely upon his thighs. When he spoke, his voice was flat, almost bored, and the very lack of emotion in his tone was more chilling than the most murderous rage.

"Mornaday, when this business, whatever it is, is finished, I will find you. And there will be things to say." To a disinterested observer, it might have sounded like casual conversation, but I knew it for the threat it was, and so did Mornaday.

Mornaday's smile faltered only a little, but I noticed his lips went white even as he forced a cordial tone. "I should look forward to it. But if I have my way, there will be no chance. I do not want you in this country, Mr. Stoker. Nor do I want Miss Speedwell here."

"You know her name?" Stoker looked from Mornaday to me. "Did you tell him that we are not really married?"

"I did not," I replied. "How he came to know my name is entirely beyond my ken."

"My methods are my own," Mornaday said silkily. "Now, Miss Speedwell, I have in mind to be a chief inspector someday. That will not happen with blots upon my record, and you will not be a blot."

"Then why help us?" I asked, drawing the blanket about my sodden body more tightly. As I warmed a little, I was aware of a distinctly unpleasant aroma beginning to emanate from my person, and Stoker's was worse. The Thames was a filthy place, I reflected, and we would both be thoroughly fortunate if we did not contract one of the more virulent wasting diseases after our dunking.

Mornaday's reply to my question was prompt. "Because the police do not always get it right. My superior likes Mr. Stoker for the murder of the baron, and he suspects you of being an accomplice. I believe he is wrong. And I very much like it when he is wrong." His mouth curved into an arch smile.

"Unfortunately, it is never wise to point out the shortcomings of one's superiors. So I have acquired the habit of occasionally circumventing him by conducting my own investigation and removing his suspects from under his nose. I followed you to the traveling show on a hunch of my own. I observed you there and formed my impression that neither of you was responsible for the baron's murder."

"Did you bribe the professor to let you have the position as groom?"

"I did. I spun him a tale about thwarted love and disappointed hopes. I persuaded him that Mr. Stoker had stolen my fiancée. He was most susceptible. I suspect him of being a romantic, and he was very quick to believe the worst of Mr. Stoker. In fact, he insisted upon it."

"And you promised him more money if he discovered any relevant information. As you did Salome," I accused.

Mornaday clucked his tongue. "Very well, yes. I paid them both to discover what they could. And it was remarkably little," he said with a repressive glance at Stoker. "The promise of a few coins to the professor, a few more to Salome, and they were more than willing to turn over whatever information they discovered. The professor still bears a grudge over some old quarrel, and Salome's head for business is hard as nails. She would sell her own mother for a copper." He glanced to Stoker. "You really ought to choose your friends more carefully, old man."

"You needn't worry," Stoker returned with equal coolness. "It isn't as though you were going to be one."

"If you do not believe in our culpability in the baron's murder, then how did that notice get into the newspapers?" I asked. Mornaday winced.

"As we had so few leads in the case, my superior was willing to let me take a short holiday. I did not tell him I was chasing down a hunch, and so, when he grew impatient, there was nothing to stop him from pursuing what he believed to be his likeliest suspect. I followed you back to London and picked up your trail again at the baron's house when you broke in."

I could see his disapproval. "We had reasons," I said coolly.

"I am sure that you did. I have no doubt you went there with the idea of playing amateur detective and solving the baron's murder in order to make certain Mr. Stoker was not unjustly accused of a crime he did not commit."

"And how is it that you were on hand to effect such a timely rescue today?" Stoker asked.

Mornaday smiled again. "I have a number of contacts in the community of watermen. By a little judicious bribery in the right quarters, I happened to learn that Mr. de Clare had secured the hire of a boat for himself, and that he insisted upon something light and fast. It seemed logical that he meant to attempt to spirit Miss Speedwell away, and it was a small matter to find myself a boat that was even faster. Once I had done that, I needed only to keep a close watch upon him and follow along to intervene when required." He gave us a severe look. "But we are beyond that now. You must believe me when I tell you that you must leave London. My superior is growing suspicious of my frequent absences. I cannot always be there to stand at your back, and these miscreants will not relinquish their pursuit."

He gestured to the helmsman, who began to make for a short boat landing just before a great cluster of docks and ships. "Those are the West India docks beyond. You should be able to pick up a hansom here. I cannot take you further. And I cannot say more. Please, for the sake of your lives, go. Anywhere but England."

"What about Ireland?" I asked deliberately.

He swore softly. "Whatever you think you may know about Ireland, forget it. I have told you I cannot say more, but yes, Mr. de Clare and his friends are Irish, and you must give them a wide berth if you wish to live long enough to celebrate your next birthday." He turned anguished eyes to Stoker. "You must make her see reason. Get her safely out of the country."

Stoker shrugged. "I cannot even persuade her to stay in the house. What makes you think I can force her to leave the country?"

I put a quelling hand to Stoker's arm. "Do not alarm Mr. Mornaday, Stoker. Can you not see he is aggrieved on our behalf? And we owe him so much already." The helmsman brought us gently up to the little landing, and Mornaday handed us onto the dock before pointing out the quickest route to a main thoroughfare.

I extended my hand to him. "Thank you for your many kindnesses. I hope if we meet again it will be under very different circumstances," I told him. He saluted and the little boat slipped away as swiftly as it had come, nimbly dodging the larger craft upon the water as it made its way upriver.

Stoker turned to me with an expression of frank skepticism. "You are not actually thinking of leaving the country." It was not even a question, and I gave a little sigh of pleasure that he was beginning to know me so well.

"Of course not. But why give Mr. Mornaday something to worry about? He seems such a nice fellow."

"A nice fellow!" Stoker snorted. "He bribed people I once considered friends to give information about us—a deed that will not go unpunished."

"Something to save for a rainy day," I promised him. "In the meantime, we must return to Bishop's Folly and get into some dry clothes and apply ourselves to the mystery at hand. We have much to talk about."

TWENTY-THREE

In spite of Mornaday's blithe assurances that we should easily secure a cab, we walked some distance before finding an empty hansom whose driver seemed entirely incurious about taking up two bedraggled passengers. Stoker gave him the address of Bishop's Folly and we settled against the seat quite close together—for warmth rather than from any more affectionate motivation.

After a moment, Stoker began to smile.

"What is so funny?" I demanded.

"You. I never imagined you would actually understand my signal."

"You mean your melodramatic attempts at Morse code by drumming your fists on the deck? It's a wonder every boatman on the Thames didn't understand it."

He rolled his eyes heavenward. "Forgive me for failing to find a more subtle means of informing you of my intentions, but I was improvising. I've never been abducted before. I shall do better next time."

I gave an unladylike snort of laughter. "I think we managed, all things considered. And for a first-timer at abduction, you did very well indeed."

His gaze narrowed. "Veronica, have you been abducted before?"

I waved an airy hand, thinking of my intemperate Corsican friend and a few rather delicate situations in Sarawak and Mexico. "Oh, heaps of times."

He opened his mouth to speak but thought better of it, and we journeyed back to Bishop's Folly in soggy silence.

I was surprised to find upon reaching the Belvedere how quickly the place had come to seem like a home of sorts—borrowed, temporary, but a home nonetheless. I stoked the fire in the snug and put the kettle on while Stoker rummaged about and unearthed a bit of slender rope. He secured one end to a caryatid's wrist and the other to a narwhal's tusk, fashioning a makeshift and rather exotic clothesline. I made first use of the little domestic office to tidy myself and was just hanging my things upon the clothesline to dry when Stoker emerged from his own efforts, toweling his hair, his shirt opened loosely at the throat.

"All of my sweets, at the bottom of the Thames," he grumbled. I rummaged among the tins of provisions and found a bit of honeycomb candy. The pieces were stuck together, but he occupied himself happily in breaking them apart and when he put the first piece into his mouth, he closed his eyes and sighed in unadulterated pleasure.

I took an inventory of all that I had lost. "A hatpin, my violet hat, and Lady Cordelia's revolver, all gone," I mourned. But my little velvet mouse had survived the dunking. I had placed him in a warm and discreet spot next to the stove whilst Stoker had been occupied drying himself. Naturally, I did not think of Chester as a child's keepsake; he was a mascot of sorts and nothing more, but Stoker would no doubt make a fuss and I was in no mood to be laughed at.

I was annoyed enough to find my compass had been thoroughly wetted, and I dried it carefully, clucking as I turned it this way and that in an effort to get the arrow to move.

"Blast. I think the water has got inside and ruined it," I muttered.

Stoker came to my side and peered over my shoulder. "Let me. I do like to tinker a bit," he said, taking the compass from me. "Where did you get this?"

"Aunt Lucy. She told me it would always show me the way home again, and I have worn it every day since."

He turned it this way and that, examining it thoroughly. "An expensive piece. Heavy for its size."

"Well, Aunt Lucy was like that—if she had a tuppence, she would rather spend it on a flower than bread. Aunt Nell was just the opposite, practical to a fault. She deplored Aunt Lucy's spendthrift ways. In fact, she hated that compass, no doubt because it *was* expensive."

"Hated it?" he asked, but his voice was detached, his focus entirely upon the piece he held.

"Yes, I was wearing it the first time I came into her room after her apoplexy. She looked at it and was so enraged, the doctor had to give her an injection of morphia to settle her down. I did not wear it in front of her again so as not to upset her."

"Interesting," he murmured. He raised it to his ear and shook it hard.

"Stoker! What are you doing? You will ruin it," I protested.

He held it to my ear. "Listen." He gave another shake and I heard a faint but unmistakable rattle.

"What on earth—"

I put out my hand for the compass, running my thumb along the side. For the first time I noticed a seam at the edge.

The day's events had loosened it a little, and one bit stood just proud of the rest. I tried to slip a fingernail behind it.

"Too thick," I muttered. Stoker retrieved the knife from the lanyard he had put aside when he changed his clothes. "Try this."

I slid the finely honed edge under the seam and gave a gentle push. It popped free so suddenly I nearly dropped the entire thing. Wedged tightly into the back of the compass was a key. I used the knife blade to pry it free.

"Did either of the aunts leave you anything with a lock? A box? A small trunk?"

"Nothing. Only this—a perfectly anonymous key," I said in some frustration.

"Not entirely anonymous," he said, turning it over for my inspection. Along the length of the key were incised a series of letters. "BOLOXST," I read aloud. "But what does it mean? It sounds like a rude word."

"I highly doubt your aunt would have given you a key with a variation of 'bollocks' on it. A surname, perhaps? Did you ever meet anyone of their acquaintance with that name?"

"Boloxst? No, it's a ridiculous notion. No one has ever been called Boloxst," I said.

"It does seem unlikely," he agreed. "Perhaps it is an anagram."

We set to work with paper and pencils and an hour later gave it up as a blind alley. "I've nothing more interesting than 'stool,'" I remarked. "Hardly illuminating."

"Indeed. If one were going to leave behind a keyhole, it would scarcely be in a stool. Perhaps it *is* a foreign name."

I peered at the letters again. "If one really concentrates, it looks almost Flemish."

"No," he said flatly. "We've already got the Irish involved, thanks to the villainous Mr. de Clare. I will not tolerate Flemings as well."

"You are irritable, and heavens, I can see why! We haven't eaten in hours and we've let the kettle boil dry."

Stoker took his turn at providing victuals and we ate cold meat and mustard on bread as we drank our tea. "Go over it again," I instructed. "Everything we know."

"Your mother was an Irish actress who changed her name to pursue a career," he began promptly.

"Hold a moment. Perhaps there is something there. Her name before she changed it was de Clare. Do we know anything about the de Clares?"

He shrugged. "Old family—in the Domesday Book just like the Templeton-Vanes. Some king or other sent them off to Ireland, and a branch has been there ever since."

I shook my head. "I do not understand. If she were a de Clare, then she—and my duplicitous uncle—would be nobility. What objection could my father's family have to her as a bride?"

"Her career. Actresses have gained a little in respectability since the days of the Restoration, but families like mine wouldn't countenance one marrying in for a second. Besides, the de Clares have been in Ireland for centuries, breeding like rabbits. There are doubtless dozens of cadet lines which have come down quite far in the world. She mightn't have been born any better than a merchant's daughter or a farmer's." His eyes took on a speculative gleam. "You would have to ask your uncle. I should like to meet up with him again—I owe him a thrashing."

I gave him a repressive look and he shrugged. "Or you might try to trace her relations. Perhaps there are other siblings or even a grandparent still living."

"Absolutely not. I am not going to Ireland."

"Why not?"

"Have you been to Ireland? The climate is appalling. Nothing but mist."

"What is your objection to mist?"

I regarded him with the same disdain with which I had beheld my first Turkish toilet. "It is gloomy. Butterflies like the sun. Ireland is for the *moth* people."

"You are a lepidopterist," he said repressively. "You are not supposed to discriminate against moths."

"I am entitled to my prejudices," I replied before returning to the subject at hand. "Still, there seems little enough point in going to Ireland when the Irish have come to us. My uncle and his henchman are all Hibernian." I paused, considering the peculiar green spice my uncle smelled of. "Why do you suppose my uncle chews caraway? I wonder what it signifies."

"That he has digestive issues," Stoker supplied promptly. "Caraway seeds are a carminative. I have occasionally prescribed them to patients with an excess of wind."

"You mean—"

"Yes," he said, cutting me off sharply before I could finish the thought.

"How unfortunate," I murmured. I dared not meet his eyes for fear I would dissolve into laughter at the notion of an abductor who suffered from excessive wind. I primmed my mouth. "So, we have a mother and uncle and assorted miscreants from Ireland, where I was born. We assume that my mother left me in the care of the Harbottles, and they found it expedient to leave Ireland. But why? Who would profit from menacing an infant in those circumstances?"

Our eyes met and we spoke in unison. "The father."

"I did not like to believe it, but perhaps you were right. It does have a certain pretty symmetry," I observed. "We can assume my father was also Irish, perhaps better bred than my mother, perhaps from a conservative family. After my birth, he marries this other woman instead of my mother. Lily Ashbourne dies, possibly by his hand. Who, then, is left to tie him to her memory? His child. A loose end he must knot.

Fearing him, the Harbottles flee Ireland and move constantly throughout my childhood, eluding him and the threat he poses." I floundered. "Then what?"

Stoker promptly picked up the thread. "He cannot find you. Perhaps he has come close throughout the years. Perhaps he has put men loyal to himself onto your trail. He may have collected a few clues. It is possible the Harbottles were less than careful when they ought to have been."

"The baron knew their assumed name, and we know he had a connection to my father," I added. "My father may have discovered our whereabouts through him. The baron never knew where we were living, but when Aunt Nell died, I placed a notice in the London newspaper. I did not believe they had connections anywhere, but I wanted to make quite certain any possible debts were settled. That is how the baron found us."

We were silent a moment, both of us considering the implications.

"I have thought of something else that might have kept them apart," Stoker put in. "It might be that your mother was born to a respectable, even a wealthy family. But in Ireland, even money isn't enough to span one unbridgeable divide."

"Religion," I supplied.

He gave a short nod. "Precisely. We know from the papers that your mother was a practicing Catholic. What if your father was a Protestant? Those resentments run deep." That much was true. I had missed some of the more sensational headlines during my travels, but a quick perusal of the newspapers in Stoker's workroom had enlightened me. It had been only two years since Irishmen detonated dynamite at the Tower and Westminster Hall, and shortly before there had been the Phoenix Park Murders—the fatal stabbings of the Chief Secretary for Ireland and his Permanent Undersecretary. The fact that the secretary had been a member of the powerful Cavendish family had not protected him. Even the royal family was not safe. An Irishman had come close to assassinating the queen's own son in Australia not so many years before. And these were merely the most recent acts in centuries of violent conflict.

I sighed. "I suppose it is not difficult to believe that a Protestant fellow from a good family would never dare marry a Catholic actress. He would be marked down as a traitor by his side, as would she. They should both be in danger, depending how deeply their families felt about Home Rule." I dropped my head into my hands. "God, what a filthy muddle."

"And there might be more," he said.

I lifted my head to look him squarely in the eye. "I have this day been abducted, nearly drowned, and stabbed a man with a hatpin. I am unsinkable, Stoker. Do your worst."

"It did occur to me that your father might be in league with your uncle," he said flatly. "And if that is the case, he might well be responsible for Max's death."

I sputtered. "Impossible."

"You cannot say that," he told me in a reasonable tone. "You do not know him."

"I know that it is highly illogical to think on the one hand my father might be responsible for Lily Ashbourne's death and on the other that he might be conspiring with her brother!"

He shrugged. "Illogical but not impossible. And we've no proof your father had anything to do with her death. For all we know, he was forced into the marriage and heartbroken at giving Lily up."

"Oh, make up your mind!" I slapped my palms to the table and thrust myself out of my chair.

To his everlasting credit, he said nothing, letting me pace back and forth until I had run out my irritation. I gave a sigh of impatience and settled back into my chair.

"Don't pout," Stoker warned. "Your face will settle into

permanent creases of sulkiness."

"I am not sulking. I am thinking." After a few minutes, I gave up. "Very well. You have a point. My father may or may not be a villain. He may or may not have played a part in my mother's death. And he may or may not be implicated in the baron's death. We have done nothing but make the waters murky, Stoker."

"I know." He rubbed his temples. "We are scientists. It is our vocation to think critically and we have been going at this entirely backward."

I tipped my head. "You just admitted I am a scientist rather than a dilettante who chases pretty things with wings."

"You do chase pretty things with wings," he returned. "You do not like the poor hairy moths."

"Don't be ridiculous. I mightn't like all of the moths, but some of them are quite resplendent. *Hyalophora cecropia*, for instance—"

He raised a hand. "You needn't justify yourself to me. As you say, we are entitled to our prejudices. I should be far happier to work upon a lioness than a vulture. We are mere humans, Veronica. We are destined to prefer beauty to ugliness."

His mouth twisted upon these last words, and I wondered if he was thinking of his own altered beauty and if he felt somehow diminished by it.

Suddenly, I surged from my chair, this time in triumph. "I know what the inscription on the key means."

"What?" he demanded.

"Where would you go to leave something of value?"

"A bank," was the prompt reply.

"And what city are we in?"

"London." Understanding kindled in his face. "BOL. Bank of London."

"Exactly."

"And OXST?" His eyes lit and he gave me a grin. "Oxford Street branch."

I curled my hands into triumphant fists. "Yes! I know it is right. I *know* it."

"Veronica," he said gently, "what do you hope to find there?"

"Proof that my father did not harm my mother," I replied. "Proof that he did. Something, *anything* that I can hold on to and know is real."

He gave me a searching look, then a grudging nod. "That I can understand."

"What did Mornaday mean when he spoke of your family history?" I asked.

He considered his hands as he formed his answer. "Let us simply say that Inspector Mornaday knows things that are none of his business—things that ought to have been buried years ago."

"I should not have pried."

He gave me a ghostly smile. "It isn't your knowing that I mind. It's the telling." I said nothing and after a moment he went on. "My family and I are not close. That is why I use only a variation of my given name rather than the name Lord Templeton-Vane gave me," he told me with a curl of his lip. "I do not speak to them and they do not speak to me. It is better that way. Old sins are never forgot, but they may be packed away."

A thousand questions hung upon my lips, but I asked him none. Instead I changed the subject.

"You wagered me a guinea that my birth is somehow linked to the baron's death. If we discover everything we can about my father, then if you are correct, we will surely stand a better chance of finding the baron's killer."

"True," he said absently.

"And it is very kind of Inspector Mornaday to play the

ally. He has bought us time, perhaps even enough to establish your innocence."

Stoker fixed me with a searching look. "Are you really so naïve? Kindness has nothing to do with it."

"Well, I admit he would certainly profit from it professionally if he manages to conclude this case successfully," I acknowledged.

He gave a snort of laughter. "Mornaday is more compelled by his libido than his ambition. Ah, that was a palpable hit. It has brought a blush to your cheek." He poured out a fresh cup of tea for himself and added a splash of whiskey.

Something about his tone and his casual dismissal of Mornaday irritated me. The fellow had delivered us, not once but twice, and it required little imagination to think Stoker resented his interference. I had little sympathy with such overweening masculine pride, and I resolved to prick it.

I raised my chin. "It has done nothing of the sort," I retorted. "If Inspector Mornaday hopes for a carnal reward at the end of this, his hopes might not be entirely misplaced."

Stoker spluttered upon his tea. "What?"

"You heard me. He is a handsome fellow," I said, warming to my theme. "Handsome enough I might even be persuaded to break my rule against dalliances with Englishmen. He has expressive eyes and a pleasing way about him. And I believe I have already mentioned his lovely hands."

Stoker swore fluently and shoved his teacup aside.

"Where are you going?" I asked sweetly.

"Out."

"Mind you don't stray too far. I promised Lady Cordelia we should dine with her and his lordship tonight."

The only response was the slamming of the Belvedere door behind him. I smiled and poured out another cup of tea.

TWENTY-FOUR

STOKER WAS IN SUCH a filthy temper when he returned that I felt rather sorry for the Beauclerks for inflicting him upon them. He said scarcely a dozen words at dinner, restricting himself to complimenting Lady Cordelia on the lamb and Lord Rosemorran on the acquisition of a rather fine pelt of a Himalayan bear. It was left to the Beauclerks and to me to carry the flag of civility, and we managed quite nicely.

We settled onto the subject of travel, and his lordship was most interested to find I had been to Switzerland, a country of particular interest to him.

"And how did you find Switzerland, Miss Speedwell?" he asked as we started in on some elegant fish roulades.

"Very pleasant, so long as one is able to overlook the preponderance of goiter," I replied.

That led to a thoroughly engrossing discussion on the efficacy of the Chinese methods of dealing with goiter, the Boxer Rebellion, opium addiction, the problem of crime in the East End, and the difficulty of finding a cook who could produce a really good blancmange.

Through our conversational meanderings, I also learned that Lady Cordelia claimed membership in the Hippolyta Club, founded to celebrate the achievements of remarkable women. I had long been intrigued by its reputation for accepting the most distinguished members, whose intelligence was equaled only by their accomplishments. Some of the less respectful society wags had christened it the Curiosity Club on the basis that its members were constantly sticking in their noses where ladies' noses ought not to be, but the members had adopted the epithet as a badge of honor. For her part, Lady Cordelia had been nominated on the strength of a paper she had written upon the subject of hyperintegers, mathematics being her particular passion. Scarcely able to multiply beyond the twelves myself, I was immensely impressed, and I turned to Lord Rosemorran, inviting him to share my respect.

"Oh yes, Cordelia and her numbers. Very useful for keeping the estate accounts," he said with a fond look.

I looked back at Lady Cordelia, who was quietly dissecting her lamb into tiny pieces. It was the rankest chauvinism that he reduced her intellectual accomplishments to columns in a ledger, but I realized from her placid looks that Lady Cordelia must be well accustomed to his benign neglect, and I sighed for her. She gave me a small, conspiratorial smile, and I found myself liking her very much indeed.

For his part, Lord Rosemorran was keen to display his newest treasure, a stuffed Eurasian eagle owl he had purchased at auction. "Belonged to Voltaire. Was it Voltaire?" he asked, rummaging in his pocket for the card with the specimen's description. "Ah well. It makes little difference now he's mine. I mean to call him Tacitus." He nudged me in the ribs with his elbow. "D'ye mark the joke? Rather good one that, calling a stuffed owl Tacitus."

He was still chuckling when we took our leave, and while Stoker tarried a moment to discuss the new trophy with his lordship, Lady Cordelia walked me through the morning room to make the acquaintance of her lovebirds, Crates and Hipparchia. They had the freedom of an enormous cage of wrought iron, some ten feet in length, but they cuddled close together on a single perch, rather like their namesakes.

I said as much to Lady Cordelia and she smiled her gentle Madonna's smile. "They are devoted to one another," she said. She was dressed, as ever, in deepest black, and as she spoke, she twisted a ring upon her finger. It was a mourning ring set with a single lock of hair the color of a russet apple.

She saw my glance and squared her shoulders, concealing her hands in the folds of her skirts. "How go your investigative efforts, Miss Speedwell?"

"We are moving forward," I told her. "There was a development today, in fact, during the course of which I am sorry to say that I lost your revolver. You must allow me to replace it."

She shook her head. "Do not trouble yourself. I only hope it proved useful."

"Indeed it did."

"Good," she said. "You must let me know if you require further protection of firearms. His lordship has quite a collection."

"For the love of God, do not encourage her," Stoker instructed as he strode up to join us.

"I am not encouraging," she said calmly. "I am abetting." She turned to me. "You are striking a blow for all of us with your adventures, Miss Speedwell. I hope you know that."

I thought of her then, her brilliant mathematician's mind wasted upon grocers' bills and linen counts, and I pressed her hand in return. "I will do my best not to let down the side, Lady Cordelia."

* * *

When Stoker and I returned to the snug in the Belvedere, I poured us each a stiff measure of whiskey, but when I attempted to introduce the subject of the latest developments in our adventure, he held up a repressive hand.

"No."

"No?"

"Not tonight. As you noted earlier, we have been the victims of a thwarted abduction, swum halfway across the Thames, received cryptic revelations from Mornaday, and I cannot speak for you, but my head throbs. I am going to drink this and then go to bed, where I intend to sleep at least twelve hours. We have all of tomorrow to bat theories around like so many shuttlecocks. Until then, I am my own man."

With that pronouncement, he took his glass and stalked off to the sofa, where he arranged himself with some difficulty, his long legs half-hanging over the arm.

"All right," I agreed amiably. "We shall not speak of the murder or any of its attendant questions."

We were silent awhile, companionably so. Stoker read a journal of zoology while I occupied myself with my own mammalian studies. I had become aware of an annoyingly insistent biological demand, which I had initially attributed to the excitement of our recent adventures. The urge for physical congress is closely linked to that of survival, I reasoned, and we had been fleeing from danger.

It had also been, I thought sadly, far too long since my last erotic indulgence. I began to count backward on my fingers to my last journey, but the task soon proved depressing. To say that I longed for a little male companionship would be an understatement so extreme as to be criminal. I fairly vibrated with need, and I knew from experience that my body's demands would only grow more urgent unless they were slaked. And while Stoker might be a little lacking in finesse, I had little doubt he could employ his admirably nimble hands and well-proportioned frame to great effect. He also had the advantage of proximity, I reflected.

Too great a proximity. He was a fellow countryman, and therefore entirely out of bounds to me, I reminded myself with mingled disappointment and relief. I would have appreciated the satisfaction of a carnal paroxysm—in my experience, they bring a sparkle to the eye as well as brightness to the complexion and a spring to the step—but using Stoker to achieve that end was a means I could not begin to contemplate. Tumbling in the sheets with a man was one thing; facing him the next morning over the toast rack was another matter entirely.

Still, I found myself curious about how he managed his own physiological needs. He had shown himself immensely responsive—even against his will—to Salome's efforts. And during our brief embrace in the shadows, he had given every indication of an extremely passionate nature held firmly in check. I pondered the question for some time before my curiosity got the better of me.

"It occurs to me, Stoker, I have made no secret of the fact that I am accustomed to a certain amount of regular and health-giving exercise of the intimate variety whilst abroad," I began. "And I think I must arrange a trip abroad soon if my health is not to suffer the consequences. It has been too long." I tipped my head as I looked him over from tousled hair to scuffed boots. "How long has it been for you?"

He turned a shocked face to me. "That is bloody well none of your business!"

I shrugged. "Why? We are both scientists. I see no reason we cannot speak frankly of biological things. I find myself quite often distracted by such thoughts, and I merely wondered how you managed. Is there a technique you find effective in managing your urges?"

He raised his hands as if to ward off evil. "Stop. Now. I beg you."

I blinked. "You mean you do not wish to talk about it?"

"That is precisely what I mean."

I gave him a repressive look. "Oh, come now, Stoker. Don't be coy. Tell me. How long has it been for you?"

To my astonishment, he blushed. "It has been some time, years in fact—" He ground to a stop.

"How very extraordinary," I murmured.

"Is it? A gentleman is supposed to hold himself to a certain standard," he reminded me coldly.

"And yet you go to such lengths to pretend you do not deserve the title in other respects, it is curious you should cling so tightly to your scruples in this."

"It is not when you consider—" He broke off.

"When I consider what?" I prodded gently.

He said nothing for a long moment, and when he spoke, it was with a seriousness of purpose that would not be gainsaid. "I have my reasons," he told me. "And I must beg you to respect them." He hesitated and went on in a rough voice. "I have not always conducted myself as a gentleman; that much is true. But I am set upon a different path now. I no longer believe that degrading myself with slatterns and tavern wenches is appropriate."

I very nearly laughed, but his expression was so earnest, I could not. Instead I sat up. "Slatterns and tavern wenches? That's a curious sort of company to keep."

"Brazil is a curious place."

"Brazil? You have not lain with a woman since *Brazil*? Stoker, that was years ago."

"And?" he demanded.

"You must engage in horizontal refreshment. It isn't healthy to congest oneself like that."

"I am not congested," he retorted.

"Really? That brings me back to my question. You are a man with demonstrably strong passions, and yet you live like a monk. What about the solitary sensual pursuits? Do you ever engage in—"

"Not. Another. Word," he thundered. "I cannot believe you would ask me such a thing. And I am not discussing this further."

I pulled a face. "Very well."

It was his turn to blink in surprise. "Really? You concede? Just like that?"

"Heavens, Stoker. What did you expect? I asked for the truth and you have given as much as you feel comfortable sharing. Furthermore, I have discovered that whether you like it or not, you are a gentleman. And, I suspect, a romantic."

He snorted. "A romantic?"

"Indeed. Otherwise you would have made frequent and athletic use of any number of London's professional ladies of light virtue. While as a pragmatist, I do not always understand romanticism, I respect it."

"Well, then," he said uncertainly.

"Indeed. Good night, Stoker."

Retreating behind a rather splendid coromandel screen, I availed myself of the narrow campaign bed that had once belonged to the Duke of Wellington. Its proportions were modest, but it was comfortably furnished with a proper featherbed. I settled in, reflecting upon the curious character of the man with whom I had thrown in my lot. I could hear him turning the pages of the journal as he read, occasionally giving a low sigh as he arranged himself more comfortably. At length he blew out the lamp and we lay in darkness, separated by the screen. It was oddly companionable.

Something about his quickness of mind, his determination to live by his own lights, had called to me. I recognized his nature as my own. It was as if we were two castaways from a far-off land, adrift among strangers whose ways we could not entirely understand. But something within us spoke the same language, for all our clashes of words. He did not trust me entirely; that much was certain. And I frequently frustrated him to the point of madness. But I knew that whatever bedeviled him, he had need of me—and it seemed a betrayal to turn my back upon one of my own kind. I had seldom met another such as we, and I had learned that to be a child of the wilderness was a lonely thing.

Lying in the dark, I had intended to puzzle out the clues we had and assemble them in perfect order to present to Stoker the following morning as a dazzling solution in the manner of Arcadia Brown, Lady Detective. But just as I began to arrange the clues in my mind, I heard Stoker's voice.

"Cold water."

"I beg your pardon?"

He gave a gusty sigh. "Try cold water. Bathing in it, not drinking. A swim is the best if you can manage it. It will put you right off of those sorts of thoughts."

"Thank you, Stoker. I shall make a note of that."

He snorted by way of response. Smiling into the darkness, I surrendered to the soothing delights of goose down and linen sheets and sank into a sleep like death.

When I woke, I could tell it was morning although the light was watery and grey. The fine weather had broken and a dull day lay before us with the steady drum of rain upon the roof. I rose and washed and dressed, taking a bit of cheese and a cold ham roll for my breakfast. Stoker was still slumbering upon the sofa, and I took a moment to admire the prospect presented by a virile, attractive man caught in the vulnerability of sleep. I would have happily played Diana to his Endymion, but in the light of our previous discussion, I kept my hands chastely to myself and began to prowl with only the mollusks and the stuffed birds and paintings for company. I browsed the books and perused the collections, delighted to find a private translation of Maria Sibylla Merian's *Der Raupen wunderbare Verwandlung und sonderbare Blumennahrung.* I had just settled in happily with the first volume of *The Caterpillars' Marvelous Transformation and Strange Floral Food* when I became increasingly aware that I was not alone. From behind a molting egret standing upon one leg, a quizzical pair of dark eyes assessed me.

"Who are you?"

"I might ask you the same thing," I said coolly.

A child of perhaps six years stepped out from behind the bird. Her Sunday frock was streaked with something that looked suspiciously like golden treacle and her hair ribbon was dangling loose as if she had just been dragged through a bush backward.

"I am Rosie," she said solemnly.

"No, she isn't." Lady Cordelia's maid, Sidonie, appeared as if out of thin air, taking the child by the hand. "She is *Lady* Rose. Her father is Lord Rosemorran."

The child looked at me closely. "Who are you?" she demanded with an imperiousness that would have done credit to an empress. As a rule, I did not much like children, but I might learn to like this one, I decided.

"I am an adult person who is not answerable to children."

Before she could formulate a response, Stoker appeared.

"Hello, Lady Rose," he said, sweeping her a formal bow.

"Stoker!" the child crowed. She flung herself at him for an

embrace, but Sidonie put a dampening hand upon her shoulder.

"Lady Rose, you have the manners of a savage. Greet Mr. Stoker properly." She herself gave him a nod, darting a gaze up at him through lowered lashes. "Mr. Stoker, it is good to see you again. I hope that you are well."

"Very," he said solemnly before turning to the child. "And how are you, little Rose?"

"Tolerable."

Tolerable! The child had the soul of a dowager in an infant's body. She indicated me with a graceful wave of her hand. "Do you know this person?"

"I do indeed," he said.

"Her eyes are peculiar. I have never seen eyes that color. What color is that?"

"It is the precise color of the wing frills on a White-browed purpletuft, *Iodopleura isabellae*, from South America," he replied with such unthinking swiftness that I gave him a searching look.

"A White-browed purpletuft? I am afraid I am not familiar with that bird," I said quietly.

"It was something I happened to notice. Nothing more," he replied in haste. He flushed a little, and if his remark did not cause Sidonie to take notice, the sudden color of his complexion did. She gave me a look of frank speculation as Stoker turned again to the child. "Miss Speedwell is a friend of mine and of your father's and your aunt Cordelia's," he added significantly.

It was the mention of Lady Cordelia's name that did the trick. She sketched me the briefest of curtsies.

I gave her a casual nod just as her aunt appeared. "There you are! Rose, you have been stealing treacle from the kitchens again, haven't you?"

"No," the child said, widening her eyes innocently.

Lady Cordelia bent and put a finger to the child's cheek,

then popped it into her own mouth. "Treacle. Sidonie, take Lady Rose to her room. I shall be up directly."

The pair of them left, little Rose dragging her feet until Stoker slipped her a sweet behind Lady Cordelia's back. Sidonie cast a lovelorn look over her shoulder at Stoker as she went.

"I do hope my niece hasn't been disturbing you," Lady Cordelia said to me. "She and her brother arrived late last night rather unexpectedly, and we are between governesses at present."

"Not at all," I said, very nearly meaning it. Lady Rose had the potential to be an interesting young acquaintance.

"She was just discovering that Miss Speedwell lacks the maternal instincts," Stoker said blandly.

Lady Cordelia gave me an appraising look. "Miss Speedwell is not the only one."

I would dearly have loved to pursue that line of discussion further, but Lady Cordelia was clearly harried.

"Forgive me, but I must attend to the children. According to Cook, Rose has drunk an entire tin of treacle and will no doubt be sick very shortly, and little Arthur keeps trying to ride Betony."

"Doesn't his lordship spend time with his children?" I asked. "It is Sunday, after all."

Her voice was carefully neutral. "Sunday is Ambrose's day of contemplation. He withdraws from all company and spends the day in his rooms, reading."

"How fortunate," I remarked. "For him."

She inclined her head and left us then, and I turned on Stoker with scorn. "O, the perfidy of men."

"What have I done?" he protested.

"Nothing at present, but you are the only representative of your sex I have at hand to abuse. Take your lumps for your brothers."

He settled himself into the armchair opposite. "Ah, I

understand. You think his lordship should play nursemaid to his own children."

"I think he ought to take a greater interest in the formation of their intellect and character as well as their discipline. Why must it be left to poor Lady Cordelia to herd them about like so many recalcitrant sheep? Lady Rose is a pretty child and precocious as well, but it ought not to fall solely to her aunt to guide her."

"You are seeing the Beauclerks at their worst," he told me. "It is always difficult on Lady C. when a governess gives notice."

"And who is responsible for engaging the governess? No doubt Lady Cordelia. Who runs the household? Manages the servants? Supervises the children's education? Settles the accounts? Lady Cordelia. I think his lordship takes wretched advantage of her generosity."

Stoker threw his head back and laughed. "If you believe that, you don't know Lady Cordelia. Believe me, if she wanted things to be different, they would be. Yes, she is responsible for everything of significance that happens here at the Folly as well as at their Cornish estate. As you say, she supervises the children, the households, the accounts, and I daresay even Lord Rosemorran himself. But it suits her."

I gave a snort of derision. "Believe it if it consoles you. I still say she is thwarted in her true ambitions."

"And what are they?"

"I don't know yet. I only know she doesn't bore me as much as other ladies of my acquaintance."

He gave me a thoughtful look. "You are making a friend there."

"Perhaps. It is something of a relief to find another woman of intelligence and sound common sense. I have not met many, I can assure you."

"For which you blame my gender," he finished.

"Who else? It is men who have kept women downtrodden and poorly educated, so burdened by domesticity and babies they can scarcely raise their heads. You put us on pedestals and wrap us in cotton wool, cluck over us as being too precious and too fragile for any real labor of the mind, yet where is the concern for the Yorkshire woman working herself into an early grave in a coal mine? The factory girl who chokes herself to an untimely death on bad air? The wife so worn by repeated childbearing that she is dead at thirty? No, my dear Stoker, your sex has held the reins of power for too long. And I daresay you will not turn them loose without a fight."

He raised his hands. "Not from me. I say liberate the women and let them go out and earn wages and write laws and have the vote. They cannot do worse than their lords and masters."

I narrowed my eyes. "You are not joking."

"No, I am not. I have known enough of women to understand they are as duplicitous and vicious as men. If they are capable of being our equals in malice, why not in our better qualities as well? There are no masculine virtues, Veronica. And none sacred to women either. We are all of us just people, and most badly flawed ones at that."

"Yes, some of us are suspiciously lacking in virtue," I said with a significant look. "For example, I believe the maid, Sidonie, would like very much to misbehave with you."

He mumbled a reply to the effect that I was daft, and I raised a brow at him. "Surely you are not so unaware of your effect upon the girl. She stares like a moonstruck calf whenever you are near. Even Lady Cordelia made mention of it."

"I might have noticed," he said grudgingly.

It occurred to me then that Stoker's raffish appearance—the pierced lobe, the unruly locks, the glowering expressions—were not merely expressions of his own tastes and values; they might well be a sort of protective coloration, taken on to shield himself from the predation of voracious ladies. Of course, they would also serve to attract an entirely different sort of woman, the kind not easily put off by a little handsome savagery. For those of us who liked our men well roughened, his appearance was the fulfillment of a lifetime's dreaming of pirates and ne'er-do-well rogues. I might have enlightened him on the devastating effect of going about looking like a highwayman, but the risk he might scrub himself up to look like a parson was too horrifying to contemplate.

"Lucky for you that Lady Cordelia seems to have the girl firmly in hand. She is a good friend to you. I am rather surprised she doesn't harbor a tendresse for you herself."

"Our relationship is not like that," he said firmly. "Lady Cordelia is only, has ever only been, a friend."

"She is very attractive," I mused. "And you have your own charms. I am surprised the two of you have never even had a passing dalliance, a moment of . . . something."

He hesitated, then sat forward, glancing about again to make certain we were not overheard. "Lady Cordelia is everything I admire in a lady. She is kind and patient and endlessly selfless. But while I admire her virtues, I cannot help that they leave me cold. Give me a flawed woman with warm blood in her veins instead of ice water any day."

For a moment his gaze lingered upon me, intense and full of unspoken meaning. But he turned quickly away to examine a bit of Egyptian enamelware someone had left lying around. "But why has she never pursued *you*? I mean, you are entirely disreputable in appearance, but you are from a good family. You are an Honourable. That is not too far down for an earl's daughter to lower herself if she has a mind."

"We are friends, and that is all we shall ever be," he repeated firmly.

He fell silent again, and I might have returned to my book, but I did not.

"Stoker, what do you think we are going to find tomorrow?"

"I do not know," he said slowly. "But I know whatever it is, whatever ugly truths are resting in that bank, you will face them squarely. You have an odd sort of courage, Veronica. It will see you through."

"Whatever happens tomorrow, I am glad you will be there."

"You may rely upon it," he said, but his familiar, mocking smile was not in evidence for once, and I believed he meant it.

TWENTY-FIVE

We spent the rest of that rainy Sunday installed in the Belvedere, eating sandwiches that Lady Cordelia sent and poking about the collections. I was highly amused to discover Stoker laughing over a print of Cabanel's *Fallen Angel*—no doubt appreciating the resemblance—and we quarreled happily over the proper arrangement the earl should take for organizing his glorious but haphazard collection. (I favored chronological order, while Stoker championed a thematic approach.) When he was not looking, I managed to unearth a color plate of the White-browed purpletuft. It was an altogether unremarkable bird, but the puffs of violet feathers were so strikingly beautiful that I stared at it for a long time, thoughtfully tracing each tiny plume with a fingertip.

We retired early, and I believe both of us slept poorly, for we were awake and ready to leave far earlier than our errand required. The packet we had taken from the baron's study went into Stoker's pocket for safekeeping. He had replaced the back of the compass and tinkered with it until it worked again, and this I pinned once more to my bodice. I had the oddest sense that at last we were embarking upon the final leg of our adventure, and it was with mingled excitement and nostalgia that I took my leave of the Belvedere. Whatever befell us, our interlude together could not last much longer, and I would miss it.

There were no signs of pursuers as we made our way to Oxford Street, although we took the precaution of a circuitous route. I was being given a thorough education on London's various alleys and byways and parks, and although I always preferred countryside or wilderness, there was something arresting about the great city. Bunting had been hung in honor of the Jubilee, and the streets were teeming with a certain energy I suspected the city had not known before. There was anticipation, as the royal procession was only a few days away and dignitaries were arriving from the furthest reaches of the globe to fete the queen. Her image scowled from commemorative plates and flags, from placards and tea towels, Her Majesty, Victoria Regina, the Empress-Queen.

I studied a tooth mug on display in a window near the bank as we waited for that establishment to open. "She is really not a very attractive woman," I observed to Stoker. "All popeyes and lack of chin."

"The Hanoverian influence," he said shortly. "It would take some very strong genes to counter the German strain."

"Hm. Perhaps a healthy dose of French blood," I began, but before I could finish my thought, the door of the bank rattled.

"Ready?" Stoker asked.

I gave him a brisk nod and set off, knowing that he would be at my heels, faithful as a hound. The edifice before us was not the main Bank of London; that building was in Threadneedle Street, where it had stood for some two hundred years. This branch had been opened during the Regency, designed with all the elegant restraint that implied. Along the way, someone had decided this was no longer sufficiently imposing for a bank and had festooned the symmetrical façade with a succession of neo-Gothic embellishments culminating in a tiny clock tower that chimed out the hour as we approached. As soon as we were inside, I requested an audience with the bank manager, and within a very few minutes we had been escorted to his office. He was a cadaverously thin man with great flapping ears, ears that caught all the secrets his clients cared to whisper, I wagered.

I proffered the key. "This key fits an item that was left in your care by a Miss Harbottle. I am here to retrieve whatever is in your keeping."

The careful face gave nothing away. He did not take the key but merely gave me a long, level look. "I was told only to release the contents of the box to a Miss Veronica Speedwell."

"I am she."

A thin smile touched his lips. "You will understand that I must necessarily take precautions, Miss Speedwell. Miss Harbottle requested a proof of your identity."

"What proof do you require?"

The smile deepened, and there was an unmistakable twinkle in the sad eyes. "She said that I was not to release the box to you unless you introduced me to Chester."

"Who the devil is Chester?" Stoker demanded.

I put up a hand to quell his questions. I reached into my pocket and drew out the tiny grey velvet mouse. "May I present Chester?"

The manager bowed. "Precisely as described to me. In that case, I will fetch the box."

Stoker's brows were still raised when the manager returned a few moments later with a plain strongbox. "Your key fits this lock, Miss Speedwell. The box belongs to us, but you are free to remove the contents. I can offer you a quarter of an hour's privacy before my first appointment."

He withdrew with enormous tact while I fitted the key to the lock. It turned with only a slight protest, yielding almost at once. Inside the box was a packet similar to the one we had found in the baron's study. This one had been wrapped in a single large sheet of foolscap and tied with black tape. A blob of black sealing wax showed that it had never been opened since it had been placed in the bank for safekeeping.

I lifted my eyes to Stoker. "What if it is proof that my father murdered my mother?" I asked. "What then?"

"Then we will decide what to do with it," he said firmly.

I broke the seal. Within the packet were a handful of papers, but these were not like the ones we had taken from the baron's study. His collection had been newspaper cuttings and letters and photographs. These were official documents, stiff with the weight of authority.

"It is my birth certificate," I breathed. "It details the birth of a baby girl in Ireland on 21 June 1862—my birthdate. The mother is Lily Ashbourne." I stopped speaking abruptly, the words stuck in my throat.

"And the father?" Stoker asked.

I could not speak. I handed him the paper.

"Yes, here is the date and the mother, just as you said, and the father—" He looked at me, nearly dropping the paper. "This cannot be."

I swallowed hard. "But it is."

"'Mother, Lily Ashbourne,'" he read slowly.

I held up a hand. "Don't," I commanded, my voice sharp.

But he did not stop.

"'Father, His Royal Highness, Prince Albert Edward, The Prince of Wales.'"

I was not aware of intending to sit, but I found myself supported by a small armchair, Stoker kneeling at my side. "Illegitimate daughter of the Prince of Wales," I managed finally in a voice very unlike my own.

"Jesus Christ," Stoker said, and I knew from his tone it was not a blasphemy but a prayer.

"What more?" I demanded.

His face was pale, his eyes fathomless as he held out a second document to me. "Not illegitimate."

"That is not possible," I said. But I took the paper from him with trembling fingers and read the words for myself, a simple string of vowels and consonants that, linked together, changed everything I thought I knew in the space of a heartbeat.

Certificate of Marriage. All of the details were there—the names of bride and groom, the date, the signature of the priest.

"Surely it was bigamous," I protested. "Surely this cannot be authentic."

"It can and it is," Stoker said stubbornly. "And it means Mornaday was correct. You are in danger, Veronica. Terrible danger."

Over the course of our relationship, I had had many reasons to be grateful for Stoker's presence, but never as much as that day. I was stunned, unable to think, and it was Stoker who thrust the documents into his pocket, pulled me to my feet, and propelled me from the bank and into the watery sunshine. The city was the same; the same odors of horse and coal smoke still hung in the air; the same bustle of tradesmen and nannies pushing prams and fashionable carriages jostling with market carts still rang in my ears. But everything had changed.

He guided me along Oxford Street towards Hyde Park. We passed a bookshop, and sudden inspiration lit his face. "Walk on towards the park," he ordered. "Give the Marble Arch a wide berth, for God's sake. The police have a small station there and the last thing we want is to attract their attention. Don't look around. Just keep walking. Once you are inside the park, turn left onto the first path. Take a seat on the first bench you come to. I shall join you as soon as I can."

I did not even have the presence of mind to ask what he meant to do. I merely walked on as he had commanded, nearly getting myself run over as I crossed the teeming street into the park without looking twice. The curses of the cabmen were still ringing in my ears when I found a bench. I forced myself to sit calmly, reciting the names of every butterfly I had captured while I waited. I had just reached *Euchloe cardimines* when Stoker appeared, holding his arm somewhat awkwardly against his chest.

"Why did you stop in the bookshop?"

"Because we needed this," he said, drawing out a slim volume with a green kid cover. *A Brief History of the British Royal Family with Notes Regarding European Connections.* "I would have preferred Debrett's but it was too bloody huge to fit under my coat."

"You stole it?"

"I haven't any money on me. Do not scruple—I will send them the price of it in due course, but our necessity was greater than the bookseller's, I believe."

He rifled the pages until he came to the entry he was seeking. "'HRH, The Prince of Wales, Albert Edward. Date of birth . . .'" He trailed off, then gave an exclamation of triumph. "Here it is, 'Marriage to HRH Princess Alexandra of Denmark, 10 March 1863.'"

He sat back, the book falling to his lap. "Ten days before my mother died," I said tonelessly.

"It fits," he agreed. He took the rest of the documents from his coat pocket. "There is a statement from the priest, signed and witnessed. He presided over your parents' marriage and your birth as well as your mother's death. The same priest whose obituary we found in the baron's study."

"He was the one person who had been there for everything," I said.

"Not quite." He pointed to the names of the witnesses on the marriage certificate. "Baron Maximilian von Stauffenbach and Nan Williams, spinster. Your erstwhile aunt Lucy. No doubt she confided everything to her sister, whom you knew as Nell Harbottle. When Nell and the baron died, those were the last links with this marriage, your birth."

"Except me."

"Except you." He replaced the papers carefully and tucked the book into his coat. "You realize what this means, Veronica."

"Do not say it," I warned.

"The Prince of Wales' marriage to Princess Alexandra is bigamous. Their children, all of them, are therefore illegitimate. You are the only legitimate child of the Prince of Wales."

I took the book from him and passed a finger down the line of issue to the Prince and Princess of Wales. Albert Victor, born just two years after my own birth. George. Louise. Victoria. Maud. And a poor little mite called Alexander who had died within a day of being born. Five living children, all styled princes and princesses—my half brothers and sisters, and every last one of them illegitimate because their parents had been married ten days before my mother's death.

"It is not possible," I protested fiercely. "It cannot be."

"We have the documents. We have *you*," he pointed out.

"But my parents' marriage cannot possibly be legal."

"There might be difficulties with the heir to the throne marrying without his sovereign's consent," he conceded.

I leaped upon the point. "And if that is the case, then all of this goes away."

"No, it does not," he said patiently. "Even if your parents' marriage could be set aside and you were found to be illegitimate, this is still a scandal that could tarnish the monarchy irreparably. The Prince of Wales has always managed to escape condemnation for his affairs, but this is too much, Veronica. His other liaisons have all been nine days' wonders because his fixers managed to sweep them under the carpet. But they cannot sweep aside a marriage certificate and a grown daughter. Whether the marriage was legal or not, the prince married Princess Alexandra whilst believing himself married to your mother. He committed bigamy—knowingly."

He paused to let me absorb the information. I gave him a nod and he went on, still patient as he led me through the mire we had found ourselves in. "The Princess of Wales is the daughter of the Danish king, remember. How do you think her father will feel when her honor is thrown in the gutter? If Denmark supports her—and it most assuredly will—the Germans and Austrians will be right there to oppose them. They have been spoiling for a fight with Denmark since that ridiculous tussle over the Danish succession. And do you really think the Austrian and German empires will take sides without the Russians wading into the conflict? If they get involved, that will draw in the Ottoman Empire. Then Greece and Sweden will come. This one fact—your legitimacy—is the first domino in a series of events that could topple thrones, Veronica. There are people who would give a great deal to keep that from happening."

"Or take a great deal," I said, thinking of the baron, dead in his own home by some miscreant's hand. My uncle's? My father's? I thought of the elegant Prince of Wales and pushed that thought aside. I could not believe the bon vivant of the British royal family would stoop so low as to order a man's murder in cold blood. "But how are we to discover the truth?

We cannot simply present these documents to a solicitor and ask."

"That is exactly what we are going to do," he said, his face set in grim determination. He tore the entry on the Prince of Wales from the *Brief History* and stuffed it into his pocket before rising and taking me by the hand.

"Where are we going?"

"Chancery Lane. We are going to Lincoln's Inn."

As much of a blow as the morning's revelations had been, they did not prevent me from arguing against the plan. "Stoker, we cannot simply appear in Lincoln's Inn to speak to a barrister without an appointment."

"We can speak with this one."

"You know a barrister? Why in the name of heaven have we been doing this on our own without professional guidance, then?"

"Because I swore to myself I would never speak to him again on this earth."

"And yet you believe he will help us in a matter as grave as this one?"

"He will."

"How can you be so certain?"

"He is my brother."

We arrived at length at Inns of Court and the professional quarters of Sir Rupert Templeton-Vane. Stoker strode in past the protesting clerks and entered his brother's private office without knocking. The gentleman behind the desk must have been surprised, but he recovered swiftly, and as he rose to his full height, I detected a resemblance. There was something alike in the graceful bones of their faces, but Sir Rupert was a muted copy. Where Stoker was a portrait in oils, his brother was a watercolor, with auburn hair and hazel eyes to Stoker's black locks and dark blue eyes. Sir Rupert's complexion was warmer, lacking the Celtic pallor of Stoker's skin, but their expressions were similar, and I thought as I looked at Sir Rupert there was a cool ruthlessness about his mouth that might make him an implacable enemy if one was foolish enough to earn his enmity.

"Revelstoke," he said, greeting his brother calmly. "But I believe you prefer Stoker, do you not?"

"I see you have been knighted," Stoker returned. "That must have made his lordship proud."

Sir Rupert gave him a thin smile.

"Well, I know only the direst of circumstances would prompt you to call upon me, and therefore I must assume that you require my help. Given our last parting, I can further assume you would only do so if the matter were one of life and death."

"Your last parting?" I asked Stoker.

"I broke his nose," he explained with characteristic brevity.

Sir Rupert touched that appendage lightly. "It never healed quite as it was. I saw the best doctors in Harley Street, but there is still a very slight bump. Can you see it?" he asked me, turning his face in profile.

"It lends character to an already handsome face," I told him truthfully.

"How very kind of you. Stoker, are you going to present your companion so I can greet her properly? Or have you come to inform me that I am a brother-in-law again? In which case I can assure you she is a distinct improvement upon the last."

I could feel Stoker fairly vibrating with rage at his brother's cool detachment. The fellow was playing with him, no doubt taking great pleasure in poking the lion, but I was in no mood for such childish sibling tricks.

"Sir Rupert, I am Veronica Speedwell, and I am not your brother's wife. In fact, I am not entirely certain of who I am."

The elegant brows rose again. "Miss Speedwell, you intrigue me. Tell me more."

I looked pointedly at the chairs in front of his desk and his color heightened. "Forgive me. I have been monstrously discourteous. Please, make yourself comfortable, Miss Speedwell, and I will ring for tea. Stoker, sit down. I never did like your trick of looming over me."

We did as he instructed and in a very few minutes a clerk appeared with a tray of excellent French porcelain and elegant little confections. "I have a weakness for the pastry chef's art," he admitted to me as he passed a plate of the tiny cakes. I held up a hand.

"Thank you, but no."

"For Christ's sake, Rip, we did not come here for a tea party. We need help."

Sir Rupert's nostrils flared delicately. "I never liked that name, and you know it. And there is no reason to dispense with civilities just because you find yourself in a spot of bother."

"A spot of bother—do you hear the man?" Stoker demanded of me, thrusting his hands into his hair.

"Well, to be fair, we haven't explained ourselves yet," I pointed out. I held a hand out for the papers. Stoker surrendered them, and I let them rest on the edge of the desk for a moment, just out of Sir Rupert's reach.

"First, I need your word, as a gentleman, a Christian, a professional—whatever you care to swear upon, whatever you hold dear. I need your word that what we show you today will never leave the confines of this office. You will never speak of it, never write of it, never send a message by smoke signal or semaphore flag or any other means to any person of what we are about to tell you."

Sir Rupert's lightly arch manner dropped away and he leaned forward in his chair. "My dear Miss Speedwell," he said, in a perfectly earnest voice, "my brother and I may have a relationship that is slightly less cordial than that of Cain and Abel, but I give you my word that I have never betrayed a confidence entrusted to me, and I shall not begin with yours. I swear to this upon everything I hold sacred, and the one thing that Stoker does—our mother's grave."

I looked to Stoker and his expression was unfathomable. "Show him," he said, his voice suddenly rough.

"Sir Rupert, I will preface this by explaining that I am an orphan, or so I believed." I sketched briefly for him my upbringing by the Harbottle sisters and the discovery that I was the daughter of the actress Lily Ashbourne. I related the few facts we knew regarding her lover's marriage and her subsequent death.

I paused then, not entirely certain of how to proceed. "But Stoker and I have also come into possession of documents which reveal my father's identity."

Without another word I handed them over. He skimmed them quickly with a practiced and professional gaze, one hand cradling his cup of tea. When he came to the marriage certificate, he dropped the cup with an almighty crash and jumped to his feet.

"Do you have any idea what this means?" he demanded. He turned swiftly to Stoker. "I knew you hated me, but I thought even you would balk at attempting to destroy my career."

Stoker held up a hand. "Quiet or the clerks will hear you."

"Quiet! You expect me to be quiet when you have just unleashed seven devils upon me?"

"Sir Rupert," I said softly. "Please, calm yourself. No one ever need know that you advised us. I will promise that to you, and Stoker will as well. Stoker?" I nudged.

He waited, longer than I would have liked, but eventually he gave a curt nod. "I promise."

Somewhat mollified, Sir Rupert picked up the papers. "I cannot believe this," he breathed, looking at them as if they were holy relics. "The Prince of Wales, married to an actress and father of a child. A *legitimate* child."

"Yes," I said, attempting to draw him back to the present. "You have struck directly at the heart of the matter. That is the question for which we require an answer. Am I legitimate?"

He considered, furrowing his brow for a long moment. Then he rose and went to his books, selecting a weighty volume bound in dark calf. He applied himself to this book, and seven others, reading with his brows knit firmly together as we drank our tea and finished off the cakes. Finally, he sat back and made his pronouncement.

"I do not know," he admitted.

Stoker glowered. "Dammit, Rupert, the one time I come to you—"

His brother held up a hand. "I am not attempting to be obstructionist, I assure you. The trouble is that there are complicated precedents." He turned to me. "In the first place, the Royal Marriages Act of 1772 outlaws any marriage of a member of the royal family to which the sovereign has not given specific consent. Since Her Majesty most certainly did not consent to this marriage, it is null and void. Furthermore, the priest who conducted it and Miss Ashbourne both committed serious crimes in attempting it."

I felt suddenly buoyant, light as air, almost dizzy with relief. "It is finished, then."

Sir Rupert held up a hand. "Not quite so fast, Miss Speedwell. I am afraid there is an additional complication. The Act of Settlement in 1701 prohibits any person in the line of succession from marrying a Roman Catholic."

"Yet another reason why my parents' marriage was invalid. Surely that is good news," I pointed out.

"So one might think. But Miss Ashbourne was Roman Catholic and married in the Catholic Church by a priest of good standing. Her marriage would not have been recognized by the Church of England or the law of the land, but it *would* have been valid in the eyes of the Catholic Church."

"But surely that does not matter," I protested.

"Oh, but I am afraid it very much does," he countered. "When King George IV was Prince Regent, he married Maria Fitzherbert, a Roman Catholic, in her church's rites. The pope himself declared the marriage valid."

"But that was decades ago and it created no trouble."

"Yes, because Mrs. Fitzherbert did not press the issue, nor did she present the prince with a child. There was no rival claimant for the throne and no succession crisis ensued. This," he said with a jab of his finger to my papers, "is a cat of a very different color."

I gave a short, mirthless laugh. "You do not know me, Sir Rupert, but I beg you will believe I have no interest in pressing a claim to the English throne."

"It is not about what you would press, Miss Speedwell," he said gently. "It is about what you would represent. In the eyes of any Catholic, you would be their rightful heiress. The Prince of Wales has married bigamously in their interpretation. His children by Princess Alexandra are, canonically, bastards and unable to succeed. That leaves you as the only legitimate child of the heir to the throne in the hearts of every Catholic subject in Her Majesty's empire. It is enough to start a revolution—in one place in particular," he said meaningfully.

"Ireland," Stoker supplied. "And her mother was Irish. Christ and his apostles," he swore. "The separatists could not have asked for a prettier gift—a legitimately born Catholic alternative to the British royal family—and with Irish blood in her veins no less."

Sir Rupert looked at me intently. "Miss Speedwell, whether you like it or not, these documents prove that you are, in fact, the most dangerous person in the British Empire."

TWENTY-SIX

After his pronouncement, Sir Rupert collapsed back into his chair. We sat in bewildered silence for a long moment before he swore—something more profane than I had ever heard issue from Stoker's lips, although at least he followed his lapse with an apology—and retrieved a bottle from his desk. He poured a generous measure of excellent whiskey into crystal glasses and handed them to us, taking a double measure for himself.

He swallowed it down in a single go, and Stoker regarded him with something like cautious admiration. "Careful, there. The Templeton-Vane men have always done that a bit too easily."

Sir Rupert wiped his mouth upon a pristine handkerchief and gave his younger brother a shake of the head. "No. It was Mother who liked a tipple. She could drink Father under the table."

Stoker bridled. "She did not."

"Of course she did. Kept the best of Father's single malt in a perfume bottle on her dressing table. She used to bribe the butler for it."

Stoker stared at him openmouthed, and Sir Rupert gentled his tone. "There is a lot you have yet to learn about our family."

"The Templeton-Vanes are the very last subject I would wish to discuss with you," Stoker replied coldly.

Sir Rupert steepled his hands under his chin. "One of these days, you will put aside your childish resentments, Revelstoke. But in light of Miss Speedwell's current predicament, I think we ought to call a truce."

Emotions warred upon Stoker's face, but his tone was as even as his brother's. "Agreed. From the information you have given us, it should be a simple matter to determine who is best served by removing the threat she represents."

Sir Rupert nodded. "Indeed. First—"

Stoker rose. "Not you. Us," he said, putting a hand underneath my elbow and encouraging me to my feet.

Sir Rupert rose with automatic courtesy. "But you cannot possibly do this alone!"

"We will and we must," Stoker told him. "I am grateful to you, Rupert, really. You have been quite decent, and it is rather refreshing to take my leave of you without either one of us dripping blood upon the carpets. But this is as far as you can come."

He glanced meaningfully at the photograph resting on a small easel on Sir Rupert's desk. It depicted a woman—sternly pretty with a small mouth and exquisite hands—and three little boys.

"You have a wife," I said, suddenly understanding Stoker's reluctance to involve his brother further. "And children. You have already declared I am the most dangerous person in the Empire," I told him with a lightness I did not feel. "I would not have that danger touch you or yours."

I put out my hand. "Thank you for your assistance, Sir Rupert. I will not forget it. And if it is ever in my power to do you a service, you may be assured I shall."

He clasped my hand slowly. "In that case, Godspeed, Miss Speedwell." He gave me a ghost of a smile at the bit of wordplay and released my hand. The brothers did not touch but exchanged nods, and we made as if to leave. At the last moment, Stoker turned back, tossing the *Brief History* onto his brother's desk. "One last thing, old man. I stole that from Wibberley's, the little bookshop in Oxford Street. Oh, and there is a page gone missing. See that it is paid for, will you?"

Sir Rupert gave a short laugh, like the bark of a fox, and we left him then, emerging into Chancery Lane just as the street began to fill with solicitors and barristers and clerks, all bound for their luncheon tables.

Stoker took my arm. "Put down your veil. I don't like how crowded the street has become, and we must have a think."

I drew the light silk veil over my features. "I have just the spot," I told him. "Where no one would ever think to look for us."

An hour later we were in the Tower of London listening to the Yeoman Warder's speech of welcome. We had paid our admission by cobbling together a few coins. Most had gone to fish and chips, fragrantly greasy and eaten straight from the newspaper, with Stoker complaining all the while that respectable ladies did not eat in the street.

"Since when do such trivialities concern you?" I demanded.

"They do not, but they will draw attention to you," he reminded me. I shrugged and finished every delectable bite of my crispy cod.

"That was sublime," I told him as we threw away the greasy

newspapers and joined the queue to enter the Tower. I listened eagerly to the Yeoman Warder's patter, then quickly assessed our options. With Stoker hard upon my heels, I directed my steps to the squat bulk of St. Thomas's Tower. We emerged at the top to find clouds gathering and a cold river mist rising.

Stoker gave me a quizzical look. "What the devil are we doing here?"

"I have never been to the Tower of London," I told him simply. "It might be my last chance."

"Veronica—" he began, but I waved him off.

"I am not prey to martyrdom, Stoker. I have no intention of letting these ruffians abscond with me. But I would be a fool not to take advantage of the opportunity for new experiences, you must agree."

He gave a gusty sigh. "Very well. But why *here*? It is bloody cold."

"You have answered your own question. We are not likely to be followed or overheard, and I always find a brisk breeze clears my head. So we shall stand up here and let the wind buffet us while we work it out."

He peered over the edge of the tower to the swirling green waters of the Thames.

"Traitors' Gate," I observed. "Just think of all the Tudors who came this way to meet their fates—Anne Boleyn, Catherine Howard, the Countess of Salisbury, poor little Lady Jane Grey. Not a comforting thought."

"Yes, well, royalty has a history of going to bloodthirsty lengths to retain its hold on power," he commented dryly. He dropped his head. "Damn me for a fool. I'm sorry."

"Don't be. You are not wrong. The history of our country is quite forthcoming on the fate of traitors and pretenders. Even unwilling ones," I said, thinking of the sad little puppet Jane Grey. "But that was a different time. We live in a modern age,

Stoker. And in a world with steamships and telegraphs and suspension bridges, I find it difficult to believe anyone would be put to death for the misfortune of having the wrong blood."

"Are you willing to take that chance?" he asked.

"No." I took one last shuddering glance at the padlocked gate and turned to Stoker. "So let us begin. Who would have motive to wish me harm?"

"The royal family," he said promptly.

I considered, then shook my head. "I think not."

"They have the most to lose if you make your claim," he pointed out.

"But look at them—*really* look at them. What are they? They may be royal, but they have the values of middle-class Germans. They believe in God and duty and respectability. Granted, my father may have erred against that in his liaison with my mother, but consider what he did. When he believed himself in love for the first time, he did not simply seduce the girl. *He married her.* No one in the whole of the Empire could have known better than he what he was risking in doing so. But he did it. He may have regretted it afterward when he realized the enormity of it all, but he did not simply sin with her and damn the consequences. The Prince of Wales is a romantic."

Stoker snorted. "Have you paid attention to the newspapers? Your princely father has seduced the wives of half the court. He has been named in divorce proceedings, Veronica. That is hardly the sort of thing one would expect from a romantic."

"It is precisely the sort of thing I would expect," I countered. "He thinks with his heart. He is in love with women and the idea of love. He believes himself chivalrous. He married Lily because it was wildly improbable, like something out of myth—or his own family history. Have you forgot Edward IV? He married a widowed nobody and made her Queen of England. No doubt the Prince of Wales thought he could do the same, and somehow, between marrying Lily and announcing his betrothal to Princess Alexandra, he changed his mind. But what?"

Stoker retrieved the page he had torn from the *Brief History* and scrutinized it for a long moment. "He changed his mind—or something changed it for him," Stoker said slowly. "And I've just realized what it was. The date your parents married—it was the autumn of 1861. By the following year, he became engaged to Princess Alexandra. Do you remember what happened in December of 1861?" he asked, brandishing the page.

"Hardly," I replied. "I was, you will recall, in utero at the time."

"In December of 1861, Prince Albert died."

I stared at him, comprehension turning to certainty as Stoker elaborated. "The Prince Consort fell ill after he visited the Prince of Wales at university. The royal court never addressed the rumors, but they walked together for hours in a chilling rain. What would drive a man of not terribly robust health to take his son for a private walk where no one could overhear them in killing weather?"

"A scandal about to break," I finished breathlessly. "He had learned of the marriage."

"Or at least heard something of their liaison. Enough to send him straight down to school to upbraid his son, even though they would have been together in just a few weeks for Christmas."

"And what a burden that would be for an impressionable, romantic youth," I went on. "Married in haste to an unsuitable woman, waiting for an opportunity to introduce her to his family and win their blessing, and then his beloved father, the bulwark of the entire family, is dead—because of him, because the shock of the news *killed* him."

"That impressionable, romantic youth would be

devastated," Stoker said. "He would carry that guilt to the end of his days. And it would poison everything and everyone to do with that marriage."

"Of course. He wouldn't have been able to bear to look at her after that." I stopped and did a quick bit of arithmetic. "Lily would have been three months into her pregnancy with me. Surely the Prince of Wales knew about it. Perhaps he even planned to tell them at Christmas during the happy family gathering, brazening the thing out—'I have wonderful news! I am married and she is expecting an heir!'—but then death comes for his father first, shattering everything. The queen is utterly devastated by grief, destroyed by it, withdrawing almost totally from society. The prince could never have told her then—it surely would have killed her. And he bears the burden of her blame for his father's death."

"Meanwhile she has been planning his marriage to a beautiful Danish princess," Stoker said, picking up the thread. "And what choice does he have but to acquiesce? He must agree to the betrothal to atone for killing his father."

"And so he relinquishes his future with Lily and her child in order to do his duty as his mother, as England, would define it. He gives them up in order to expiate the sin of killing his own father. He breaks all ties with the woman he loves and his child and marries for reasons of state."

Stoker rubbed his chin. "Plausible. I would go so far as to say probable. But that still does not tell us what his role has been in all of this. Or what your uncle's purpose in seeking you out has been."

"That depends entirely on whether he knows the identity of Lily's husband," I pointed out. "I suspect if we were to pry into Edmund de Clare's associates in Ireland we would find separatists among them. He comes from an old Catholic family. It is entirely logical that he would support Home Rule."

"And men have done quite a lot in order to be the power behind the throne," he said with a nod towards the surrounding towers. "These stones alone have seen their share of ruthless uncles."

"Which would also account for why my uncle was so keen to remove you from the scene but without harming me," I pointed out. "He would want me in good health."

"With an eye to?"

"Abducting me to Ireland seems the likeliest," I said finally. "Some Catholic stronghold where he can tuck me away and keep me under his thumb while he presents my claims."

"Christ," Stoker said with a grimace, "there are enough islands and hideaways, he could keep you hidden a hundred years or more and no one would find you. And in the meantime, he could be filling your head with tales of family and God and free Ireland."

"And doubtless marrying me off to a suitable separatist fellow of his choosing," I said with a shudder.

"You might have a point. If he marries you off and gets you breeding, he could do even more with your child than he could with you. He wouldn't even need you then," he said in a sepulchral voice.

"If you are trying to frighten me, I assure you, my imagination is every bit as Gothic as yours. I can well imagine the poisoned tea or the slim dagger in the night and the claims that I succumbed to a fever while everyone rallies around my infant," I said repressively. "But we can agree that dear uncle Edmund has no immediate designs upon my life."

"But he would have had ample reason for wanting the baron dead," Stoker pointed out. "De Clare would need more than you in his power—he would need the proofs of your claims. If Max refused to surrender them . . ." His voice trailed off and I gave a shudder. I hated to think that a man—a man I had liked and who had been kind to me—had been killed for me.

"But he is not the only possibility," Stoker said with some relish. "There is another candidate just as likely."

I stared at him in dawning comprehension.

"It cannot be Mornaday! He has come too often to our aid."

Stoker shrugged. "So it seems. But has he been coming to our aid or merely thwarting your uncle's attempts to spirit you out of England? Think of it. Your uncle, aside from having his men lay unfriendly arms upon me, has shown only an inclination to talk to you. That you have refused him has driven him to increasingly more desperate actions—actions which have not harmed so much as a hair upon your head."

"Bosh!" I declared. "He tried to have you drowned in the Thames, in case you have forgot."

"Only because he thought I was your abductor. And to an outsider, it would seem as if I had taken you into my power and kept you there."

"You're forgetting the incident at Paddington Station," I reminded him triumphantly. "I eluded him entirely of my own volition. If I had truly been your captive, why wouldn't I have seized the opportunity to go with my uncle and escape your clutches?"

"Perhaps he thinks I've mesmerized you. Perhaps he thinks I have made dire threats of violence should you attempt to go. Perhaps he thinks you've fallen prey to my considerable charms and are in love with me—to your own detriment."

I pulled a face. "Be serious."

"I am. We cannot know what your uncle believes the situation to be. We can only hypothesize based upon his actions. And his actions are those of a man who wishes to talk."

"And Mornaday's are those of a man who wishes to enact a rescue," I countered.

"We have only his word for the fact that he is with Scotland Yard," Stoker said. "We did not ask him to present his credentials."

"We were half drowned," I reminded him. "It was an awkward time to insist upon formalities. Besides, if Mornaday had some nefarious purpose, why intervene at all?"

"To prevent your uncle from persuading you to leave the country."

"Oh, that is preposterous! Mornaday is no more a villain than you are," I said with a touch of waspishness.

"You cannot discount a theory simply because it does not suit your prejudices," he reminded me. "That is bad science."

"And this is not science. It is something entirely different. You still have not explained *how* Mornaday might be involved if he is not a detective from Scotland Yard. What is his purpose?"

He shrugged. "To get within his power the previously unknown daughter of the Prince of Wales."

"How does he even know of my existence? For whom does he work?"

"Occam's razor," he said. "The simplest explanation is the likeliest. If only a handful of people knew of your existence and most are dead, the one still alive is the most logical person to have told him."

"My father. You believe *my father* set Mornaday on my trail? Do you think he had Max killed as well?"

"I don't know."

His brow was furrowed and I resisted the urge to throw something at him. "You are seriously considering the possibility that the Prince of Wales, a man devoted to card games and shooting pheasants and genteel debauchery, has orchestrated a plot to murder his father's oldest friend and run me to ground?"

"His father's oldest friend," Stoker said, repeating the

words as if tasting them on his tongue. "I hadn't thought of it in quite that way, but you're right. It was Max he turned to when he needed a witness for his marriage to Lily. And no doubt Max was the one who paid money—the prince's money—into the Harbottle accounts for your keep."

"You see? Would a man really kill the family friend who has done so much for him?" I demanded.

"I should think it would give him all the more reason," was Stoker's reply.

TWENTY-SEVEN

In due course, the chill breeze off the Thames drove us down from the tower and we walked the Outer Ward, making a slow loop between the inner buildings of the Tower and its surrounding fortifications. There were visitors aplenty that day, and we threaded our way between groups chattering in German and Italian and French, guidebooks in hand as they pointed out the various attractions.

"Pity for them the Menagerie has been emptied out," Stoker said. "It must have been quite the experience to stand in this place and hear the roaring of lions."

"They didn't belong here," I protested. "They should never have been brought to this country."

He raised a brow. "You find that different from what we do as naturalists?"

"I do. We preserve the natural dignity of the animal," I said firmly. "We study them in the name of scientific inquiry. The creatures that were kept here were simply trophies, balm to the royal sense of self-importance."

"Yes, well, royal senses of self-importance require a lot of balming," he reminded me. "And we still haven't finished deciding who is behind the plot against you."

"Not the royal family, of that I am certain, in spite of your dim view of my father," I began. "But I will concede that they have handlers, men who are highly placed and willing to turn a blind eye to a bit of bloody work if it will preserve the stability of the monarchy."

"A courtier, then. Very likely. And how does Mornaday fit into this?"

I considered. "He might be a private detective, but he might also be precisely as he claims—an inspector with Scotland Yard. That would make him a reluctant ally to whichever puppet master pulls his strings. He claims he was tasked by his superior at Scotland Yard with monitoring our activities—perhaps even ordered to secure us. He has refused because he believes I am no threat, but his masters will not be appeased. He is torn between the conflicting claim of duty and his own instincts. In that case, he does the only possible thing: he warns us to flee. He might be rapped on the knuckles for failing in his job, but he will not be ruined. And we escape the clutches of whatever forces at Scotland Yard are working against us."

"Not 'whatever forces,'" Stoker corrected grimly. "There is only one division of Scotland Yard that would concern itself with royal scandal—Special Branch."

"I thought Special Branch were formed to deal with the Irish problem."

"Originally, yes. But they have expanded their purview over the past few years. Special Branch are discreet to the point of secrecy. If someone close to the royal family wanted something investigated on their behalf, they would go to Special Branch."

"How convenient to have so many people to clear up one's indiscretions," I said with a trace of bitterness. I felt a rush of cold wind. It was an atmospheric place, the Tower. The very stones seemed heavy with the memory of pain.

We fell to silence, and I amused myself watching a Tower raven strut about, preening his handsome feathers as smugly as a lord. Legend held that if the ravens left the Tower, the monarchy itself would fall, and from his demeanor, it seemed as if this fellow knew his own importance.

One of the guards strode past and the raven quorked irritably at him, scolding him in his throaty little voice. Stoker started to laugh, but I grasped his arm, digging my fingers into his muscle.

"Stoker, what if Mornaday's urging us to flee was a warning?"

"Of course it was a warning," he said, rolling his eyes. "A rather poor one considering it came after we had already been abducted."

"Not that," I told him impatiently. "What if Mornaday knows of something else, some *other* danger."

"What sort of danger?"

"If Special Branch meant to clear up this particular indiscretion, the only way to do the job thoroughly would be to eliminate me before the Irish could take me in hand. And we have given them the perfect scapegoat."

"What on earth are you—" He broke off as the truth began to reveal itself to him. "Kill you and lay the blame for it at my door," he said flatly.

"Exactly. They could manufacture a dozen motives. Lovers' quarrel, a falling out over money, some fever of the brain. Don't you see? It answers all of their requirements. It removes me as a threat and it eliminates the one other person who knows the truth—you. And they daren't leave you alive for a trial. They cannot risk the truth about my birth coming out in the testimony. They will have to kill you as well. A prison suicide—taking your own life in remorse or a thwarted attempt at escape.

And everyone will believe it because of your reputation."

He said nothing, but his complexion had gone very white.

"Stoker, I know you do not wish to discuss your past, but—"

"But you're quite right," he said, his voice low and harsh. "According to public record, I am a violent man—at least if you believe what the newspapers have said about me. Half of society thinks I am mad and the other half thinks I am the devil. They could not have chosen a better villain for their melodrama."

He faltered then, and I put a hand to his arm, rousing him from the painful reverie into which he had fallen. "What shall we do?"

"We might take Mornaday's advice and flee," he said slowly. "We could go abroad, somewhere on the Continent, and from there make our way around the world, as far from here as possible."

"And run for the whole of our lives? Stoker, we would never be free of them. Can you really imagine a life like that? Jumping at shadows and wondering, every moment, if it would be our last. I could not live such a farce, and I do not believe you could either."

"Even if it saved your life?" he demanded.

I shook my head. "Not even then."

"Veronica," he said quietly. "Do not think that I was suggesting anything improper in urging flight. If we leave together, I will not tarnish your reputation further. I will marry you."

I tipped my head. "Stoker, I have received seventeen marriage proposals and that is by far the most halfhearted."

"I mean it. I will take care of you," he said, tugging a little at his collar.

"Generally when a gentleman proposes marriage he looks rather less like he's awaiting the tumbril to carry him off to the guillotine. You may put your mind at ease. I have as little inclination to marry as you do. Nor do I intend to flee. But I believe you will be just as much a victim of this malicious plot as I will. And I cannot have that."

I drew in a deep breath of the damp river air and blew it out slowly. "I have a little money put by in the bank. Not much," I warned, "but it is enough to see you out of the country and well on your way. Madeira, perhaps. Or the Canary Islands. From there you can work your way to Africa and eventually Australia. Australia is full of unsuitable people—you will fit in beautifully. And just think of all the lovely animals you can stuff. You should go there for the platypus alone," I said with considerable more brightness than I felt.

"And what do you intend to do?" he asked slowly.

"Stay and fight them, of course," I replied.

He did not answer for a long moment, but when he did his voice was chilly with the coldest rage I had ever heard. "In spite of what society believes me capable of, I do not strike women," he said, each word clipped and hard. "But I can tell you if anything drove me to it, it would be precisely that sort of insult to my honor."

I opened my mouth to speak, but he went on, each word as pointed as a sword. "I am many things, Veronica Speedwell, and most of them I take no pride in, but I am still—and will ever be—a gentleman and a former sailor of Her Majesty's Navy. And the one thing a sailor does not do is desert his comrades under fire. If we stay, we go down together, and we go down fighting."

I put out my hand. "There is no one I would rather have at my back. To the end, then."

He grasped my hand and shook it. "To the end."

* * *

Of course, as had become our habit, we quarreled over what the end should be—or at least Stoker quarreled and I carried on doing precisely as I wished.

"We must return to your workshop to set our plans in motion," I informed him.

"What plans?"

"To flush them out," I declared. "All of them. I am going to bring them to us, the Irish, Mornaday and his superiors, all of them."

His voice was strangled. "Do you mean to get us killed?"

I spoke with grim finality. "No. But I mean to be free of this once and for all. And to do that, I must bring them all together at one time."

"And how precisely do you propose to do that?"

"Why, by sending them invitations, of course. Steel yourself, Stoker. Veronica Speedwell is about to introduce herself properly."

Stoker was every bit as tiresome about the plan as I expected. He raised objections on the grounds of my safety, his safety, common sense, and half a dozen other topics that I dispatched with a coolness that would have been a credit to any battlefield commander. If my knees trembled a little, I dared not show it to Stoker. I had little doubt he possessed a predator's sense for weakness. If he smelled it upon me, he would not stop until he had forced me to give up my plan, and that was something I could not afford. I must bring an end to this matter, once and for all, no matter the cost.

It was not until I calmly informed him that I would go without him that he capitulated with very bad grace. He brooded for the rest of the day, and it occurred to me that a man as large as Stoker in a foul mood was a formidable creature indeed. But if we were to have any sort of working partnership moving forward, he would have to learn that I could not be cowed by any display of masculine posturing. Nor could I be moved by appeals to logic, emotion, or femininity, all of which he tried, and all of which I rejected. I had discovered that, in light of his stubbornness, the most expedient way of dealing with him was simply to do as I pleased and trust he would follow. His own innate sense of chivalry as well as his natural curiosity would make certain of that.

Against Stoker's better judgment we repaired to his workshop. I had argued successfully that it was far closer to the Tower than Bishop's Folly and had the added benefit of leaving the Beauclerks entirely out of it. Our things had been left at the Folly, but at least we retained possession of the most important—the packets of information that proved my true identity. I rewrapped them together carefully, using a piece of plain brown paper from Stoker's supply to bundle them all. I tied them with a bit of butcher's twine as Stoker coaxed up the fire in his stove. Absently, I crumbled a bit of the broken sealing wax in my fingers.

"Don't," he ordered. "It is getting on the floor and Huxley oughtn't eat it."

I was not surprised he had turned pernickety. The specter of impending death will do that to some people. In my case, it made me rather fidgety, and I paced the room, picking up specimens and putting them down again.

"This plover is molting," I told him.

He removed it from my grasp and brushed the feathers from my fingers. "A plover is a nonpasserine. This is a cuckooshrike. And you could have seen it is a passerine from its toes if you had cared to look."

I pulled a face at him but left him to his wretched cuckooshrike. I never much cared for birds anyway. Instead I plucked one of his ancient newspapers at random and began to read.

We had been there only a short while when Badger arrived to look in on Huxley. "Mr. S.! I didn't look to see you back already."

Stoker gave the boy a smile. "Neither did I. Miss Speedwell has a pair of notes she would like for you to deliver. And a shilling for your trouble. Any questions?"

The boy's eyes shone. "Nay."

"And here is a little something more. We shall need food for tonight and tomorrow. Nothing tricky—just a few meat pies and a bit of cheese, maybe some oysters. Bring a loaf and a few bottles of beer as well."

"Aye, Mr. S." He tugged the brim of his cap and disappeared, taking Huxley with him for a walk. We did not speak while he was gone. Stoker worked at his elephant while I returned to his stacks of outdated newspapers, assembling everything I could find on Special Branch, Irish separatists, and the men who concerned themselves with directing the business of the court.

Badger returned in a few hours' time with a basket of food and Huxley, now thoroughly exercised. I put down a dish of fresh water and the dog drank deeply, thrusting his entire face into the bowl, then flopped down onto the floor, where he promptly went to sleep.

"Any trouble?" I asked.

"No, miss. I handed one over at the Empress of India Hotel, the other at Scotland Yard," he told me with an avid gleam. Clearly his trip to the Yard had impressed him mightily.

"Excellent. Thank you."

He turned to go, and Stoker put a hand to his shoulder. "Badger, thank you for your care of Huxley whilst I was away. He looks fit."

The boy grinned. "It weren't nowt," he assured Stoker.

"Just the same, it is appreciated."

He hesitated then, and I saw genuine regard for the boy on

his face. "Tonight, lad. Don't come here."

Badger's brow furrowed. "Sir?"

"It may not be safe."

Badger's pointed little chin seemed to sharpen. "I'm good in a fight if you need a fellow to stand at your back."

Stoker turned to me with anguished eyes. I stepped forward.

"You are a stalwart companion," I told him. "But this is something Mr. Stoker and I have to do alone."

"All right, then," he said, but with a grudging air.

He left then and Stoker's shoulders sagged. "Bloody hell. That about did me in. Such a small fellow for such a stout heart."

"He will grow up to be a man like you," I told him. "Loyal above all else."

Stoker turned his back and returned to his elephant. I was not surprised. We like to believe it is the power of language that gives us superiority over animals, but words have their limitations.

For the rest of that day we carried on, Stoker with his elephant and notebooks, me with the newspapers, each of us piecing together the disparate parts. While Stoker stitched and glued his pachyderm and devoted hours to writing up his notes, I assembled a portrait of the men who were likely at the heart of the plot against us. Mornaday had been mentioned in the newspapers a number of times, and it was apparent from his various successes that he was a force to be reckoned with. He was clever and resourceful, often using disguises in the quest to run his prey to ground. I clucked my tongue in annoyance at this. I had rather liked him for a villain, and here his credentials were firmly established. He *was* a proper detective, blast the man. But I consoled myself with the notion that he could be both detective and blackguard, using his position to accomplish dark deeds in the service of some shadowy overseer. He had been promoted as a result of unmasking the Kennington Slasher, and there was a photograph of Mornaday standing at the gallows when the fellow was hanged—next to his superior, Sir Hugo Montgomerie.

I handed the paper to Stoker. "It appears that Mornaday is indeed a detective," I told him. "He has received commendations."

He scrutinized the photograph. Like all newspaper likenesses, this one was blurry and indistinct, but it was enough. It was clearly Mornaday, but it was not this familiar face that caused Stoker to curse. "Bloody hell. Sir Hugo Montgomerie. Head of Special Branch."

"You know him?"

"In a manner of speaking," he said darkly. "Our paths crossed once. Many years ago."

"How?" I demanded. "And no more of your evasions. I have let you keep your secrets, but not this one. It might be pertinent."

"It isn't," he insisted. But he began to tell me the story anyway. "I was rather unhappy as a boy, which you may well understand having met my brother."

"I can see the two of you are not close," I temporized.

He gave a snort. "If I were to avail myself of a coat of arms, it would feature a black sheep rampant. In any event, after one particularly gruesome scene, I left home."

"How old were you?"

"Eleven, twelve," he said carelessly. "I've forgot."

"And that's when you went to the traveling show," I supplied, putting the pieces together at last.

A whisper of nostalgia flickered over his features. "They were kind enough to take me in. The professor was not such a tightfisted bastard in those days," he added. "I learned conjuring tricks and knife throwing and a few other useful things."

"Like the carnal pleasures," I put in, thinking of Salome's

revelations. "Goodness me, Stoker, at eleven or twelve? You *were* a prodigy."

"*May* I finish?"

"Do carry on," I urged.

"In any event, I stayed with them for some time, almost half a year before my father's pet detective managed to track me. It was Montgomerie. He was not with the Yard at the time, and he bloody well wasn't *Sir* Hugo. But it explains how quickly Scotland Yard got onto me as a suspect in Max's death. Montgomerie was a meticulous sort of fellow. I've little doubt he kept his case notes from my disappearance—and when Max was murdered it would have been short work to discover that I had been one of his associates."

"And easy to confirm that you were still in contact as soon as they waded through the baron's business papers and realized you were his tenant."

I glanced around the workshop. "You said he intended to leave his fortune to one of his favorite institutions? What will they do with it?"

Stoker shrugged. "I am sure they will sell it off to someone or other for use as a warehouse again. The river is badly silted up at the dock, but that can always be dredged."

"And you will lose your home."

"This is not home, Veronica," he said in a hollow voice. "It is merely a place where I live."

He returned to his elephant then, hammering ferociously at one of the supports, and I thought of the first time I had goaded him out of his silence by pricking his temper. But it was not his rage I wanted then. For the first time in a very long time, I wanted something quite different from another human being—and as I explored that want I recognized it as a longing for reassurance.

"Stoker."

Something in my tone must have conveyed itself, for he put down his hammer and turned. "Yes?"

"Do you ever think about death?" They were not the words I intended to speak, but they would do to begin. Huxley climbed into my lap and I petted him, running my fingers through his coarse hair.

He spread his hands, encompassing the whole of his workshop. "Every day. I am surrounded by it."

"I mean your own."

"I have. I've come closer than most," he reminded me.

"In Brazil?" Huxley gave a damp snuffle and settled onto my lap.

"And other places," he told me. "Have you thought about it?"

"Never. Not in Corsica or Mexico or Sarawak. Not even in Sumatra when that bloody volcano was erupting. I always thought everything would be all right. I always believed when I closed my eyes at night that I would wake again in the morning. I knew the sun was just over the horizon, and I believed I would live to see it rise again. I suppose you think I'm very stupid," I finished, trailing off.

"On the contrary, Veronica. I think that is the only way to live."

If only his voice had not been quite so gentle; if only he had comprehended me just a little less. I would never have voiced my doubts. It is easy to stiffen one's upper lip and carry on when you dare not share your cowardice for fear of being misunderstood. But it is a difficult thing to heft one's burden alone when there is someone willing to share it.

"Stoker, what if I've blundered?" I asked suddenly, the words bursting out in a torrent. "What if I've miscalculated and it all goes awry? They might—" I did not say the words. I could not.

"Yes," he agreed. "They might."

"And that doesn't frighten you?" I demanded. My voice rose and Huxley shifted, grumbling a little as only an annoyed bulldog can.

"It scares the bloody hell out of me, if I'm honest," he replied. "But you cannot think like that. You've made your gamble. You've thrown the dice and now we wait to see if you've won."

"But if I've lost—" I broke off and tried again, forcing the words past the lump in my throat. "I accused you of being rash when you fled London after the baron's death, but I am no better. I have risked both our lives in this and I had no right to bring you any further into this fight."

"I have been in it," he reminded me. "From the first. And I will be there at the last. Whatever happens."

He dug in his pocket for one of his scarlet handkerchiefs. "Here, use this before you give Huxley pneumonia from wetting him with your tears."

His tone was mocking, but his gaze was unperturbed. A calmness had settled over him, a serenity that I had never seen.

"Is this what it's like? Before a battle, I mean. You must have seen a few in the navy."

"A few," he admitted. "There's always a moment, after the frantic preparation and before the firing, when everything goes quiet. You can feel the men around you praying. I never could. For me there was only the silence."

"What did you do with your silence?"

He gave me a small smile. "What do you think? I recited a few lines of Keats to myself. I thought of the life I might never live, the life I wanted to live. And I thought of my commander, the man into whose hands I had entrusted my life."

"Do you think he prayed?"

"He did. He was a righteous man, whatever that means. But I don't believe we won because God was on our side or because our men prayed more or cared more. We won because we had bigger guns."

"So might was right," I observed.

"That's how it often is in the world," he reminded me. "But sometimes right wins simply because justice demands it."

"You sound terribly certain."

"So should you," he admonished. "A captain can never show fear. It's bad for morale."

I gave a sharp laugh. "And I am the captain of this little endeavor? Are you content to be led into battle by me?"

"You're as fine a man as any I knew in the navy," he assured me. "And if I did not give you command, you would only take it."

"True," I admitted. I toyed with Huxley's ears. "Thank you. I feel better now."

He gave me a long look. "Good." He bent to retrieve his hammer.

"Stoker?"

"Yes, Veronica?"

"What do you think the odds are that we will survive this meeting?" The lump from my throat was gone, and my voice no longer trembled.

He considered this a moment. "One in five," he pronounced.

My heart plunged to my feet. "And still you are willing to bet on us?"

His smile was dazzling. "Any man who bets against us is a fool."

My invitations had specified nine o'clock in the evening at Stoker's warehouse. The time and place had been chosen with care. I had selected an evening appointment to allow the gentlemen sufficient time to receive the invitation and prepare. I had decided upon Stoker's workshop because it was the nearest we could come to a higher-ground advantage. We knew they were coming, and forewarned was forearmed, I pointed out to Stoker. He grumbled extensively about sitting ducks, but he had secured the back windows; the little yard behind was surrounded by a high, stout wall that admitted no entrance, and the sole front door was heavily barricaded. There was no way they could gain entry without our knowing they were coming.

The early evening, predictably, crawled and then raced and then slowed again. Time played tricks upon us so that one moment we were lamenting the length of the day, and the next we were hurrying to finish our preparations.

"Little wonder it seems long," he pointed out. "It is almost Midsummer Day."

I did not reply. I was busy admiring our handiwork. Together we had cleared a large space in the center of the workshop. We had extinguished the lamps, and shadows gathered in the far corners of the place. From the gloom sharp teeth gleamed and eyes glimmered—hints of the mounts we had pushed to the perimeter of the room. The shelves we could not shift easily were left in place, but the great jars of floating specimens lent an unearthly note, like something straight out of Mary Shelley's masterpiece. One could easily imagine the touch of a galvanic wire bringing all of them suddenly, horribly to life.

Now the cauldron was centered in the middle of the workshop, drawing the eye and demanding attention.

"We needn't do this, you know," he informed me at one point. "There is a perfectly serviceable stove."

"You are forgetting the power of theater," I said. "I want to create an effect they will always remember."

"Perhaps you are your mother's child after all," he replied. But Stoker himself was not averse to a little theatricality, I noted. He had divested himself of coat, waistcoat, and neckcloth when we returned to his workshop and he made no effort to resume them again. Instead, he rolled his sleeves to the elbow, baring the asklepian tattoo upon his forearm. He had put on his eye patch as well; that might have been from fatigue—although it did occur to me he enjoyed the air of menace it conferred upon his appearance.

Once the cauldron was in place, we kindled a fire within it, burning stacks upon stacks of the old newspapers and broken shelves until the flames rose red and hot into the darkening air of the warehouse. We flung open the windows overlooking the Thames, long windows that stretched from near the floor, barely above the level of the water, to twelve feet or more overhead. Stoker had climbed like a monkey to open the skylights, and the smoke from the fire streamed out.

"'Yet man is born unto trouble as the sparks fly upward,'" I quoted.

"Yes, well, it doesn't feel particularly auspicious to quote Job," Stoker said with a repressive look. He turned to me just as the clock struck nine. "It is time."

I did not make any special effort with my appearance. My hands were sooty and dirty with newsprint, so I washed them. But I left my hair tumbling half out of its chignon, and I did not put on my jacket. My shirtwaist was white, like Lily Ashbourne's most famous costume, and I wanted them to see the resemblance for themselves.

The clock had not finished striking the nine solemn tones when we heard them. First it was a dull thud as they struck the main door. Stoker had removed the barricade by then, but we did not go to let them in. I wanted them to come to me, and the few minutes it took for them to force their way in only heightened their anticipation.

Stoker turned to me, and I noted a single-mindedness

of purpose I had not yet seen within him. This was not the wreck of a man I had met only days before. This was a new creation—focused, determined, and bent upon resolving this matter, for better or worse.

He gave me a short nod. "To battle stations, Veronica. They have come."

TWENTY-EIGHT

Stoker and I were standing behind the cauldron when they arrived. The hellish light illuminated our faces, and I watched them enter through air that shimmered with heat.

Edmund de Clare was first, accompanied by his henchman, Silent John, and a pair of other fellows I recognized from our pleasure cruise along the Thames.

I stepped out from behind the cauldron but went no further. "Stop there," I instructed. He obeyed and I gave him a long, slow look from head to toe. Expensive tailoring that had seen better days. Shoes in need of a shine. An imperfect shave from an indifferent barber. And then I understood him—all of his life had been a series of near misses. Here was a man who had been close to greatness, close to wealth, close to happiness. And they had eluded him.

At his approach Huxley whimpered and crawled under the sofa. It occurred to me that the dog was an excellent judge of character.

"Good evening, Uncle." If he was surprised that I had put

the pieces together, he betrayed no sign of it.

"And you are Lily's daughter," he said in his rich, melodious voice. I remembered reading that Lily's greatest asset as an actress had not been her lovely face, but rather her extraordinary speaking voice. It must have been a family trait, I reflected. "I knew it the first day I saw you, from the carriage in the lane in Little Byfield, and then at Paddington Station—to hear you speak in her voice. You have no idea how difficult it has been to restrain myself from telling you outright who I was. But I knew you would never believe me. Who could believe such a thing, even from a blood uncle?" he said, his voice almost faltering.

It was an admirable touch, and it told me he was still determined to play the devoted kinsman. He must have realized I could not know for certain whether he was my enemy or not, and he was clearly a gambling man. He would play every last card in his hand—and probably a few from up his sleeve. The break in the voice might have fooled a woman who was not attentive to the rest of his face, the almost imperceptible muscle movements at the eyes, which told me he was nervous—and angry. Still, I might have believed in his sincerity had it not been for his henchmen, quietly attempting to circle around the cauldron and surround us.

"Call off your hounds," I told him. "You are in no position to bully us."

His expression reddened with swift anger, but he darted a wary glance to Stoker and waved off his men. They fell back and I nodded. "Excellent. You are the first arrivals, but I daresay more are on their way."

Just then, as if unable to resist such a perfect cue, Mornaday slipped into the room behind them.

"Quite," he said brightly. He had produced a revolver and was pointing it directly at my uncle. "I think we can all agree to be civilized about this, can't we?"

The de Clare henchmen were looking quite nervous at this latest development, but before they could act, a tall shadow detached itself from behind Mornaday, stepping into the light. The gentleman was perhaps fifty but fit as a whippet, and something about the expression on his face told me he was by far a more formidable opponent than Mornaday.

"Steady, de Clare," he told my uncle. "If you were thinking that Inspector Mornaday is only one man, you were wrong. I have a dozen men outside this building and I am longing to hang you. Please, do me the favor of murdering an English police officer and let me watch you dance at the end of a rope."

He turned to me, and we exchanged long, appraising looks. I felt Stoker stiffen beside me, and that was all the confirmation I required. "Sir Hugo Montgomerie, I believe?"

His nod was brisk. "It is past time I made your acquaintance, Miss Speedwell." He flicked an indifferent glance to Stoker. "Templeton-Vane. It has been a long time."

"Not quite long enough," Stoker observed blandly.

I nodded towards the de Clares. "Sir Hugo, clearly you know my uncle, Edmund de Clare. I am not certain of the identity of the other fellows. I assume they are cousins of some fashion."

"They are," Sir Hugo acknowledged. "Your uncle is at the center of a group that is agitating quite vehemently for Irish Home Rule. All of his sons and nephews are involved as well. They've been a nuisance to the English authorities there, and I am delighted to make his personal acquaintance at last."

My uncle lifted that pugnacious chin with all the native drama of a Celt. "Do what you like to us. Ireland will be free of your kind and we will be martyrs to the cause."

"But I don't think you want to be a martyr, do you?" I asked. "Martyrdom is well and good, but you would far rather be the power behind the throne. I presume we can speak freely here? All of us know exactly who I am and what claims I might make?"

We exchanged glances like wolves circling a fresh kill. But it was too late for posturing.

"Let us have it plainly, then," I went on. "My mother was the Irish actress Lily Ashbourne, sister of Edmund de Clare," I said with a nod to the gentleman. "Somehow, during the course of her travels, she made the acquaintance of the Prince of Wales. I have had quite a bit of time to read the old newspapers here, and I discovered something interesting—in 1860 both His Royal Highness and Lily Ashbourne were on tours of North America. In fact, they happened to be at Niagara Falls at precisely the same time. The prince toured the falls and that night he attended the theater in town—the theater where Lily Ashbourne was performing her most dynamic role, Phaedra. I suspect that is when they met."

"It was," Mornaday confirmed. "I have read the statement he made to Sir Hugo's predecessor."

"He made a statement?"

Sir Hugo gave me a cool nod. "When Prince Albert discovered the liaison, he instructed a high-ranking detective at Scotland Yard to investigate Miss Ashbourne and determine whether she seemed likely to pose a threat to the royal family. He was quite concerned about a lawsuit demanding maintenance. The detective in question was in due course made head of Special Branch upon its creation. When he died and I succeeded him, those files were turned over to me."

"But a maintenance suit was not the greatest of Prince Albert's worries," I guessed.

"No," Sir Hugo acknowledged. "It was the worry that Miss Ashbourne would bring a paternity suit. I have the letters from the Prince Consort describing his fears of just such an eventuality. He believed his son's actions would destroy the royal family and, in due course, possibly even the monarchy."

"And well it might have," I agreed. "Particularly if he had known the truth—that Lily Ashbourne and the Prince of Wales had been married before their child was born."

Mornaday sucked in his breath, and Edmund de Clare gave a shout of pure triumph. In the flickering light, Sir Hugo seemed to turn pale. "There was never proof."

I brandished the packet I had assembled of the papers Stoker and I had recovered. "There is now."

Sir Hugo's expression did not falter, but I knew he understood what it was. Edmund de Clare stared, gape mouthed, as though I had just fished the Holy Grail out of my pocket.

"Is that—"

"Yes," I told him. "It is. This is the information for which the Baron von Stauffenbach was murdered."

De Clare blanched in spite of the heat of the fire. "That was an accident!" he protested. Sir Hugo turned to him inquiringly and de Clare went on, the words burbling forth, as if, having begun to speak, he could not stop himself. "He wouldn't tell me what I wanted to know and the lad struck him too hard," he said, jerking his chin towards Silent John. The fellow was sweating profusely, and I believed my uncle was telling the truth. No hardened criminal would look so likely to faint when faced with his crimes.

"Be that as it may, someone ought to answer for his death," I said levelly.

"And he will," my uncle swore. "If you come with us, I will turn him over to the police, I swear it."

Silent John gave a hoarse cry of dismay at being turned on so easily, but one of the other Irish cuffed him sharply to silence. Sir Hugo turned to Edmund de Clare with a genial look.

"And how do you propose to leave this place with Miss Speedwell? I have already told you I have a dozen constables outside who will prevent it."

Edmund's eyes gleamed. "And I have fifty stout Irish lads out there who say you won't."

Stoker spoke up then, addressing Sir Hugo. "They mean to start a riot. Your men fire on them and who do you think will come pouring out of these buildings to help them? The Irish your lot cleaned out of Piccadilly and pushed into the East End. This is their patch, and they will defend their own."

Edmund bared his teeth in a smile. "Quite right, my lad. And all it takes is one word to them out there about who she is, and you will unleash hell on earth in the middle of London—and two days before the Jubilee. Do you think you can keep the story quiet then? I know that is what you want, and I can promise you, you will live to fight another day if you let us go."

Sir Hugo did not respond. I did not give him the chance. I stepped forward. "What makes you think I will go willingly?" I asked my uncle.

He gentled his smile, and I saw a flash then of the potent charm Lily Ashbourne must have wielded. The softest touch of a Kerry accent slipped into his voice. "Because you will be free. What do you think they will do to you, girl, if we don't take you? You think they will let you go? Nay. They will lock you up and throw away the key, pretend you don't exist, because you are dangerous. Look at Sir High-and-Mighty Hugo Montgomerie there. Cool as milk to look at, but he is sweating like a pig on the inside. He knows what's at stake for his royal masters, and he knows it is his neck if he fails them. He's got no choice, little one. He must kill you to save himself. Do you hear me, child? *They will kill you.*" He edged a small step forward, pitching his voice low and coaxing. "But we are your family. You are a de Clare, in blood and bone, just as much as you are one of them. Come home to us, come home *with* us, and let us take care of you."

I gave him a slow smile. "That was masterfully done, Mr. de Clare. I marvel afresh at the Celtic propensity for persuasion. But you have not persuaded me," I finished with a cool glance. "I would be no safer with you than I would be in Sir Hugo's clutches. Tell me, which one of my cousins have you decided shall have me in marriage to breed you a male heir of your own blood?" I asked, nodding towards his compatriots.

He bridled. "Now, hold yourself, there is no call—"

I held up a hand. "You are changeable as a weathercock. I know exactly what you want me for, and it is not to play Happy Families, so spare us the sentimental rubbish. You want a figurehead for your revolution. Well, I shall not play the puppet for you or anyone. I might not approve of everything this Government does," I added with a reproachful look at Sir Hugo, "but I would rather be a private citizen here than a queen anywhere else."

"Spoken like a loyal subject of Her Majesty," Sir Hugo put in silkily. "But I am afraid that will not allay the threat you present. Miss Speedwell, you must see that I have no choice. Irish mob or not," he said, flicking a distasteful look at my uncle, "I must take you into custody."

"I understand your predicament, Sir Hugo. You are not working at your own behest, are you? You must have anticipated my misguided uncle would come with reinforcements. And yet you mustered only a dozen men. That seems either monstrously naïve or very secretive. I am guessing the latter. I think my uncle has the right of it—someone else is pulling your strings, and you cannot risk taking too many men from their regular duties at Scotland Yard or the story would be made public. So your master works behind the scenes—an adviser to the royal family, I surmise. Someone accustomed to using force to get his way, someone ruthless and entirely devoted to the family. If he weren't already cold in his grave, I would have suspected that wretched Scotsman, Brown. But there is someone. And he is playing the tune to which you dance."

Sir Hugo did not care for my characterization of himself as puppet. He gave me a thin smile. "You are even more clever than Inspector Mornaday's report indicated. But your deductions are irrelevant. Whoever has taken an interest in you has the interests of the Crown at heart, and those interests must be paramount."

"I agree," I said calmly. "I *quite* agree that the Crown must not be permitted to be threatened or even embarrassed, particularly not now, when the eyes of the world are upon the queen as she celebrates her Jubilee. It would be unthinkable."

"I am glad you are prepared to be reasonable," he remarked.

"The question is, are you?"

Once more I raised the packet. "These are all the papers that are pertinent to my identity. In this packet is my parents' marriage certificate—a certificate whose witnesses are now all dead. In this packet is the registration of my birth, also witnessed by a man who is dead. Every single person who had direct knowledge of the circumstances of my birth and could give testimony under oath to my parentage is deceased."

"All except your father," Edmund de Clare pointed out.

"And I think we may expect his lips to be sealed upon the matter." I turned to Sir Hugo. "Everything that represents the danger I am to the Crown is in this packet."

Deliberately, I lifted my arm higher and held his gaze for an instant before I dropped it into the flames. My uncle dashed forward, but before he could reach the cauldron, Stoker, on cue and according to plan, threw in a bottle of formaldehyde, shattering the glass and causing the flames to blaze upward, nearly licking the ceiling as a ball of fire roared out of the cauldron.

"You needn't bother yourself," I told my uncle. "That was formaldehyde, the most flammable substance in this place. The papers were destroyed the moment it touched them."

De Clare's face went utterly blank as the shock of his loss settled upon him. In that instant, reason deserted him. He went for Stoker, his hands at Stoker's throat. The surprise of the attack had caught Stoker off guard and bowled him over onto his back, my uncle throttling him as they went down heavily. Stoker drove one knee upward into my uncle's chest, sending him flying backward through the air and squarely against the cauldron. My uncle dangled a moment above the flames, flailing wildly. Stoker made a grab at him, catching de Clare's waistcoat in his fist and pulling him from danger, but it was too late. The trailing tails of his coat dragged through the fire, igniting instantly. Stoker released him and de Clare staggered back against the cauldron.

He pushed himself free unsteadily, the fire a ghoulish nimbus as he staggered towards the windows. His progress was jerky, like that of an automaton whose clockworks have begun to fail. He stopped and started, careering from table to shelves, grasping at anything in his path—furniture, mounted animals, teetering stacks of books. I like to think it was horror that paralyzed Sir Hugo, for he was closest and might have stopped my uncle and smothered the flames. But he stood motionless, watching, mouth agape, along with the rest of us, as Edmund de Clare flung himself out the window and into the fetid green waters of the Thames. We heard the splash as he entered the water, and then a terrible silence.

Before Sir Hugo or Mornaday could stop them, the rest of the Irish seized their chance, bolting out the window after Edmund and diving straight into the river. But the escape of the miscreants was the least of our worries. Edmund's frantic stagger through the workshop had set piles of papers and tanned skins alight, and the flames raced along, seizing specimens and books and newspapers in their greedy grip.

Stoker turned to me. "Get out, now! The whole place is going up!" The Wardian cases began to explode from the heat, shattering glass and chemicals over everything, the specimens dying a second death as the sawdust within them—saturated in flammable solutions—ignited with a fury.

Stoker shoved me at Mornaday and the detective responded, wrapping his arms about me to hurry me from the burning building, with Sir Hugo hard upon our heels. We reached the pavement outside to find the neighbors emerging from their lodgings, faces either aghast or avid with interest as they realized the warehouse was on fire.

I gulped in deep drafts of the smoky air as I did a swift inventory of my person. Appendages and hair were unscorched, although my costume was a little the worse for wear, streaked with soot and singed a little at the hem where my skirt had brushed a burning stack of natural history journals on the way out.

I turned to Stoker, when I realized he was not beside me. I whirled to see him making his way back into the burning building.

"Stoker!" I shouted. "What are you doing?"

He gave me one last look. "I am going back for my bloody dog!"

Terror gripped my throat as Mornaday and Sir Hugo thrust me further into the crisp, clear evening air, where we were attended by Sir Hugo's men. They were dressed in plain clothes, not the proper uniforms of police officers, but they were obedient to Sir Hugo, bringing blankets and nips of whiskey from pocket flasks and asking repeatedly if they should attempt to summon the fire brigade. Sir Hugo instructed them against it. He watched in perfect composure as the building burned, his lips pressed together in an expression of detached satisfaction. I could understand why. This was a preferable solution to the problem of Edmund de Clare. A trial for the baron's murder would have meant publicity. This way, Edmund de Clare would vanish into the waters of the Thames, and his plot would disappear with him. Whether his claim of having a host of men waiting outside had been a prevarication or the truth, we would never know. No one came forward, and in other circumstances I would have been amused to think that Edmund de Clare had bluffed the head of Scotland Yard.

I knew precisely how to puncture Sir Hugo's sangfroid. "You are content to let Stoker's home burn?" I asked, not troubling to conceal the acid in my tone.

"There are greater considerations afoot," he replied with maddening calm. He had a neat little beard of the sort that Stuart kings used to wear, and he stroked it, no doubt in satisfaction.

I gave him a grim smile. "Yes, well, mind you have your men trawl that section of the Thames for Edmund de Clare's body, although they shan't find it. It's rather shallow just there. I daresay he managed to get away quite handily."

To my enormous pleasure, Sir Hugo blinked. "Shallow?"

"Deep enough to prevent him from sustaining further injury from the jump, but not so deep as to present any real danger of drowning is my guess," I elaborated. "He has a boat, you know. And while he may not be the cleverest of criminal masterminds, a man with even rudimentary common sense would have taken the precaution of arranging his means of leaving our little rendezvous tonight. What better route than the river? You did not expect it, I daresay. And with Silent John and those other two ruffians to aid him, I suspect he is already halfway down the Thames."

Behind him, Mornaday hid his smile behind a hand at his superior's discomfiture. Sir Hugo's nostrils flared slightly. It was an elegant nose and he used it to good effect.

"My dear Miss Speedwell, I hardly think—"

"I'm only surprised Inspector Mornaday did not tell you all about it."

"You knew he had a boat?" Sir Hugo whirled on Mornaday and fixed him with a cold eye that promised retribution of the most painful sort. I turned away. As much as it would please me to see Mornaday get his comeuppance, I could no longer hide my concern for Stoker's fate. He had been in that burning building far too long. I kept my eyes fixed upon the door, watching the smoke billow forth and the hellish flames grow higher and higher. I heard the riverside wall give way, bricks and beams tumbling into the Thames just where my uncle had gone in, and another woman might have prayed. But I could not. I looked down at my hands and saw crescents of blood, the relics of my fingernails digging into my palms.

My focus narrowed onto the smoke that rolled and hissed like a living thing, and then it parted a moment, and a figure emerged. It was Stoker, a little the worse for wear, but cradling a yawning Huxley, who was snuffling about in search of a sausage.

My knees threatened to give way. "Fool," I muttered.

Stoker shrugged. "He is family."

The undercover police officers kept the peace, pushing the avid spectators back as the fire burned itself out. Because the warehouse was detached, no other businesses or lodgings were put in danger, and in due course, Sir Hugo permitted the fire brigade to be summoned to finish off the job.

I turned to see Mornaday looking distinctly cowed after his upbraiding and Sir Hugo staring at me in something like disbelief. I had the feeling that very few people ever surprised him.

"That was your only chance to claim a throne," he said.

"That was never what I wanted." I pulled the blanket closer about my shoulders. "I think we can agree that I am no longer a threat? To the Crown or to your master?"

He hesitated. "In spite of my better judgment, I will do

my best to be persuasive upon the point to the parties most concerned. We will speak again tomorrow. I will send word of the time," he said, dismissing me with a flick of the finger. It was then I realized instinctively that Sir Hugo had always known my whereabouts. Whatever games he played, they were deep ones, and I wondered precisely how far his tentacles could reach.

Whilst Sir Hugo was directing his men, Stoker and Huxley and I slipped away. "He said he wants to see us again. You left without giving him our direction. He shan't like that," Stoker noted as we trudged through the darkening streets on weary feet.

"He will know where to find us," was my only reply.

TWENTY-NINE

I COLLAPSED INTO BED WITHOUT washing, the smell of smoke heavy in my hair, soot still staining my hands. I was more exhausted than I had ever been in the whole of my life. The revelations of the past few days finally came crashing down upon me, and when I woke it was to find the late morning sun streaming across the floor of the Belvedere. Stoker handed me a cup of tea, bitter and dark.

"You look like hell," he said quietly. For his part, he was washed and dressed as tidily as I had ever seen him. I sipped at my tea, grateful for the warmth of it seeping into my bones. His expression was inscrutable. "I have seen Lady C. and told her we are back."

"For the moment," I said waspishly. For the first time in my life, having no fixed home was something thorny and unpleasant, but it was nothing compared to the guilt I felt over having played a part in destroying his.

Stoker did not respond to this. He merely gave me a long look. "Finish your tea and then have a wash. It is time to go."

I lifted my eyes from the cup. "Montgomerie?"

He nodded and we said no more. I washed and dressed and finished my tea, and Stoker and I presented ourselves at police headquarters for our interview with Sir Hugo. I had expected endless miles of corridors and functionaries to navigate, but we were met at an unmarked street door by one of his men and whisked up a private stair and directly into Sir Hugo's office—as discreet an entrance as it was possible to make at Scotland Yard.

Sir Hugo was settled behind his desk, and I was surprised to find he used a slender Regency writing table instead of a more traditional—and expected—barricade of mahogany. The effect was one of intimacy. Even opposite him, we were seated near enough that I could make out the lines at the corners of his eyes. He looked a little fatigued, but not much the worse for wear after our ordeal. His beard was neatly groomed, and his clothes were expertly tailored. I suspected Sir Hugo of having a private income as well as his stipend as head of the Yard—or perhaps his shadowy master rewarded him handsomely, I reflected with some cynicism.

Mornaday stood quietly in the corner, his posture not entirely relaxed. I wondered how harshly he had been disciplined for his easy treatment of us. Stoker sat in a chair scarcely large enough to contain him, and I perched on the edge of mine, tipping my head inquiringly at Sir Hugo.

To my astonishment, he smiled, a rather beautiful smile, and when he spoke, it was with something approaching sincerity. "Miss Speedwell, it might surprise you to know I am pleased that you emerged unscathed from the activities of last night."

"It would," I acknowledged.

"I am not your enemy," he said, his tone warmer than I had yet heard it. "In fact, we have a thing or two in common. For instance, I am a butterfly collector myself. Inspector

Mornaday tells me you have a very fine ring net, although I must say I am partial to a clap net myself."

I returned the smile. "Sir Hugo, I know when a man wants something from me. You needn't exercise your charm on my account—particularly as I suspect that only my destroying those papers prevented you from taking my life."

He gaped at me. "My dear Miss Speedwell—"

"You deny it? Was there really no plot at all to kill me and lay the blame squarely upon Mr. Stoker? Forgive me, Mr. Templeton-Vane, as you know him," I amended.

Sir Hugo continued to gawp as I went on in the same gentle tone. "I believe there was. Furthermore, I believe that only my prompt action last night prevented you from carrying it out."

"I am a gentleman," he returned coldly. "I would never have gone through—" Too late, he realized he had acknowledged the plot. I dared not look at Stoker.

Sir Hugo cleared his throat and began again. "Miss Speedwell, I do not deny that there were certain parties that believed only your complete removal would ensure the security of this nation, and indeed the empire itself. I disagreed, most strenuously," he said with special emphasis, "and I would never have countenanced such an action, either from myself or any of my subordinates."

He fell to silence and I let his words sit for a moment between us. At last, I gave him a grudging nod. "My instincts seldom fail me, Sir Hugo, and I believe you to be a man of honor who would balk at murdering a woman whose only crime is an accident of birth." His stiffness eased a trifle, but I leaned forward, skewering him with a glance. "I also believe that you are very glad I destroyed those proofs so you did not have to test your own conscience."

Before he could respond, I sat back, folding my hands in my lap. "Now that we have dispensed with the pretenses, why don't you tell us what you want with us."

His mouth slackened. "Very well. I will be as forthright as you wish, Miss Speedwell." He opened the blotter on his desk and removed a piece of paper, folded over. He slid it across the desk towards me.

I opened the paper to find it was nearly blank. Except for a figure penned in neat, exact numbers. "What is this?"

"Your pension. I have spoken with my superior," he said, his mouth twitching upon the word. Clearly he remembered my taunts of the night before—remembered and resented. "Destroying the proofs of your possible legitimacy was taken as a gesture of good faith," he told me with deliberate stress upon the word "possible." "You must consider this a reciprocal gesture of goodwill."

I pushed the paper back across the desk and rose. "Thank you, Sir Hugo. But you may inform your superior that I do not require hush money. I burned the papers to prove I have no intention of pressing a claim. My word should be good enough."

He rose swiftly to his feet, as did Stoker. "Miss Speedwell, I am not a man who likes to revisit his opinions. I form them swiftly and they are invariably correct. But Inspector Mornaday has been eloquent on your behalf. While I must question your judgment in the company you choose to keep," he added with a flick of a glance towards Stoker, "I would like to believe you do not mean to bring harm to the family."

"Then believe it."

He touched the page. "Accepting this token of their gratitude would go a long way towards accomplishing that."

"No, Sir Hugo. It would go a long way towards putting me in their debt—a position I have no intention of occupying."

He looked appealingly at Stoker. "Can you not exercise some influence in this?"

Stoker shrugged. "I could sooner influence the sun to set in the east, Sir Hugo. She is entirely her own woman."

The rush of gratitude I felt for Stoker's understanding nearly made me dizzy. Never before had I encountered a man so willing to abandon his allegedly God-given right to dominion over the fairer sex.

Sir Hugo returned his attention to me, raising an imperious brow. "Without your cooperation in this matter, I do not know how far I can go towards ensuring the continued goodwill of my superior."

I lifted my chin and gave him my most imperious stare. "I am willing to take my chances, but know this, Sir Hugo—if there are any further acts of hostility, you may rest assured they will not begin with me."

I turned on my heel and walked out, calling over my shoulder, "Adieu for now, Sir Hugo."

Mornaday hurried to show us out, shepherding us down the staircase and opening the door that led onto the pavement. "That was unexpected," he told me with a grin. "But I have come to expect the unexpected from you, Miss Speedwell."

I put out my hand. "Thank you, Inspector Mornaday, for all your efforts on our behalf."

He took my hand, shaking it slowly. His look was inscrutable and he gathered Stoker in with it. "I do not know how bad this is all going to get. I believe you are safe for now. Just, keep yourself quiet, will you? The less you draw attention to yourselves, the sooner they will feel secure and the sooner they will believe you mean them no harm."

Stoker gave him a searching glance. "I still owe you a thrashing, Mornaday. But I am prepared to forgo the pleasure in exchange for a bit of information."

Mornaday's eyes widened a fraction as they settled on Stoker's shoulders, broad and set as they were with murderous intent. "I am listening," he said quickly.

"I would like to know who is sitting in the shadows watching all of this. Tell us the name of the fellow giving Sir Hugo's orders. We might like to look out for him."

Mornaday cast a look back over his shoulder, shaking his head. "More than my job is worth, man. More than my *life* is worth. But I can tell you this—you have it wrong. There is no 'him.' It is a 'her.'"

With that he retreated into the building and pulled the door shut behind him.

Stoker and I spoke little upon our journey back to Bishop's Folly, and when we reached the estate, a heaviness had settled upon us both. I felt tired down to my marrow, a weariness so deep the sleep of a hundred years seemed inadequate to remedy it. I was aware with creeping horror that the lowness I felt was not simply because our adventure was at an end, but because so much was left imperfectly finished. There would be no justice for the baron's murderer, at least not at the present. Whatever my father's presence in my life had been hitherto, it was now clear that his interest in me would never extend to a meeting. I realized then that he was the person to whom Max had referred when he said the secrets were not his to tell. He intended to consult someone, and who besides the prince himself would command Max's discretion and loyalty? Perhaps the baron had even planned to arrange a meeting between us. I could imagine him accomplishing this rapprochement. If anyone could have persuaded the prince to come face-to-face with the daughter he had abandoned, it would have been the baron. But with the loss of this sole intermediary to remind him of his hapless youth, the prince could put it behind him, leaving the uncomfortable knowledge of my existence to Special Branch to mind for him—perhaps with an annual report he might skim and then toss aside before he settled to a good roast beef dinner and a game of whist.

But above all this was the knowledge that my time with Stoker was finished too, and that realization burned the rest to ash. Unsolved puzzles abounded at present, and Stoker himself was not the least of these. I still had not yet divined the cause of his friendship with Lady Cordelia or his antipathy for his family. I had not discovered his wife's fate or heard the story of the man he had murdered. I was convinced he carried within him a thousand fathoms, and I had plumbed so few. I wanted to know everything about him, but I felt like Schliemann standing upon the buried walls of Troy. The truth was there, waiting to be unearthed. If only I had time . . . We were free to go our separate ways, no longer bound by investigation or curiosity or whatever strange sympathy had held us together. We were free, but this liberty felt like the bitterest imprisonment. The thought of living the rest of my life without his irascible temper to challenge me, his idle verses to cheer me, his pockets full of sweets and his mind full of secrets and sorrows . . . but it would profit me nothing to dwell upon these.

And so I sat down to dinner and made polite chat with the Beauclerks. Stoker and I exchanged glances, both of us keenly aware that our time at Bishop's Folly must be at an end. I waited for him to explain that the investigation into the baron's murder was in abeyance—some prevarication would be required here—and that we no longer required their hospitality. But he said nothing, and the words stuck in my throat as well. His lordship had just received a mummy he was tremendously enthused about, and he was happy to carry the weight of conversation, but Stoker could bear no more company. He excused himself as soon as the sweet was served, and Lady Cordelia rose as well.

"I ought to look in on the children," she said vaguely,

taking herself upstairs and leaving me alone with his lordship.

He shoved the decanter of port in my direction. "I may not be very good with people, Miss Speedwell, but even I could sense an atmosphere tonight. Tell me your troubles, if you like."

Before I could stop myself, the words began to pour out of me, a trickle at first, then a torrent, aided by a sympathetic ear and quantities of a very excellent port. Naturally, I did not relate the most dangerous details of our adventure, but I told him enough for him to understand we had been in peril of our lives and that the peril seemed to have passed, at least for now. I told him of Stoker's losses and my own dullness of feeling now that the escapade was finished, of my lowness of spirit and my horror at having large ambitions and not a generous enough purse to fund them.

To my astonishment, his lordship proved an excellent listener, and when I had concluded, he ordered strong tea for us both. It had grown late—or early, I realized, as the streaks of dawn had begun to gild the sky. Morning came early at midsummer, and we had talked through the night. But I felt cleansed now, purged of my worries, and as light as ether.

"It was very good of you not to give us away to the police," I told him. "You are a true friend to Stoker."

He looked uncomfortable, as all Englishmen do when complimented. "He has been a good friend to me. Or rather, my sister. The precise nature of their relationship eludes me, but Cordelia has informed me Stoker offered her friendship and succor at a time when she was most in need of it. Whatever that means," he added with a rueful smile.

If I had hoped to hear revelations concerning the origin of their relationship, I was doomed to disappointment. His lordship was not a man to pry—as I had just learned to my own advantage. He had been a restful companion and a good listener as well as kindly.

As if intuiting my questions about why Lady Cordelia had not confided in him, he shook his head. "I am no good with ladies' troubles."

"You have done remarkably well with mine," I pointed out.

He flushed a little, the same becoming rose shade as his sister when something excited her emotions. "I find listening to you to be very interesting. I have not much experience with ladies, you know. My sister, of course. And my aunt. My wife. But they were all calm, unruffled. Very capable women. None of them has had need of me to solve their problems, so I have little skill with it. I only hope I can learn before my children require me," he added with a furrowed brow. I saw then that I had judged him a little harshly. It was not his intention to burden his sister with the care of his children, any more than it had been his intention to leave his offspring too often to their own devices. He lacked the skills to communicate with them, but not the will, and with the will, all else could be made right.

"I have no doubt you will surpass your own expectations," I said, feeling a rush of sudden sympathy for this gentle man. "Your instincts are excellent. You have proven that by trusting Stoker and me rather than exposing us to the police."

"I can only quote Xenocrates, dear lady. 'I have often regretted my speech, never my silence.'"

"A worthy philosophy, my lord. Let us drink to Xenocrates."

We lifted our cups of tea and toasted Xenocrates, and in that moment, I felt Inspiration whisper in my ear. The plan came to me as fully formed as Athena sprung from the brow of Zeus, and I outlined it for his lordship in detail. There was no chance to think twice about the propriety of what I was asking. I must cast the dice and see how they fell, I told myself. I had not thought the thing through, but for every question Lord Rosemorran put to me, I had a ready response, and when

I finally fell silent, leaving him to deliberate upon my question, he stared at me with mingled awe and disbelief.

"My dear Miss Speedwell," he began. "I hardly know how to reply."

"Say 'yes,'" I commanded. And to his credit, he laughed.

"Very well. One can hardly say 'no' to a force of nature. I accept your proposal."

And we toasted that as well.

After another revivifying cup of tea, I made my toilette and left Bishop's Folly without meeting Stoker or Huxley or any of the Beauclerks. Even Betony seemed to have something better to do that morning. I had taken pains with my appearance, wearing my black silk and pinning on my large black hat with the luscious roses. I collected more than a few admiring glances as I made my way into the heart of a euphoric London. It was Jubilee Day, and the bunting swung gaily overhead—ropes of flowers and banners of blue, white, and red proclaiming VICTORIA OUR QUEEN. The crowds were thick with spectators and hawkers crying their wares, selling food and lemonade and Jubilee memorabilia. The snorting of horses, the smell of hot grease, the chants of the crowd—all mingled to riotous effect as all of London had turned out to wish her well upon the anniversary of her accession.

I found a lamppost and by means of a tuppence bribe persuaded the youth ensconced there to give up his place to me. I stood on the base, one arm holding fast to the lamp as I watched the procession roll past. First, the soldiers, resplendent in brass-buttoned scarlet tunics, and marching in step to the bands that played with sharp precision. The sober dignitaries came next in their carriages, foreign heads of state—from the European sons-in-law who had married into the family to the maharajas who had conceded their kingdoms to its matriarch. The Europeans sat stiffly correct in their morning suits and chivalric orders, but the Indians were resplendent in vibrant silks and gems that glittered in the sunlight. Then came the Court, various officials and ladies-in-waiting, each decked in their finest, the duchesses blazing with jewels as feathers bobbed from their plumed hats, the gentlemen laden with various orders. They waved and nodded and smiled at the crowds, whipping them into a frenzy of anticipation. I saw Sir Hugo, riding discreetly, dressed in sober black and keeping a weather eye upon the crowd as the cheers rose higher and louder.

And then they came—the family. Carriage after carriage rolled past with them, *her* children and grandchildren, a family occasion that happened to be a matter of state. There were the children of the Prince of Wales, my half siblings, clustered together in their privilege, and I expected a pang at the thought that we should never know each other. But there was nothing in my heart save silence.

Next came the Prince of Wales himself, beautifully tailored and genial, lifting a manicured hand as he smiled to the crowd. This was the man Lily Ashbourne had loved and lost and died for heartbreak over. I wondered what she would have thought of him. Would she have recognized the boy she once knew in the greying man he now was? And I wondered, too, if he ever thought of her. Was she a passing fancy? A fevered dream? Or was she a regret he would carry to the end of his days? I could read no answers in his serenely satisfied expression, and in an instant he was gone, borne away in his golden carriage amidst the patriotic cheers.

Finally, she came, in the grandest carriage of all. The equipage was pulled by half a dozen cream horses, perfectly matched. She was smaller than I had expected—and plumper, like an autumn pigeon with its feathers fluffed out against the coming winter. She wore an unapologetically ugly black bonnet and carried a bouquet of roses. I had only ever seen her in profile, on coins and stamps, and it astonished me to find she was smiling. Her teeth were small and not particularly good, but she was clearly happy at this outpouring of joy, reveling in the love and approval of her subjects. She did not turn her head my way as she passed. There was no moment of recognition between us. And I knew there never would be. Whatever unpleasantness her children caused her was their business. She would make it none of hers.

The carriage passed by swiftly, the horses' hooves clipping briskly as they trotted forward, carrying her on to St. Paul's for the ceremony of thanksgiving in honor of her reign. The crowd surged forward, moving in her wake to get one final glimpse of their queen. I did not follow them. One look had been enough.

I made my way slowly back towards Bishop's Folly. I was halfway across Green Park when he found me. I ought not to have been surprised. He had, after all, told me once he could track a jaguar through a jungle for forty miles and never lose it. It would have been child's play to him to trail my enormous beflowered hat.

"Been to see your granny?" Stoker asked blandly.

I gave him a small smile, which he did not return. "Not that she noticed. But yes. I needed to see her, just once. And now it is finished. I can move forward and put all of this behind me."

"Can you? There are still one or two questions as yet unanswered," he pointed out. There was a distance in him I could not bridge, a coldness that had settled over him as soon as the danger had passed. He had retreated once more into the guise of a stranger. I did not know why he had sought me out. Perhaps he merely wanted to weave in as many loose strands as we could. I owed him as much, I thought bleakly.

I sighed. "More than one or two questions without answers. What is the identity of the puppet master—or *mistress*, rather—pulling at Sir Hugo's strings? What has become of Edmund de Clare and have we heard the last of him? And was he telling the truth when he said the baron's death was an accident?"

Stoker fell in step beside me, almost but not quite touching me. "Max believed in chivalry and courage and all manner of old-fashioned things. He died defending the daughter of the woman he loved. He would have chosen that death. And I think he did."

"What do you mean?"

"He had the chance to throw the doors wide-open on this when he brought you to London. You were in a carriage with him for hours. He might have told you who you were, asked point-blank if you knew of the documents. But he kept it all shrouded in mystery because I think he wanted to face them. It was his own misfortune that he underestimated Edmund de Clare's desperation."

"I suppose," I said slowly. "If only he had told me."

His expression hardened. "Would you have believed him? A strange man you have never met, telling you that you are the legitimate daughter of the Prince of Wales? You would have bolted out of that carriage at the first chance. And he would have lost you forever."

I nodded slowly. "You are probably correct. I like to think I would have been too intrigued by his tale to be frightened into flight, but none of us are as brave as we believe."

"I am not certain of that," he told me, the words breaking fiercely from him as if he spoke against his will. "I think you are braver than any man I have ever known."

His eyes were a shade too brilliant for comfort. Some new emotion had been kindled, wrestling against the coldness, and it discomfited me. I did not know what to say, so, as was my wont in times of confusion, I turned to the butterfly—always darting just out of reach, using its mazy flight as defense as well as a means of moving forward. I reached into my pocket and changed the subject.

"Speaking of money, here is your winnings from our wager. I had not forgot. You were entirely correct. The connection was there, only I failed to see it. That is the hallmark of a good partnership, you know—when one partner sees the forest and the other studies the trees. In any event, here you are. A bright, shiny new guinea for your watch chain."

I proffered the coin and he took it. "I shall wear it with pride. And if I ever run out of money, I will always have the means to buy a bottle of gin," he told me with a hint of his old raffishness. "Well, I suppose it is time to move on," he said briskly.

"Of course," I replied. "This little adventure of ours has cost us dearly. We have almost no money, your collections and home have been lost, and we were very nearly murdered. You would be the most illogical man in all of nature if you did not wish to put it behind you. But having said that, I wonder if perhaps there is not just a little of the daring adventurer left in you."

He went very still. "What do you mean?"

"I made a proposal to Lord Rosemorran last night."

I outlined the details, explaining carefully the scheme that his lordship and I had devised, and all the while Stoker listened intently, interrupting only once to ask a question.

"He is serious this time?"

"Indeed. He wants to make the Belvedere at Bishop's Folly into a proper museum. And he cannot do that until the collections are cataloged and expertly prepared for display. Once that is done, expeditions will have to go out and secure the specimens to fill in the collections. It is enough work to keep us busy for twenty, nay, thirty years if we like. We have a home base here in London and expeditions when we long to go out into the field—*funded* expeditions," I corrected. "His lordship means to collect subscriptions from his wealthiest friends to underwrite the cost. Between expeditions we will each draw an appropriate salary, and his lordship will turn over the Belvedere for our work. He is also prepared to offer us a place to live. He mentioned the smaller buildings on the estate, the little follies Lady Cordelia pointed out to me when we arrived. His lordship says it will be a small matter to have them fitted out properly for us each to have a small residence of our own. I have already claimed the Gothic chapel," I warned him, "so mind you do not cast your eyes upon it."

I held my breath as he considered, and in that moment of stillness it seemed all of eternity slipped past. Empires rose and fell and wars were fought and children were born and lived and grew old and died before he answered, and the worst of it was that I could not show him by word or gesture how very much his reply would mean to me. We were stalwart companions at arms, partners in adventure. I asked nothing more of him than that.

He stared at me, his expression inscrutable. "I feel as if I have been dropped into a whirlwind."

"You have not answered," I pointed out.

"I would be a fool to refuse," he said simply. "And I am no fool."

The tightness in my chest eased and I could breathe once more. This was not the end, then. Whatever this strange connection was between us—it was not yet finished.

He shook his head as if to clear it. "I am glad this is not the end," he said, echoing my thoughts, and then he hesitated a moment, his gaze intent, his hands curling into fists as if to keep himself from reaching out.

But the moment passed, and when he spoke, I had the

oddest sensation it was not what he intended to say. His voice was casual and his manner relaxed. "Well, Veronica, I can say in all sincerity I have never known anyone like you. You have thought of everything."

"I tried," I said modestly.

"It must be difficult for people to surprise you," he said, looking out over the great green sweep of the park.

"It seldom happens," I admit.

"Well, then I shall take great pride in this," he said, withdrawing a packet of papers from his pocket. He handed it to me.

"What is this?" But I already knew.

"Call it a birthday present. I noticed the date on the documents. You are five and twenty today. Happy birthday, Veronica." Still I stared at the packet in my hand, almost unable to comprehend what he had done. "Those are the original papers proving your identity," he told me gently. "Both the papers your mother turned over to Max and the set the Harbottles left for you in the bank."

For a long moment I could not speak, and when I did, the words came out in a torrent. "But I burned those! You saw me."

"You burned the packet I gave you. That is what I was doing when you thought I was writing up my notes on the elephant mount. I was creating a dummy version for you to destroy. I did agree that destroying the packet was the only way to buy your freedom," he assured me, "but I thought it would accomplish the same thing if you only *appeared* to destroy it."

"But why—"

He looked into the distance, his gaze fixed far away. "Everyone deserves the truth, Veronica. What you do with it is your affair. But you should not have the choice made for you just because some people are frightened by the facts. Burn it, publish it, throw it in the Thames—the decision must be yours and no one else's."

I turned the packet over, running my finger across the tape. I thought of the lives damaged and destroyed by what it represented—my mother, dead of a broken heart. Prince Albert, my father, the baron—all had been touched by the truth in those lines. A high price had been paid for the actions of a boy not yet twenty and the girl he loved.

"It is time to let the ghosts rest in peace," I said finally.

"You mean to destroy it, then?" he asked.

I slipped the packet into my pocket and put my arm through his. "Someday," I told him. "But not just yet. For now it is enough that I have it and we are safe. Now, back we go to Bishop's Folly, where we can begin to plan our museum. It's a pity Lord Rosemorran's grand elephant was destroyed in the fire. It would have made a lovely piece for the entrance."

"The entrance!" The firm muscle of his arm twitched in outrage. "You must be mad. That elephant would have been my masterpiece. He has another, even larger, and this one I will finish, and when I do, it will go in the center of the museum as the star attraction."

"Of all the ludicrous ideas," I began.

We bickered happily all the way back to Bishop's Folly, as I had expected we would. Whatever Stoker and I undertook, we should never do so without a feisty discussion and a pitched battle of wits. But, far from discomfiting me, that notion caused my spirits to rise and my steps to quicken with anticipation. Exploration beckoned and we would answer its clarion call to continents uncharted and seas unsailed; we would travel them together and perhaps even unravel a mystery or two as well. A thousand adventures lay before us, and I could not wait to begin them. As the excellent Arcadia Brown, Lady Detective, so often proclaimed, "Excelsior!"

ACKNOWLEDGMENTS

I WOULD LIKE TO OFFER my heartfelt gratitude for all those who have contributed to this book.

Kindnesses and professional generosity have been extended by: Susanna Kearsley, Lauren Willig, Robyn Carr, Benjamin Dreyer, Erica Monroe, Delilah Dawson, Holly Faur, Ali Trotta, Christine Rose Elle, Alan Bradley, Paula Breen, the Writerspace team, and Dr. Rory Schwan.

Most particularly, I owe a tremendous debt to Blake Leyers for her skill and support in shepherding this project through the early days and its many incarnations.

Many thanks to my former home, MIRA/Harlequin, and to my new publishing family at Penguin/NAL. Particular thanks to Kara Welsh, Craig Burke, Claire Zion, Leslie Schwartz, Diana Kirkland, and Sharon Gamboa for an exceptionally warm welcome. I am especially grateful to Daniel Lagin, Colleen Reinhart, and Anthony Ramondo for their extraordinary efforts to make this book as beautiful as I imagined it could be. For her innumerable gifts and peerless skill, my editor, Ellen

Edwards, deserves all the praise and thanks I can offer.

What I owe my parents, my daughter, and most especially my husband can never be expressed, much less repaid.

As ever, many thanks to the readers, booksellers, librarians, and lovers of books who share their enthusiasm.

ABOUT THE AUTHOR

Deanna Raybourn is the author of the award-winning *New York Times* bestselling Lady Julia Grey series and several standalone novels. The Lady Julia series has been nominated for five RITA Awards, an Agatha Award, and numerous Dilys Wynn, Last Laugh, Daphne du Maurier, and *Romantic Times* Reviewers' Choice Awards. Deanna lives in Virginia with her husband and daughter.

ALSO AVAILABLE FROM TITAN BOOKS

PRAISE FOR THE INDIA BLACK NOVELS

[A] breezy, fast-paced debut."
Publishers Weekly

"Readers will enjoy this impressive debut novel, which provides a colorful portrait of Victorian society as seen through the eyes of a strong, intelligent woman."
Booklist

"This saucy debut is a satisfying amusement, with the happy promise of more to come."
Kirkus Reviews

"Expect to stay up late reading this fascinating and at times hilarious novel of espionage and intrigue; you won't want to put it down."
RT Book Reviews

ALSO AVAILABLE FROM TITAN BOOKS

PRAISE FOR THE MORIARTY NOVELS

"Michael Kurland has made Moriarty more interesting than Doyle ever made Holmes."
Isaac Asimov

"As successful as its predecessors at bringing fin de siecle Europe to brilliant life... the action veers and twists like that in a contemporary spy thriller."
Booklist

"A deliciously complex and abundantly rewarding novel... remarkable talent... Surprises abound... This is no ordinary Holmes pastiche... Uncommon are the pleasures such writing affords."
Publishers Weekly

"A fabulous whodunit."
Midwest Book Review